R. A. Torrey Classic Treasury

TABLE OF CONTENTS

How To Pray

~ ※ ~

By *R. A. Torrey*

~ ※ ~

Chapter I: The Importance of Prayer

In the 6th chapter of Ephesians in the 18th verse we read words which put the tremendous importance of prayer with startling and overwhelming force:

"Praying always with all prayer and supplication in the Spirit, and watching thereunto with all perseverance and supplication for all saints."

When we stop to weigh the meaning of these words, then note the connection in which they are found, the intelligent child of God is driven to say,

"I must pray, pray, pray. I must put all my energy and all my heart into prayer. Whatever else I do, I must pray."

The Revised Version is, if possible, stronger than the Authorized:

"With all prayer and supplication praying at all seasons in the spirit, and watching thereunto in all perseverance and supplication for all the saints."

Note the *alls*: "with *all* prayer," "at *all* seasons," "in *all* perseverance," "for *all* the saints." Note the piling up of strong words, "prayer," "supplication," "perseverance." Note once more the strong expression, "watching thereunto," more literally, "being sleepless thereunto." Paul realized the natural slothfulness of man, and especially his natural slothfulness in prayer. How seldom we pray things through! How often the church and the individual get right up to the verge of a great blessing in prayer and just then let go, get drowsy, quit. I wish that these words "being sleepless unto prayer" might burn into our hearts. I wish the whole verse might burn into our hearts.

But why is this constant, persistent, sleepless, overcoming prayer so needful?

1. First of all, *because there is a devil.*

He is cunning, he is mighty, he never rests, he is ever plotting the downfall of the child of God; and if the child of God relaxes in prayer, the devil will succeed in ensnaring him.

This is the thought of the context. The 12th verse reads:

"For our wrestling is not against flesh and blood, but against the principalities, against the powers, against the world rulers of this darkness, against the spiritual hosts of wickedness in the heavenly places." Then comes the 13th verse: "Wherefore take up the whole armor of God, that ye may be able to withstand in the evil day, and, having done all, to stand." Next follows a description of the different parts of the Christian's armor, which we are to put on if we are to stand against the devil and his mighty wiles. Then Paul brings all to a climax in the 18th verse, telling us that to all else we must add prayer—constant, persistent, untiring, sleepless prayer in the Holy Spirit, or all else will go for nothing.

2. A second reason for this constant, persistent, sleepless, overcoming prayer is that *prayer is God's appointed way for obtaining things, and the great secret of all lack in our experience, in our life and in our work is neglect of prayer.*

James brings this out very forcibly in the 4th chapter and 2nd verse of his epistle: "Ye have not because ye ask not." These words contain the secret of the poverty and powerlessness of the average Christian—neglect of prayer.

"Why is it," many a Christian is asking, "I make so little progress in my Christian life?"

"Neglect of prayer," God answers. "You have not because you ask not."

"Why is it," many a minister is asking, "I see so little fruit from my labors?"

Again God answers, "Neglect of prayer. You have not because you ask not."

"Why is it," many a Sunday-School teacher is asking, "that I see so few converted in my Sunday-School class?"

Still God answers, "Neglect of prayer. You have not because you ask not."

"Why is it," both ministers and churches are asking, "that the church of Christ makes so little headway against unbelief and error and sin and worldliness?"

Once more we hear God answering, "Neglect of prayer. You have not because you ask not."

3. The third reason for this constant, persistent, sleepless, overcoming prayer is that *those men whom God set forth as a pattern of what He expected Christians to be—the apostles—regarded prayer as the most important business of their lives.*

When the multiplying responsibilities of the early church crowded in upon them, they "called the multitude of the disciples unto them, and said, It is not reason that we should leave the Word of God, and serve tables. Wherefore, brethren, look ye out among you seven men of honest report, full of the Holy Ghost and wisdom, whom we may appoint over this business. *But we will give ourselves continually to prayer* and to the ministry of the Word." It is evident from what Paul wrote to the churches and to individuals about praying for them, that very much of his time and strength and thought was given to prayer. (Rom. 1:9; Eph. 1:15, 16; Col. 1:9; 1 Thess. 3:10; 2 Tim. 1:3).

All the mighty men of God outside the Bible have been men of prayer. They have differed from one another in many things, but in this they have been alike.

4. But there is a still weightier reason for this constant, persistent, sleepless, overcoming prayer. It is, *prayer occupied a very prominent place and played a very important part in the earthly life of our Lord.*

Turn, for example, to Mark 1:35. We read, "And in the morning, rising up a great while before day, He went out, and departed into a solitary place, and there prayed." The preceding day had been a very busy and exciting one, but Jesus shortened the hours of needed sleep that He might arise early and give Himself to more sorely needed prayer.

Turn again to Luke 6:12, where we read, "And it came to pass in those days that He went out into a mountain to pray, and continued all night in prayer to God." Our Savior found it necessary on occasion to take a whole night for prayer.

The words "pray" and "prayer" are used at least twenty-five times in connection with our Lord in the brief record of His life in the four Gospels, and His praying is mentioned in places where the words are not used. Evidently prayer took much of the time and strength of Jesus, and a man or woman who does not spend much time in prayer, cannot properly be called a follower of Jesus Christ.

5. There is another reason for constant, persistent, sleepless, overcoming prayer that seems if possible even more forcible than this, namely, *praying is the most important part of the present ministry of our risen Lord.*

Christ's ministry did not close with His death. His atoning work was finished then, but when He rose and ascended to the right hand of the Father, He entered upon other work for us just as important in its place as His atoning work. It cannot be divorced from His atoning work; it rests upon that as its basis, but it is necessary to our complete salvation.

What that great present work is, by which He carries our salvation on to completeness, we read in Heb. 7:25, "Wherefore He is able also to save them to the uttermost that come unto God by Him, seeing *He ever liveth to make intercession for them.*" This verse tells us that Jesus is able to save us unto the uttermost, not merely *from* the uttermost, but *unto* the uttermost, unto entire completeness, absolute perfection, because He not merely died, but because He also "ever liveth." The verse also tells us for what purpose He now lives, "*to make intercession for us*," to pray. Praying is the principal thing He is doing in these days. It is by His prayers that He is saving us.

The same thought is found in Paul's remarkable, triumphant challenge in Rom. 8:34—"Who is he that shall condemn? It is Christ Jesus that died, yea rather, that was raised from the dead, who is at the right hand of God, *who also maketh intercession for us*."

If we then are to have fellowship with Jesus Christ in His present work, we must spend much time in prayer; we must give ourselves to earnest, constant, persistent, sleepless, overcoming prayer. I know of nothing that has so impressed me with a sense of the importance of praying at all seasons, being much and constantly in prayer, as the thought that that is the principal occupation at present of my risen Lord. I want to have fellowship with Him, and to that end I have asked the Father that whatever else He may make me, to make me at all events an intercessor, to make me a man who knows how to pray, and who spends much time in prayer.

This ministry of intercession is a glorious and a mighty ministry, and we can all have part in it. The man or the woman who is shut away from the public meeting by sickness can have part in it; the busy mother; the woman who has to take in washing for a living can have part—she can mingle prayers for the saints, and for her pastor, and for the unsaved, and for foreign missionaries, with the soap and water as she bends over the washtub, and not do the washing any more poorly on that account; the hard driven man of business can have part in it, praying as he hurries from duty to duty. But of course we must, if we would maintain this spirit of constant prayer, take time—and take plenty of it—when we shall shut ourselves up in the secret place alone with God for nothing but prayer.

6. The sixth reason for constant, persistent, sleepless, overcoming prayer is that *prayer is the means that God has appointed for our receiving mercy, and obtaining grace to help in time of need.*

Heb. 4:16 is one of the simplest and sweetest verses in the Bible,—"Let us therefore come boldly unto the throne of grace, that we may obtain mercy, and find grace to help in time of need." These words make it very plain that God has appointed a way by which we shall seek and obtain mercy and grace. That way is prayer; bold, confident, outspoken approach to the throne of grace, the most holy place of God's presence, where our sympathizing High Priest, Jesus Christ, has entered in our behalf. (Verses 14, 15.)

Mercy is what we need, grace is what we must have, or all our life and effort will end in complete failure. Prayer is the way to get them. There is infinite grace at our disposal, and we make it ours experimentally by prayer. Oh, if we only realized the fullness of God's grace, that is ours for the asking, its height and depth and length and breadth, I am sure that we would spend more time in prayer. The measure of our appropriation of grace is determined by the measure of our prayers.

Who is there that does not feel that he needs more grace? Then ask for it. Be constant and persistent in your asking. Be importunate and untiring in your asking. God delights to have us "shameless" beggars in this direction; for it shows our faith in Him, and He is mightily pleased with faith. Because of our "shamelessness" He will rise and give us as much as we need (Luke 11:8). What little streams of mercy and grace most of us know, when we might know rivers overflowing their banks!

7. The next reason for constant, persistent, sleepless, overcoming prayer is that *prayer in the name of Jesus Christ is the way Jesus Christ Himself has appointed for His disciples to obtain fullness of joy.*

He states this simply and beautifully in John 16:24, "Hitherto have ye asked nothing in My name; ask, and ye shall receive, that your joy may be fulfilled." "Made full" is the way the Revised Version reads. Who is there that does not wish his joy filled full? Well, the way to have it filled full is by praying in the name of Jesus. We all know people whose joy is filled full, indeed, it is just running over, is shining from their eyes, bubbling out of their very lips, and running off their finger tips when they shake hands with you. Coming in contact with them is like coming in contact with an electrical machine charged with gladness. Now people of that sort are always people that spend much time in prayer.

Why is it that prayer in the name of Christ brings such fullness of joy? In part, because we get what we ask. But that is not the only reason, nor the greatest. It makes God real. When we ask something definite of God, and He gives it, how real God becomes! He is right there! It is blessed to have a God who is real, and not merely an idea. I remember how once I was taken suddenly and seriously sick all alone in my study. I dropped upon my knees and cried to God for help. Instantly all pain left me—I was perfectly well. It seemed as if God stood right there, and had put out His hand and touched me. The joy of the healing was not so great as the joy of meeting God.

There is no greater joy on earth or in heaven, than communion with God, and prayer in the name of Jesus brings us into communion with Him. The Psalmist was surely not speaking only of future blessedness, but also of present blessedness when he said,

"In Thy presence is fullness of joy." (Ps. 16.11.) O the unutterable joy of those moments when in our prayers we really press into the presence of God!

Does some one say. "I have never known any such joy as that in prayer"?

Do you take enough leisure for prayer to actually get into God's presence? Do you really give yourself up to prayer in the time which you do take?

8. The eighth reason for constant, persistent, sleepless, overcoming prayer is that *prayer*, in *every care and anxiety and need of life, with thanksgiving, is the means that God has appointed for obtaining freedom from all anxiety, and the peace of God which passeth all understanding.*

"Be careful for nothing," says Paul, "but in everything by prayer and supplication with thanksgiving let your requests be made known unto God, and the peace of God which passeth all understanding, shall keep your hearts and minds through Christ Jesus." (Phil. 4:6, 7.) To many this seems at the first glance, the picture of a life that is beautiful, but beyond the reach of ordinary mortals; not so at all. The verse tells us how the life is attainable by every child of God: "Be careful for nothing," or as the Revised Version reads, "In nothing be anxious." The remainder of the verse tells us how, and it is very simple: "But in everything by prayer and supplication with thanksgiving let your requests be made known unto God." What could be plainer or more simple than that? Just keep in constant touch with God, and when any trouble or vexation, great or small, comes up, speak to Him about it, never forgetting to return thanks for what He has already done. What will the result be? "The peace of God which passeth all understanding shall guard your hearts and your thoughts in Christ Jesus."

That is glorious, and as simple as it is glorious! Thank God, many are trying it. Don't you know any one who is always serene? Perhaps he is a very stormy man by his natural make-up, but troubles and conflicts and reverses and bereavements may sweep around him, and the peace of God which passeth all understanding guards his heart and his thoughts in Christ Jesus.

We all know such persons. How do they manage it?

Just by prayer, that is all. Those persons who know the deep peace of God, the unfathomable peace that passeth all understanding, are always men and women of much prayer.

Some of us let the hurry of our lives crowd prayer out, and what a waste of time and energy and nerve force there is by the constant worry! One night of prayer will save us from many nights of insomnia. Time spent in prayer is not wasted, but time invested at big interest.

9. The ninth reason for constant, persistent, sleepless, overcoming prayer is that *prayer is the method that God Himself has appointed for our obtaining the Holy Spirit.*

Upon this point the Bible is very plain. Jesus says, "If ye then, being evil, know how to give good gifts unto your children, how much more shall your heavenly Father give the Holy Spirit to them that ask Him?" (Luke 11:13.) Men are telling us in these days, very good men too, "You must not pray for the Holy Spirit," but what are they going to do with the plain statement of Jesus Christ, "How much more will your heavenly Father give the Holy Spirit *to them that ask Him*?"

Some years ago when an address on the baptism with the Holy Spirit was announced, a brother came to me before the address and said with much feeling,

"Be sure and tell them not to pray for the Holy Spirit."

"I will surely not tell them that, for Jesus says, 'How much more shall your heavenly Father give the Holy Spirit to them that ask Him'."

"Oh, yes," he replied, "but that was before Pentecost."

"How about Acts 4:31? Was that before Pentecost, or after?"

"After, of course."

"Read it."

"'And when *they had prayed*, the place was shaken where they were assembled together; and they were all *filled with the Holy Ghost*, and they spake the Word of God with boldness.'"

"How about Acts 8:15? Was that before Pentecost or after?"

"After."

"Please read."

"'Who, when they were come down *prayed* for them, that they might receive the Holy Ghost.'"

He made no answer. What could he answer? It is plain as day in the Word of God that before Pentecost and after, the first baptism and the subsequent fillings with the Holy Spirit were received in answer to definite prayer. Experience also teaches this.

Doubtless many have received the Holy Spirit the moment of their surrender to God before there was time to pray, but how many there are who know that their first definite baptism with the Holy Spirit came while they were on their knees or faces before God, alone or in company with others, and who again and again since that have been filled with the Holy Spirit in the place of prayer!

I know this as definitely as I know that my thirst has been quenched while I was drinking water. Early one morning in the Chicago Avenue Church prayer room, where several hundred people had been assembled a number of hours in prayer, the Holy Spirit fell so manifestly, and the whole place was so filled with His presence, that no one could speak or pray, but sobs of joy filled the place. Men went out of that room to different parts of the country, taking trains that very morning, and reports soon came back of the outpouring of God's Holy Spirit in answer to prayer. Others went out into the city with the blessing of God upon them. This is only one instance among many that might be cited from personal experience.

If we would only spend more time in prayer, there would be more fullness of the Spirit's power in our work. Many and many a man who once worked unmistakably in the power of the Holy Spirit is now filling the air with empty shoutings, and beating it with his meaningless gesticulations, because he has let prayer be crowded out. We must spend much time on our knees before God, if we are to continue in the power of the Holy Spirit.

10. The tenth reason for constant, persistent, sleepless, overcoming prayer is that *prayer is the means that Christ has appointed whereby our hearts shall not become overcharged with surfeiting and drunkenness and cares of this life, and so the day of Christ's return come upon us suddenly as a snare.*

One of the most interesting and solemn passages upon prayer in the Bible is along this line. (Luke 21:34-36) "Take heed to yourselves, lest at any time your hearts be overcharged with surfeiting and drunkenness and cares of this life, and so that day come upon you unawares. For as a snare shall it come on all them that dwell in the face of the whole earth. Watch ye therefore, and *pray always*, that ye may be accounted worthy to escape all these things that shall come to pass, and to stand before the Son of man." According to this passage there is only one way in which we can be prepared for the coming of the Lord when He appears, that is, through much prayer.

The coming again of Jesus Christ is a subject that is awakening much interest and much discussion in our day; but it is one thing to be interested in the Lord's return, and to talk about it, and quite another thing to be prepared for it. We live in an atmosphere that has a constant tendency to unfit us for Christ's coming. The world tends to draw us down by its gratifications and by its cares. There is only one way by which we can rise triumphant above these things—by constant watching unto prayer, that is, by sleeplessness unto prayer. "Watch" in this passage is the same strong word used in Eph. 6:18, and "always" the same strong phrase "in every season." The man who spends little time in prayer, who is not steadfast and constant in prayer, will not be ready for the Lord when He comes. But we may be ready. How? Pray! Pray! Pray!

11. There is one more reason for constant, persistent, sleepless, overcoming prayer, and it is a mighty one: *because of what prayer accomplishes*. Much has really been said upon that already, but there is much also that should be added.

(1) Prayer promotes our spiritual growth as almost nothing else, indeed as nothing else but Bible study; and true prayer and true Bible study go hand in hand.

It is through prayer that my sin is brought to light, my most hidden sin. As I kneel before God and pray, "Search me, O God, and know my heart; try me, and know my thoughts; and see if there be any wicked way in me," (Ps.139:23, 24), God shoots the penetrating rays of His light into the innermost recesses of my heart, and the sins I never suspected are brought to view. In answer to prayer, God washes me from mine iniquity and cleanses me from my sin (Ps. 51:2). In answer to prayer my eyes are opened to behold wondrous things out of God's Word (Ps. 119:18). In answer to prayer I get wisdom to know God's way (Jas. 1:5) and strength to walk in it. As I meet God in prayer and gaze into His face, I am changed into His own image from glory to glory (2 Cor. 3:18). Each day of true prayer life finds me liker to my glorious Lord.

John Welch, son-in-law to John Knox, was one of the most faithful men of prayer this world ever saw. He counted that day ill-spent in which seven or eight hours were not used alone with God in prayer and the study of His Word. An old man speaking of him after his death said, "He was a type of Christ."

How came he to be so like his Master?

His prayer life explains the mystery.

(2) Prayer brings power into our work.

If we wish power for any work to which God calls us, be it preaching, teaching, personal work, or the rearing of our children, we can get it by earnest prayer.

A woman with a little boy who was perfectly incorrigible, once came to me in desperation and said:

"What shall I do with him?"

I asked, "Have you ever tried prayer?"

She said that she had prayed for him, she thought. I asked if she had made his conversion and his character a matter of definite, expectant prayer. She replied that she had not been definite in the matter. She began that day, and at once there was a marked change in the child, and he grew up into Christian manhood.

How many a Sunday-school teacher has taught for months and years, and seen no real fruit from his labors, and then has learned the secret of intercession, and by earnest pleading with God, has seen his scholars brought one by one to Christ! How many a poor preacher has become a mighty man of God by casting away his confidence in his own ability and gifts, and giving himself up to God to wait upon Him for the power that comes from on high! John Livingstone spent a night, with some others likeminded, in prayer to God and religious conversation, and when he preached next day in the Kirk of Shotts five hundred people were converted, or dated some definite uplift in their life to that occasion. Prayer and power are inseparable.

(3) Prayer avails for the conversion of others.

There are few converted in this world unless in connection with some one's prayers. I formerly thought that no human being had anything to do with my own conversion, for I was not converted in church or Sunday-school, or in personal conversation with any one. I was awakened in the middle of the night and converted. As far as I can remember I had not the slightest thought of being converted, or of anything of that character, when I went to bed and fell asleep; but I was awakened in the middle of the night and converted probably inside of five minutes. A few minutes before I was about as near eternal perdition as one gets. I had one foot over the brink and was trying to get the other one over. I say I thought no human being had anything to do with it, but I had forgotten my mother's prayers, and I afterward learned that one of my college classmates had chosen me as one to pray for until I was saved.

Prayer often avails where everything else fails. How utterly all of Monica's efforts and entreaties failed with her son, but her prayers prevailed with God, and the dissolute youth became St. Augustine, the mighty man of God. By prayer the bitterest enemies of the Gospel have become its most valiant defenders, the greatest scoundrels the truest sons of God, and the vilest women the purest saints. Oh, the power of prayer to reach down, down, down, where hope itself seems vain, and lift men and women up, up, up into fellowship with and likeness to God. It is simply wonderful! How little we appreciate this marvelous weapon!

(4) Prayer brings blessings to the church.

The history of the church has always been a history of grave difficulties to overcome. The devil hates the church and seeks in every way to block its progress; now by false doctrine, again by division, again by inward corruption of life. But by prayer, a clear way can be made through everything. Prayer will root out heresy, allay misunderstanding, sweep away jealousies and animosities, obliterate immoralities, and bring in the full tide of God's reviving grace. History abundantly proves this. In the hour of darkest portent, when the case of the church, local or universal, has seemed beyond hope, believing men and believing women have met together and cried to God and the answer has come.

It was so in the days of Knox, it was so in the days of Wesley and Whitfield, it was so in the days of Edwards and Brainerd, it was so in the days of Finney, it was so in the days of the great revival of 1857 in this country and of 1859 in Ireland, and it will be so again in your day and mine. Satan has marshalled his forces. Christian science with its false Christ—a woman—lifts high its head. Others making great pretensions of apostolic methods, but covering the rankest dishonesty and hypocrisy with these pretensions, speak with loud assurance. Christians equally loyal to the great fundamental truths of the Gospel are glowering at one another with a devil-sent suspicion. The world, the flesh and the devil are holding high carnival. It is now a dark day, *but*—now "it is time for Thee, Lord, to work; for they have made void Thy law." (Ps. 119:126). And He is getting ready to work, and now He is listening for the voice of prayer. Will He hear it? Will He hear it from you? Will He hear it from the church as a body? I believe He will.

Chapter II: Praying unto God

We have seen something of the tremendous importance and the resistless power of prayer, and now we come directly to the question—how to pray with power.

1. In the 12th chapter of the Acts of the Apostles we have the record of a prayer that prevailed with God, and brought to pass great results. In the 5th verse of this chapter, the manner and method of this prayer is described in few words:

"Prayer was made without ceasing of the church *unto God* for him."

The first thing to notice in this verse is the brief expression "unto God." The prayer that has power is the prayer that is offered unto God.

But some will say, "Is not all prayer unto God?"

No. Very much of so-called prayer, both public and private, is not unto God. In order that a prayer should be really unto God, there must be a definite and conscious approach to God when we pray; we must have a definite and vivid realization that God is bending over us and listening as we pray. In very much of our prayer there is really but little thought of God. Our mind is taken up with the thought of what we need, and is not occupied with the thought of the mighty and loving Father of whom we are seeking it. Oftentimes it is the case that we are occupied neither with the need nor with the One to whom we are praying, but our mind is wandering here and there throughout the world. There is no power in that sort of prayer. But when we really come into God's presence, really meet Him face to face in the place of prayer, really seek the things that we desire *from Him*, then there is power.

If, then, we would pray aright, the first thing that we should do is to see to it that we really get an audience with God, that we really get into His very presence. Before a word of petition is offered, we should have the definite and vivid consciousness that we are talking to God, and should believe that He is listening to our petition and is going to grant the thing that we ask of Him. This is only possible by the Holy Spirit's power, so we should look to the Holy Spirit to really lead us into the presence of God, and should not be hasty in words until He has actually brought us there.

One night a very active Christian man dropped into a little prayer-meeting that I was leading. Before we knelt to pray, I said something like the above, telling all the friends to be sure before they prayed, and while they were praying, that they really were in God's presence, that they had the thought of Him definitely in mind, and to be more taken up with Him than with their petition. A few days after I met this same gentleman, and he said that this simple thought was entirely new to him, that it had made prayer an entirely new experience to him.

If then we would pray aright, these two little words must sink deep into our hearts, "*unto God.*"

2. The second secret of effective praying is found in the same verse, in the words "*without ceasing.*"

In the Revised Version, "without ceasing" is rendered "earnestly." Neither rendering gives the full force of the Greek. The word means literally "stretched-out-ed-ly." It is a pictorial word, and wonderfully expressive. It represents the soul on a stretch of earnest and intense desire. "Intensely" would perhaps come as near translating it as any English word. It is the word used of our Lord in Luke 22:44 where it is said, "He prayed more earnestly: and His sweat was as it were great drops of blood falling down to the ground."

We read in Heb. 5:7 that "in the days of His flesh" Christ "offered up prayers and supplications with strong crying and tears." In Rom. 15:30, Paul beseeches the saints in Rome to *strive* together with him in their prayers. The word translated "strive" means primarily to contend as in athletic games or in a fight. In other words, the prayer that prevails with God is the prayer into which we put our whole soul, stretching out toward God in intense and agonizing desire. Much of our modern prayer has no power in it because there is no heart in it. We rush into God's presence, run through a string of petitions, jump up and go out. If someone should ask us an hour afterward for what we prayed, oftentimes we could not tell. If we put so little heart into our prayers, we cannot expect God to put much heart into answering them.

We hear much in our day of the rest of faith, but there is such a thing as the fight of faith in prayer as well as in effort. Those who would have us think that they have attained to some sublime height of faith and trust because they never know any agony of conflict or of prayer, have surely gotten beyond their Lord, and beyond the mightiest victors for God, both in effort and prayer, that the ages of Christian history have known. When we learn to come to God with an intensity of desire that wrings the soul, then shall we know a power in prayer that most of us do not know now.

But how shall we attain to this earnestness in prayer?

Not by trying to work ourselves up into it. The true method is explained in Rom. 8:26, "And in like manner the Spirit also helpeth our infirmity: for we know not how to pray as we ought; but the Spirit Himself maketh intercession for us with groanings which cannot be uttered." The earnestness that we work up in the energy of the flesh is a repulsive thing. The earnestness wrought in us by the power of the Holy Spirit is pleasing to God. Here again, if we would pray aright, we must look to the Spirit of God to teach us to pray.

It is in this connection that fasting comes. In Dan. 9:3 we read that Daniel set his face "unto the Lord God, to seek by prayer and supplications, with fasting, and sackcloth, and ashes." There are those who think that fasting belongs to the old dispensation; but when we look at Acts 14:23, and Acts 13:2, 3, we find that it was practiced by the earnest men of the apostolic day.

If we would pray with power, we should pray with fasting. This of course does not mean that we should fast every time we pray; but there are times of emergency or special crisis in work or in our individual lives, when men of downright earnestness will withdraw themselves even from the gratification of natural appetites that would be perfectly proper under other circumstances, that they may give themselves up wholly to prayer. There is a peculiar power in such prayer. Every great crisis in life and work should be met in that way. There is nothing pleasing to God in our giving up in a purely Pharisaic and legal way things which are pleasant, but there is power in that downright earnestness and determination to obtain in prayer the things of which we sorely feel our need, that leads us to put away everything, even the things in themselves most right and necessary, that we may set our faces to find God, and obtain blessings from Him.

3. A third secret of right praying is also found in this same verse, Acts 12:5. It appears in the three words "*of the church*."

There is power in *united prayer*. Of course there is power in the prayer of an individual, but there is vastly increased power in united prayer. God delights in the unity of His people, and seeks to emphasize it in every way, and so He pronounces a special blessing upon united prayer. We read in Matt. 18:19, "If two of you shall agree on earth as touching anything that they shall ask, it shall be done for them of My Father which is in heaven." This unity, however, must be real. The passage just quoted does not say that if two shall agree in asking, but if two shall agree *as touching* anything they shall ask. Two persons might agree to ask for the same thing, and yet there be no real agreement as touching the thing they asked. One might ask it because he really desired it, the other might ask it simply to please his friend. But where there is real agreement, where the Spirit of God brings two believers into perfect harmony as concerning that which they may ask of God, where the Spirit lays the same burden on two hearts; in all such prayer there is absolutely irresistible power.

Chapter III: Obeying and Praying

1. One of the most significant verses in the Bible on prayer is 1 John 3:22. John says, "And whatsoever we ask, we receive of Him, because we keep His commandments, and do those things that are pleasing in His sight."

What an astounding statement! John says in so many words, that everything he asked for he got. How many of us can say this: "Whatsoever I ask I receive"? But John explains why this was so, "Because we keep His commandments, and do those things that are pleasing in His sight." In other words, the one who expects God to do as he asks Him, must on his part *do whatever God bids him*. If we give a listening ear to all God's commands to us, He will give a listening ear to all our petitions to Him. If, on the other hand, we turn a deaf ear to His precepts, He will be likely to turn a deaf ear to our prayers. Here we find the secret of much unanswered prayer. We are not listening to God's Word, and therefore He is not listening to our petitions.

I was once speaking to a woman who had been a professed Christian, but had given it all up. I asked her why she was not a Christian still. She replied, because she did not believe the Bible. I asked her why she did not believe the Bible.

"Because I have tried its promises and found them untrue."

"Which promises?"

"The promises about prayer."

"Which promises about prayer?"

"Does it not say in the Bible, 'Whatsoever ye ask believing ye shall receive'?"

"It says something nearly like that."

"Well, I asked fully expecting to get and did not receive, so the promise failed."

"Was the promise made to you?"

"Why, certainly, it is made to all Christians, is it not?"

"No, God carefully defines who the 'ye's' are, whose believing prayers He agrees to answer."

I then turned her to 1 John 3:22, and read the description of those whose prayers had power with God.

"Now," I said, "were you keeping His commandments and doing those things which are pleasing in His sight?"

She frankly confessed that she was not, and soon came to see that the real difficulty was not with God's promises, but with herself. That is the difficulty with many an unanswered prayer to-day: the one who offers it is not obedient.

If we would have power in prayer, we must be earnest students of His Word to find out what His will regarding us is, and then having found it, do it. One unconfessed act of disobedience on our part will shut the ear of God against many petitions.

2. But this verse goes beyond the mere keeping of God's commandments. John tells us that we must *do those things that are pleasing in His sight.*

There are many things which it would be pleasing to God for us to do which He has not specifically commanded us. A true child is not content with merely doing those things which his father specifically commands him to do. He studies to know his father's will, and if he thinks that there is any thing that he can do that would please his father, he does it gladly, though his father has never given him any specific order to do it. So it is with the true child of God. He does not ask merely whether certain things are commanded or certain things forbidden. He studies to know his Father's will in all things.

There are many Christians to-day who are doing things that are not pleasing to God, and leaving undone things which would be pleasing to God. When you speak to them about these things they will confront you at once with the question, "Is there any command in the Bible not to do this thing?" And if you cannot show them some verse in which the matter in question is plainly forbidden, they think they are under no obligation whatever to give it up; but a true child of God does not demand a specific command. If we make it our study to find out and to do the things which are pleasing to God, He will make His study to do the things which are pleasing to us. Here again we find the explanation of much unanswered prayer: We are not making it the study of our lives to know what would please our Father, and so our prayers are not answered.

Take as an illustration of questions that are constantly coming up, the matter of theater going, dancing and the use of tobacco. Many who are indulging in these things will ask you triumphantly if you speak against them, "Does the Bible say, 'Thou shalt not go to the theater'?" "Does the Bible say, 'Thou shalt not dance'?" "Does the Bible say, 'Thou shalt not smoke'?" That is not the question. The question is, Is our heavenly Father well pleased when He sees one of His children in the theater, at the dance, or smoking? That is a question for each to decide for himself, prayerfully, seeking light from the Holy Spirit. "Where is the harm in these things?" many ask. It is aside from our purpose to go into the general question, but beyond a doubt there is this great harm in many a case; they rob our prayers of power.

3. Psalm 145:18 throws a great deal of light on the question of how to pray: "The Lord is nigh unto all them that call upon Him, to all that call upon Him in truth."

That little expression "in truth" is worthy of study. If you will take your concordance and go through the Bible, you will find that this expression means "in reality," "in sincerity." The prayer that God answers is the prayer that is real, the prayer that asks for something that is sincerely desired.

Much prayer is insincere. People ask for things which they do not wish. Many a woman is praying for the conversion of her husband, who does not really wish her husband to be converted. She thinks that she does, but if she knew what would be involved in the conversion of her husband, how it would necessitate an entire revolution in his manner of doing business, and how consequently it would reduce their income and make necessary an entire change in their method of living, the real prayer of her heart would be, if she were to be sincere with God:

"O God, do not convert my husband."

She does not wish his conversion at so great cost.

Many a church is praying for a revival that does not really desire a revival. They think they do, for to their minds a revival means an increase of membership, an increase of income, an increase of reputation among the churches, but if they knew what a real revival meant, what a searching of hearts on the part of professed Christians would be involved, what a radical transformation of individual, domestic and social life would be brought about, and many other things that would come to pass if the Spirit of God was poured out in reality and power; if all this were known, the real cry of the church would be:

"O God, keep us from having a revival."

Many a minister is praying for the baptism with the Holy Spirit who does not really desire it. He thinks he does, for the baptism with the Spirit means to him new joy, new power in preaching the Word, a wider reputation among men, a larger prominence in the church of Christ. But if he understood what a baptism with the Holy Spirit really involved, how for example it would necessarily bring him into antagonism with the world, and with unspiritual Christians, how it would cause his name to be "cast out as evil," how it might necessitate his leaving a good comfortable living and going down to work in the slums, or even in some foreign land; if he understood all this, his prayer quite likely would be—if he were to express the real wish of his heart,—

"O God, save me from being baptized with the Holy Ghost."

But when we do come to the place where we really desire the conversion of friends at any cost, really desire the outpouring of the Holy Spirit whatever it may involve, really desire the baptism with the Holy Ghost come what may, where we desire anything "in truth" and then call upon God for it "in truth," God is going to hear.

Chapter IV: Praying in the Name of Christ and According to the Will of God

1. It was a wonderful word about prayer that Jesus spoke to His disciples on the night before His crucifixion, "Whatsoever ye shall ask *in My name*, that will I do, that the Father may be glorified in the Son. If ye shall ask anything in My name, I will do it."

Prayer in the name of Christ has power with God. God is well pleased with His Son Jesus Christ. He hears Him always, and He also hears always the prayer that is really in His name. There is a fragrance in the name of Christ that makes acceptable to God every prayer that bears it.

But what is it to pray in the name of Christ?

Many explanations have been attempted that to ordinary minds do not explain. But there is nothing mystical or mysterious about this expression. If one will go through the

Bible and examine all the passages in which the expression "in My name" or "in His name" or synonymous expressions are used, he will find that it means just about what it does in modern usage. If I go to a bank and hand in a check with my name signed to it, I ask of that bank *in my own name*. If I have money deposited in that bank, the check will be cashed; if not, it will not be. If, however, I go to a bank with somebody else's name signed to the check, I am asking *in his name*, and it does not matter whether I have money in that bank or any other, if the person whose name is signed to the check has money there, the check will be cashed.

If, for example, I should go to the First National Bank of Chicago, and present a check which I had signed for $50.00, the paying teller would say to me:

"Why, Mr. Torrey, we cannot cash that. You have no money in this bank."

But if I should go to the First National Bank with a check for $5,000.00 made payable to me, and signed by one of the large depositors in that bank, they would not ask whether I had money in that bank or in any bank, but would honor the check at once.

So it is when I go to the bank of heaven, when I go to God in prayer. I have nothing deposited there, I have absolutely no credit there, and if I go in my own name I will get absolutely nothing; but Jesus Christ has unlimited credit in heaven, and He has granted to me the privilege of going to the bank with His name on my checks, and when I thus go, my prayers will be honored to any extent.

To pray then in the name of Christ is to pray on the ground, not of my credit, but His; to renounce the thought that I have any claims on God whatever, and approach Him on the ground of God's claims. Praying in the name of Christ is not merely adding the phrase "I ask these things in Jesus' name" to my prayer. I may put that phrase in my prayer and really be resting in my own merit all the time. On the other hand, I may omit that phrase but really be resting in the merit of Christ all the time. But when I really do approach God, not on the ground of my merit, but on the ground of Christ's merit, not on the ground of my goodness, but on the ground of the atoning blood (Heb. 10:19), God will hear me. Very much of our modern prayer is vain because men approach God imagining that they have some claim upon God whereby He is under obligations to answer their prayers.

Years ago when Mr. Moody was young in Christian work, he visited a town in Illinois. A judge in the town was an infidel. This judge's wife besought Mr. Moody to call upon her husband, but Mr. Moody replied:

"I cannot talk with your husband. I am only an uneducated young Christian, and your husband is a book infidel."

But the wife would not take no for an answer, so Mr. Moody made the call. The clerks in the outer office tittered as the young salesman from Chicago went in to talk with the scholarly judge.

The conversation was short. Mr. Moody said:

"Judge, I can't talk with you. You are a book infidel, and I have no learning, but I simply want to say if you are ever converted, I want you to let me know."

The judge replied: "Yes, young man, if I am ever converted I will let you know. Yes, I will let you know."

The conversation ended. The clerks tittered still louder when the zealous young Christian left the office, but the judge was converted within a year. Mr. Moody visiting the town again asked the judge to explain how it came about. The judge said:

"One night, when my wife was at prayer meeting, I began to grow very uneasy and miserable. I did not know what was the matter with me, but finally retired before my wife came home. I could not sleep all that night. I got up early, told my wife that I would eat no breakfast, and went down to the office. I told the clerks they could take a holiday, and shut myself up in the inner office. I kept growing more and more miserable, and finally I got down and asked God to forgive my sins, but I would not say 'for Jesus' sake,' for I was a Unitarian and I did not believe in the atonement. I kept praying 'God forgive my sins'; but no answer came. At last in desperation I cried, 'O God, for Christ's sake forgive my sins,' and found peace at once."

The judge had no access to God until he came in the name of Christ, but when he thus came, he was heard and answered at once.

2. Great light is thrown upon the subject "How to Pray" by 1 John 5:14, 15: "And this is the boldness which we have toward Him, that if we ask anything *according to His will*, He heareth us; and if we know that He heareth us whatsoever we ask, we know that we have the petitions which we have asked of Him."

This passage teaches us plainly that if we are to pray aright, we must pray according to God's will, then will we beyond a peradventure get the thing we ask of Him.

But can we know the will of God? Can we know that any specific prayer is according to His will?

We most surely can.

How?

(1) First by the Word. God has revealed His will in His Word.

When anything is definitely promised in the Word of God, we know that it is His will to give that thing. If then when I pray, I can find some definite promise of God's Word and lay that promise before God, I know that He hears me, and if I know that He hears me, I know that I have the petition that I have asked of Him. For example, when I pray for wisdom I know that it is the will of God to give me wisdom, for He says so in James 1:5: "If any of you lack wisdom, let him ask of God, that giveth to all men liberally, and upbraideth not; and it shall be given him." So when I ask for wisdom I know that the prayer is heard, and that wisdom will be given me. In like manner when I pray for the Holy Spirit I know from Luke 11:13 that it is God's will, that my prayer is heard, and that I have the petition that I have asked of Him: "If ye then, being evil, know how to give good gifts unto your children, how much more shall your heavenly Father give the Holy Spirit to them that ask Him?"

Some years ago a minister came to me at the close of an address on prayer at a Y.M.C.A. Bible school, and said,

"You have produced upon those young men the impression that they can ask for definite things and get the very things that they ask."

I replied that I did not know whether that was the impression that I produced or not, but that was certainly the impression that I desired to produce.

"But," he replied, "that is not right. We cannot be sure, for we don't know God's will."

I turned him at once to James 1:5, read it and said to him, "Is it not God's will to give us wisdom, and if you ask for wisdom do you not know that you are going to get it?"

"Ah!" he said, "we don't know what wisdom is."

I said, "No, if we did, we would not need to ask; but whatever wisdom may be, don't you know that you will get it?"

Certainly it is our privilege to know. When we have a specific promise in the Word of God, if we doubt that it is God's will, or if we doubt that God will do the thing that we ask, we make God a liar.

Here is one of the greatest secrets of prevailing prayer: To study the Word to find what God's will is as revealed there in the promises, and then simply take these promises and spread them out before God in prayer with the absolutely unwavering expectation that He will do what He has promised in His Word.

(2) But there is still another way in which we may know the will of God, that is, by the teaching of His Holy Spirit. There are many things that we need from God which are not covered by any specific promise, but we are not left in ignorance of the will of God even then. In Rom. 8:26, 27 we are told, "And in like manner the Spirit also helpeth our infirmity: for we know not how to pray as we ought; but the Spirit Himself maketh intercession for us with groanings which cannot be uttered; and He that searcheth the hearts knoweth what is the mind of the spirit, because He maketh intercession for the saints *according to the will of God*." Here we are distinctly told that the Spirit of God prays in us, draws out our prayer, in the line of God's will. When we are thus led out by the Holy Spirit in any direction, to pray for any given object, we may do it in all confidence that it is God's will, and that we are to get the very thing we ask of Him, even though there is no specific promise to cover the case. Often God by His Spirit lays upon us a heavy burden of prayer for some given individual. We cannot rest, we pray for him with groanings which cannot be uttered. Perhaps the man is entirely beyond our reach, but God hears the prayer, and in many a case it is not long before we hear of his definite conversion.

The passage 1 John 5:14, 15 is one of the most abused passages in the Bible: "This is *the confidence* that we have in Him, that, if we ask anything according to His will, He heareth us; and if we know that He hear us, whatsoever we ask, we know that we have the petitions that we desired of Him." The Holy Spirit beyond a doubt put it into the Bible to encourage our faith. It begins with "This is *the confidence* that we have in Him," and closes with "*We know* that we have the petitions that we desired of Him;" but one of the most frequent usages of this passage, which was so manifestly given to beget confidence, is to introduce an element of uncertainty into our prayers. Oftentimes when one waxes confident in prayer, some cautious brother will come and say:

"Now, don't be too confident. If it is God's will He will do it. You should put in, 'If it be Thy will.'"

Doubtless there are many times when we do not know the will of God, and in all prayer submission to the excellent will of God should underlie it; but when we know God's will, there need be no "ifs"; and this passage was not put into the Bible in order that we might introduce "ifs" into all our prayers, but in order that we might throw our "ifs" to the wind, and have "*confidence*" and "*know* that we have the petitions which we have asked of Him."

Chapter V: Praying in the Spirit

1. Over and over again in what has already been said, we have seen our dependence upon the Holy Spirit in prayer. This comes out very definitely in Eph. 6:18, "Praying always with all prayer and supplication *in the Spirit*," and in Jude 20, "Praying *in the Holy Ghost*." Indeed the whole secret of prayer is found in these three words, "in the Spirit." It is the prayer that God the Holy Spirit inspires that God the Father answers.

The disciples did not know how to pray as they ought, so they came to Jesus and said, "Lord teach us to pray." We know not how to pray as we ought, but we have another Teacher and Guide right at hand to help us (John 14:16, 17), "The Spirit helpeth our infirmity" (Rom. 8:26). He teaches us how to pray. True prayer is prayer in the Spirit; that is, the prayer the Spirit inspires and directs. When we come into God's presence we should recognize "our infirmity," our ignorance of what we should pray for or how we should pray for it, and in the consciousness of our utter inability to pray aright we should look up to the Holy Spirit, casting ourselves utterly upon Him to direct our prayers, to lead out our desires and to guide our utterance of them.

Nothing can be more foolish in prayer than to rush heedlessly into God's presence, and ask the first thing that comes into our mind, or that some thoughtless friend has asked us to pray for. When we first come into God's presence we should be silent before Him. We should look up to Him to send His Holy Spirit to teach us how to pray. We must wait for the Holy Spirit, and surrender ourselves to the Spirit, then we shall pray aright.

Oftentimes when we come to God in prayer, we do not feel like praying. What shall one do in such a case? Cease praying until he does feel like it? Not at all. When we feel least like praying is the time when we most need to pray. We should wait quietly before God and tell Him how cold and prayerless our hearts are, and look up to Him and trust Him and expect Him to send the Holy Spirit to warm our hearts and draw them out in prayer. It will not be long before the glow of the Spirit's presence will fill our hearts, and we will begin to pray with freedom, directness, earnestness and power. Many of the most blessed seasons of prayer I have ever known have begun with a feeling of utter deadness and prayerlessness, but in my helplessness and coldness I have cast myself upon God, and looked to Him to send His Holy Spirit to teach me to pray, and He has done it.

When we pray in the Spirit, we will pray for the right things and in the right way. There will be joy and power in our prayer.

2. If we are to pray with power we must pray *with faith*. In Mark 11:24 Jesus says, "Therefore I say unto you, What things soever ye desire, when ye pray, believe that ye receive them, and ye shall have them." No matter how positive any promise of God's Word may be, we will not enjoy it in actual experience unless we confidently expect its fulfillment in answer to our prayer. "If any of you lack wisdom," says James, "let him ask of God that giveth to all men liberally, and upbraideth not; and it shall be given him." Now that promise is as positive as a promise can be, but the next verse adds,

"But let him ask in faith, nothing doubting: for he that doubteth is like the surge of the sea driven by the wind and tossed. For let not that man think that he shall receive anything of the Lord." There must then be confident unwavering expectation. But there is a faith that goes beyond expectation, that believes that the prayer is heard and the promise granted. This comes out in the Revised Version of Mark 11:24, "Therefore I say unto you, All things whatsoever ye pray and ask for, believe that ye *have* received them, and ye shall have them."

But how can one get this faith?

Let us say with all emphasis, it cannot be pumped up. Many a one reads this promise about the prayer of faith, and then asks for things that he desires and tries to make himself believe that God has heard the prayer. This ends only in disappointment, for it is not real faith and the thing is not granted. It is at this point that many people make a collapse of faith altogether by trying to work up faith by an effort of their will, and as the thing they made themselves believe they expected to get is not given, the very foundation of faith is oftentimes undermined.

But how does real faith come?

Rom 10:17 answers the question: "So then faith cometh by hearing, and hearing *by the Word of God*." If we are to have real faith, we must study the Word of God and find out what is promised, then simply believe the promises of God. Faith must have a warrant.

Trying to believe something that you want to believe is not faith. Believing what God says in His Word is faith. If I am to have faith when I pray, I must find some promise in the Word of God on which to rest my faith. Faith furthermore comes through the Spirit. The Spirit knows the will of God, and if I pray in the Spirit, and look to the Spirit to teach me God's will, He will lead me out in prayer along the line of that will, and give me faith that the prayer is to be answered; but in no case does real faith come by simply determining that you are going to get the thing that you want to get.

If there is no promise in the Word of God, and no clear leading of the Spirit, there can be no real faith, and there should be no upbraiding of self for lack of faith in such a case. But if the thing desired is promised in the Word of God, we may well upbraid ourselves for lack of faith if we doubt; for we are making God a liar by doubting His Word.

Chapter VI: Always Praying and Not Fainting

In two parables in the Gospel of Luke, Jesus teaches with great emphasis the lesson that men ought always to pray and not to faint. The first parable is found in Luke 11:5-8, and the other in Luke 18:1-8.

"And He said unto them, Which of you shall have a friend, and shall go unto him at midnight, and say unto him: 'Friend, lend me three loaves; for a friend of mine in his journey is come to me, and I have nothing to set before him?' And he from within shall answer and say: 'Trouble me not: the door is now shut, and my children are with me in bed. I cannot rise and give thee.' I say unto you, Though he will not rise and give him because he is his friend, yet because of his importunity he will rise and give him as many as he needeth." (Luke 11:5-8)

"And He spake a parable unto them to this end, that men always ought to pray and not to faint, saying: There was in a city a judge which feared not God, neither regarded man; and there was a widow in that city; and she came to him, saying:

"'Avenge me of mine adversary.'

"And he would not for a while; but afterward he said within himself: 'Though I fear not God, nor regard man, yet because this widow troubleth me I will avenge her, lest by her continual coming she weary me.'

"And the Lord said, Hear what the unjust judge saith. And shall not God avenge his own elect, which cry day and night unto Him, though He bear long with them? I tell you that He will avenge them speedily. Nevertheless when the Son of man cometh, shall He find faith on the earth?" (Luke 18:1-8)

In the former of these two parables Jesus sets forth the necessity of importunity in prayer in a startling way. The word rendered "importunity" means literally "shamelessness," as if Jesus would have us understand that God would have us draw nigh to Him with a determination to obtain the things we seek that will not be put to shame by any seeming refusal or delay on God's part. God delights in the holy boldness that will not take "no" for an answer. It is an expression of great faith, and nothing pleases God more than faith.

Jesus seemed to put the Syro-Phoenician woman away almost with rudeness, but she would not be put away, and Jesus looked upon her shameless importunity with pleasure, and said, "O woman, great is thy faith; be it unto thee even as thou wilt." (Matt. 15:28) God does not always let us get things at our first effort. He would train us and make us strong men by compelling us to work hard for the best things. So also He does not always give us what we ask in answer to the first prayer; He would train us and make us strong men of prayer by compelling us to pray hard for the best things. He makes us *pray through.*

I am glad that this is so. There is no more blessed training in prayer than that that comes through being compelled to ask again and again and again even through a long period of years before one obtains that which he seeks from God. Many people call it submission to the will of God when God does not grant them their requests at the first or second asking, and they say:

"Well, perhaps it is not God's will."

As a rule this is not submission, but spiritual laziness. We do not call it submission to the will of God when we give up after one or two efforts to obtain things by action; we call it lack of strength of character. When the strong man of action starts out to accomplish a thing, if he does not accomplish it the first, or second or one hundredth time, he keeps hammering away until he does accomplish it; and the strong man of prayer when he starts to pray for a thing keeps on praying until he prays it through, and obtains what he seeks. We should be careful about what we ask from God, but when we do begin to pray for a thing we should never give up praying for it until we get it, or until God makes it very clear and very definite to us that it is not His will to give it.

Some would have us believe that it shows unbelief to pray twice for the same thing, that we ought to "take it" the first time that we ask. Doubtless there are times when we are able through faith in the Word or the leading of the Holy Spirit to *claim* the first time that which we have asked of God; but beyond question there are other times when we must pray again and again and again for the same thing before we get our answer. Those who have gotten beyond praying twice for the same thing have gotten beyond their Master, (Matt. 26:44). George Muller prayed for two men daily for upwards of sixty years. One of these men was converted shortly before his death, I think at the last service that George Muller held, the other was converted within a year after his death. One of the great needs of the present day is men and women who will not only start out to pray for things, but pray on and on and on until they obtain that which they seek from the Lord.

Chapter VII: Abiding in Christ

"If ye abide in Me, and My words abide in you, ye shall ask what ye will, and it shall be done unto you." (John 15:7) The whole secret of prayer is found in these words of our Lord. Here is prayer that has unbounded power: "Ask *what ye will*, and it shall be done unto you."

There is a way then of asking and getting precisely what we ask and getting all we ask. Christ gives two conditions of this all-prevailing prayer:

1. The first condition is, "If ye abide in Me."

What is it to abide in Christ?

Some explanations that have been given of this are so mystical or so profound that to many simple-minded children of God they mean practically nothing at all; but what Jesus meant was really very simple.

He had been comparing Himself to a vine, His disciples to the branches in the vine. Some branches continued in the vine, that is, remained in living union with the vine, so that the sap or life of the vine constantly flowed into these branches. They had no independent life of their own. Everything in them was simply the outcome of the life of the vine flowing into them. Their buds, their leaves, their blossoms, their fruit, were really not theirs, but the buds, leaves, blossoms and fruit of the vine. Other branches were completely severed from the vine, or else the flow of the sap or life of the vine into them was in some way hindered. Now for us to abide in Christ is for us to bear the same relation to Him that the first sort of branches bear to the vine; that is to say, to abide in Christ is to renounce any independent life of our own, to give up trying to think our thoughts, or form our resolutions, or cultivate our feelings, and simply and constantly look to Christ to think His thoughts in us, to form His purposes in us, to feel His emotions and affections in us. It is to renounce all life independent of Christ, and constantly to look to Him for the inflow of His life into us, and the outworking of His life through us. When we do this, and in so far as we do this, our prayers will obtain that which we seek from God.

This must necessarily be so, for our desires will not be our own desires, but Christ's, and our prayers will not in reality be our own prayers, but Christ praying in us. Such prayers will always be in harmony with God's will, and the Father heareth Him always. When our prayers fail it is because they are indeed our prayers. We have conceived the desire and framed the petition of ourselves, instead of looking to Christ to pray through us.

To say that one should be abiding in Christ in all his prayers, looking to Christ to pray through Him rather than praying himself, is simply saying in another way that one should pray "in the Spirit." When we thus abide in Christ, our thoughts are not our own thoughts, but His, our joys are not our own joys, but His, our fruit is not our own fruit, but His; just as the buds, leaves, blossoms and fruit of the branch that abides in the vine are not the buds, leaves, blossoms and fruit of the branch, but of the vine itself whose life is flowing into the branch and manifests itself in these buds, leaves, blossoms and fruit.

To abide in Christ, one must of course already be in Christ through the acceptance of Christ as an atoning Savior from the guilt of sin, a risen Savior from the power of sin, and a Lord and Master over all his life. Being in Christ, all that we have to do to abide (or continue) in Christ is simply to renounce our self-life—utterly renouncing every thought, every purpose, every desire, every affection of our own, and just looking day by day and hour by hour for Jesus Christ to form His thoughts, His purposes, His affections, His desires in us. Abiding in Christ is really a very simple matter, though it is a wonderful life of privilege and of power.

2. But there is another condition stated in this verse, though it is really involved in the first: "And My words abide in you."

If we are to obtain from God all that we ask from Him, Christ's words must abide or continue in us. We must study His words, fairly devour His words, let them sink into our thought and into our heart, keep them in our memory, obey them constantly in our life, let them shape and mold our daily life and our every act.

This is really the method of abiding in Christ. It is through His words that Jesus imparts Himself to us. The words He speaks unto us, they are spirit and they are life. (John 6:33) It is vain to expect power in prayer unless we meditate much upon the words of Christ, and let them sink deep and find a permanent abode in our hearts. There are many who wonder why they are so powerless in prayer, but the very simple explanation of it all is found in their neglect of the words of Christ. They have not hidden His words in their hearts; His words do not abide in them. It is not by seasons of mystical meditation and rapturous experiences that we learn to abide in Christ; it is by feeding upon His word, His written word as found in the Bible, and looking to the Holy Spirit to implant these words in our hearts and to make them a living thing in our hearts. If we thus let the words of Christ abide in us, they will stir us up in prayer. They will be the mold in which our prayers are shaped, and our prayers will be necessarily along the line of God's will, and will prevail with Him. Prevailing prayer is almost an impossibility where there is neglect of the study of the Word of God.

Mere intellectual study of the Word of God is not enough; there must be meditation upon it. The Word of God must be revolved over and over and over in the mind, with a constant looking to God by His Spirit to make that Word a living thing in the heart. The prayer that is born of meditation upon the Word of God is the prayer that soars upward most easily to God's listening ear.

George Muller, one of the mightiest men of prayer of the present generation, when the hour for prayer came would begin by reading and meditating upon God's Word until out of the study of the Word a prayer began to form itself in his heart. Thus God Himself was a real author of the prayer, and God answered the prayers which He Himself had inspired.

The Word of God is the instrument through which the Holy Spirit works, it is the sword of the Spirit in more senses than one; and the one who would know the work of the Holy Spirit in any direction must feed upon the Word. The one who would pray in the Spirit must meditate much upon the Word, that the Holy Spirit may have something through which He can work. The Holy Spirit works His prayers in us through the Word, and neglect of the Word makes praying in the Holy Spirit an impossibility. If we would feed the fire of our prayers with the fuel of God's Word, all our difficulties in prayer would disappear.

Chapter VIII: Praying with Thanksgiving

There are two words often overlooked in the lesson about prayer which Paul gives us in Phil. 4:6, 7, "In nothing be anxious; but in everything by prayer and supplication with thanksgiving let your requests be made known unto God. And the peace of God, which passeth all understanding, shall guard your hearts and your thoughts in Christ Jesus." The two important words often overlooked are, "*with thanksgiving.*"

In approaching God to ask for new blessings, we should never forget to return thanks for blessings already granted. If any one of us would stop and think how many of the prayers which we have offered to God have been answered, and how seldom we have gone back to God to return thanks for the answers thus given, I am sure we would be overwhelmed with confusion. We should be just as definite in returning thanks as we are in prayer. We come to God with most specific petitions, but when we return thanks to Him, our thanksgiving is indefinite and general.

Doubtless one reason why so many of our prayers lack power is because we have neglected to return thanks for blessings already received. If any one were to constantly come to us asking help from us, and should never say "Thank you" for the help thus given, we would soon tire of helping one so ungrateful. Indeed, regard for the one we were helping would hold us back from encouraging such rank ingratitude. Doubtless our heavenly Father out of a wise regard for our highest welfare oftentimes refuses to answer petitions that we send up to Him in order that we may be brought to a sense of our ingratitude and taught to be thankful.

God is deeply grieved by the thanklessness and ingratitude of which so many of us are guilty. When Jesus healed the ten lepers and only one came back to give Him thanks, in wonderment and pain He exclaimed,

"Were not the ten cleansed? But where are the nine?" (Luke 17:17)

How often must He look down upon us in sadness at our forgetfulness of His repeated blessings, and His frequent answer to our prayers.

Returning thanks for blessings already received increases our faith and enables us to approach God with new boldness and new assurance. Doubtless the reason so many have so little faith when they pray, is because they take so little time to meditate upon and thank God for blessings already received. As one meditates upon the answers to prayers already granted, faith waxes bolder and bolder, and we come to feel in the very depths of our souls that there is nothing too hard for the Lord. As we reflect upon the wondrous goodness of God toward us on the one hand, and upon the other hand upon the little thought and strength and time that we ever put into thanksgiving, we may well humble ourselves before God and confess our sin.

The mighty men of prayer in the Bible, and the mighty men of prayer throughout the ages of the church's history have been men who were much given to thanksgiving and praise. David was a mighty man of prayer, and how his Psalms abound with thanksgiving and praise. The apostles were mighty men of prayer; of them we read that "they were continually in the temple, praising and blessing God." Paul was a mighty man of prayer, and how often in his epistles he bursts out in definite thanksgiving to God for definite blessings and definite answers to prayers. Jesus is our model in prayer as in everything else. We find in the study of His life that His manner of returning thanks at the simplest meal was so noticeable that two of His disciples recognized Him by this after His resurrection.

Thanksgiving is one of the inevitable results of being filled with the Holy Spirit and one who does not learn "in everything to give thanks" cannot continue to pray in the Spirit. If we would learn to pray with power we would do well to let these two words sink deep into our hearts: "WITH THANKSGIVING."

Chapter IX: Hindrances to Prayer

We have gone very carefully into the positive conditions of prevailing prayer; but there are some things which hinder prayer. These God has made very plain in His Word.

1. The first hindrance to prayer we will find in James 4:3, "Ye ask and receive not *because ye ask amiss, that ye may spend it in your pleasures.*"

A selfish purpose in prayer robs prayer of power. Very many prayers are selfish. These may be prayers for things for which it is perfectly proper to ask, for things which it is the will of God to give, but the motive of the prayer is entirely wrong, and so the prayer falls powerless to the ground. The true purpose in prayer is that God may be glorified in the answer. If we ask any petition merely that we may receive something to use in our pleasures or in our own gratification in one way or another, we "ask amiss" and need not expect to receive what we ask. This explains why many prayers remain unanswered.

For example, many a woman is praying for the conversion of her husband. That certainly is a most proper thing to ask; but many a woman's motive in asking for the conversion of her husband is entirely improper, it is selfish. She desires that her husband may be converted because it would be so much more pleasant for her to have a husband who sympathized with her; or it is so painful to think that her husband might die and be lost forever. For some such selfish reason as this she desires to have her husband converted. The prayer is purely selfish. Why should a woman desire the conversion of her husband? First of all and above all, that God may be glorified; because she cannot bear the thought that God the Father should be dishonored by her husband trampling underfoot the Son of God.

Many pray for a revival. That certainly is a prayer that is pleasing to God, it is along the line of His will; but many prayers for revivals are purely selfish. The churches desire revivals in order that the membership may be increased, in order that the church may have a position of more power and influence in the community, in order that the church treasury may be filled, in order that a good report may be made at the presbytery or conference or association. For such low purposes as these, churches and ministers oftentimes are praying for a revival, and oftentimes too God does not answer the prayer. Why should we pray for a revival? For the glory of God, because we cannot endure it that God should continue to be dishonored by the worldliness of the church, by the sins of unbelievers, by the proud unbelief of the day; because God's Word is being made void; in order that God may be glorified by the outpouring of His Spirit on the Church of Christ. For these reasons first of all and above all, we should pray for a revival.

Many a prayer for the Holy Spirit is a purely selfish prayer.

It certainly is God's will to give the Holy Spirit to them that ask Him—He has told us so plainly in His Word (Luke 11:13), but many a prayer for the Holy Spirit is hindered by the selfishness of the motive that lies back of the prayer. Men and women pray for the Holy Spirit in order that they may be happy, or in order that they may be saved from the wretchedness of defeat in their lives, or in order that they may have power as Christian workers, or for some other purely selfish motive. Why should we pray for the Spirit? In order that God may no longer be dishonored by the low level of our Christian lives and by our ineffectiveness in service, in order that God may be glorified in the new beauty that comes into our lives and the new power that comes into our service.

2. The second hindrance to prayer we find in Is. 59:1, 2: "Behold, the Lord's hand is not shortened, that it cannot save; neither His ear heavy, that it cannot hear. But *your iniquities have separated between you and your God, and your sins have hid His face from you, that He will not hear.*"

Sin hinders prayer. Many a man prays and prays and prays, and gets absolutely no answer to his prayer. Perhaps he is tempted to think that it is not the will of God to answer, or he may think that the days when God answered prayer, if He ever did, are over. So the Israelites seem to have thought. They thought that the Lord's hand was shortened, that it could not save, and that His ear had become heavy that it could no longer hear.

"Not so," said Isaiah, "God's ear is just as open to hear as ever, His hand just as mighty to save; but there is a hindrance. That hindrance is your own sins. Your iniquities have separated between you and your God, and your sins have hid His face from you that He will not hear."

It is so to-day. Many and many a man is crying to God in vain, simply because of sin in his life. It may be some sin in the past that has been unconfessed and unjudged, it may be some sin in the present that is cherished, very likely is not even looked upon as sin, but there the sin is, hidden away somewhere in the heart or in the life, and God "will not hear."

Any one who finds his prayers ineffective should not conclude that the thing which he asks of God is not according to His will, but should go alone with God with the Psalmist's prayer, "Search me, O God, and know my heart: try me, and know my thoughts: and see if there be any wicked way in me" (Ps. 139:23, 24), and wait before Him until He puts His finger upon the thing that is displeasing in His sight. Then this sin should be confessed and put away.

I well remember a time in my life when I was praying for two definite things that it seemed that I must have, or God would be dishonored; but the answer did not come. I awoke in the middle of the night in great physical suffering and great distress of soul. I cried to God for these things, reasoned with Him as to how necessary it was that I get them, and get them at once; but no answer came. I asked God to show me if there was anything wrong in my own life. Something came to my mind that had often come to it before, something definite but which I was unwilling to confess as sin. I said to God,

"If this is wrong I will give it up"; but still no answer came. In my innermost heart, though I had never admitted it, I knew it was wrong.

At last I said:

"This is wrong. I have sinned. I will give it up."

I found peace. In a few moments I was sleeping like a child. In the morning I woke well in body, and the money that was so much needed for the honor of God's name came.

Sin is an awful thing, and one of the most awful things about it is the way it hinders prayer, the way it severs the connection between us and the source of all grace and power and blessing. Any one who would have power in prayer must be merciless in dealing with his own sins. "If I regard iniquity in my heart, the Lord will not hear me." (Ps. 66:18) So long as we hold on to sin or have any controversy with God, we cannot expect Him to heed our prayers. If there is anything that is constantly coming up in your moments of close communion with God, that is the thing that hinders prayer: put it away.

3. The third hindrance to prayer is found in Ez. 14:3, "Son of man, these men have taken their idols into their heart, and put the stumbling block of their iniquity before their face: should I be inquired of at all by them?" *Idols in the heart cause God to refuse to listen to our prayers.*

What is an idol? An idol is anything that takes the place of God, anything that is the supreme object of our affection. God alone has the right to the supreme place in our hearts. Everything and everyone else must be subordinate to Him.

Many a man makes an idol of his wife. Not that a man can love his wife any too much, but he can put her in the wrong place, he can put her before God; and when a man regards his wife's pleasure before God's pleasure, when he gives her the first place and God the second place, his wife is an idol, and God cannot hear his prayers.

Many a woman makes an idol of her children. Not that we can love our children too much. The more dearly we love Christ, the more dearly we love our children; but we can put our children in the wrong place, we can put them before God, and their interests before God's interests. When we do this our children are our idols.

Many a man makes an idol of his reputation or his business. Reputation or business is put before God. God cannot hear the prayers of such a man.

One great question for us to decide, if we would have power in prayer is, Is God absolutely first? Is He before wife, before children, before reputation, before business, before our own lives? If not, prevailing prayer is impossible.

God often calls our attention to the fact that we have an idol, by not answering our prayers, and thus leading us to inquire as to why our prayers are not answered, and so we discover the idol, put it away, and God hears our prayers.

4. The fourth hindrance to prayer is found in Prov. 21:13, "*Whoso stoppeth his ears at the cry of the poor,* he also shall cry himself, but shall not be heard."

There is perhaps no greater hindrance to prayer than stinginess, the lack of liberality toward the poor and toward God's work. It is the one who gives generously to others who receives generously from God. "Give, and it shall be given unto you; good measure, pressed down, shaken together, running over, shall they give into your bosom. For with what measure ye mete it shall be measured to you again." (Luke 6:38) The generous man is the mighty man of prayer. The stingy man is the powerless man of prayer.

One of the most wonderful statements about prevailing prayer (already referred to) 1 John 3:22, "Whatsoever we ask we receive of Him, because we keep His commandments, and do those things that are pleasing in His sight," is made in direct connection with generosity toward the needy. In the context we are told that it is when we love, not in word or in tongue, but in deed and in truth, when we open our hearts toward the brother in need, it is then and only then we have confidence toward God in prayer.

Many a man and woman who is seeking to find the secret of their powerlessness in prayer need not seek far; it is nothing more nor less than downright stinginess. George Muller, to whom reference has already been made, was a mighty man of prayer because he was a mighty giver. What he received from God never stuck to his fingers; he immediately passed it on to others. He was constantly receiving because he was constantly giving. When one thinks of the selfishness of the professing church to-day, how the orthodox churches of this land do not average $1.00 per year per member for foreign missions, it is no wonder that the church has so little power in prayer. If we would get from God, we must give to others. Perhaps the most wonderful promise in the Bible in regard to God's supplying our need is Phil. 4:19, "And my God shall fulfill every need of yours according to His riches in glory in Christ Jesus." This glorious promise was made to the Philippian church, and made in immediate connection with their generosity.

5. The fifth hindrance to prayer is found in Mark 11:25, "And when ye stand praying, *forgive*, if ye have ought against any; that your Father also which is in heaven may forgive you your trespasses."

An unforgiving spirit is one of the commonest hindrances to prayer. Prayer is answered on the basis that our sins are forgiven; and God cannot deal with us on the basis of forgiveness while we are harboring ill-will against those who have wronged us. Any one who is nursing a grudge against another has fast closed the ear of God against his own petition. How many there are crying to God for the conversion of husband, children, friends, and wondering why it is that their prayer is not answered, when the whole secret is some grudge that they have in their hearts against some one who has injured them, or who they fancy has injured them. Many and many a mother and father are allowing their children to go down to eternity unsaved, for the miserable gratification of hating somebody.

6. The sixth hindrance to prayer is found in 1 Peter 3:7, "Ye husbands, in like manner, dwell with your wives according to knowledge, giving honor unto the woman, as unto the weaker vessel as being also joint-heirs of the grace of life; to the end that your prayers be not hindered." Here we are plainly told that *a wrong relation between husband and wife is a hindrance to prayer.*

In many and many a case the prayers of husbands are hindered because of their failure of duty toward their wives. On the other hand, it is also doubtless true that the prayers of wives are hindered because of their failure in duty toward their husbands. If husbands and wives should seek diligently to find the cause of their unanswered prayers, they would often find it in their relations to one another.

Many a man who makes great pretentions to piety, and is very active in Christian work, shows but little consideration in his treatment of his wife, and is oftentimes unkind, if not brutal; then he wonders why it is that his prayers are not answered. The verse that we have just quoted explains the seeming mystery. On the other hand, many a woman who is very devoted to the church, and very faithful in attendance upon all services, treats her husband with the most unpardonable neglect, is cross and peevish toward him, wounds him by the sharpness of her speech, and by her ungovernable temper; then wonders why it is that she has no power in prayer.

There are other things in the relations of husbands and wives which cannot be spoken of publicly, but which doubtless are oftentimes a hindrance in approaching God in prayer. There is much of sin covered up under the holy name of marriage that is a cause of spiritual deadness, and of powerlessness in prayer. Any man or woman whose prayers seem to bring no answer should spread their whole married life out before God, and ask Him to put His finger upon anything in it that is displeasing in His sight.

7. The seventh hindrance to prayer is found in James 1:5-7, "But if any of you lacketh wisdom, let him ask of God, who giveth to all liberally and upbraideth not; and it shall be given him. But let him ask *in faith, nothing doubting*: for he that doubteth is like the surge of the sea driven by the wind and tossed. For let not that man think that he shall receive anything of the Lord."

Prayers are hindered by unbelief. God demands that we shall believe His Word absolutely. To question it is to make Him a liar. Many of us do that when we plead His promises, and is it any wonder that our prayers are not answered? How many prayers are hindered by our wretched unbelief! We go to God and ask Him for something that is positively promised in His Word, and then we do not more than half expect to get it. "Let not that man think that he shall receive anything of the Lord."

Chapter X: When to Pray

If we would know the fulness of blessing that there is in the prayer life, it is important not only that we pray in the right way, but also that we pray at the right time. Christ's own example is full of suggestiveness as to the right time for prayer.

1. In the 1st chapter of Mark, the 35th verse, we read, "And *in the morning*, rising up *a great while before day,* He went out, and departed into a solitary place, and there prayed."

Jesus chose the early morning hour for prayer. Many of the mightiest men of God have followed the Lord's example in this. In the morning hour the mind is fresh and at its very best. It is free from distraction, and that absolute concentration upon God which is essential to the most effective prayer is most easily possible in the early morning hours. Furthermore, when the early hours are spent in prayer, the whole day is sanctified, and power is obtained for overcoming its temptations, and for performing its duties. More can be accomplished in prayer in the first hours of the day than at any other time during the day. Every child of God who would make the most out of his life for Christ, should set apart the first part of the day to meeting God in the study of His Word and in prayer. The first thing we do each day should be to go alone with God and face the duties, the temptations, and the service of that day, and get strength from God for all. We should get victory before the hour of trial, temptation or service comes. The secret place of prayer is the place to fight our battles and gain our victories.

2. In the 6th chapter of Luke in the 12th verse, we get further light upon the right time to pray. We read, "And it came to pass in those days, that He went out into a mountain to pray, and continued *all night* in prayer to God."

Here we see Jesus praying in the night, spending the entire night in prayer. Of course we have no reason to suppose that this was the constant practice of our Lord, nor do we even know how common this practice was, but there were certainly times when the whole night was given up to prayer. Here too we do well to follow in the footsteps of the Master.

Of course there is a way of setting apart nights for prayer in which there is no profit; it is pure legalism. But the abuse of this practice is no reason for neglecting it altogether. One ought not to say, "I am going to spend a whole night in prayer," with the thought that there is any merit that will win God's favor in such an exercise; that is legalism. But we oftentimes do well to say, "I am going to set apart this night for meeting God, and obtaining His blessing and power; and if necessary, and if He so leads me, I will give the whole night to prayer." Oftentimes we will have prayed things through long before the night has passed, and we can retire and find more refreshing and invigorating sleep than if we had not spent the time in prayer. At other times God doubtless will keep us in communion with Himself away into the morning, and when He does this in His infinite grace, blessed indeed are these hours of night prayer!

Nights of prayer to God are followed by days of power with men. In the night hours the world is hushed in slumber, and we can easily be alone with God and have undisturbed communion with Him. If we set apart the whole night for prayer, there will be no hurry, there will be time for our own hearts to become quiet before God, there will be time for the whole mind to be brought under the guidance of the Holy Spirit, there will be plenty of time to pray things through. A night of prayer should be put entirely under God's control. We should lay down no rules as to how long we will pray, or as to what we shall pray about, but be ready to wait upon God for a short time or a long time as He may lead, and to be led out in one direction or another as He may see fit.

3. Jesus Christ prayed *before all the great crises in his earthly life.*

He prayed before choosing the twelve disciples; before the sermon on the mount; before starting out on an evangelistic tour; before His anointing with the Holy Spirit and His entrance upon His public ministry; before announcing to the twelve His approaching death; before the great consummation of His life at the cross. (Luke 6:12, 13; Luke 9:18, 21, 22; Luke 3:21, 22; Mark 1:35-38; Luke 22:39-46.) He prepared for every important crisis by a protracted season of prayer. So ought we to do also. Whenever any crisis of life is seen to be approaching, we should prepare for it by a season of very definite prayer to God. We should take plenty of time for this prayer.

4. Christ prayed not only before the great events and victories of His life, but He also prayed *after its great achievements and important crises.*

When He had fed the five thousand with the five loaves and two fishes, and the multitude desired to take Him and make Him king, having sent them away He went up into the mountain apart to pray, and spent hours there alone in prayer to God (Matt. 14:23; Jn. 6:15). So He went on from victory to victory.

It is more common for most of us to pray before the great events of life than it is to pray after them, but the latter is as important as the former. If we would pray after the great achievements of life, we might go on to still greater; as it is we are often either puffed up or exhausted by the things that we do in the name of the Lord, and so we advance no further. Many and many a man in answer to prayer has been endued with power and thus has wrought great things in the name of the Lord, and when these great things were accomplished, instead of going alone with God and humbling himself before Him, and giving Him all the glory for what was achieved, he has congratulated himself upon what has been accomplished, has become puffed up, and God has been obliged to lay him aside. The great things done were not followed by humiliation of self, and prayer to God, and so pride has come in and the mighty man has been shorn of his power.

5. Jesus Christ gave a special time to prayer *when life was unusually busy*. He would withdraw at such a time from the multitudes that thronged about Him, and go into the wilderness and pray. For example, we read in Luke 5:15, 16, "But so much the more went abroad the report concerning Him: and great multitudes came together to hear, and to be healed of their infirmities. But He withdrew Himself in the deserts and prayed."

Some men are so busy that they find no time for prayer. Apparently the busier Christ's life was, the more He prayed. Sometimes He had no time to eat (Mark 3:20), sometimes He had no time for needed rest and sleep (Mark 6:31, 33, 46), but He always took time to pray; and the more the work crowded the more He prayed.

Many a mighty man of God has learned this secret from Christ, and when the work has crowded more than usual they have set an unusual amount of time apart for prayer. Other men of God, once mighty, have lost their power because they did not learn this secret, and allowed increasing work to crowd out prayer.

Years ago it was the writer's privilege, with other theological students, to ask questions of one of the most useful Christian men of the day. The writer was led to ask,

"Will you tell us something of your prayer life?"

The man was silent a moment, and then, turning his eyes earnestly upon me, replied:

"Well, I must admit that I have been so crowded with work of late that I have not given the time I should to prayer."

Is it any wonder that that man lost power, and the great work that he was doing was curtailed in a very marked degree? Let us never forget that the more the work presses on us, the more time must we spend in prayer.

6. Jesus Christ prayed *before the great temptations of His life*.

As He drew nearer and nearer to the cross, and realized that upon it was to come the great final test of His life, Jesus went out into the garden to pray. He came "unto a place called Gethsemane, and saith unto the disciples, Sit ye here while I go and pray yonder." (Matt. 26:36) The victory of Calvary was won that night in the garden of Gethsemane. The calm majesty of His bearing in meeting the awful onslaughts of Pilate's Judgment Hall and of Calvary, was the outcome of the struggle, agony and victory of Gethsemane. While Jesus prayed the disciples slept, so He stood fast while they fell ignominiously.

Many temptations come upon us unawares and unannounced, and all that we can do is to lift a cry to God for help then and there; but many of the temptations of life we can see approaching from the distance, and in such cases the victory should be won before the temptation really reaches us.

7. In 1 Thess. 5:17 we read, "Pray *without ceasing*," and in Eph. 6:18, "praying *at all seasons*."

Our whole life should be a life of prayer. We should walk in constant communion with God. There should be a constant upward looking of the soul to God. We should walk so habitually in His presence that even when we awake in the night it would be the most natural thing in the world for us to speak to Him in thanksgiving or in petition.

Chapter XI: The Need of a General Revival

If we are to pray aright in such a time as this, much of our prayer should be for a general revival. If there was ever a time in which there was need to cry unto God in the words of the Psalmist, "Wilt Thou not revive us again, that Thy people may rejoice in Thee?" (Ps. 85:6) it is this day in which we live. It is surely time for the Lord to work, for men have made void His law (Ps. 119:126). The voice of the Lord given in the written

Word is set at naught both by the world and the church. Such a time is not a time for discouragement—the man who believes in God and believes in the Bible can never be discouraged; but it is a time for Jehovah Himself to step in and work. The intelligent Christian, the wide-awake watchman on the walls of Zion, may well cry with the Psalmist of old, "It is time for Jehovah to work, for they have made void Thy law." (Ps. 119:126)

The great need of the day is a general revival.

Let us consider first of all what a general revival is.

A revival is a time of quickening or impartation of life. As God alone can give life, a revival is a time when God visits His people and by the power of His Spirit imparts new life to them, and through them imparts life to sinners dead in trespasses and sins. We have religious excitements gotten up by the cunning methods and hypnotic influence of the mere professional evangelist; but these are not revivals and are not needed. They are the devil's imitations of a revival. *New life from God*—that is a revival. A general revival is a time when this new life from God is not confined to scattered localities, but is general throughout Christendom and the earth.

The reason why a general revival is needed is that spiritual dearth and desolation and death is general. It is not confined to any one country, though it may be more manifest in some countries than in others. It is found in foreign mission fields as well as in home fields. We have had local revivals. The life-giving Spirit of God has breathed upon this minister and that, this church and that, this community and that; but we need, we sorely need, a revival that shall be widespread and general.

Let us look for a few moments at the results of a revival. These results are apparent in ministers, in the church and in the unsaved.

1. The results of a revival in a minister are:

(1) The minister has a new love for souls. We ministers as a rule have no such love for souls as we ought to have, no such love for souls as Jesus had, no such love for souls as Paul had. But when God visits His people the hearts of ministers are greatly burdened for the unsaved. They go out in great longing for the salvation of their fellow men. They forget their ambition to preach great sermons and for fame, and simply long to see men brought to Christ.

(2) When true revivals come ministers get a new love for God's Word and a new faith in God's Word. They fling to the winds their doubts and criticisms of the Bible and of the creeds, and go to preaching the Bible and especially Christ crucified. Revivals make ministers who are loose in their doctrines orthodox. A genuine wide-sweeping revival would do more to turn things upside down and thus get them right side up than all the heresy trials ever instituted.

(3) Revivals bring to ministers new liberty and power in preaching. It is no week-long grind to prepare a sermon, and no nerve-consuming effort to preach it after it has been prepared. Preaching is a joy and a refreshment, and there is power in it in times of revival.

2. The results of a revival on Christians generally are as marked as its results upon the ministry.

(1) In times of revival Christians come out from the world and live separated lives. Christians who have been dallying with the world, who have been playing cards and dancing and going to the theater and indulging in similar follies, give them up. These things are found to be incompatible with increasing life and light.

(2) In times of revival Christians get a new spirit of prayer. Prayer-meetings are no longer a duty, but become the necessity of a hungry, importunate heart. Private prayer is followed with new zest. The voice of earnest prayer to God is heard day and night. People

no longer ask, "Does God answer prayer?" They know He does, and besiege the throne of grace day and night.

(3) In times of revival Christians go to work for lost souls.

They do not go to meeting simply to enjoy themselves and get blessed. They go to meeting to watch for souls and to bring them to Christ. They talk to men on the street and in the stores and in their homes. The cross of Christ, salvation, heaven and hell become the subjects of constant conversation. Politics and the weather and new bonnets and the latest novels are forgotten.

(4) In times of revival Christians have new joy in Christ. Life is joy, and new life is new joy. Revival days are glad days, days of heaven on earth.

(5) In times of revival Christians get a new love for the Word of God. They want to study it day and night. Revivals are bad for saloons and theaters, but they are good for bookstores and Bible agencies.

3. But revivals also have a decided influence on the unsaved world.

(1) First of all, they bring deep conviction of sin. Jesus said that when the Spirit was come He would convince the world of sin (Jn. 16:7, 8). Now we have seen that a revival is a coming of the Holy Spirit, and therefore there must be a new conviction of sin, and there always is. If you see something men call a revival, and there is no conviction of sin, you may know at once that it is bogus. It is a sure mark.

(2) Revivals bring also conversion and regeneration. When God refreshes His people, He always converts sinners also. The first result of Pentecost was new life and power to the one hundred and twenty disciples in the upper room; the second result was three thousand conversions in a single day. It is always so. I am constantly reading of revivals here and there, where Christians were greatly helped but there were no conversions. I have my doubts about that kind. If Christians are truly refreshed, they will get after the unsaved by prayer and testimony and persuasion, and there will be conversions.

WHY A GENERAL REVIVAL IS NEEDED

We see what a general revival is, and what it does; let us now face the question why it is needed at the present time.

I think that the mere description of what it is and what it does shows that it is needed, sorely needed, but let us look at some specific conditions that exist to-day that show the need of it. In showing these conditions one is likely to be called a pessimist. If facing the facts is to be called a pessimist, I am willing to be called a pessimist. If in order to be an optimist one must shut his eyes and call black white, and error truth, and sin righteousness, and death life, I don't want to be called an optimist. But I am an optimist all the same. Pointing out the real condition will lead to a better condition.

1. Look first at the ministry.

(1) Many of us who are professedly orthodox ministers are practically infidels. That is plain speech, but it is also indisputable fact. There is no essential difference between the teachings of Tom Paine and Bob Ingersoll and the teachings of some of our theological professors. The latter are not so blunt and honest about it; they phrase it in more elegant and studied sentences; but it means the same. Much of the so-called new learning and higher criticism is simply Tom Paine infidelity sugar-coated. Prof. Howard Osgood, who is a real scholar and not a mere echo of German infidelity, once read a statement of some positions, and asked if they did not fairly represent the scholarly criticism of to-day, and when it was agreed that they did, he startled his audience by saying:

"I am reading from Tom Paine's 'Age of Reason.'"

There is little new in the higher criticism. Our future ministers oftentimes are being educated under infidel professors, and being immature boys when they enter the college or seminary, they naturally come out infidels in many cases, and then go forth to poison the church.

(2) Even when our ministers are orthodox—as thank God so very many are!—they are oftentimes not men of prayer. How many modern ministers know what it is to wrestle in prayer, to spend a good share of a night in prayer? I do not know how many, but I do know that many do not.

(3) Many of us who are ministers have no love for souls. How many preach because they *must* preach, because they feel that men every where are perishing, and by preaching they hope to save some? And how many follow up their preaching as Paul did, by beseeching men everywhere to be reconciled to God?

Perhaps enough has been said about us ministers; but it is evident that a revival is needed for our sake or some of us will have to stand before God overwhelmed with confusion in an awful day of reckoning that is surely coming.

2. Look now at the church:

(1) Look at the doctrinal state of the church. It is bad enough. Many do not believe in the whole Bible. The book of Genesis is a myth, Jonah is an allegory, and even the miracles of the Son of God are questioned. The doctrine of prayer is old-fashioned, and the work of the Holy Spirit is sneered at. Conversion is unnecessary, and hell is no longer believed in. Then look at the fads and errors that have sprung up out of this loss of faith, Christian Science, Unitarianism, Spiritualism, Universalism, Babism, Metaphysical Healing, etc., etc., a perfect pandemonium of doctrines of devils.

(2) Look at the spiritual state of the church. Worldliness is rampant among church members. Many church members are just as eager as any in the rush to get rich. They use the methods of the world in the accumulation of wealth, and they hold just as fast to it as any when they have gotten it.

Prayerlessness abounds among church members on every hand. Some one has said that Christians on the average do not spend more than five minutes a day in prayer.

Neglect of the Word of God goes hand in hand with neglect of prayer to God. Very many Christians spend twice as much time every day wallowing through the mire of the daily papers as they do bathing in the cleansing laver of God's Holy Word. How many Christians average an hour a day spent in Bible study?

Along with neglect of prayer and neglect of the Word of God goes a lack of generosity. The churches are rapidly increasing in wealth, but the treasuries of the missionary societies are empty. Christians do not average a dollar a year for foreign missions. It is simply appalling.

Then there is the increasing disregard for the Lord's Day. It is fast becoming a day of worldly pleasure, instead of a day of holy service. The Sunday newspaper with its inane twaddle and filthy scandal takes the place of the Bible; and visiting and golf and bicycle, the place of the Sunday-school and church service.

Christians mingle with the world in all forms of questionable amusements. The young man and young woman who does not believe in dancing with its rank immodesties, the card table with its drift toward gambling, and the theater with its ever-increasing appeal to lewdness, is counted an old fogy.

Then how small a proportion of our membership has really entered into fellowship with Jesus Christ in His burden for souls! Enough has been said of the spiritual state of the church.

3. Now look at the state of the world.

(1) Note how few conversions there are. The Methodist church, which has led the way in aggressive work has actually lost more members than it has gained the last year. Here and there a church has a large number of accessions upon confession of faith, but these churches are rare exceptions; and where there are such accessions, in how few cases are the conversions deep, thorough and satisfactory.

(2) There is lack of conviction of sin. Seldom are men overwhelmed with a sense of their awful guilt in trampling under foot the Son of God. Sin is regarded as a "misfortune" or as "infirmity," or even as "good in the making"; seldom as enormous wrong against a holy God.

(3) Unbelief is rampant. Many regard it as a mark of intellectual superiority to reject the Bible, and even faith in God and immortality. It is about the only mark of intellectual superiority many possess, and perhaps that is the reason they cling to it so tenaciously.

(4) Hand in hand with this widespread infidelity goes gross immorality, as has always been the case. Infidelity and immorality are Siamese twins. They always exist and always grow and always fatten together. This prevailing immorality is found everywhere.

Look at the legalized adultery that we call divorce. Men marry one wife after another, and are still admitted into good society; and women do likewise. There are thousands of supposedly respectable men in America living with other men's wives, and thousands of supposedly respectable women living with other women's husbands.

This immorality is found in the theater. The theater at its best is bad enough, but now "Sapphos," and the "Degenerates," and all the unspeakable vile accessories of the stage rule the day, and the women who debauch themselves by appearing in such plays are defended in the newspapers and welcomed by supposedly respectable people.

Much of our literature is rotten, but decent people will read books as bad as "Trilby" because it is the rage. Art is oftentimes a mere covering for shameless indecency. Women are induced to cast modesty to the winds that the artist may perfect his art and defile his morals.

Greed for money has become a mania with rich and poor. The multi-millionaire will often sell his soul and trample the rights of his fellow men under foot in the mad hope of becoming a billionaire, and the laboring man will often commit murder to increase the power of the union and keep up wages. Wars are waged and men shot down like dogs to improve commerce, and to gain political prestige for unprincipled politicians who parade as statesmen.

The licentiousness of the day lifts its serpent head everywhere. You see it in the newspapers, you see it on the bill- boards, you see it on the advertisements of cigars, shoes, bicycles, patent medicines, corsets and everything else. You see it on the streets at night. You see it just outside the church door. You find it not only in the awful cesspools set apart for it in the great cities, but it is crowding further and further up our business streets and into the residence portions of our cities. Alas! now and then you find it, if you look sharp, in supposedly respectable homes; indeed it will be borne to your ears by the confessions of broken-hearted men and women. The moral condition of the world in our day is disgusting, sickening, appalling.

We need a revival, deep, widespread, general, in the power of the Holy Ghost. It is either a general revival or the dissolution of the church, of the home, of the state. A revival, new life from God, is the cure, and the only cure. That will stem the awful tide of immorality and unbelief. Mere argument will not do it; but a wind from heaven, a new outpouring of the Holy Ghost, a true God-sent revival will. Infidelity, higher criticism,

Christian Science, Spiritualism, Universalism, all will go down before the outpouring of the Spirit of God. It was not discussion but the breath of God that relegated Tom Paine, Voltaire, Volney and other of the old infidels to the limbo of forgetfulness; and we need a new breath from God to send the Wellhausens and the Kuenens and the Grafs and the parrots they have trained to occupy chairs and pulpits in England and America to keep them company. I believe that breath from God is coming.

The great need of to-day is a general revival. The need is clear. It admits of no honest difference of opinion. What then shall we do? Pray. Take up the Psalmist's prayer, "Revive us again, that Thy people may rejoice in Thee." Take up Ezekiel's prayer, "Come from the four winds, O breath (breath of God), and breathe upon these slain that they may live." Hark, I hear a noise! Behold a shaking! I can almost feel the breeze upon my cheek. I can almost see the great living army rising to their feet. Shall we not pray and pray and pray and pray, till the Spirit comes, and God revives His people?

Chapter XII: The Place of Prayer Before and During Revivals

No treatment of the subject How to Pray would be at all complete if it did not consider the place of prayer in revivals.

The first great revival of Christian history had its origin on the human side in a ten-days' prayer-meeting. We read of that handful of disciples, "These all with one accord continued steadfastly in prayer." (Acts 1:14) The result of that prayer-meeting we read of in the 2nd chapter of the Acts of the Apostles,

"They were all filled with the Holy Ghost, and began to speak with other tongues, as the Spirit gave them utterance." (v.4) Further on in the chapter we read that "there were added unto them in that day about three thousand souls." (v.41) This revival proved genuine and permanent. The converts "continued steadfastly in the apostles' teaching and fellowship, in the breaking of bread and the prayers." (v.42) "And the Lord added to them day by day those that were being saved." (v.47)

Every true revival from that day to this has had its earthly origin in prayer. The great revival under Jonathan Edwards in the 18th century began with his famous call to prayer. The marvelous work of grace among the Indians under Brainerd had its origin in the days and nights that Brainerd spent before God in prayer for an enduement of power from on high for this work.

A most remarkable and widespread display of God's reviving power was that which broke out at Rochester, New York, in 1830, under the labors of Charles G. Finney. It not only spread throughout the State but ultimately to Great Britain as well. Mr. Finney himself attributed the power of this work to the spirit of prayer that prevailed. He describes it in his autobiography in the following words:

"When I was on my way to Rochester, as we passed through a village, some thirty miles east of Rochester, a brother minister whom I knew, seeing me on the canal-boat, jumped aboard to have a little conversation with me, intending to ride but a little way and return. He, however, became interested in conversation, and upon finding where I was going, he made up his mind to keep on and go with me to Rochester. We had been there but a few days when this minister became so convinced that he could not help weeping aloud at one time as we passed along the street. The Lord gave him a powerful spirit of prayer, and his heart was broken. As he and I prayed together, I was struck with his faith in regard to what the Lord was going to do there. I recollect he would say, 'Lord, I do not know how it is; but I seem to know that Thou art going to do a great work in this city.'

The spirit of prayer was poured out powerfully, so much so that some persons stayed away from the public services to pray, being unable to restrain their feelings under preaching.

"And here I must introduce the name of a man, whom I shall have occasion to mention frequently, Mr. Abel Clary. He was the son of a very excellent man, and an elder of the church where I was converted. He was converted in the same revival in which I was. He had been licensed to preach; but his spirit of prayer was such, he was so burdened with the souls of men, that he was not able to preach much, his whole time and strength being given to prayer. The burden of his soul would frequently be so great that he was unable to stand, and he would writhe and groan in agony. I was well acquainted with him, and knew something of the wonderful spirit of prayer that was upon him. He was a very silent man, as almost all are who have that powerful spirit of prayer.

"The first I knew of his being in Rochester, a gentleman who lived about a mile west of the city, called on me one day and asked me if I knew a Mr. Abel Clary, a minister. I told him that I knew him well. 'Well,' he said, 'he is at my house, and has been there for some time, and I don't know what to think of him.' I said, 'I have not seen him at any of our meetings.' 'No,' he replied, 'he cannot go to meeting, he says. He prays nearly all the time, day and night, and in such agony of mind that I do not know what to make of it. Sometimes he cannot even stand on his knees, but will lie prostrate on the floor, and groan and pray in a manner that quite astonishes me.' I said to the brother, 'I understand it: please keep still. It will all come out right; he will surely prevail.'

"I knew at the time a considerable number of men who were exercised in the same way. A Deacon P—, of Camden, Oneida county; a Deacon T—, of Rodman, Jefferson county; a Deacon B—, of Adams, in the same county; this Mr. Clary and many others among the men, and a large number of women partook of the same spirit, and spent a great part of their time in prayer. Father Nash, as we called him, who in several of my fields of labor came to me and aided me, was another of those men that had such a powerful spirit of prevailing prayer. This Mr. Clary continued in Rochester as long as I did, and did not leave it until after I had left. He never, that I could learn, appeared in public, but gave himself wholly to prayer.

"I think it was the second Sabbath that I was at Auburn at this time, I observed in the congregation the solemn face of Mr. Clary. He looked as if he was borne down with an agony of prayer. Being well acquainted with him, and knowing the great gift of God that was upon him, the spirit of prayer, I was very glad to see him there. He sat in the pew with his brother, the doctor, who was also a professor of religion, but who had nothing by experience, I should think, of his brother Abel's great power with God.

"At intermission, as soon as I came down from the pulpit, Mr. Clary, with his brother, met me at the pulpit stairs, and the doctor invited me to go home with him and spend the intermission and get some refreshments. I did so.

"After arriving at his house we were soon summoned to the dinner table. We gathered about the table, and Dr. Clary turned to his brother and said, 'Brother Abel, will you ask the blessing?' Brother Abel bowed his head and began, audibly, to ask a blessing. He had uttered but a sentence or two when he broke instantly down, moved suddenly back from the table, and fled to his chamber. The doctor supposed he had been taken suddenly ill, and rose up and followed him. In a few moments he came down and said, 'Mr. Finney, brother Abel wants to see you.' Said I, 'What ails him?' Said he, 'I do not know but he says, you know. He appears in great distress, but I think it is the state of his mind.' I understood it in a moment, and went to his room. He lay groaning upon the bed, the Spirit making intercession for him, and in him, with groanings that could not be uttered. I had barely entered the room, when he made out to say, 'Pray, brother Finney.' I knelt down and helped him in prayer, by leading his soul out for the conversion of sinners. I continued to pray until his distress passed away, and then I returned to the dinner table.

"I understood that this was the voice of God. I saw the spirit of prayer was upon him, and I felt his influence upon myself, and took it for granted that the work would move on powerfully. It did so. The pastor told me afterward that he found that in the six weeks that I was there, five hundred souls had been converted."

Mr. Finney in his lectures on revivals tells of other remarkable awakenings in answer to the prayers of God's people. He says in one place, "A clergyman in W——n told me of a revival among his people, which commenced with a zealous and devoted woman in the church. She became anxious about sinners, and went to praying for them; she prayed, and her distress increased; and she finally came to her minister, and talked with him, and asked him to appoint an anxious meeting, for she felt that one was needed. The minister put her off, for he felt nothing of it. The next week she came again, and besought him to appoint an anxious meeting, she knew there would be somebody to come, for she felt as if God was going to pour out His Spirit. He put her off again. And finally she said to him, 'If you do not appoint an anxious meeting I shall die, for there is certainly going to be a revival.' The next Sabbath he appointed a meeting, and said that if there were any who wished to converse with him about the salvation of their souls, he would meet them on such an evening. He did not know of one, but when he went to the place, to his astonishment he found a large number of anxious inquirers."

In still another place he says, "The first ray of light that broke in upon the midnight which rested on the churches in Oneida county, in the fall of 1825, was from a woman in feeble health, who, I believe had never been in a powerful revival. Her soul was exercised about sinners. She was in agony for the land. She did not know what ailed her, but she kept praying more and more, till it seemed as if her agony would destroy her body. At length she became full of joy and exclaimed, 'God has come! God has come! There is no mistake about it, the work is begun, and is going over all the region!' And sure enough the work began, and her family were almost all converted, and the work spread all over that part of the country."

The great revival of 1857 in the United States began in prayer and was carried on by prayer more than by anything else. Dr. Cuyler in an article in a religious newspaper some years ago said, "Most revivals have humble beginnings, and the fire starts in a few warm hearts. Never despise the day of small things. During all my own long ministry, nearly every work of grace had a similar beginning. One commenced in a meeting gathered at a few hours' notice in a private house. Another commenced in a group gathered for Bible study by Mr. Moody in our mission chapel. Still another—the most powerful of all—was kindled on a bitter January evening at a meeting of young Christians under my roof. Dr. Spencer, in his 'Pastor's Sketches', (the most suggestive book of its kind I have ever read), tells us that a remarkable revival in his church sprang from the fervent prayers of a godly old man who was confined to his room by lameness. That profound Christian, Dr. Thomas H. Skinner, of the Union Theological Seminary, once gave me an account of a remarkable coming together of three earnest men in his study when he was the pastor of the Arch Street Church in Philadelphia. They literally wrestled in prayer. They made a clean breast in confession of sin, and humbled themselves before God. One and another church officer came in and joined them. The heaven-kindled flame soon spread through the whole congregation in one of the most powerful revivals ever known in that city."

In the early part of the seventeenth century there was a great religious awakening in Ulster, Ireland. The lands of the rebel chiefs which had been forfeited to the British crown, were settled up by a class of colonists who for the most part were governed by a spirit of wild adventure. Real piety was rare. Seven ministers, five from Scotland and two from England, settled in that country, the earliest arrivals being in 1613. Of one of these ministers named Blair it is recorded by a contemporary, "He spent many days and nights in prayer, alone and with others, and was vouchsafed great intimacy with God." Mr. James Glendenning, a man of very meager natural gifts, was a man similarly minded as regards prayer. The work began under this man Glendenning. The historian of the time says, "He was a man who never would have been chosen by a wise assembly of ministers nor sent to begin a reformation in this land. Yet this was the Lord's choice to begin with him the admirable work of God which I mention on purpose that all may see how the glory is only the Lord's in making a holy nation in this profane land, and that it was 'not by might, nor by power, nor by man's wisdom, but by My Spirit, saith the Lord.'" In his preaching at Oldstone multitudes of hearers felt in great anxiety and terror of conscience. They looked on themselves as altogether lost and damned, and cried out, "Men and brethren, what shall we do to be saved?" They were stricken into a swoon by the power of His Word. A dozen in one day were carried out of doors as dead. These were not women, but some of the boldest spirits of the neighborhood; "some who had formerly feared not with their swords to put a whole market town into a fray." Concerning one of them, the historian writes, "I have heard one of them, then a mighty strong man, now a mighty Christian, say that his end in coming into church was to consult with his companions how to work some mischief."

This work spread throughout the whole country. By the year 1626 a monthly concert of prayer was held in Antrim. The work spread beyond the bounds of Down and Antrim to the churches of the neighboring counties. So great became the religious interest that Christians would come thirty or forty miles to the communions, and continue from the time they came until they returned without wearying or making use of sleep. Many of them neither ate nor drank, and yet some of them professed that they "went away most fresh and vigorous, their souls so filled with the sense of God."

This revival changed the whole character of northern Ireland.

Another great awakening in Ireland in 1859 had a somewhat similar origin. By many who did not know, it was thought that this marvelous work came without warning and preparation, but Rev. William Gibson, the moderator of the General Assembly of the Presbyterian Church in Ireland in 1860, in his very interesting and valuable history of the work tells how there had been preparation for two years. There had been constant discussion in the General Assembly of the low estate of religion, and of the need of a revival. There had been special sessions for prayer. Finally four young men, who became leaders in the origin of the great work, began to meet together in an old schoolhouse in the neighborhood of Kells. About the spring of 1858 a work of power began to manifest itself. It spread from town to town, and from county to county. The congregations became too large for the buildings, and the meetings were held in the open air, oftentimes attended by many thousands of people. Many hundreds of persons were frequently convicted of sin in a single meeting. In some places the criminal courts and jails were closed for lack of occupation. There were manifestations of the Holy Spirit's power of a most remarkable character, clearly proving that the Holy Spirit is as ready to work to-day as in apostolic days, when ministers and Christians really believe in Him and begin to prepare the way by prayer.

Mr. Moody's wonderful work in England and Scotland and Ireland that afterwards spread to America had its origin on the manward side in prayer. Mr. Moody made little impression until men and women began to cry to God. Indeed his going to England at all was in answer to the importunate cries to God of a bed-ridden saint. While the spirit of prayer continued the revival abode in strength, but in the course of time less and less was made of prayer and the work fell off very perceptibly in power. Doubtless one of the great secrets of the unsatisfactoriness and superficiality and unreality of many of our modern so-called revivals, is that more dependence is put upon man's machinery than upon God's power, sought and obtained by earnest, persistent, believing prayer. We live in a day characterized by the multiplication of man's machinery and the diminution of God's power. The great cry of our day is work, work, work, new organizations, new methods, new machinery; the great need of our day is prayer. It was a master stroke of the devil when he got the church so generally to lay aside this mighty weapon of prayer. The devil is perfectly willing that the church should multiply its organizations, and deftly contrive machinery for the conquest of the world for Christ if it will only give up praying. He laughs as he looks at the church to-day and says to himself:

"You can have your Sunday-schools and your Young People's Societies, your Young Men's Christian Associations and your Women's Christian Temperance Unions, your Institutional Churches and your Industrial Schools, and your Boy's Brigades, your grand choirs and your fine organs, your brilliant preachers and your revival efforts too, if you don't bring the power of Almighty God into them by earnest, persistent, believing, mighty prayer."

Prayer could work as marvelous results today as it ever could, if the church would only betake itself to it.

There seem to be increasing signs that the church is awakening to this fact. Here and there God is laying upon individual ministers and churches a burden of prayer that they have never known before. Less dependence is being put upon machinery and more dependence upon God. Ministers are crying to God day and night for power. Churches and portions of churches are meeting together in the early morning hours and the late night hours crying to God for the latter rain. There is every indication of the coming of a mighty and widespread revival. There is every reason why, if a revival should come in any country at this time, it should be more widespread in its extent than any revival of history. There is the closest and swiftest communication by travel, by letter, and by cable between all parts of the world. A true fire of God kindled in America would soon spread to the uttermost parts of the earth. The only thing needed to bring this fire is prayer.

It is not necessary that the whole church get to praying to begin with. Great revivals always begin first in the hearts of a few men and women whom God arouses by His Spirit to believe in Him as a living God, as a God who answers prayer, and upon whose heart He lays a burden from which no rest can be found except in importunate crying unto God.

May God use this book to arouse many others to pray that the greatly-needed revival may come, and come speedily.

LET US PRAY

The Person and Work of The Holy Spirit

~ ※ ~

By *R. A. Torrey*

~ ※ ~

I: The Personality of the Holy Spirit

Before one can correctly understand the work of the Holy Spirit, he must first of all know the Spirit Himself. A frequent source of error and fanaticism about the work of the Holy Spirit is the attempt to study and understand His work without first of all coming to know Him as a Person.

It is of the highest importance from the standpoint of worship that we decide whether the Holy Spirit is a Divine Person, worthy to receive our adoration, our faith, our love, and our entire surrender to Himself, or whether it is simply an influence emanating from God or a power or an illumination that God imparts to us. If the Holy Spirit is a person, and a Divine Person, and we do not know Him as such, then we are robbing a Divine Being of the worship and the faith and the love and the surrender to Himself which are His due.

It is also of the highest importance from the practical standpoint that we decide whether the Holy Spirit is merely some mysterious and wonderful power that we in our weakness and ignorance are somehow to get hold of and use, or whether the Holy Spirit is a real Person, infinitely holy, infinitely wise, infinitely mighty and infinitely tender who is to get hold of and use us. The former conception is utterly heathenish, not essentially different from the thought of the African fetish worshipper who has his god whom he uses. The latter conception is sublime and Christian. If we think of the Holy Spirit as so many do as merely a power or influence, our constant thought will be, "How can I get more of the Holy Spirit," but if we think of Him in the Biblical way as a Divine Person, our thought will rather be, "How can the Holy Spirit have more of me?" The conception of the Holy Spirit as a Divine influence or power that we are somehow to get hold of and use, leads to self-exaltation and self-sufficiency. One who so thinks of the Holy Spirit and who at the same time imagines that he has received the Holy Spirit will almost inevitably be full of spiritual pride and strut about as if he belonged to some superior order of Christians. One frequently hears such persons say, "I am a Holy Ghost man," or "I am a Holy Ghost woman." But if we once grasp the thought that the Holy Spirit is a Divine Person of infinite majesty, glory and holiness and power, who in marvelous condescension has come into our hearts to make His abode there and take possession of our lives and make use of them, it will put us in the dust and keep us in the dust. I can think of no thought more humbling or more overwhelming than the thought that a person of Divine majesty and glory dwells in my heart and is ready to use even me.

It is of the highest importance from the standpoint of experience that we know the Holy Spirit as a person. Thousands and tens of thousands of men and women can testify to the blessing that has come into their own lives as they have come to know the Holy Spirit, not merely as a gracious influence (emanating, it is true, from God) but as a real Person, just as real as Jesus Christ Himself, an ever-present, loving Friend and mighty Helper, who is not only always by their side but dwells in their heart every day and every hour and who is ready to undertake for them in every emergency of life. Thousands of ministers, Christian workers and Christians in the humblest spheres of life have spoken to me, or written to me, of the complete transformation of their Christian experience that came to them when they grasped the thought (not merely in a theological, but in an experimental way) that the Holy Spirit was a Person and consequently came to know Him.

There are at least four distinct lines of proof in the Bible that the Holy Spirit is a person.

I. *All the distinctive characteristics of personality are ascribed to the Holy Spirit in the Bible.*

What are the distinctive characteristics, or marks, of personality? Knowledge, feeling or emotion, and will. Any entity that thinks and feels and wills is a person. When we say that the Holy Spirit is a person, there are those who understand us to mean that the Holy Spirit has hands and feet and eyes and ears and mouth, and so on, but these are not the characteristics of personality but of corporeity. All of these characteristics or marks of personality are repeatedly ascribed to the Holy Spirit in the Old and New Testaments. We read in 1 Cor. ii. 10, 11, "But God hath revealed them unto us by His Spirit: for the Spirit searcheth all things, yea, the deep things of God. For what man knoweth the things of a man, save the spirit of man which is in him? even so the things of God knoweth no man, but the Spirit of God." Here knowledge is ascribed to the Holy Spirit. We are clearly taught that the Holy Spirit is not merely an influence that illuminates our minds to comprehend the truth but a Being who Himself knows the truth.

In 1 Cor. xii. 11, we read, "But all these worketh that one and the selfsame Spirit, dividing to every man severally as *He will*." Here will is ascribed to the Spirit and we are taught that the Holy Spirit is not a power that we get hold of and use according to our will but a Person of sovereign majesty, who uses us according to His will. This distinction is of fundamental importance in our getting into right relations with the Holy Spirit. It is at this very point that many honest seekers after power and efficiency in service go astray. They are reaching out after and struggling to get possession of some mysterious and mighty power that they can make use of in their work according to their own will. They will never get possession of the power they seek until they come to recognize that there is not some Divine power for them to get hold of and use in their blindness and ignorance but that there is a Person, infinitely wise, as well as infinitely mighty, who is willing to take possession of them and use them according to His own perfect will. When we stop to think of it, we must rejoice that there is no Divine power that beings so ignorant as we are, so liable to err, to get hold of and use. How appalling might be the results if there were. But what a holy joy must come into our hearts when we grasp the thought that there is a Divine Person, One who never errs, who is willing to take possession of us and impart to us such gifts as He sees best and to use us according to His wise and loving will.

We read in Rom. viii. 27, "And He that searcheth the hearts knoweth what is *the mind of the Spirit*, because He maketh intercession for the saints according to the will of God." In this passage mind is ascribed to the Holy Spirit. The Greek word translated "mind" is a comprehensive word, including the ideas of thought, feeling and purpose. It is the same that is used in Rom. viii. 7 where we read that "the carnal mind is enmity against God: for it is not subject to the law of God, neither indeed can be." So then in this passage we have all the distinctive marks of personality ascribed to the Holy Spirit.

We find the personality of the Holy Spirit brought out in a most touching and suggestive way in Rom. xv. 30, "Now I beseech you, brethren, for the Lord Jesus Christ's sake, and for the *love of the Spirit*, that ye strive together with me in your prayers to God for me." Here we have "*love*" ascribed to the Holy Spirit. The reader would do well to stop and ponder those five words, "*the love of the Spirit*." We dwell often upon the love of God the Father. It is the subject of our daily and constant thought. We dwell often upon the love of Jesus Christ the Son. Who would think of calling himself a Christian who passed a day without meditating on the love of his Savior, but how often have we meditated upon "*the love of the Spirit*"? Each day of our lives, if we are living as Christians ought, we kneel down in the presence of God the Father and look up into His face and say, "I thank Thee, Father, for Thy great love that led Thee to give Thine only begotten Son to die upon the cross of Calvary for me." Each day of our lives we also look up into the face of our Lord and Savior, Jesus Christ, and say, "Oh, Thou glorious Lord and Savior, Jesus Thou Son of God, I thank Thee for Thy great love that led Thee not to count it a thing to be grasped to be on equality with God but to empty Thyself and forsaking all the glory of heaven, come down to earth with all its shame and to take my sins upon Thyself and die in my place upon the cross of Calvary." But how often do we kneel and say to the Holy Spirit, "Oh, Thou eternal and infinite Spirit of God, I thank Thee for Thy great love that led Thee to come into this world of sin and darkness and to seek me out and to follow me so patiently until Thou didst bring me to see my utter ruin and need of a Savior and to reveal to me my Lord and Savior, Jesus Christ, as just the Savior whom I need." Yet we owe our salvation just as truly to the love of the Spirit as we do to the love of the Father and the love of the Son. If it had not been for the love of God the Father looking down upon me in my utter ruin and providing a perfect atonement for me in the death of His own Son on the cross of Calvary, I would have been in hell to-day. If it had not been for the love of Jesus Christ, the eternal Word of God, looking upon me in my utter ruin and in obedience to the Father, putting aside all the glory of heaven for all the shame of earth and taking my place, the place of the curse, upon the cross of Calvary and pouring out His life utterly for me, I would have been in hell to-day. But if it had not been for the love of the Holy Spirit, sent by the Father in answer to the prayer of the Son (John xiv. 16) leading Him to seek me out in my utter blindness and ruin and to follow me day after day, week after week, and year after year, when I persistently turned a deaf ear to His pleadings, following me through paths of sin where it must have been agony for that holy One to go, until at last I listened and He opened my eyes to see my utter ruin and then revealed Jesus to me as just the Savior that would meet my every need and then enabled me to receive this Jesus as my own Savior; if it had not been for this patient, long-suffering, never-tiring, infinitely-tender love of the Holy Spirit, I would have been in hell to-day. Oh, the Holy Spirit is not merely an influence or a power or an illumination but is a Person just as real as God the Father or Jesus Christ His Son.

The personality of the Holy Spirit comes out in the Old Testament as truly as in the New, for we read in Neh. ix. 20, "Thou gavest also Thy good Spirit to instruct them, and withheldest not Thy manna from their mouth, and gavest them water for their thirst." Here both intelligence and goodness are ascribed to the Holy Spirit. There are some who tell us that while it is true the personality of the Holy Spirit is found in the New Testament, it is not found in the Old. But it is certainly found in this passage. As a matter of course, the doctrine of the personality of the Holy Spirit is not as fully developed in the Old Testament as in the New. But the doctrine is there.

There is perhaps no passage in the entire Bible in which the personality of the Holy Spirit comes out more tenderly and touchingly than in Eph. iv. 30, "And grieve not the Holy Spirit of God, whereby ye are sealed unto the day of redemption." Here grief is ascribed to the Holy Spirit. The Holy Spirit is not a blind, impersonal influence or power that comes into our lives to illuminate, sanctify and empower them. No, He is immeasurably more than that, He is a holy Person who comes to dwell in our hearts, One who sees clearly every act we perform, every word we speak, every thought we entertain, even the most fleeting fancy that is allowed to pass through our minds; and if there is anything in act, or word or deed that is impure, unholy, unkind, selfish, mean, petty or untrue, this infinitely holy One is deeply grieved by it. I know of no thought that will help one more than this to lead a holy life and to walk softly in the presence of the holy One.

How often a young man is kept back from yielding to the temptations that surround young manhood by the thought that if he should yield to the temptation that now assails him, his holy mother might hear of it and would be grieved by it beyond expression. How often some young man has had his hand upon the door of some place of sin that he is about to enter and the thought has come to him, "If I should enter there, my mother might hear of it and it would nearly kill her," and he has turned his back upon that door and gone away to lead a pure life, that he might not grieve his mother. But there is One who is holier than any mother, One who is more sensitive against sin than the purest woman who ever walked this earth, and who loves us as even no mother ever loved, and this One dwells in our hearts, if we are really Christians, and He sees every act we do by day or under cover of the night; He hears every word we utter in public or in private; He sees every thought we entertain, He beholds every fancy and imagination that is permitted even a momentary lodgement in our mind, and if there is anything unholy, impure, selfish, mean, petty, unkind, harsh, unjust, or in anywise evil in act or word or thought or fancy, He is grieved by it. If we will allow those words, "Grieve not the Holy Spirit of God," to sink into our hearts and become the motto of our lives, they will keep us from many a sin. How often some thought or fancy has knocked for an entrance into my own mind and was about to find entertainment when the thought has come, "The Holy Spirit sees that thought and will be grieved by it" and that thought has gone. II. *Many acts that only a Person can perform are ascribed to the Holy Spirit.*

If we deny the personality of the Holy Spirit, many passages of Scripture become meaningless and absurd. For example, we read in 1 Cor. ii. 10, "But God hath revealed them unto us by His Spirit: for *the Spirit searcheth* all things, yea, the deep things of God." This passage sets before us the Holy Spirit, not merely as an illumination whereby we are enabled to grasp the deep things of God, but a Person who Himself searches the deep things of God and then reveals to us the precious discoveries which He has made.

We read in Rev. ii. 7, "He that hath an ear, let him hear what *the Spirit saith* unto the churches; To him that overcometh will I give to eat of the tree of life, which is in the midst of the paradise of God." Here the Holy Spirit is set before us, not merely as an impersonal enlightenment that comes to our mind but a Person who speaks and out of the depths of His own wisdom, whispers into the ear of His listening servant the precious truth of God.

In Gal. iv. 6 we read, "And because ye are sons, God hath sent forth the Spirit of His Son into your hearts, *crying*, Abba, Father." Here the Holy Spirit is represented as crying out in the heart of the individual believer. Not merely a Divine influence producing in our own hearts the assurance of our sonship but one who cries out in our hearts, who bears witness together with our spirit that we are sons of God. (See also Rom. viii. 16.)

The Holy Spirit is also represented in the Scripture as one who prays. We read in Rom. viii. 26, R. V., "And in like manner the Spirit also helpeth our infirmity; for we know not how to pray as we ought; but *the Spirit Himself maketh intercession* for us with groanings which cannot be uttered." It is plain from this passage that the Holy Spirit is not merely an influence that moves us to pray, not merely an illumination that teaches us how to pray, but a Person who Himself prays in and through us. There is wondrous comfort in the thought that every true believer has two Divine Persons praying for him, Jesus Christ, the Son who was once upon this earth, who knows all about our temptations, who can be touched with the feeling of our infirmities and who is now ascended to the right hand of the Father and in that place of authority and power ever lives to make intercession for us (Heb. vii. 25; 1 John ii. 1); and another Person, just as Divine as He, who walks by our side each day, yes, who dwells in the innermost depths of our being and knows our needs, even as we do not know them ourselves, and from these depths makes intercession to the Father for us. The position of the believer is indeed one of perfect security with these two Divine Persons praying for him.

We read again in John xv. 26, "But when the Comforter is come, whom I will send unto you from the Father, even the Spirit of truth, which proceedeth from the Father, *He shall testify* of Me." Here the Holy Spirit is set before us as a Person who gives His testimony to Jesus Christ, not merely as an illumination that enables the believer to testify of Christ, but a Person who Himself testifies; and a clear distinction is drawn in this and the following verse between the testimony of the Holy Spirit and the testimony of the believer to whom He has borne His witness, for we read in the next verse, "And *ye also* shall bear witness because ye have been with Me from the beginning." So there are two witnesses, the Holy Spirit bearing witness to the believer and the believer bearing witness to the world.

The Holy Spirit is also spoken of as a teacher. We read in John xiv. 26, "But the Comforter, which is the Holy Ghost, whom the Father will send in My name, *He shall teach* you all things, and bring all things to your remembrance, whatsoever I have said unto you." And in a similar way, we read in John xvi. 12-14, "I have yet many things to say unto you, but ye cannot bear them now. Howbeit when He, the Spirit of truth, is come, *He will guide* you into all truth: for He shall not speak of Himself; but whatsoever He shall hear, that shall He speak: and He will show you things to come. He shall glorify Me: for He shall receive of Mine, and shall show it unto you." And in the Old Testament, Neh. ix. 20, "Thou gavest also Thy good Spirit to instruct them." In all these passages it is perfectly clear that the Holy Spirit is not a mere illumination that enables us to apprehend the truth, but a Person who comes to us to teach us day by day the truth of God. It is the privilege of the humblest believer in Jesus Christ not merely to have his mind illumined to comprehend the truth of God, but to have a Divine Teacher to daily teach him the truth he needs to know (cf. 1 John ii. 20, 27). The Holy Spirit is also represented as the Leader and Guide of the children of God. We read in Rom. viii. 14, "For as many as are *led by the Spirit* of God they are the sons of God." He is not merely an influence that enables us to see the way that God would have us go, nor merely a power that gives us strength to go that way, but a Person who takes us by the hand and gently leads us on in the paths in which God would have us walk.

The Holy Spirit is also represented as a Person who has authority to command men in their service of Jesus Christ. We read of the Apostle Paul and his companions in Acts xvi. 6, 7, "Now when they had gone throughout Phrygia and the region of Galatia, and were *forbidden of the Holy Ghost* to preach the Word in Asia, after they were come to Mysia, they assayed to go into Bithynia: but the Spirit suffered them not." Here it is a Person who takes the direction of the conduct of Paul and his companions and a Person whose authority they recognized and to whom they instantly submit.

Further still than this the Holy Spirit is represented as the One who is the supreme authority in the church, who calls men to work and appoints them to office. We read in Acts xiii. 2, "As they ministered to the Lord, and fasted, the Holy Ghost said, Separate Me Barnabas and Saul for the work where unto I have called them." And in Acts xx. 28, "Take heed therefore unto yourselves, and to all the flock, over the which the Holy Ghost hath made you overseers, to feed the Church of God, which He hath purchased with His own blood." There can be no doubt to a candid seeker after truth that it is a Person, and a person of Divine majesty and sovereignty, who is here set before us.

From all the passages here quoted, it is evident that many acts that only a person can perform are ascribed to the Holy Spirit.

III. *An office is predicated of the Holy Spirit that can only be predicated of a person.*

Our Savior says in John xiv. 16, 17, "And I will pray the Father, and He shall give you another Comforter, that He may abide with you forever; Even the Spirit of truth: whom the world cannot receive, because it seeth Him not, neither knoweth Him: but ye know Him; for He dwelleth with you, and shall be in you." Our Lord had announced to the disciples that He was about to leave them. An awful sense of desolation took possession of them. Sorrow filled their hearts (John xvi. 6) at the contemplation of their loneliness and absolute helplessness when Jesus should thus leave them alone. To comfort them the Lord tells them that they shall not be left alone, that in leaving them He was going to the Father and that He would pray the Father and He would give them another Comforter to take the place of Himself during His absence. Is it possible that Jesus Christ could have used such language if the other Comforter who was coming to take His place was only an impersonal influence or power? Still more, is it possible that Jesus could have said as He did in John xvi. 7, "Nevertheless I tell you the truth: *It is expedient for you that I go away*: for if I go not away, the Comforter will not come unto you; but if I depart, I will send Him unto you," if this Comforter whom He was to send was simply an impersonal influence or power? No, one Divine Person was going, another Person just as Divine was coming to take His place, and it was expedient for the disciples that the One go to represent them before the Father, for another just as Divine and sufficient was coming to take His place. This promise of our Lord and Savior of the coming of the other Comforter and of His abiding with us is the greatest and best of all for the present dispensation. This is *the* promise of the Father (Acts i. 4), the promise of promises. We shall take it up again when we come to study the names of the Holy Spirit.

IV. *A treatment is predicated to the Holy Spirit that could only be predicated of a Person.*

We read in Isa. lxiii. 10, R. V., "But they *rebelled and grieved* His Holy Spirit: therefore He was turned to be their enemy, and He fought against them." Here we are told that the Holy Spirit is rebelled against and grieved (cf. Eph. iv. 30). Only a person can be rebelled against and only a person of authority. Only a person can be grieved. You cannot grieve a mere influence or power. In Heb. x. 29, we read, "Of how much sorer punishment, suppose ye, shall he be thought worthy, who hath trodden underfoot the Son of God, and hath counted the blood of the covenant, wherewith he was sanctified, an unholy thing, and hath *done despite unto* the Spirit of grace?" Here we are told that the Holy Spirit is "done despite unto" ("treated with contumely"—Thayer's Greek-English Lexicon of the New Testament). There is but one kind of entity in the universe that can be treated with contumely (or insulted) and that is a person. It is absurd to think of treating an influence or a power or any kind of being except a person with contumely. We read again in Acts v. 3, "But Peter said, Ananias, why hath Satan filled thine heart *to lie to* the Holy Ghost, and to keep back part of the price of the land?" Here we have the Holy Spirit represented as one who can be lied to. One cannot lie to anything but a person.

In Matt. xii. 31, 32, we read, "Wherefore I say unto you, All manner of sin and blasphemy shall be forgiven unto men: but the blasphemy against the Holy Ghost shall not be forgiven unto men. And whosoever speaketh a word against the Son of man, it shall be forgiven him: but whosoever speaketh against the Holy Ghost, it shall not be forgiven him, neither in this world, neither in the world to come." Here we are told that the Holy Spirit is blasphemed against. It is impossible to blaspheme anything but a person. If the

Holy Spirit is not a person, it certainly cannot be a more serious and decisive sin to blaspheme Him than it is to blaspheme the Son of man, our Lord and Savior, Jesus Christ Himself.

Here then we have four distinctive and decisive lines of proof *that the Holy Spirit is a Person.* Theoretically most of us believe this but do we, in our real thought of Him and in our practical attitude towards Him treat Him as if He were indeed a Person? At the close of an address on the Personality of the Holy Spirit at a Bible conference some years ago, one who had been a church-member many years, a member of one of the most orthodox of our modern denominations, said to me, "I never thought of *It* before as a Person." Doubtless this Christian woman had often sung:

> *"Praise God from whom all blessings flow,*
> *Praise Him all creatures here below,*
> *Praise Him above, ye heavenly host,*
> *Praise Father, Son and Holy Ghost."*

Doubtless she had often sung:

> *"Glory be to the Father, and to the Son, and to the Holy Ghost,*
> *As it was in the beginning, is now, and ever shall be,*
> *World without end, Amen."*

But it is one thing to sing words; it is quite another thing to realize the meaning of what we sing. If this Christian woman had been questioned in regard to her doctrine, she would doubtless have said that she believed that there were three Persons in the Godhead, Father, Son and Holy Spirit, but a theological confession is one thing, a practical realization of the truth we confess is quite another. So the question is altogether necessary, no matter how orthodox you may be in your creedal statements, Do you regard the Holy Spirit as indeed as real a Person as Jesus Christ, as loving and wise and strong, as worthy of your confidence and love and surrender as Jesus Christ Himself? The Holy Spirit came into this world to be to the disciples of our Lord after His departure, and to us, what Jesus Christ had been to them during the days of His personal companionship with them (John xiv. 16, 17). Is He that to you? Do you know Him? Every week in your life you hear the apostolic benediction, "The grace of the Lord Jesus Christ and the love of God and the communion of the Holy Ghost be with you all" (2 Cor. xiii. 14), but while you hear it, do you take in the significance of it? Do you know the communion of the Holy Ghost? The fellowship of the Holy Ghost? The partnership of the Holy Ghost? The comradeship of the Holy Ghost? The intimate personal friendship of the Holy Ghost? Herein lies the whole secret of a real Christian life, a life of liberty and joy and power and fullness. To have as one's ever-present Friend, and to be conscious that one has as his ever-present Friend, the Holy Spirit and to surrender one's life in all its departments entirely to His control, this is true Christian living. The doctrine of the Personality of the Holy Spirit is as distinctive of the religion that Jesus taught as the doctrines of the Deity and the atonement of Jesus Christ Himself. But it is not enough to believe the doctrine—one must know the Holy Spirit Himself. The whole purpose of this chapter (God help me to say it reverently) is to introduce you to my Friend, the Holy Spirit.

II: The Deity of the Holy Spirit

In the preceding chapter we have seen clearly that the Holy Spirit is a Person. But what sort of a Person is He? Is He a finite person or an infinite person? Is He God? This question also is plainly answered in the Bible. There are in the Scriptures of the Old and New Testaments five distinct and decisive lines of proof of the Deity of the Holy Spirit.

I. *Each of the four distinctively Divine attributes is ascribed to the Holy Spirit.*

What are the distinctively Divine attributes? Eternity, omnipresence, omniscience and omnipotence. All of these are ascribed to the Holy Spirit in the Bible.

We find *eternity* ascribed to the Holy Spirit in Heb. ix. 14, "How much more shall the blood of Christ, who through the *eternal* Spirit offered Himself without spot to God, purge your conscience from dead works to serve the living God?"

Omnipresence is ascribed to the Holy Spirit in Ps. cxxxix. 7-10, "Whither shall I go from Thy Spirit? or whither shall I flee from Thy presence? If I ascend up into heaven, Thou art there: if I make my bed in hell, behold, Thou art there. If I take the wings of the morning, and dwell in the uttermost parts of the sea; even there shall Thy hand lead me, and Thy right hand shall hold me."

Omniscience is ascribed to the Holy Spirit in several passages. For example, we read in 1 Cor. ii. 10, 11, "But God hath revealed them unto us by His Spirit: for the Spirit *searcheth all things*, yea, the deep things of God. For what man knoweth the things of a man, save the spirit of man which is in him? *Even so the things of God knoweth no man, but the Spirit of God.*" Again in John xiv. 26, "But the Comforter, which is the Holy Ghost, whom the Father will send in My name, He shall *teach you all things*, and bring all things to your remembrance, whatsoever I have said unto you." Still further we read in John xvi. 12, 13, R. V., "I have yet many things to say unto you, but ye cannot bear them now. Howbeit when He, the Spirit of truth is come, He shall *guide you into all the truth*: for He shall not speak from Himself; but what things soever He shall hear, these shall He speak: and He shall declare unto you the things that are to come."

We find *omnipotence* ascribed to the Holy Spirit in Luke i. 35, "And the angel answered and said unto her, The Holy Ghost shall come upon thee, and the *power of the Highest* shall overshadow thee: therefore also that holy thing which shall be born of thee shall be called the Son of God."

II. *Three distinctively Divine works are ascribed to the Holy Spirit.*

When we think of God and His work, the first work of which we always think is that of creation. In the Scriptures creation is ascribed to the Holy Spirit. We read in Job xxxiii. 4, "The Spirit of God *hath made me*, and the *breath of the Almighty* hath given me life." We read still again in Ps. civ. 30, "Thou sendest forth Thy Spirit, *they are created*: and Thou renewest the face of the earth." In connection with the description of creation in the first chapter of Genesis, the activity of the Spirit is referred to (Gen. i. 1-3).

The impartation of life is also a Divine work and this is ascribed in the Scriptures to the Holy Spirit, We read in John vi. 6, A. R. V., "It is the Spirit that giveth life: the flesh profiteth nothing." We read also in Rom. viii. 11, "But if the Spirit of Him that raised up Jesus from the dead dwell in you, He that raised up Christ from the dead shall also quicken your mortal bodies *by His Spirit* that dwelleth in you." In the description of the creation of man in Gen. ii. 7, it is the breath of God, that is the Holy Spirit, who imparts life to man, and man becomes a living soul. The exact words are, "And the Lord God formed man of the dust of the ground, and breathed into his nostrils *the breath of life*; and man became a living soul." The Greek word which is rendered "spirit" means "breath" and though the Holy Spirit as a Person does not come out distinctly in this early reference to Him in Gen. ii. 7, nevertheless, this passage interpreted in the light of the fuller revelation of the New Testament clearly refers to the Holy Spirit.

The authorship of Divine prophecies is also ascribed to the Holy Spirit. We read in 2 Pet. i. 21, R. V., "For no prophecy ever came by the will of man: but men spake from God, *being moved by the Holy Ghost.*" Even in the Old Testament, there is a reference to the Holy Spirit as the author of prophecy. We read in 2 Sam. xxiii. 2, 3, "*the Spirit of the Lord spake* by me, and His word was in my tongue. The God of Israel said, the Rock of Israel spake to me, He that ruleth over men must be just, ruling in the fear of God."

So we see that the three distinctly Divine works of creation, the impartation of life, and prophecy are ascribed to the Holy Spirit.

III. *Statements which in the Old Testament distinctly name the Lord or Jehovah as their subject are applied to the Holy Spirit in the New Testament, i. e., the Holy Spirit occupies the position of Deity in New Testament thought.*

A striking illustration of this is found in Isa. vi. 8-10, "Also I heard the voice of the Lord, saying, Whom shall I send, and who will go for us? Then said I, Here am I; send me. And He said, Go, and tell this people, Hear ye indeed, but understand not; and see ye indeed, but perceive not. Make the heart of this people fat, and make their ears heavy, and shut their eyes; lest they see with their eyes, and hear with their ears, and understand with their heart, and convert and be healed." In verse five we are told that it was Jehovah (whenever the word Lord is spelled in capitals in the Old Testament, it stands for Jehovah in the Hebrew and is so rendered in the American Revision) whom Isaiah saw and who speaks. But in Acts xxviii. 25-27 there is a reference to this statement of Isaiah's and whereas in Isaiah we are told it is Jehovah who speaks, in the reference in Acts we are told that it was the Holy Spirit who was the speaker. The passage in Acts reads as follows, "And when they agreed not among themselves, they departed after that Paul had spoken one word, Well spake the Holy Ghost by Esaias the prophet unto our fathers, saying, Go unto this people, and say, Hearing ye shall hear, and shall not understand; and seeing ye shall see and not perceive: For the heart of this people is waxed gross, and their ears are dull of hearing, and their eyes have they closed; lest they should see with their eyes, and hear with their ears, and understand with their heart, and should be converted, and I should heal them." So we see that what is distinctly ascribed to Jehovah in the Old Testament is ascribed to the Holy Spirit in the New: *i. e.*, the Holy Spirit is identified with Jehovah. It is a noteworthy fact that in the Gospel of John, the twelfth chapter and the thirty-ninth to forty-first verses where another reference is made to this passage in Isaiah, this same passage is ascribed to Christ (note carefully the forty-first verse). So in different parts of Scripture, we have the same passage referred to Jehovah, referred to the Holy Spirit, and referred to Jesus Christ. May we not find the explanation of this in the threefold "Holy" of the seraphic cry in Isaiah vi. 3, where we read, "And one cried unto another, and said, Holy, holy, holy, is the Lord of hosts: the whole earth is full of His glory." In this we have a distinct suggestion of the tri-personality of the Jehovah of Hosts, and hence the propriety of the threefold application of the vision. A further suggestion of this tri-personality of Jehovah of Hosts is found in the eighth verse of the chapter where the Lord is represented as saying, "Whom shall I send, and who will go for *us*?"

Another striking illustration of the application of passages in the New Testament to the Holy Spirit which in the Old Testament distinctly name Jehovah as their subject is found in Ex. xvi. 7. Here we read, "And in the morning, then ye shall see the glory of the Lord; for that He heareth your murmurings against the Lord: and what are we that ye murmur against us?" Here the murmuring of the children of Israel is distinctly said to be against Jehovah. But in Heb. iii. 7-9, where this instance is referred to, we read, "Wherefore, *as the Holy Ghost saith*, To-day if ye will hear His voice, harden not your hearts, and in the provocation, in the day of temptation in the wilderness: When your fathers tempted *Me*, proved *Me*, and saw My works forty years." The murmurings which Moses in the Book of Exodus says were against Jehovah, we are told in the Epistle to the Hebrews were against the Holy Spirit. This leaves it beyond question that the Holy Spirit occupies the position of Jehovah (or Deity) in the New Testament (cf. also Ps. xcv. 8-11).

IV. *The name of the Holy Spirit is coupled with that of God in a way it would be impossible for a reverent and thoughtful mind to couple the name of any finite being with that of the Deity.*

We have an illustration of this in 1 Cor. xii. 4-6, "Now there are diversities of gifts, but the *same Spirit*. And there are differences of administrations, but the *same Lord*. And there are diversities of operations, but it is the *same God* which worketh all in all." Here we find God, and the Lord and the Spirit associated together in a relation of equality that would be shocking to contemplate if the Spirit were a finite being. We have a still more striking illustration of this in Matt. xxviii. 19, "Go ye therefore, and teach all nations, baptizing them in the name of the *Father*, and of the *Son*, and of the *Holy Ghost*." Who, that had grasped the Bible conception of God the Father, would think for a moment of coupling the name of the Holy Spirit with that of the Father in this way if the Holy Spirit were a finite being, even the most exalted of angelic beings? Another striking illustration is found in 2 Cor. xiii. 14, "The grace of *the Lord Jesus Christ*, and the love of *God*, and the communion of *the Holy Ghost*, be with you all. Amen." Can any one ponder these words and catch anything like their real import without seeing clearly that it would be impossible to couple the name of the Holy Spirit with that of God the Father in the way in which it is coupled in this verse unless the Holy Spirit were Himself a Divine Being?

V. *The Holy Spirit is called God.*

The final and decisive proof of the Deity of the Holy Spirit is found in the fact that He is called God in the New Testament. We read in Acts v. 3, 4, "But Peter said, Ananias, why hath Satan filled thine heart to lie to the Holy Ghost, and to keep back part of the price of the land? Whiles it remained, was it not thine own? And after it was sold, was it not in thine own power? Why hast thou conceived this thing in thine heart? Thou hast not lied unto men but *unto God*." In the first part of this passage we are told that Ananias lied to the Holy Spirit. When this is further explained, we are told it was not unto men but unto God that he had lied in lying to the Holy Spirit, *i. e.*, the Holy Spirit to whom he lied is called God.

To sum it all up, by the ascription of all the distinctively Divine attributes, and several distinctly Divine works, by referring statements which in the Old Testament clearly name Jehovah, the Lord, or God as their subject to the Holy Spirit in the New Testament, by coupling the name of the Holy Spirit with that of God in a way that would be impossible to couple that of any finite being with that of Deity, by plainly calling the Holy Spirit God, in all these unmistakable ways, God in His own Word distinctly proclaims that the Holy Spirit is a Divine Person.

III: The Distinction of the Holy Spirit from the Father and from His Son, Jesus Christ

We have seen thus far that the Holy Spirit is a Person and a Divine Person. And now another question arises, Is He as a Person separate and distinct from the Father and from the Son? One who carefully studies the New Testament statements cannot but discover that beyond a question He is. We read in Luke iii. 21, 22, "Now when all the people were baptized, it came to pass that Jesus also being baptized, and praying, the heaven was opened, and the Holy Ghost descended in a bodily shape like a dove upon Him, and a voice came from heaven, which said, Thou art My beloved Son; in Thee I am well pleased." Here the clearest possible distinction is drawn between Jesus Christ, who was on earth, and the Father who spoke to Him from heaven as one person speaks to another person, and the Holy Spirit who descended in a bodily form as a dove from the Father, who was speaking, to the Son, to whom He was speaking, and rested upon the Son as a Person separate and distinct from Himself. We see a clear distinction drawn between the name of the Father and that of the Son and that of the Holy Spirit in Matt, xxviii. 19, where we read, "Go ye therefore, and teach all nations, baptizing them in the name of the Father, *and* of the Son, *and* of the Holy Ghost." The distinction of the Holy Spirit from the Father and the Son comes out again with exceeding clearness in John xiv. 16. Here we read, "And *I* will pray *the Father*, and He shall give you *another Comforter*, that He may abide with you forever." Here we see the one Person, the Son, praying to another Person, the Father, and the Father to whom He prays giving another Person, another Comforter, in answer to the prayer of the second Person, the Son. If words mean anything, and certainly in the Bible they mean what they say, there can be no mistaking it, that the Father and the Son and the Spirit are three distinct and separate Persons.

Again in John xvi. 7, a clear distinction is drawn between Jesus who goes away to the Father and the Holy Spirit who comes from the Father to take His place. Jesus says, "Nevertheless I tell you the truth; It is expedient for you that I go away: for if I go not away, *the Comforter* will not come unto you; but if I depart, I will send Him unto you." A similar distinction is drawn in Acts ii. 33, where we read, "Therefore being by the right hand of God exalted, and having received of the Father the promise of the Holy Ghost, He hath shed forth this, which ye now see and hear." In this passage, the clearest possible distinction is drawn between the Son exalted to the right hand of the Father and the Father to whose right hand He is exalted, and the Holy Spirit whom the Son receives from the Father and sheds forth upon the Church.

To sum it all up, again and again the Bible draws the clearest possible distinction between the three Persons, the Holy Spirit, the Father and the Son. They are three separate personalities, having mutual relations to one another, acting upon one another, speaking of or to one another, applying the pronouns of the second and third persons to one another.

IV: The Subordination of the Spirit to the Father and to the Son

From the fact that the Holy Spirit is a Divine Person, it does not follow that the Holy Spirit is in every sense equal to the Father. While the Scriptures teach that in Jesus Christ dwelt all the fullness of the Godhead in a bodily form (Col. ii. 9) and that He was so truly and *fully* Divine that He could say, "I and the Father are one" (John x. 30) and "He that hath seen Me hath seen the Father" (John xiv. 9), they also teach with equal clearness that Jesus Christ was not equal to the Father in every respect, but subordinate to the Father in many ways. In a similar way, the Scriptures teach us that though the Holy Spirit is a Divine Person, He is subordinate to the Father and to the Son. In John xiv. 26, we are taught that the Holy Spirit is sent by the Father and in the name of the Son. Jesus declares very clearly, "But the Comforter, which is the Holy Ghost, whom *the Father will send* in My name, He shall teach you all things, and bring all things to your remembrance, whatsoever I have said unto you." In John xv. 26 we are told that it is Jesus who sends the Spirit from the

Father. The exact words are, "But when the Comforter is come, *whom I will send* unto you from the Father, even the Spirit of truth, which proceedeth from the Father, He shall testify of Me." Just as we are elsewhere taught that Jesus Christ was sent by the Father (John vi. 29; viii. 29, 42), we are here taught that the Holy Spirit in turn is sent by Jesus Christ.

The subordination of the Holy Spirit to the Father and the Son comes out also in the fact that He derives some of His names from the Father and from the Son. We read in Rom. viii. 9, "But ye are not in the flesh, but in the Spirit, if so be that *the Spirit of God* dwell in you. Now if any man have not *the Spirit of Christ*, he is none of His." Here we have two names of the Spirit, one derived from His relation to the Father, "the Spirit of God," and the other derived from His relation to the Son, "the Spirit of Christ."

In Acts xvi. 7, R. V., He is spoken of as "the Spirit of Jesus."

The subordination of the Spirit to the Son is also seen in the fact that the Holy Spirit speaks "not from Himself but speaks the words which He hears." We read in John xvi. 13, R. V., "Howbeit when He, the Spirit of truth, is come, He shall guide you into all the truth: for He *shall not speak from Himself*; but *what things soever He shall hear*, these shall He speak: and He shall declare unto you the things that are to come." In a similar way, Jesus said of Himself, "My teaching is not Mine, but His that sent Me." (John vii. 16; viii. 26, 40).

The subordination of the Spirit to the Son comes out again in the clearly revealed fact that it is the work of the Holy Spirit not to glorify Himself but to glorify Christ. Jesus says in John xvi. 14, "He shall glorify Me: for He shall receive of Mine, and shall shew it unto you." In a similar way, Christ sought not His own glory, but the glory of Him that sent Him, that is the Father (John vii. 18).

From all these passages, it is evident that the Holy Spirit in His present work, while possessed of all the attributes of Deity, is subordinated to the Father and to the Son. On the other hand, we shall see later that in His earthly life, Jesus lived and taught and worked in the power of the Holy Spirit.

V: The Person and Work of the Holy Spirit as Revealed in His Names

At least twenty-five different names are used in the Old and New Testaments in speaking of the Holy Spirit. There is the deepest significance in these names. By the careful study of them, we find a wonderful revelation of the Person and work of the Holy Spirit.

I. *The Spirit.*

The simplest name by which the Holy Spirit is mentioned in the Bible is that which stands at the head of this paragraph—"*The Spirit.*" This name is also used as the basis of other names, so we begin our study with this. The Greek and Hebrew words so translated mean literally, "Breath" or "Wind." Both thoughts are in the name as applied to the Holy Spirit.

1. The thought of breath is brought out in John xx. 22 where we read, "And when He had said this, *He breathed on them*, and saith unto them, Receive ye the Holy Ghost." It is also suggested in Gen. ii. 7, "And the Lord God formed man of the dust of the ground, and *breathed* into his nostrils the breath of life; and man became a living soul." This becomes more evident when we compare with this Ps. civ. 30, "Thou sendest forth *Thy*

Spirit, they are created: and Thou renewest the face of the earth." And Job xxxiii. 4, "*The Spirit of God hath made me*, and *the breath* of the Almighty hath given me life." What is the significance of this name from the standpoint of these passages? It is that the Spirit is the outbreathing of God, His inmost life going forth in a personal form to quicken. When we receive the Holy Spirit, we receive the inmost life of God Himself to dwell in a personal way in us. When we really grasp this thought, it is overwhelming in its solemnity. Just stop and think what it means to have the inmost life of that infinite and eternal Being whom we call God, dwelling in a personal way in you. How solemn and how awful and yet unspeakably glorious life becomes when we realize this.

2. The thought of the Holy Spirit as "the Wind" is brought out in John iii. 6-8, "That which is born of the flesh is flesh; and that which is born of the Spirit is spirit. Marvel not that I said unto thee, Ye must be born again. The wind bloweth where it listeth, and thou hearest the sound thereof, but canst not tell whence it cometh, and whither it goeth: so is every one that is born of the Spirit." In the Greek, it is the same word that is translated in one part of this passage "Spirit" and the other part of the passage "wind." And it would seem as if the word ought to be translated the same way in both parts of the passage. It would then read, "That which is born of the flesh is flesh and that which is born of the 'Wind' is wind. Marvel not that I said unto thee, Ye must be born again. The wind bloweth where it listeth and thou hearest the sound thereof, but canst not tell whence it cometh or whither it goeth: so is every one that is born of the 'Wind.' " The full significance of this name as applied to the Holy Spirit (or Holy Wind) it may be beyond us to fathom, but we can see at least this much of its meaning:

(1) The Spirit like the wind is *sovereign*. "The wind bloweth where it listeth" (John iii. 8). You cannot dictate to the wind. It does as it wills. Just so with the Holy Spirit—He is sovereign—we cannot dictate to Him. He "divides to each man" severally even "*as He will*" (1 Cor. xii. 11, R. V.). When the wind is blowing from the north you may long to have it blow from the south, but cry as clamorously as you may to the wind, "Blow from the south" it will keep right on blowing from the north. But while you cannot dictate to the wind, while it blows as it will, you may learn the laws that govern the wind's motions and by bringing yourself into harmony with those laws, you can get the wind to do your work. You can erect your windmill so that whichever way the wind blows from the wheels will turn and the wind will grind your grain, or pump your water. Just so, while we cannot dictate to the Holy Spirit we can learn the laws of His operations and by bringing ourselves into harmony with those laws, above all by submitting our wills absolutely to His sovereign will, the sovereign Spirit of God will work through us and accomplish His own glorious work by our instrumentality.

(2) The Spirit like the wind is *invisible but none the less perceptible and real and mighty*. You hear the sound of the wind (John iii. 8) but the wind itself you never see. You hear the voice of the Spirit but He Himself is ever invisible. (The word translated "sound" in John iii. 8 is the word which elsewhere is translated "voice." See R. V.) We not only hear the voice, of the wind but we see its mighty effects. We feel the breath of the wind upon our cheeks, we see the dust and the leaves blowing before the wind, we see the vessels at sea driven swiftly towards their ports; but the wind itself remains invisible. Just so with the Spirit; we feel His breath upon our souls, we see the mighty things He does, but Himself we do not see. He is invisible, but He is real and perceptible. I shall never forget a solemn hour in Chicago Avenue Church, Chicago. Dr. W. W. White was making a farewell address before going to India to work among the students there. Suddenly, without any apparent warning, the place was filled with an awful and glorious Presence.

To me it was very real, but the question arose in my mind, "Is this merely subjective, just a feeling of my own, or is there an objective Presence here?" After the meeting was over, I asked different persons whether they were conscious of anything and found that at the same point in the meeting they, too, though they saw no one, became distinctly conscious of an overwhelming Presence, the Presence of the Holy Spirit. Though many years have passed, there are those who speak of that hour to this day. On another occasion in my own home at Chicago, when kneeling in prayer with an intimate friend, as we prayed it seemed as if an unseen and awful Presence entered the room. I realized what Eliphaz meant when he said, "Then a spirit passed before my face; the hair of my flesh stood up" (Job iv. 15). The moment was overwhelming, but as glorious as it was awful. These are but two illustrations of which many might be given. None of us have seen the Holy Spirit at any time, but of His presence we have been distinctly conscious again and again and again. His mighty power we have witnessed and His reality we cannot doubt. There are those who tell us that they do not believe in anything which they cannot see. Not one of them has ever seen the wind but they all believe in the wind. They have felt the wind and they have seen its effects, and just so we, beyond a question, have felt the mighty presence of the Spirit and witnessed His mighty workings.

(3) The Spirit like the wind is *inscrutable*. "Thou canst not tell whence it cometh and whither it goeth." Nothing in nature is more mysterious than the wind. But more mysterious still is the Holy Spirit in His operations. We hear of how suddenly and unexpectedly in widely separated communities He begins to work His mighty work. Doubtless there are hidden reasons why He does thus begin His work, but often-times these reasons are completely undiscoverable by us. We know not whence He comes nor whither He goes. We cannot tell where next He will display His mighty and gracious power.

(4) The Spirit, like the wind, is *indispensable*. Without wind, that is "air in motion," there is no life and so Jesus says, "Verily, verily, I say unto you, except a man be born of water and of the Spirit, he cannot enter into the kingdom of God." If the wind should absolutely cease to blow for a single hour, most of the life on this earth would cease to be. Time and again when the health reports of the different cities of the United States are issued, it has been found that the five healthiest cities in the United States were five cities located on the great lakes. Many have been surprised at this report when they have visited some of these cities and found that they were far from being the cleanest cities, or most sanitary in their general arrangement, and yet year after year this report has been returned. The explanation is simply this, it is the wind blowing from the lakes that has brought life and health to the cities. Just so when the Spirit ceases to blow in any heart or any church or any community, death ensues, but when the Spirit blows steadily upon the individual or the church or the community, there is abounding spiritual life and health.

(5) Closely related to the foregoing thought, like the wind the Holy Spirit is *life giving*. This thought comes out again and again in the Scriptures. For example, we read in John vi. 63, A. R. V., "It is the Spirit that giveth life," and in 2 Cor. iii. 6, we read, "The letter killeth, but the Spirit giveth life." Perhaps the most suggestive passage on this point is Ezek. xxxvii. 8, 9, 10, "And when I beheld, lo, the sinews and the flesh came up upon them, and the skin covered them above: but there was *no breath* in them. Then said He unto me, Prophesy unto *the wind*, prophesy, son of man, and say to *the wind*, Thus saith the Lord God; Come from the four winds, O breath, and breathe upon these slain, that they may live. So I prophesied as He commanded me, and *the breath came into them, and they lived*, and stood upon their feet, an exceeding great army" (cf. John iii. 5). Israel, in the

prophet's vision, was only bones, very many and very dry (vs. 2, 11), until the prophet proclaimed unto them the word of God; then there was a noise and a shaking and the bones came together, bone to his bone, and the sinews and the flesh came upon the bones, but still there was no life, but when the wind blew, the breath of God's Spirit, then "they stood up upon their feet an exceeding great army." All life in the individual believer, in the teacher, the preacher, and the church is the Holy Spirit's work. You will sometimes make the acquaintance of a man, and as you hear him talk and observe his conduct, you are repelled and disgusted. Everything about him declares that he is a dead man, a moral corpse and not only dead but rapidly putrefying. You get away from him as quickly as you can. Months afterwards you meet him again. You hesitate to speak to him; you want to get out of his very presence, but you do speak to him, and he has not uttered many sentences before you notice a marvelous change. His conversation is sweet and wholesome and uplifting; everything about his manner is attractive and delightful. You soon discover that the man's whole conduct and life has been transformed. He is no longer a putrefying corpse but a living child of God. What has happened? The Wind of God has blown upon him; he has received the Holy Spirit, the Holy Wind. Some quiet Sabbath day you visit a church. Everything about the outward appointments of the church are all that could be desired. There is an attractive meeting-house, an expensive organ, a gifted choir, a scholarly preacher. The service is well arranged but you have not been long at the gathering before you are forced to see that there is no life, that it is all form, and that there is nothing really being accomplished for God or for man. You go away with a heavy heart. Months afterwards you have occasion to visit the church again; the outward appointments of the church are much as they were before but the service has not proceeded far before you note a great difference. There is a new power in the singing, a new spirit in the prayer, a new grip in the preaching, everything about the church is teeming with the life of God. What has happened? The Wind of God has blown upon that church; the Holy Spirit, the Holy Wind, has come. You go some day to hear a preacher of whose abilities you have heard great reports. As he stands up to preach you soon learn that nothing too much has been said in praise of his abilities from the merely intellectual and rhetorical standpoint. His diction is faultless, his style beautiful, his logic unimpeachable, his orthodoxy beyond criticism. It is an intellectual treat to listen to him, and yet after all as he preaches you cannot avoid a feeling of sadness, for there is no real grip, no real power, indeed no reality of any kind, in the man's preaching. You go away with a heavy heart at the thought of this waste of magnificent abilities. Months, perhaps years, pass by and you again find yourself listening to this celebrated preacher, but what a change! The same faultless diction, the same beautiful style, the same unimpeachable logic, the same skillful elocution, the same sound orthodoxy, but now there is something more, there is reality, life, grip, power in the preaching. Men and women sit breathless as he speaks, sinners bowed with tears of contrition, pricked to their hearts with conviction of sin; men and women and boys and girls renounce their selfishness, and their sin and their worldliness and accept Jesus Christ and surrender their lives to Him. What has happened? The Wind of God has blown upon that man. He has been filled with the Holy Wind.

(6) Like the wind, the Holy Spirit is *irresistible*. We read in Acts i. 8, "But *ye shall receive power*, after that the Holy Ghost is come upon you: and ye shall be witnesses unto Me both in Jerusalem, and in all Judea, and in Samaria, and unto the uttermost parts of the earth." When this promise of our Lord was fulfilled in Stephen, we read, "And they were *not able to resist* the wisdom *and the Spirit* by which he spake." A man filled with the Holy Spirit is transformed into a cyclone. What can stand before the wind? When St.

Cloud, Minn., was visited with a cyclone years ago, the wind picked up loaded freight cars and carried them away off the track. It wrenched an iron bridge from its foundations, twisted it together and hurled it away. When a cyclone later visited St. Louis, Mo., it cut off telegraph poles a foot in diameter as if they had been pipe stems. It cut off enormous trees close to the root, it cut off the corner of brick buildings where it passed as though they had been cut by a knife; nothing could stand before it; and so, nothing can stand before a Spirit-filled preacher of the Word. None can resist the wisdom and the Spirit by which he speaks. The Wind of God took possession of Charles G. Finney, an obscure country lawyer, and sent him through New York State, then through New England, then through England, mowing down strong men by his resistless, Spirit-given logic. One night in Rochester, scores of lawyers, led by the justice of the Court of Appeals, filed out of the pews and bowed in the aisles and yielded their lives to God. The Wind of God took possession of D. L. Moody, an uneducated young business man in Chicago, and in the power of this resistless Wind, men and women and young people were mowed down before his words and brought in humble confession and renunciation of sin to the feet of Jesus Christ, and filled with the life of God they have been the pillars in the churches of Great Britain and throughout the world ever since. The great need to-day in individuals, in churches and in preachers is that the Wind of God blow upon us.

Much of the difficulty that many find with John iii. 5, "Jesus answered, Verily, verily, I say unto thee, Except a man be born of water and of the Spirit, he cannot enter into the kingdom of God," would disappear if we would only bear in mind that "Spirit" means "Wind" and translate the verse literally all through, "Except a man be born of water and Wind (there is no 'the' in the original), he cannot enter the kingdom of God." The thought would then seem to be, "Except a man be born of the cleansing and quickening power of the Spirit (or else of the cleansing Word—cf. John xv. 3; Eph. v. 26; Jas. i. 18; 1 Pet. i. 23—and the quickening power of the Holy Spirit)."

II. *The Spirit of God.*

The Holy Spirit is frequently spoken of in the Bible as the Spirit of God. For example we read in 1 Cor. iii. 16, "Know ye not that ye are the temple of God, and that the Spirit of God dwelleth in you." In this name we have the same essential thought as in the former name, but with this addition, that His Divine origin, nature and power are emphasized. He is not merely "The Wind" as seen above, but "The Wind *of God*."

III. *The Spirit of Jehovah.*

This name is used of the Holy Spirit in Isa. xi. 2, A. R. V., "And the Spirit of Jehovah shall rest upon him." The thought of the name is, of course, essentially the same as the preceding with the exception that God is here thought of as the Covenant God of Israel. He is thus spoken of in the connection in which the name is found; and, of course, the Bible, following that unerring accuracy that it always exhibits in its use of the different names for God, in this connection speaks of the Spirit as the Spirit of Jehovah and not merely as the Spirit of God.

IV. *The Spirit of the Lord Jehovah.*

The Holy Spirit is called the Spirit of the Lord Jehovah in Isa. lxi. 1-3, A. R. V., "The Spirit of the Lord Jehovah is upon Me; because Jehovah hath anointed Me to preach good tidings to the meek; He hath sent Me to bind up the broken-hearted, to proclaim liberty to the captives, etc." The Holy Spirit is here spoken of, not merely as the Spirit of Jehovah, but the Spirit of the Lord Jehovah because of the relation in which God Himself is spoken of in this connection, as not merely Jehovah, the covenant God of Israel, but as Jehovah

Israel's Lord as well as their covenant-keeping God. This name of the Spirit is even more expressive than the name "The Spirit of God."

V. *The Spirit of the Living God.*

The Holy Spirit is called *"The Spirit of the living God"* in 2 Cor. iii. 3, "Forasmuch as ye are manifestly declared to be the epistle of Christ ministered by us, written not with ink, but with *the Spirit of the living God*; not in tables of stone, but in fleshy tables of the heart." What is the significance of this name? It is made clear by the context. The Apostle Paul is drawing a contrast between the Word of God written with ink on parchment and the Word of God written on "tables that are hearts of flesh" (R. V.) by the Holy Spirit, who in this connection is called "the Spirit of the living God," because He makes God a living reality in our personal experience instead of a mere intellectual concept. There are many who believe in God, and who are perfectly orthodox in their conception of God, but after all God is to them only an intellectual theological proposition. It is the work of the Holy Spirit to make God something vastly more than a theological notion, no matter how orthodox; He is the Spirit *of the living God*, and it is His work to make God a living God to us, a Being whom we know, with whom we have personal acquaintance, a Being more real to us than the most intimate human friend we have. Have you a real God? Well, you may have. The Holy Spirit is the Spirit of the living God, and He is able and ready to give to you a living God, to make God real in your personal experience. There are many who have a God who once lived and acted and spoke, a God who lived and acted at the creation of the universe, who perhaps lived and acted in the days of Moses and Elijah and Jesus Christ and the Apostles, but who no longer lives and acts. If He exists at all, He has withdrawn Himself from any active part in nature or the history of man. He created nature and gave it its laws and powers and now leaves it to run itself. He created man and endowed him with his various faculties but has now left him to work out his own destiny. They may go further than this: they may believe in a God, who spoke to Abraham and to Moses and to David and to Isaiah and to Jesus and to the Apostles, but who speaks no longer. We may read in the Bible what He spoke to these various men but we cannot expect Him to speak to us. In contrast with these, it is the work of the Holy Spirit, the Spirit *of the living God*, to give us to know a God who lives and acts and speaks to-day, a God who is ready to come as near to us as He came to Abraham, to Moses or to Isaiah, or to the Apostles or to Jesus Himself. Not that He has any new revelations to make, for He guided the Apostles into all the truth (John xvi. 13, R. V.): but though there has been a complete revelation of God's truth made in the Bible, still God lives to-day and will speak to us as directly as He spoke to His chosen ones of old. Happy is the man who knows the Holy Spirit as the Spirit of the living God, and who, consequently, has a real God, a God who lives to-day, a God upon whom he can depend to-day to undertake for him, a God with whom he enjoys intimate personal fellowship, a God to whom he may raise his voice in prayer and who speaks back to him.

VI. *The Spirit of Christ.*

In Rom. viii. 9, "But ye are not in the flesh, but in the Spirit, if so be that the Spirit of God dwell in you. Now if any man have not *the Spirit of Christ*, he is none of His." The Holy Spirit is called *the Spirit of Christ*. The Spirit of Christ in this passage does not mean a Christlike spirit. It means something far more than that, it means that which lies back of a Christlike spirit; it is a name of the Holy Spirit. Why is the Holy Spirit called *the Spirit of Christ*? For several reasons:

(1) *Because He is Christ's gift.* The Holy Spirit is not merely the gift of the Father, but the gift of the Son as well. We read in John xx. 22 that Jesus "breathed on them and

saith unto them, Receive ye the Holy Ghost." The Holy Spirit is therefore the breath of Christ, as well as the breath of God the Father. It is Christ who breathes upon us and imparts to us the Holy Spirit. In John xiv. 15 and the following verses Jesus teaches us that it is in answer to His prayer that the Father gives to us the Holy Spirit. In Acts ii. 33 we read that Jesus "Being by the right hand of God exalted and having received of the Father the promise of the Holy Spirit," shed Him forth upon believers; that is, that Jesus, having been exalted to the right hand of God, in answer to His prayer, receives the Holy Spirit from the Father and sheds forth upon the Church Him whom He hath received from the Father. In Matt. iii. 11 we read that it is Jesus who baptizes with the Holy Spirit. In John vii. 37-39 Jesus bids all that are thirsty to *come unto Him* and drink, and the context makes it clear that the water that He gives is the Holy Spirit, who becomes in those who receive Him a source of life and power flowing out to others. It is the glorified Christ who gives to the Church the Holy Spirit. In the fourth chapter of John and the tenth verse Jesus declares that He is the One who gives the living water, the Holy Spirit. In all these passages, Christ is set forth as the One who gives the Holy Spirit, so the Holy Spirit is called "the Spirit of Christ."

(2) But there is a deeper reason why the Holy Spirit is called "the Spirit of Christ," *i. e., because it is the work of the Holy Spirit to reveal Christ to us*. In John xvi. 14, R. V., we read, "He (that is the Holy Spirit) shall glorify Me: for He shall take of Mine, and shall declare it unto you." In a similar way in John xv. 26, R. V., it is written, "But when the Comforter is come, whom I will send unto you from the Father, even the Spirit of truth, which proceedeth from the Father, He shall bear witness of Me." This is the work of the Holy Spirit to bear witness of Christ and reveal Jesus Christ to men. And as the revealer of Christ, He is called "the Spirit of Christ."

(3) But there is a still deeper reason yet why the Holy Spirit is called the Spirit of Christ, and that is *because it is His work to form Christ as a living presence within us*. In Eph. iii. 16, 17, the Apostle Paul prays to the Father that He would grant to believers according to the riches of His glory to be strengthened with might by His Spirit in the inner man, that Christ may dwell in their hearts by faith. This then is the work of the Holy Spirit, to cause Christ to dwell in our hearts, to form the living Christ within us. Just as the Holy Spirit literally and physically formed Jesus Christ in the womb of the Virgin Mary (Luke i. 35) so the Holy Spirit spiritually but really forms Jesus Christ within our hearts to-day. In John xiv. 16-18, Jesus told His disciples that when the Holy Spirit came that He Himself would come, that is, the result of the coming of the Holy Spirit to dwell in their hearts would be the coming of Christ Himself. It is the privilege of every believer in Christ to have the living Christ formed by the power of the Holy Spirit in his own heart and therefore the Holy Spirit who thus forms Christ within the heart is called the Spirit of Christ. How wonderful! How glorious is the significance of this name. Let us ponder it until we understand it, as far as it is possible to understand it, and until we rejoice exceedingly in the glory of it. VII. *The Spirit of Jesus Christ.*

The Holy Spirit is called *the Spirit of Jesus Christ* in Phil. i. 19, "For I know that this shall turn to my salvation through your prayer, and the supply of *the Spirit of Jesus Christ*." The Spirit is not merely the Spirit of the eternal Word but the Spirit of the Word incarnate. Not merely the Spirit of Christ, but the Spirit *of Jesus Christ*. It is the Man Jesus exalted to the right hand of the Father who receives and sends the Spirit. So we read in Acts ii. 32, 33, "This *Jesus* hath God raised up, whereof we all are witnesses. Therefore being by the right hand of God exalted, and having received of the Father the promise of the Holy Ghost, He hath shed forth this, which ye now see and hear."

VIII. *The Spirit of Jesus.*

The Holy Spirit is called *the Spirit of Jesus* in Acts xvi. 6, 7, R. V., "And they went through the region of Phrygia and Galatia, having been forbidden of the Holy Ghost to speak the word in Asia; and when they were come over against Mysia, they assayed to go into Bithynia; and the *Spirit of Jesus* suffered them not." By the using of this name, "*The Spirit of Jesus*" the thought of the relation of the Spirit to the *Man Jesus* is still more clear than in the name preceding this, the Spirit of Jesus Christ.

IX. *The Spirit of His Son.*

The Holy Spirit is called *the Spirit of His Son* in Gal. iv. 6, "And because ye are sons, God hath sent forth *the Spirit of His Son* into your hearts, crying, Abba, Father." We see from the context (vs. 4, 5) that this name is given to the Holy Spirit in special connection with His testifying to the sonship of the believer. It is "*the Spirit of His Son*" who testifies to our sonship. The thought is that the Holy Spirit is a filial Spirit, a Spirit who produces a sense of sonship in us. If we receive the Holy Spirit, we no longer think of God as if we were serving under constraint and bondage but we are sons living in joyous liberty. We do not fear God, we trust Him and rejoice in Him. When we receive the Holy Spirit, we do not receive a Spirit of bondage again to fear but a Spirit of adoption whereby we cry, Abba, Father (Rom. viii. 15). This name of the Holy Spirit is one of the most suggestive of all. We do well to ponder it long until we realize the glad fullness of its significance. We shall take it up again when we come to study the work of the Holy Spirit.

X. *The Holy Spirit.*

This name is of very frequent occurrence, and the name with which most of us are most familiar. One of the most familiar passages in which the name is used is Luke xi. 13, "If ye then, being evil, know how to give good gifts unto your children: how much more shall your heavenly Father give *the Holy Spirit* to them that ask Him?" This name emphasizes the essential moral character of the Spirit. He is *holy* in Himself. We are so familiar with the name that we neglect to weigh its significance. Oh, if we only realized more deeply and constantly that He is the *Holy* Spirit. We would do well if we, as the seraphim in Isaiah's vision, would bow in His presence and cry, "Holy, holy, holy." Yet how thoughtlessly oftentimes we talk about Him and pray for Him. We pray for Him to come into our churches and into our hearts but what would He find if He should come there? Would He not find much that would be painful and agonizing to Him? What would we think if vile women from the lowest den of iniquity in a great city should go to the purest woman in the city and invite her to come and live with them in their disgusting vileness with no intention of changing their evil ways. But that would not be as shocking as for you and me to ask the Holy Spirit to come and dwell in our hearts when we have no thought of giving up our impurity, or our selfishness, or our worldliness, or our sin. It would not be as shocking as it is for us to invite the Holy Spirit to come into our churches when they are full of worldliness and selfishness and contention and envy and pride, and all that is unholy. But if the denizens of the lowest and vilest den of infamy should go to the purest and most Christlike woman asking her to go and dwell with them with the intention of putting away everything that was vile and evil and giving to this holy and Christlike woman the entire control of the place, she would go. And as sinful and selfish and imperfect as we may be, the infinitely Holy Spirit is ready to come and take His dwelling in our heart if we will surrender to Him the absolute control of our lives, and allow Him to bring everything in thought and fancy and feeling and purpose and imagination and action into conformity with His will. The infinitely Holy Spirit is ready to come into our churches, however imperfect and worldly they may be now, if we are willing to put the absolute control of everything in His hands. But let us never forget that He is *the Holy* Spirit, and when we pray for Him let us pray for Him as such.

XI. *The Holy Spirit of Promise.*

The Holy Spirit is called *the Holy Spirit of promise* in Eph. i. 13, R. V., "In whom ye also, having heard the Word of truth, the Gospel of your salvation,—in whom, having also believed, ye were sealed with *the Holy Spirit of promise*." We have here the same name as that given above with the added thought that this Holy Spirit is the great promise of the Father and of the Son. The Holy Spirit is God's great all-inclusive promise for the present dispensation; the one thing for which Jesus bade the disciples wait after His ascension before they undertook His work was "the promise of the Father," that is the Holy Spirit (Acts i. 4, 5). The great promise of the Father until the coming of Christ was the coming atoning Savior and King, but when Jesus came and died His atoning death upon the cross of Calvary and arose and ascended to the right hand of the Father, then the second great promise of the Father was the Holy Spirit to take the place of our absent Lord. (See also Acts ii. 33.)

XII. *The Spirit of Holiness.*

The Holy Spirit is called *the Spirit of holiness* in Rom. i. 4, "And declared to be the Son of God with power, according to *the Spirit of holiness*, by the resurrection from the dead." At the first glance it may seem as if there were no essential difference between the two names the Holy Spirit and the Spirit of holiness. But there is a marked difference. The name of the Holy Spirit, as already said, emphasizes the essential moral character of the Spirit as holy, but the name of *the Spirit of holiness* brings out the thought that the Holy Spirit is not merely holy in Himself but He imparts holiness to others. The perfect holiness which He Himself possesses He imparts to those who receive Him (cf. 1 Pet. i. 2).

XIII. *The Spirit of Judgment.*

The Holy Spirit is called *the Spirit of judgment* in Isa. iv. 4, "When the Lord shall have washed away the filth of the daughters of Zion, and shall have purged the blood of Jerusalem from the midst thereof by *the Spirit of judgment*, and by the Spirit of burning." There are two names of the Holy Spirit in this passage; first, *the Spirit of judgment*. The Holy Spirit is so called because it is His work to bring sin to light, to convict of sin (cf. John xvi. 7-9). When the Holy Spirit comes to us the first thing that He does is to open our eyes to see our sins as God sees them. He judges our sin. (We will go into this more at length in studying John xvi. 7-11 when considering the work of the Holy Spirit.)

XIV. *The Spirit of Burning.*

This name is used in the passage just quoted above. (See XIII.) This name emphasizes His searching, refining, dross-consuming, illuminating and energizing work. The Holy Spirit is like a fire in the heart in which He dwells; and as fire tests and refines and consumes and illuminates and warms and energizes, so does He. In the context, it is the cleansing work of the Holy Spirit which is especially emphasized (Isa. iv. 3, 4).

XV. *The Spirit of Truth.*

The Holy Spirit is called *the Spirit of truth* in John xiv. 17, "Even the Spirit of truth; whom the world cannot receive, because it seeth Him not, neither knoweth Him; but ye know Him; for He dwelleth with you, and shall be in you" (cf. John xv. 26; xvi. 13). The Holy Spirit is called the Spirit of truth because it is the work of the Holy Spirit to communicate truth, to impart truth, to those who receive Him. This comes out in the passage given above, and, if possible, it comes out even more clearly in John xvi. 13, R. V., "Howbeit when He, *the Spirit of truth*, is come, He shall guide you into all the truth: for He shall not speak from Himself; but what things soever He shall hear, these shall He speak: and He shall declare unto you the things that are to come." All truth is from the Holy Spirit. It is only as He teaches us that we come to know the truth.

XVI. *The Spirit of Wisdom and Understanding.*

The Holy Spirit is called the Spirit of wisdom and understanding in Isa. xi. 2, "And the Spirit of the Lord shall rest upon him, *the Spirit* of wisdom and understanding, the Spirit of counsel and might, the Spirit of knowledge and of the fear of the Lord." The significance of the name is so plain as to need no explanation. It is evident both from the words used and from the context that it is the work of the Holy Spirit to impart wisdom and understanding to those who receive Him. Those who receive the Holy Spirit receive the Spirit "of power" and "of love" and "*of a sound mind*" or sound sense (2 Tim. i. 7).

XVII. *The Spirit of Counsel and Might.*

We find this name used of the Holy Spirit in the passage given under the preceding head. The meaning of this name too is obvious, the Holy Spirit is called "the Spirit of counsel and of might" because He gives us counsel in all our plans and strength to carry them out (cf. Acts viii. 29; xvi. 6, 7; i. 8). It is our privilege to have God's own counsel in all our plans and God's strength in all the work that we undertake for Him. We receive them by receiving the Holy Spirit, the Spirit of counsel and might.

XVIII. *The Spirit of Knowledge and of the Fear of the Lord.*

This name also is used in the passage given above (Isa. xi. 2). The significance of this name is also obvious. It is the work of the Holy Spirit to impart knowledge to us and to beget in us a reverence for Jehovah, that reverence that reveals itself above all in obedience to His commandments. The one who receives the Holy Spirit finds his delight in the fear of the Lord. (See Isa. xi. 3, R. V.) The three suggestive names just given refer especially to the gracious work of the Holy Spirit in the servant of the Lord, that is Jesus Christ (Isa. xi. 1-5).

XIX. *The Spirit of Life.*

The Holy Spirit is called *the Spirit of life* in Rom. viii. 2, "For the law of *the Spirit of life* in Christ Jesus hath made me free from the law of sin and death." The Holy Spirit is called the Spirit of life because it is His work to impart life (cf. John vi. 63, R. V.; Ezek. xxxvii. 1-10). In the context in which the name is found in the passage given above, beginning back in the seventh chapter of Romans, seventh verse, Paul is drawing a contrast between the law of Moses outside a man, holy and just and good, it is true, but impotent, and the living Spirit of God in the heart, imparting spiritual and moral life to the believer and enabling him thus to meet the requirements of the law of God, so that what the law alone could not do, in that it was weak through the flesh, the Spirit of God imparting life to the believer and dwelling in the heart enables him to do, so that the righteousness of the law is fulfilled in those who walk not after the flesh but after the Spirit. (See Rom. viii. 2-4.) The Holy Spirit is therefore called "the Spirit of life," because He imparts spiritual life and consequent victory over sin to those who receive Him.

XX. *The Oil of Gladness.*

The Holy Spirit is called the "oil of gladness" in Heb. i. 9, "Thou hast loved righteousness, and hated iniquity; therefore God, even thy God, hath anointed thee with the *oil of gladness* above thy fellows." Some one may ask what reason have we for supposing that "the oil of gladness" in this passage is a name of the Holy Spirit. The answer is found in a comparison of Heb. i. 9, with Acts x. 38 and Luke iv. 18. In Acts x. 38 we read "how God anointed Jesus of Nazareth with the Holy Ghost and with power," and in Luke iv. 18, Jesus Himself is recorded as saying, "*The Spirit of the Lord is upon* Me, because He hath *anointed* Me to preach the Gospel to the poor," etc. In both of these passages, we are told it was *the Holy Spirit with which Jesus was anointed* and as in the passage in Hebrews we are told that *it was with the oil of gladness that He was anointed*; so, of course, the only possible conclusion is that the oil of gladness means the Holy Spirit. What a beautiful and suggestive name it is for Him whose fruit is, first, "love" then "joy" (Gal. v. 22). The Holy Spirit becomes a source of boundless joy to those who receive Him; He so fills and satisfies the soul, that the soul who receives Him does not thirst forever (John iv. 14). No matter how great the afflictions with which the believer receives the Word, still he will have "*the joy of the Holy Ghost*" (1 Thess. i. 6). On the Day of Pentecost, when the disciples were baptized with the Holy Spirit, they were so filled with ecstatic joy that others looking on them thought they were intoxicated. They said, "These men are full of new wine." And Paul draws a comparison between abnormal intoxication that comes through excess of wine and the wholesome exhilaration from which there is no reaction that comes through being filled with the Spirit (Eph. v. 18-20). When God anoints one with the Holy Spirit, it is as if He broke a precious alabaster box of oil of gladness above their heads until it ran down to the hem of their garments and the whole person was suffused with joy unspeakable and full of glory.

XXI. *The Spirit of Grace.*

The Holy Spirit is called "the Spirit of grace" in Heb. x. 29, "Of how much sorer punishment, suppose ye, shall he be thought worthy, who hath trodden underfoot the Son of God, and hath counted the blood of the covenant, wherewith he was sanctified, an unholy thing, and hath done despite unto *the Spirit of grace*?" This name brings out the fact that it is the Holy Spirit's work to administer and apply the grace of God: He Himself is gracious, it is true, but the name means far more than that, it means that He makes ours experimentally the manifold grace of God. It is only by the work of the Spirit of grace in our hearts that we are enabled to appropriate to ourselves that infinite fullness of grace that God has, from the beginning, bestowed upon us in Jesus Christ. It is ours from the beginning, as far as belonging to us is concerned, but it is only ours experimentally as we claim it by the power of the Spirit of grace.

XXII. *The Spirit of Grace and of Supplication.*

The Holy Spirit is called "the Spirit of grace and of supplication" in Zech. xii. 10, R. V., "And I will pour upon the house of David, and upon the inhabitants of Jerusalem, *the Spirit of grace and of supplication*; and they shall look unto Me whom they have pierced: and they shall mourn for him, as one mourneth for his only son, and shall be in bitterness for his first-born." The phrase, "the Spirit of grace and of supplication" in this passage is beyond a doubt a name of the Holy Spirit. The name "the Spirit of grace" we have already had under the preceding head, but here there is a further thought of that operation of grace that leads us to pray intensely. The Holy Spirit is so called because it is He that teaches to pray because all true prayer is in the Spirit (Jude 20). We of ourselves know not how to pray as we ought, but it is the work of the Holy Spirit of intercession to make intercession for us with groanings which cannot be uttered and to lead us out in prayer according to the will of God (Rom. viii. 26, 27). The secret of all true and effective praying is knowing the Holy Spirit as "the Spirit of grace and of supplication."

XXIII. *The Spirit of Glory.*

The Holy Spirit is called "the Spirit of glory" in 1 Pet. iv. 14, "If ye be reproached for the name of Christ, happy are ye; for *the Spirit of glory* and of God resteth upon you: on their part He is evil spoken of, but on your part He is glorified." This name does not merely teach that the Holy Spirit is infinitely glorious Himself, but it rather teaches that He imparts the glory of God to us, just as the Spirit of truth imparts truth to us, and as the

Spirit of life imparts life to us, and as the Spirit of wisdom and understanding and of counsel and might and knowledge and of the fear of the Lord imparts to us wisdom and understanding and counsel and might and knowledge and the fear of the Lord, and as the Spirit of grace applies and administers to us the manifold grace of God, so the Spirit of glory is the administrator to us of God's glory. In the immediately preceding verse we read, "But rejoice, inasmuch as ye are partakers of Christ's sufferings: that, when His glory shall be revealed, ye may be glad also with exceeding joy." It is in this connection that He is called the Spirit of glory. We find a similar connection between the sufferings which we endure and the glory which the Holy Spirit imparts to us in Rom. viii. 16, 17, "The Spirit Himself beareth witness with our spirit, that we are children of God: and if children, then heirs; heirs of God and joint-heirs with Christ; *if so be that we suffer with* Him, that we may *be also glorified with Him*." The Holy Spirit is the administrator of glory as well as of grace, or rather of the grace that culminates in glory.

XXIV. *The Eternal Spirit.*

The Holy Spirit is called "the eternal Spirit" in Heb. ix. 14, "How much more shall the blood of Christ, who through *the eternal Spirit* offered Himself without spot to God, purge your conscience from dead works to serve the living God." The eternity and the Deity and infinite majesty of the Holy Spirit are brought out by this name. XXV. *The Comforter.*

The Holy Spirit is called "the Comforter" over and over again in the Scriptures. For example in John xiv. 26, we read, "But *the Comforter* which is the Holy Ghost, whom the Father will send in My name, He shall teach you all things, and bring all things to your remembrance, whatsoever I have said unto you." And in John xv. 26, "But when *the Comforter* is come, whom I will send unto you from the Father, even the Spirit of truth, which proceedeth from the Father, He shall testify of Me." (See also John xvi. 27.) The word translated "Comforter" in these passages means that, but it means much more beside. It is a word difficult of adequate translation into any one word in English. The translators of the Revised Version found difficulty in deciding with what word to render the Greek word so translated. They have suggested in the margin of the Revised Version "advocate" "helper" and a simple transference of the Greek word into English, "Paraclete." The word translated "Comforter" means literally, "one called to another's side," the idea being, one right at hand to take another's part. It is the same word that is translated "advocate" in 1 John ii. 1, "My little children, these things write I unto you, that ye sin not. And if any man sin, we have *an advocate* with the Father, Jesus Christ the righteous." But "advocate," as we now understand it, does not give the full force of the Greek word so rendered. Etymologically "advocate" means nearly the same thing. Advocate is Latin ("advocatus") and it means "one called to another to take his part," but in our modern usage, the word has acquired a restricted meaning. The Greek word translated "Comforter" (Parakleetos) means "one called alongside," that is one called to stand constantly by one's side and who is ever ready to stand by us and take our part in everything in which his help is needed. It is a wonderfully tender and expressive name for the Holy One. Sometimes when we think of *the Holy Spirit*, He seems to be so far away, but when we think of the Parakleetos, or in plain English our "Stand-byer" or our "part-taker," how near He is. Up to the time that Jesus made this promise to the disciples, He Himself had been their Parakleetos. When they were in any emergency or difficulty they turned to Him. On one occasion, for example, the disciples were in doubt as to how to pray and they turned to Jesus and said, "Lord, teach us to pray." And the Lord taught them the wonderful prayer that has come down through the ages (Luke xi. 1-4). On another occasion, Peter was sinking in the waves of Galilee and he cried, "Lord, save me," and immediately Jesus stretched forth His hand and caught him and saved him (Matt. xiv. 30, 31). In every extremity they turned to Him. Just so now that Jesus is gone to the Father, we have another Person, just as Divine as He is, just as wise as He, just as strong as He, just as loving as He, just as tender as He, just as ready and just as able to help, who is always right by our side. Yes, better yet, who dwells in our heart, who will take hold and help if we only trust Him to do it.

If the truth of the Holy Spirit as set forth in the name "Parakleetos" once gets into our heart and abides there, it will banish all loneliness forever; for how can we ever be lonely when this best of all Friends is ever with us? In the last eight years, I have been called upon to endure what would naturally be a very lonely life. Most of the time I am separated from wife and children by the calls of duty. For eighteen months consecutively, I was separated from almost all my family by many thousands of miles. The loneliness would have been unendurable were it not for the one all-sufficient Friend, who was always with me. I recall one night walking up and down the deck of a storm-tossed steamer in the South Seas. Most of my family were 18,000 miles away; the remaining member of my family was not with me. The officers were busy on the bridge, and I was pacing the deck alone, and the thought came to me, "Here you are all alone." Then another thought came, "I am not alone; by my side as I walk this deck in the loneliness and the storm walks the Holy Spirit" and He was enough. I said something like this once at a Bible conference in St. Paul. A doctor came to me at the close of the meeting and gently said, "I want to thank you for that thought about the Holy Spirit always being with us. I am a doctor. Oftentimes I have to drive far out in the country in the night and storm to attend a case, and I have often been so lonely, but I will never be lonely again. I will always know that by my side in my doctor's carriage, the Holy Spirit goes with me."

If this thought of the Holy Spirit as the ever-present Paraclete once gets into your heart and abides there, it will banish all fear forever. How can we be afraid in the face of any peril, if this Divine One is by our side to counsel us and to take our part? There may be a howling mob about us, or a lowering storm, it matters not. He stands between us and both mob and storm. One night I had promised to walk four miles to a friend's house after an evening session of a conference. The path led along the side of a lake. As I started for my friend's house, a thunder-storm was coming up. I had not counted on this but as I had promised, I felt I ought to go. The path led along the edge of the lake, oftentimes very near to the edge, sometimes the lake was near the path and sometimes many feet below. The night was so dark with the clouds one could not see ahead. Now and then there would be a blinding flash of lightning in which you could see where the path was washed away, and then it would be blacker than ever. You could hear the lake booming below. It seemed a dangerous place to walk but that very week, I had been speaking upon the Personality of the Holy Spirit and about the Holy Spirit as an ever-present Friend, and the thought came to me, "What was it you were telling the people in the address about the Holy Spirit as an ever-present Friend?" And then I said to myself, "Between me and the boiling lake and the edge of the path walks the Holy Spirit," and I pushed on fearless and glad. When we were in London, a young lady attended the meeting one afternoon in the Royal Albert Hall. She had an abnormal fear of the dark. It was absolutely impossible for her to go into a dark room alone, but the thought of the Holy Spirit as an ever-present Friend sank into her mind. She went home and told her mother what a wonderful thought she had heard that day, and how it had banished forever all fear from her. It was already growing very dark in the London winter afternoon and her mother looked up and said, "Very well, let us see if it is real. Go up to the top of the house and shut yourself alone in a dark room."

She instantly sprang to her feet, bounded up the stairs, went into a room that was totally dark and shut the door and sat down. All fear was gone, and as she wrote the next day, the whole room seemed to be filled with a wonderful glory, the glory of the presence of the Holy Spirit.

In the thought of the Holy Spirit as the Paraclete there is also a cure for insomnia. For two awful years, I suffered from insomnia. Night after night I would go to bed apparently almost dead for sleep; it seemed as though I must sleep, but I could not sleep; oh, the agony of those two years! It seemed as if I would lose my mind if I did not get relief. Relief came at last and for years I went on without the suggestion of trouble from insomnia. Then one night I retired to my room in the Institute, lay down expecting to fall asleep in a moment as I usually did, but scarcely had my head touched the pillow when I became aware that insomnia was back again. If one has ever had it, he never forgets it and never mistakes it. It seemed as if insomnia were sitting on the foot-board of my bed, grinning at me and saying, "I am back again for another two years." "Oh," I thought, "two more awful years of insomnia." But that very morning, I had been lecturing to our students in the Institute about the Personality of the Holy Spirit and about the Holy Spirit as an ever-present Friend, and at once the thought came to me, "What were you talking to the students about this morning? What were you telling them?" and I looked up and said, "Thou blessed Spirit of God, Thou art here. I am not alone. If Thou hast anything to say to me, I will listen," and He began to open to me some of the deep and precious things about my Lord and Savior, things, that filled my soul with joy and rest, and the next thing I knew I was asleep and the next thing I knew it was to-morrow morning. So whenever insomnia has come my way since, I have simply remembered that the Holy Spirit was there and I have looked up to Him to speak to me and to teach me and He has done so and insomnia has taken its flight.

In the thought of the Holy Spirit as the Paraclete there is a cure for a breaking heart. How many aching, breaking hearts there are in this world of ours, so full of death and separation from those we most dearly love. How many a woman there is, who a few years ago, or a few months or a few weeks ago, had no care, no worry, for by her side was a Christian husband who was so wise and strong that the wife rested all responsibility upon him and she walked care-free through life and satisfied with his love and companionship. But one awful day, he was taken from her. She was left alone and all the cares and responsibilities rested upon her. How empty that heart has been ever since; how empty the whole world has been. She has just dragged through her life and her duties as best she could with an aching and almost breaking heart. But there is One, if she only knew it, wiser and more loving than the tenderest husband, One willing to bear all the care and responsibilities of life for her, One who is able, if, she will only let Him, to fill every nook and corner of her empty and aching heart; that One is the Paraclete. I said something like this in St. Andrews' Hall in Glasgow. At the close of the meeting a sad-faced Christian woman, wearing a widow's garb, came to me as I stepped out of the hall into the reception room. She hurried to me and said, "Dr. Torrey, this is the anniversary of my dear husband's death. Just one year ago to-day he was taken from me. I came to-day to see if you could not speak some word to help me. You have given me just the word I need. I will never be lonesome again." A year and a half passed by. I was on the yacht of a friend on the lochs of the Clyde. One day a little boat put out from shore and came alongside the yacht. One of the first to come up the side of the yacht was this widow. She hurried to me and the first thing she said was, "The thought that you gave me that day in St. Andrews'

Hall on the anniversary of my husband's leaving me has been with me ever since, and the Holy Spirit does satisfy me and fill my heart."

But it is in our work for our Master that the thought of the Holy Spirit as the Paraclete comes with greatest helpfulness. I think it may be permissible to illustrate it from my own experience. I entered the ministry because I was literally forced to. For years I refused to be a Christian, because I was determined that I would not be a preacher, and I feared that if I surrendered to Christ I must enter the ministry. My conversion turned upon my yielding to Him at this point. The night I yielded, I did not say, "I will accept Christ" or "I will give up sin," or anything of that sort, I simply cried, "Take this awful burden off my heart, and I will preach the Gospel." But no one could be less fitted by natural temperament for the ministry than I. From early boyhood, I was extraordinarily timid and bashful. Even after I had entered Yale College, when I would go home in the summer and my mother would call me in to meet her friends, I was so frightened that when I thought I spoke I did not make an audible sound. When her friends had gone, my mother would ask, "Why didn't you say something to them?" And I would reply that I supposed I had, but my mother would say, "You did not utter a sound." Think of a young fellow like that entering the ministry. I never mustered courage even to speak in a public prayer-meeting until after I was in the theological seminary. Then I felt, if I was to enter the ministry, I must be able to at least speak in a prayer-meeting. I learned a little piece by heart to say, but when the hour came, I forgot much of it in my terror. At the critical moment, I grasped the back of the settee in front of me and pulled myself hurriedly to my feet and held on to the settee. One Niagara seemed to be going up one side and another down another; my voice faltered. I repeated as much as I could remember and sat down. Think of a man like that entering the ministry. In the early days of my ministry, I would write my sermons out in full and commit them to memory, stand up and twist a button until I had repeated it off as best I could and would then sink back into the pulpit chair with a sense of relief that that was over for another week. I cannot tell you what I suffered in those early days of my ministry. But the glad day came when I came to know the Holy Spirit as the Paraclete. When the thought got possession of me that when I stood up to preach, there was Another who stood by my side, that while the audience saw me God saw Him, and that the responsibility was all upon Him, and that He was abundantly able to meet it and care for it all, and that all I had to do was to stand back as far out of sight as possible and let Him do the work. I have no dread of preaching now; preaching is the greatest joy of my life, and sometimes when I stand up to speak and realize that He is there, that all the responsibility is upon Him, such a joy fills my heart that I can scarce restrain myself from shouting and leaping. He is just as ready to help us in all our work; in our Sunday-school classes; in our personal work and in every other line of Christian effort. Many hesitate to speak to others about accepting Christ. They are afraid they will not say the right thing; they fear that they will do more harm than they will good. You certainly will if *you* do it, but if you will just believe in the Paraclete and trust Him to say it and to say it in His way, you will never do harm but always good. It may seem at the time that you have accomplished nothing, but perhaps years after you will find out you have accomplished much and even if you do not find it out in this world, you will find it out in eternity.

There are many ways in which the Paraclete stands by us and helps us of which we will speak at length when we come to study His work. He stands by us when we pray (Rom. viii. 26, 27); when we study the Word (John xiv. 26; xvi. 12-14); when we do personal work (Acts viii. 29); when we preach or teach (1 Cor. ii. 4); when we are tempted

(Rom. viii. 2); when we leave this world (Acts vii. 54-60). Let us get this thought firmly fixed now and for all time that the Holy Spirit is One called to our side to take our part.

"Ever present, truest Friend,
Ever near, Thine aid to lend."

VI: The Work of the Holy Spirit in the Material Universe

There are many who think of the work of the Holy Spirit as limited to man. But God reveals to us in His Word that the Holy Spirit's work has a far wider scope than this. We are taught in the Bible that the Holy Spirit has a threefold work in the material universe.

I. The creation of the material universe and of man is effected through the agency of the Holy Spirit.

We read in Ps. xxxiii. 6, "By the word of the Lord were the heavens made; and all the host of them *by the breath of His mouth*." We have already seen in our study of the names of the Holy Spirit that the Holy Spirit is the breath of Jehovah, so this passage teaches us that all the hosts of heaven, all the stellar worlds, were made by the Holy Spirit. We are taught explicitly in Job xxxiii. 4, that the creation of man is the Holy Spirit's work. We read, "*The Spirit of God* hath made me, and *the breath of the Almighty* hath given me life." Here both the creation of the material frame and the impartation of life are attributed to the agency of the Holy Spirit. In other passages of Scripture we are taught that creation was in and through the Son of God. For example we read in Col. i. 16, R. V., "For in Him were all things created, in the heavens and upon the earth, things visible and things invisible, whether thrones or dominions or principalities or powers; all things have been created through Him and unto Him." In a similar way we read in Heb. i. 2, that God "hath at the end of these days spoken unto us in His Son, whom He appointed heir of all things, *through whom* also He made the worlds (ages)." In the passage given above (Ps. xxxiii. 6), the Word as well as the Spirit are mentioned in connection with creation. In the account of the creation and the rehabilitation of this world to be the abode of man, Father, Word and Holy Spirit are all mentioned (Gen. i. 1-3). It is evident from a comparison of these passages that the Father, Son and Holy Spirit are all active in the creative work. The Father works *in* His Son, *through* His Spirit.

II. Not only is the original creation of the material universe attributed to the agency of the Holy Spirit in the Bible but *the maintenance of living creatures* as well.

We read in Ps. civ. 29, 30, "Thou hidest Thy face, they are troubled: Thou takest away their breath, they die, and return to their dust. Thou *sendest forth Thy Spirit*, they are created: and Thou *renewest* the face of the earth." The clear indication of this passage is that not only are things brought into being through the agency of the Holy Spirit, but that they are maintained in being by the Holy Spirit. Not only is spiritual life maintained by the Spirit of God but material being as well. Things exist and continue by the presence of the Spirit of God in them. This does not mean for a moment that the universe is God, but it does mean that the universe is maintained in its being by the immanence of God in it. This is the great and solemn truth that lies at the foundation of the awful and debasing perversions of Pantheism in its countless forms.

III. But not only is the universe created through the agency of the Holy Spirit and maintained in its existence through the agency of the Holy Spirit, but *the development of the earlier, chaotic, undeveloped states of the material universe into higher orders of being is effected through the agency of the Holy Spirit*.

We read in Gen, i. 2, 3, "And the earth was (or became) without form and void; and darkness was upon the face of the deep. And *the Spirit of God moved* upon the face of the waters. And God said, Let there be light: and there was light." We may take this account to refer either to the original creation of the universe, or we may take it as the deeper students of the Word are more and more inclining to take it, as the account of the rehabilitation of the earth after its plunging into chaos through sin after the original creation described in v. 1. In either case we have set before us here the development of the earth from a chaotic and unformed condition into its present highly developed condition through the agency of the Holy Spirit. We see the process carried still further in Gen. ii. 7, "And the Lord God formed man of the dust of the ground, *and breathed* into his nostrils the breath of life; and man became a living soul." Here again it is through the agency of the breath of God, that a higher thing, human life, comes into being. Naturally, as the Bible is the history of man's redemption it does not dwell upon this phase of truth, but seemingly each new and higher impartation of the Spirit of God brings forth a higher order of being. First, inert matter; then motion; then light; then vegetable life; then animal life; then man; and, as we shall see later, then the new man; and then Jesus Christ, the supreme Man, the completion of God's thought of man, the Son of Man. This is the Biblical thought of development from the lower to the higher by the agency of the Spirit of God as distinguished from the godless evolution that has been so popular in the generation now closing. It is, however, only hinted at in the Bible. The more important phases of the Holy Spirit's work, His work in redemption, are those that are emphasized and iterated and reiterated. The Word of God is even more plainly active in each state of progress of creation. God *said* occurs ten times in the first chapter of Genesis.

VII: The Holy Spirit Convicting the World of Sin, of Righteousness and of Judgment

Our salvation begins experimentally with our being brought to a profound sense that we need a Savior. The Holy Spirit is the One who brings us to this realization of our need. We read in John xvi. 8-11, R. V., "And He, when He is come, will convict the world in respect of sin, and of righteousness, and of judgment: of sin, because they believe not on Me; of righteousness, because I go to the Father, and ye behold Me no more; of judgment, because the prince of this world hath been judged."

I. We see in this passage that *it is the work of the Holy Spirit to convict men of sin.* That is, to so convince of their error in respect to sin as to produce a deep sense of personal guilt. We have the first recorded fulfilment of this promise in Acts ii. 36, 37, "Therefore let all the house of Israel know assuredly, that God hath made that same Jesus, whom ye have crucified, both Lord and Christ. Now when they heard this, *they were pricked in their heart, and said* unto Peter and to the rest of the apostles, Men and brethren, *what shall we do*?" The Holy Spirit had come just as Jesus had promised that He would and when He came He convicted the world of sin: He pricked them to their heart with a sense of their awful guilt in the rejection of their Lord and their Christ. If the Apostle Peter had spoken the same words the day before Pentecost, no such results would have followed; but now Peter was filled with the Holy Spirit (v. 4) and the Holy Spirit took Peter and his words and through the instrumentality of Peter and his words convicted his hearers. The Holy Spirit is the only One who can convince men of sin. The natural heart is "deceitful above all things and desperately wicked," and there is nothing in which the inbred deceitfulness of our hearts comes out more clearly than in our estimations of ourselves. We are all of us sharp-sighted enough to the faults of others but we are all blind by nature to our own faults. Our blindness to our own shortcomings is oftentimes little short of ludicrous. We have a strange power of exaggerating our imaginary virtues and losing sight utterly of our defects. The longer and more thoroughly one studies human nature, the more clearly will he see how hopeless is the task of convincing other men of sin. We cannot do it, nor has God left it for us to do. He has put this work into the hands of One who is abundantly able to do it, the Holy Spirit. One of the worst mistakes that we can make in our efforts to bring men to Christ is to try to convince them of sin in any power of our own. Unfortunately, it is one of the commonest mistakes. Preachers will stand in the pulpit and argue and reason with men to make them see and realize that they are sinners. They make it as plain as day; it is a wonder that their hearers do not see it; but they do not. Personal workers sit down beside an inquirer and reason with him, and bring forward passages of Scripture in a most skillful way, the very passages that are calculated to produce the effect desired and yet there is no result. Why? Because we are trying to do the Holy Spirit's work, the work that He alone can do, convince men of sin. If we would only bear in mind our own utter inability to convince men of sin, and cast ourselves upon Him in utter helplessness to do the work, we would see results.

At the close of an inquiry meeting in our church in Chicago, one of our best workers brought to me an engineer on the Pan Handle Railway with the remark, "I wish that you would speak to this man. I have been talking to him two hours with no result." I sat down by his side with my open Bible and in less than ten minutes that man, under deep conviction of sin, was on his knees crying to God for mercy. The worker who had brought him to me said when the man had gone out, "That is very strange." "What is strange?" I asked. "Do you know," the worker said, "I used exactly the same passages in dealing with that man that you did, and though I had worked with him for two hours with no result, in ten minutes with the same passages of Scripture, he was brought under conviction of sin and accepted Christ." What was the explanation? Simply this, for once that worker had forgotten something that she seldom forgot, namely, that the Holy Spirit must do the work. She had been trying to convince the man of sin. She had used the right passages; she had reasoned wisely; she had made out a clear case, but she had not looked to the only One who could do the work. When she brought the man to me and said, "I have worked with him for two hours with no result," I thought to myself, "If this expert worker has dealt with him for two hours with no result, what is the use of my dealing with him?" and in a sense of utter helplessness I cast myself upon the Holy Spirit to do the work and He did it.

But while we cannot convince men of sin, there is One who can, the Holy Spirit. He can convince the most hardened and blinded man of sin. He can change men and women from utter carelessness and indifference to a place where they are overwhelmed with a sense of their need of a Savior. How often we have seen this illustrated. Some years ago, the officers of the Chicago Avenue Church were burdened over the fact that there was so little profound conviction of sin manifested in our meetings. There were conversions, a good many were being added to the church, but very few were coming with an apparently overwhelming conviction of sin. One night one of the officers of the church said, "Brethren, I am greatly troubled by the fact that we have so little conviction of sin in our meetings. While we are having conversions and many accessions to the church, there is not that deep conviction of sin that I like to see, and I propose that we, the officers of the church, meet from night to night to pray that there may be more conviction of sin in our meetings." The suggestion was taken up by the entire committee. We had not been praying many nights when one Sunday evening I saw in the front seat underneath the gallery a showily dressed man with a very hard face. A large diamond was blazing from his shirt front. He was sitting beside one of the deacons. As I looked at him as I preached, I thought to myself, "That man is a sporting man, and Deacon Young has been fishing to-day." It turned out that I was right. The man was the son of a woman who kept a sporting house in a Western city. I think he had never been in a Protestant service before. Deacon Young had got hold of him that day on the street and brought him to the meeting. As I preached the man's eyes were riveted upon me. When we went down-stairs to the after meeting, Deacon Young took the man with him. I was late dealing with the anxious that night. As I finished with the last one about eleven o'clock, and almost everybody had gone home, Deacon Young came over to me and said, "I have a man over here I wish you would come and speak with." It was this big sporting man. He was deeply agitated. "Oh," he groaned, "I don't know what is the matter with me. I never felt this way before in all my life," and he sobbed and shook like a leaf. Then he told me this story: "I started out this afternoon to go down to Cottage Grove Avenue to meet some men and spend the afternoon gambling. As I passed by the park over yonder, some of your young men were holding an open air meeting and I stopped to listen. I saw one man testifying whom I had known in a life of sin, and I waited to hear what he had to say. When he finished I went on down the street. I had not gone far when some strange power took hold of me and brought me back and I stayed through the meeting. Then this gentleman spoke to me and brought me over to your church, to your Yoke Fellows' Meeting. I stayed to supper with them and he brought me up to hear you preach, then he brought me down to this meeting." Here he stopped and sobbed, "Oh, I don't know what is the matter with me. I feel awful. I never felt this way before in all my life," and his great frame shook with emotion. "I know what is the matter with you," I said. "You are under conviction of sin; the Holy Spirit is dealing with you," and I pointed him to Christ, and he knelt down and cried to God for mercy, to forgive his sins for Christ's sake.

Not long after, one Sunday night I saw another man sitting in the gallery almost exactly above where this man had sat. A diamond flashed also from this man's shirt front. I said to myself, "There is another sporting man." He turned out to be a travelling man who was also a sporting man. As I preached, he leaned further and further forward in his seat. In the midst of my sermon, without any intention of giving out the invitation, simply wishing to drive a point home, I said, "Who will accept Jesus Christ to-night?" Quick as a flash the man sprang to his feet and shouted, "I will." It rang through the building like the crack of a revolver. I dropped my sermon and instantly gave out the invitation; men and women and young people rose all over the building to yield themselves to Christ. God was answering prayer and the Holy Spirit was convincing men of sin. The Holy Spirit can convince men of sin. We need not despair of any one, no matter how indifferent they may appear, no matter how worldly, no matter how self-satisfied, no matter how irreligious, the Holy Spirit can convince men of sin. A young minister of very rare culture and ability once came to me and said, "I have a great problem on my hands. I am the pastor of the church in a university town. My congregation is largely made up of university professors and students. They are most delightful people. They have very high moral ideals and are living most exemplary lives. Now," he continued, "if I had a congregation in which there were drunkards and outcasts and thieves, I could convince them of sin, but my problem is how to make people like that, the most delightful people in the world, believe that they are sinners, how to convict them of sin." I replied, "It is impossible. You cannot do it, but the Holy Spirit can." And so He can. Some of the deepest manifestations of conviction of sin I have ever seen have been on the part of men and women of most exemplary conduct and attractive personality. But they were sinners and the Holy Spirit opened their eyes to the fact.

While it is the Holy Spirit who convinces men of sin, He does it through us. This comes out very clearly in the context of the passage before us. Jesus says in the seventh verse, R. V., of the chapter, "Nevertheless I tell you the truth; It is expedient for you that I go away: for if I go not away, the Comforter will not come *unto you*; but if I go, I will send Him *unto you*." Then He goes on to say, "And when He is come (*unto you*), He will convict the world of sin." That is, our Lord Jesus sends the Holy Spirit unto us (unto believers), and when He is come unto us believers, through us to whom He has come, He convinces the world. On the Day of Pentecost, it was the Holy Spirit who convinced the 3,000 of sin, but the Holy Spirit came to the group of believers and through them convinced the outside world. As far as the Holy Scriptures definitely tell us, the Holy Spirit has no Way of getting at the unsaved world except through the agency of those who are already saved. Every conversion recorded in the Acts of the Apostles was through the agency of men or women already saved. Take, for example, the conversion of Saul of Tarsus. If there ever was a miraculous conversion, it was that. The glorified Jesus appeared visibly to Saul on his way to Damascus, but before Saul could come out clearly into the light as a saved man, human instrumentality must be brought in. Saul prostrate on the ground cried to the risen Christ asking what he must do, and the Lord told him to go into Damascus and there it would be told him what he must do. And then Ananias, "a certain disciple," was brought on the scene as the human instrumentality through whom the Holy Spirit should do His work (cf. Acts ix. 17; xxii. 16). Take the case of Cornelius. Here again was a most remarkable conversion through supernatural agency. "*An angel*" appeared to Cornelius, but the angel did not tell Cornelius what to do to be saved. The angel rather said to Cornelius, "Send men to Joppa, and *call for Simon*, whose surname is Peter, who shall tell thee words whereby *thou and all thy house shall be saved*" (Acts xi. 13, 14). So we may go right through the record of the conversions in the Acts of the Apostles and we will see they were all effected through human instrumentality. How solemn, how almost overwhelming, is the thought that the Holy Spirit has no way of getting at the unsaved with His saving power except through the instrumentality of us who are already Christians. If we realized that, would we not be more careful to offer to the Holy Spirit a more free and unobstructed channel for His all-important work? The Holy Spirit needs human lips to speak through. He needs yours, and He needs lives so clean and so utterly surrendered to Him that He can work through them.

Notice of which sin it is that the Holy Spirit convinces men—the sin of unbelief in Jesus Christ, "Of sin because they believe not on Me," says Jesus. Not the sin of stealing, not the sin of drunkenness, not the sin of adultery, not the sin of murder, but the sin of unbelief in Jesus Christ. The one thing that the eternal God demands of men is that they believe on Him whom He hath sent (John vi. 29). And the one sin that reveals men's rebellion against God and daring defiance of Him is the sin of not believing on Jesus Christ, and this is the one sin that the Holy Spirit puts to the front and emphasizes and of which He convicts men. This was the sin of which He convicted the 3,000 on the Day of Pentecost. Doubtless, there were many other sins in their lives, but the one point that the Holy Spirit brought to the front through the Apostle Peter was that the One whom they had rejected was their Lord and Christ, attested so to be by His resurrection from the dead (Acts ii. 22-36). "And *when they heard this* (namely, that He whom they had rejected was

Lord and Christ) they were pricked in their hearts." This is the sin of which the Holy Spirit convinces men to-day. In regard to the comparatively minor moralities of life, there is a wide difference among men, but the thief who rejects Christ and the honest man who rejects Christ are alike condemned at the great point of what they do with God's Son, and this is the point that the Holy Spirit presses home. The sin of unbelief is the most difficult of all sins of which to convince men. The average unbeliever does not look upon unbelief as a sin. Many an unbeliever looks upon his unbelief as a mark of intellectual superiority. Not unfrequently, he is all the more proud of it because it is the only mark of intellectual superiority that he possesses. He tosses his head and says, "I am an agnostic;" "I am a skeptic;" or, "I am an infidel," and assumes an air of superiority on that account. If he does not go so far as that, the unbeliever frequently looks upon his unbelief as, at the very worst, a misfortune. He looks for pity rather than for blame. He says, "Oh, I wish I could believe. I am so sorry I cannot believe," and then appeals to us for pity because he cannot believe, but when the Holy Spirit touches a man's heart, he no longer looks upon unbelief as a mark of intellectual superiority; he does not look upon it as a mere misfortune; he sees it as the most daring, decisive and damning of all sins and is overwhelmed with a sense of his awful guilt in that he had not believed on the name of the only begotten Son of God. II. But the Holy Spirit not only convicts of sin, *He convicts in respect of righteousness*.

He convicts the world in respect of righteousness because Jesus Christ has gone to the Father, that is He convicts (convinces with a convincing that is self-condemning) the world of Christ's righteousness attested by His going to the Father. The coming of the Spirit is in itself a proof that Christ has gone to the Father (cf. Acts ii. 33) and the Holy Spirit thus opens our eyes to see that Jesus Christ, whom the world condemned as an evil-doer, was indeed the righteous One. The Father sets the stamp of His approval upon His character and claims by raising Him from the dead and exalting Him to His own right hand and giving to Him a name that is above every name. The world at large to-day claims to believe in the righteousness of Christ but it does not really believe in the righteousness of Christ: it has no adequate conception of the righteousness of Christ. The righteousness which the world attributes to Christ is not the righteousness which God attributes to Him, but a poor human righteousness, perhaps a little better than our own. The world loves to put the names of other men that it considers good alongside the name of Jesus Christ. But when the Spirit of God comes to a man, He convinces him of the righteousness of Christ; He opens his eyes to see Jesus Christ standing absolutely alone, not only far above all men but "far above all principality and power and might and dominion, and every name that is named, not only in this world but also in that which is to come" (Eph. i. 21). III. The Holy Spirit also convicts the world of judgment.

The ground upon which the Holy Spirit convinces men of judgment is upon the ground of the fact that "the Prince of this world hath been judged" (John xvi. 11). When Jesus Christ was nailed to the cross, it seemed as if He were judged there, but in reality it was the Prince of this world who was judged at the cross, and, by raising Jesus Christ from the dead, the Father made it plain to all coming ages that the cross was not the judgment of Christ, but the judgment of the Prince of darkness. The Holy Spirit opens our eyes to see this fact and so convinces us of judgment. There is a great need to-day that the world be convinced of judgment. Judgment is a doctrine that has fallen into the background, that has indeed almost sunken out of sight. It is not popular to-day to speak about judgment, or retribution, or hell. One who emphasizes judgment and future retribution is not thought to be quite up to date; he is considered "medieval" or even "archaic," but when the Holy Spirit opens the eyes of men, they believe in judgment. In the early days of my Christian experience, I had great difficulties with the Bible doctrine of future retribution. I came again and again up to what it taught about the eternal penalties of persistent sin. It seemed as if I could not believe it: it must not be true. Time and again I would back away from the stern teachings of Jesus Christ and the Apostles concerning this matter. But one night I was waiting upon God that I might know the Holy Spirit in a fuller manifestation of His presence and His power. God gave me what I sought that night and with this larger experience of the Holy Spirit's presence and power, there came such a revelation of the glory, the infinite glory of Jesus Christ, that I had no longer any difficulties with what the Book said about the stern and endless judgment that would be visited upon those who persistently rejected this glorious Son of God. From that day to this, while I have had many a heartache over the Bible doctrine of future retribution, I have had no intellectual difficulty with it. I have believed it. The Holy Spirit has convinced me of judgment.

VIII: The Holy Spirit Bearing Witness to Jesus Christ

When our Lord was talking to His disciples on the night before His crucifixion of the Comforter who after His departure was to come to take His place, He said, "But when the Comforter is come, whom I will send unto you from the Father, even the Spirit of truth, which proceedeth from the Father, He shall bear witness of Me: and ye also bear witness, because ye have been with Me from the beginning" (John xv. 26, 27, R. V.), and the Apostle Peter and the other disciples when they were strictly commanded by the Jewish Council not to teach in the name of Jesus said, "We are witnesses of these things, and so is also the Holy Ghost" (Acts v. 32). It is clear from these words of Jesus Christ and the Apostles that it is the work of the Holy Spirit to bear witness concerning Jesus Christ. We find the Holy Spirit's testimony to Jesus Christ in the Scriptures, but beside this the Holy Spirit bears witness directly to the individual heart concerning Jesus Christ. He takes His own Scriptures and interprets them to us and makes them clear to us. All truth is from the Spirit, for He is "the Spirit of truth," but it is especially His work to bear witness to Him who is the truth, that is Jesus Christ (John xiv. 6). It is only through the testimony of the Holy Spirit directly to our hearts that we ever come to a true, living knowledge of Jesus Christ (cf. 1 Cor. xii. 3). No amount of mere reading the written Word (in the Bible) and no amount of listening to man's testimony will ever bring us to a living knowledge of Christ. It is only when the Holy Spirit Himself takes the written Word, or takes the testimony of our fellow man, and interprets it directly to our hearts that we really come to see and know Jesus as He is. On the day of Pentecost, Peter gave all his hearers the testimony of the Scriptures regarding Christ and also gave them his own testimony; he told them what he and the other Apostles knew by personal observation regarding His resurrection, but unless the Holy Spirit Himself had taken the Scriptures which Peter had brought together and taken the testimony of Peter and the other disciples, the 3,000 would not on that day have seen Jesus as He really was and received Him and been baptized in His name. The Holy Spirit added His testimony to that of Peter and that of the written Word. Mr. Moody used to say in his terse and graphic way that when Peter said, "Therefore let all the house of Israel know assuredly that God hath made that same Jesus, whom ye have crucified, both Lord and Christ (Acts ii. 36), the Holy Spirit said, 'Amen' and the people saw and believed." And it is certain that unless the Holy Spirit had come that day and through Peter and the other Apostles borne His direct testimony to the hearts of their hearers, there would have been no saving vision of Jesus on the part of the people. If you wish men to get a true view of Jesus Christ, such a view of Him that they may believe and be saved, it is not enough that you give them the Scriptures concerning Him; it is not enough that you give them your own testimony, you must seek for them the testimony of the Holy Spirit and put yourself into such relations with God that the Holy Spirit may bear His testimony through you. Neither your testimony, nor even that of the written Word alone will effect this, though it is your testimony, or that of the Word that the Holy Spirit uses. But unless your testimony and that of the Word is taken up by the Holy Spirit and He Himself testifies, they will not believe. This explains something which every experienced worker must have noticed. We sit down beside an inquirer and open our Bibles and give him those Scriptures which clearly reveal Jesus as his atoning Savior on the cross, a Savior from the guilt of sin, and as his risen Savior, a Savior from the power of sin. It is just the truth the man needs to see and believe in order to be saved, but he does not see it. We go over these Scriptures which to us are as plain as day again and again, and the inquirer sits there in blank darkness; he sees nothing, he grasps nothing. Sometimes we almost wonder if the inquirer is stupid that he cannot see it. No, he is not stupid, except with that spiritual blindness that possesses every mind unenlightened by the Holy Spirit (1 Cor. ii. 14). We go over it again and still he does not see it. We go over it again and his face lightens up and he exclaims, "I see it. I see it," and he sees Jesus and believes and is saved and knows he is saved there on the spot. What has happened? Simply this, the Holy Spirit has borne His testimony and what was dark as midnight before is as clear as day now. This explains also why it is that one who has been long in darkness concerning Jesus Christ so quickly comes to see the truth when he surrenders his will to God and seeks light from Him. When he surrenders his will to God, he has put himself into that attitude towards God where the Holy Spirit can do His work (Acts v. 32). Jesus says in John vii. 17, R. V., "If any man willeth to do His will, he shall know of the teaching, whether it be of God, or whether I speak from Myself." When a man wills to do the will of God, then the conditions are provided on which the Holy Spirit works and He illuminates the mind to see the truth about Jesus and to see that His teaching is the very Word of God. John writes in John xx. 31, "But these are written (these things in the Gospel of John) that ye might believe that Jesus is the Christ, the Son of God; and that believing ye might have life through His name." John wrote his Gospel for this purpose, that men might see Jesus as the Christ, the Son of God, through what he records, and that they might believe that He is the Christ, the Son of God, and that thus believing they might have life through His name. The best book in the world to put into the hands of one who desires to know about Jesus and to be saved is the Gospel of John. And yet many a man has read the Gospel of John over and over and over again and not seen and believed that Jesus is the Christ, the Son of God. But let the same man surrender his will absolutely to God and ask God for light as he reads the Gospel and promise God that he will take his stand on everything in the Gospel that He shows him to be true and before the man has finished the Gospel he will see clearly that Jesus is the Christ, the Son of God, and will believe and have eternal life. Why? Because he has put himself into the place where the Holy Spirit can take the things written in the Gospel and interpret them and bear His testimony. I have seen this tested and proven time and time again all around the world. Men have come to me and said to me that they did not believe that Jesus is the Christ, the Son of God, and many have gone farther and said they were agnostics and did not even know whether there was a personal God. Then I have told them to read the Gospel of John, that in that Gospel John presented the evidence that Jesus was the Christ, the Son of God. Oftentimes they have told me they have read it over and over again, and yet were not convinced that Jesus was the Christ, the Son of God. Then I have said to them, "You have not read it the right way," and I have got them to surrender their will to God (or in case where they were not sure there was a God, have got them to take their stand upon the right to follow it wherever it might carry them). Then I have had them agree to read the Gospel of John slowly and thoughtfully, and each time before they read to look up to God, if there were any God, to help them to understand what they were to read and to promise Him that they would take their stand upon whatever He showed them to be true, and follow it wherever it would carry them. And in every instance before they had finished the Gospel they had come to see that Jesus was the Christ, the Son of God, and have believed and been saved. They had put themselves in that position where the Holy Spirit could bear His testimony to Jesus Christ and He had done it and through His testimony they saw and believed.

If you wish men to see the truth about Christ, do not depend upon your own powers of expression and persuasion, but cast yourself upon the Holy Spirit and seek for them His testimony and see to it that they put themselves in the place where the Holy Spirit can testify. This is the cure for both skepticism and ignorance concerning Christ. If you yourself are not clear concerning the truth about Jesus Christ, seek for yourself the testimony of the Holy Spirit regarding Christ. Read the Scriptures, read especially the Gospel of John but do not depend upon the mere reading of the Word, but before you read it, put yourself in such an attitude towards God by the absolute surrender of your will to Him that the Holy Spirit may bear His testimony in your heart concerning Jesus Christ. What we all most need is a clear and full vision of Jesus Christ and this comes through the testimony of the Holy Spirit. One night a number of our students came back from the Pacific Garden Mission in Chicago and said to me, "We had a wonderful meeting at the mission to-night. There were many drunkards and outcasts at the front who accepted Christ." The next day I met Mr. Harry Monroe, the superintendent of the mission, on the street, and I said, "Harry, the boys say you had a wonderful meeting at the mission last night." "Would you like to know how it came about?" he replied. "Yes." "Well," he said, "I simply held up Jesus Christ and it pleased the Holy Spirit to illumine the face of Jesus Christ, and men saw and believed." It was a unique way of putting it but it was an expressive way and true to the essential facts in the case. It is our part to hold up Jesus Christ, and then look to the Holy Spirit to illumine His face or to take the truth about Him and make it clear to the hearts of our hearers and He will do it and men will see and believe. Of course, we need to be so walking towards God that the Holy Spirit may take us as the instruments through whom He will bear His testimony.

IX: The Regenerating Work of the Holy Spirit

The Apostle Paul in Titus iii. 5, R. V., writes, "Not by works done in righteousness, which we did ourselves, but according to His mercy He saved us, through the washing of regeneration and *renewing of the Holy Ghost*." In these words we are taught that *the Holy Spirit renews men, or makes men new*, and that through this renewing of the Holy Spirit, we are saved. Jesus taught the same in John iii. 3-5, "Jesus answered and said unto him, Verily, verily, I say unto thee, Except a man be born again, he cannot see the kingdom of God. Nicodemus saith unto Him, How can a man be born when he is old? Can he enter the second time into his mother's womb and be born? Jesus answered, Verily, verily, I say unto thee, Except a man be born of water and *of the Spirit*, he cannot enter into the kingdom of God."

What is regeneration? *Regeneration is the impartation of life, spiritual life, to those who are dead, spiritually dead, through their trespasses and sins* (Eph. ii. 1, R. V.). It is the Holy Spirit who imparts this life. It is true that the written Word is the instrument which the Holy Spirit uses in regeneration. We read in 1 Pet. i. 23, "Being born again, not of corruptible seed, but of incorruptible, *by the Word of God*, which liveth and abideth forever." We read in James i. 18, "Of His own will begat He us with *the Word of truth*, that we should be a kind of first fruits of His creatures." These passages make it plain that the Word is the instrument used in regeneration, but it is only as the Holy Spirit uses the instrument that the new birth results. "It is the Spirit that giveth life" (John vi. 63, A. R. V.). In 2 Cor. iii. 6, we are told that "the letter killeth, but the Spirit giveth life."[1] This is sometimes interpreted to mean that the literal interpretation of Scripture, the interpretation that takes it in its strict grammatical sense and makes it mean what it says, kills; but that some spiritual interpretation, an interpretation that "gives the spirit of the passage," by making it mean something it does not say, gives life; and those who insist upon Scripture meaning exactly what it says are called "deadly literalists." This is a favorite perversion of Scripture with those who do not like to take the Bible as meaning just what it says and who find themselves driven into a corner and are looking about for some convenient way of escape. If one will read the words in their context, he will see that this thought was utterly foreign to the mind of Paul. Indeed, one who will carefully study the epistles of Paul will find that he himself was a literalist of the literalists. If literalism is deadly, then the teachings of Paul are among the most deadly ever written. Paul will build an argument upon the turn of a word, upon a number or a tense. What does the passage mean? The way to find out what any passage means is to study in their context the words used. Paul is drawing a contrast between the Word of God outside of us, written with ink upon parchment or graven on tables of stone, and the Word of God written within us in tables that are hearts of flesh with the Spirit of the living God (v. 3) and he tells us that if we merely have the Word of God outside us in a Book or on parchment or on tables of stone, that it will kill us, that it will only bring condemnation and death, but that if we have the Word of God made a living thing in our hearts, written upon our hearts by the Spirit of the living God, that it will bring us life.[2] No number of Bibles upon our tables or in our libraries will save us, but the truth of the Bible written by the Spirit of the living God in our hearts will save us.

To put the matter of regeneration in another way; *regeneration is the impartation of a new nature, God's own nature to the one who is born again* (2 Pet. i. 4). Every human being is born into this world with a perverted nature; his whole intellectual, affectional and volitional nature perverted by sin. No matter how excellent our human ancestry, we come into this world with a mind that is blind to the truth of God. ("The natural man receiveth not the things of the Spirit of God: for they are foolishness unto him: neither can he know them, because they are spiritually discerned." 1 Cor. ii. 14.) With affections that are alienated from God, loving the things that we ought to hate and hating the things that we ought to love. ("Now the works of the flesh are manifest, which are these; Adultery, fornication, uncleanness, lasciviousness, idolatry, witchcraft, hatred, variance, emulations, wrath, strife, seditions, heresies, envyings, murders, drunkenness, revellings, and such

---

[1] Both the translators of the Authorized Version and the Revised Version, and even the translators of the American Revision, seem to have lost sight of the context, for while they spell "Spirit" in the third verse with a capital, in the sixth verse, in all three versions it is spelled with a small "s."

[2] The ministry of many an orthodox preacher and teacher is a ministry of death. It is true that the Word of the Gospel is preached but it is preached with enticing words of man's wisdom and not in the demonstration of the Spirit and of power (1 Cor. ii. 4). The Gospel comes in word only and not in power and in the Holy Spirit (1 Thess. i. 5).

like." Gal. v. 19, 20, 21.) With a will that is perverted, set upon pleasing itself, rather than pleasing God. ("Because the mind of the flesh is enmity against God; for it is not subject to the law of God, neither indeed can it be." Rom. viii. 7, R. V.) In the new birth a new intellectual, affectional and volitional nature is imparted to us. We receive the mind that sees as God sees, thinks God's thoughts after Him (1 Cor. ii. 12-14); affections in harmony with the affections of God. ("The fruit of the Spirit is love, joy, peace, long-suffering, gentleness, goodness, faith, meekness, temperance: against such there is no law." Gal. v. 22, 23); a will that is in harmony with the will of God, that delights to do the things that please Him. (Like Jesus we say, "My meat is to do the will of Him that sent Me, and to finish His work." John iv. 34; cf. John vi. 38; Gal i. 10.) It is the Holy Spirit who creates in us this new nature, or imparts this new nature to us. No amount of preaching, no matter how orthodox it may be, no amount of mere study of the Word will regenerate unless the Holy Spirit works. It is He and He alone who makes a man a new creature.

The new birth is compared in the Bible to growth from a seed. The human heart is the soil, the Word of God is the seed (Luke viii. 11; cf. 1 Pet. i. 23; Jas. i. 18; 1 Cor. iv. 15), every preacher or teacher of the Word is a sower, but the Spirit of God is the One who quickens the seed that is thus sown and the Divine nature springs up as the result. There is abundant soil everywhere in which to sow the seed, in the human hearts that are around about us upon every hand. There is abundant seed to be sown, any of us can find it in the granary of God's Word; and there are to-day many sowers: but there may be soil and seed and sowers, but unless as we sow the seed, the Spirit of God quickens it and the heart of the hearer closes around it by faith, there will be no harvest. Every sower needs to see to it that he realizes his dependence upon the Holy Spirit to quicken the seed he sows and he needs to see to it also that he is in such relation to God that the Holy Spirit may work through him and quicken the seed he sows.

The Holy Spirit does regenerate men. He has power to raise the dead. He has power to impart life to those who are morally both dead and putrefying. He has power to impart an entirely new nature to those whose nature now is so corrupt that to men they appear to be beyond hope. How often I have seen it proven. How often I have seen men and women utterly lost and ruined and vile come into a meeting scarcely knowing why they came, and as they have sat there the Word was spoken, the Spirit of God has quickened the Word thus sown in their hearts and in a moment that man or woman, by the mighty power of the Holy Spirit, has become a new creation. I know a man who seemed as completely abandoned and hopeless as men ever become. He was about forty-five years of age. He had gone off in evil courses in early boyhood. He had run away from home, had joined the navy and afterwards the army, and learned all the vices of both. He had been dishonorably discharged from the army because of his extreme dissipation and disorderliness. He had found his companionships among the lowest of the low and the vilest of the vile. When he would go up the street of a Western town at night, and merchants would hear his yell, they would close their doors in fear. But this man went one night into a revival meeting in a country church out of curiosity. He made sport of the meeting that night with a boon companion who sat by his side, but he went again the next night. The Spirit of God touched his heart. He went forward and bowed at the altar. He arose a new creation. He was transformed into one of the noblest, truest, purest, most unselfish, most gentle and most Christlike men I have ever known. I am sometimes asked, "Do you believe in sudden conversion?" I believe in something far more wonderful than sudden conversion. I believe in sudden regeneration. Conversion is merely an outward thing, the turning around. Regeneration goes down to the deepest depths of the inmost soul, transforming thoughts, affections, will, the whole inward man. I believe in sudden regeneration because the Bible teaches it and because I have seen it times without number. I believe in sudden regeneration because I have experienced it. We are sometimes told that "the religion of the future will not teach sudden miraculous conversion." If the religion of the future does not teach sudden miraculous conversion, if it does not teach something far more meaningful, sudden, miraculous regeneration by the power of the Holy Spirit, then the religion of the future will not be in conformity with the facts of experience and so will not be scientific. It will miss one of the most certain and most glorious of all truths. Man-devised religions in the past have often missed the truth and man-devised religions in the future will doubtless do the same. But the religion God has revealed in His Word and the religion that God confirms in experience teaches sudden regeneration by the mighty power of the Holy Spirit. If I did not believe in regeneration by the power of the Holy Spirit, I would quit preaching. What would be the use in facing great audiences in which there were multitudes of men and women hardened and seared, caring for nothing but the things of the world and the flesh, with no high and holy aspirations, with no outlook beyond money and fame and power and pleasure, if it were not for the regenerating power of the Holy Spirit? But with the regenerating power of the Holy Spirit, there is every use; for the preacher can never tell where the Spirit of God is going to strike and do His mighty work. There sits before you a man who is a gambler, or a drunkard, or a libertine. There does not seem to be much use in preaching to him, but you can never tell but that very night, the Spirit of God will touch that man's heart and transform him into one of the holiest and most useful of men. It has often occurred in the past and will doubtless often occur in the future. There sits before you a woman, who is a mere butterfly of fashion. She seems to have no thought above society and pleasure and adulation. Why preach to her? Without the regenerating power of the Holy Spirit, it would be foolishness and a waste of time; but you can never tell, perhaps this very night the Spirit of God will shine in that darkened heart and open the eyes of that woman to see the beauty of Jesus Christ and she may receive Him and then and there the life of God be imparted by the power of the Holy Spirit to that trifling soul.

The doctrine of the regenerating power of the Holy Spirit is a glorious doctrine. It sweeps away false hopes. It comes to the one who is trusting in education and culture and says, "Education and culture are not enough. You must be born again." It comes to the one who is trusting in mere external morality, and says, "External morality is not enough, you must be born again." It comes to the one who is trusting in the externalities of religion, in going to church, reading the Bible, saying prayers, being confirmed, being baptized, partaking of the Lord's supper, and says, "The mere externalities of religion are not enough, you must be born again." It comes to the one who is trusting in turning over a new leaf, in outward reform, in quitting his meanness; it says, "Outward reform, quitting your meanness is not enough. You must be born again." But in place of the vague and shallow hopes that it sweeps away, it brings in a new hope, a good hope, a blessed hope, a glorious hope. It says, "You may be born again." It comes to the one who has no desire higher than the desire for things animal or selfish or worldly and says, "You may become a partaker of the Divine nature, and love the things that God loves and hate the things that God hates. You may become like Jesus Christ. You may be born again."

X: The Indwelling Spirit Fully and Forever Satisfying

The Holy Spirit takes up His abode in the one who is born of the Spirit. The Apostle Paul says to the believers in Corinth in 1 Cor. iii. 16, R. V., "Know ye not that ye are a temple of God, and that the Spirit of God dwelleth in you?" This passage refers, not so much to the individual believer, as to the whole body of believers, the Church. The Church as a body is indwelt by the Spirit of God. But in 1 Cor. vi. 19, R. V., we read, "Know ye not that your body is a temple of the Holy Ghost which is in you, which ye have from God?" It is evident in this passage that Paul is not speaking of the body of believers, of the Church as a whole, but of the individual believer. In a similar way, the Lord Jesus said to His disciples on the night before His crucifixion, "And I will pray the Father, and He shall give you another Comforter, that He may abide with you forever; Even the Spirit of truth; whom the world cannot receive, because it seeth Him not, neither knoweth Him: but ye know Him; for He dwelleth with you and *shall be in you*" (John xiv. 16, 17). The Holy Spirit dwells in every one who is born again. We read in Rom. viii. 9, "If any man have not the Spirit of Christ (the Spirit of Christ in this verse, as we have already seen, does not mean merely a Christlike spirit, but is a name of the Holy Spirit) he is none of His." One may be a very imperfect believer but if he really is a believer in Jesus Christ, if he has really been born again, the Spirit of God dwells in him. It is very evident from the First Epistle to the Corinthians that the believers in Corinth were very imperfect believers; they were full of imperfection and there was gross sin among them. But nevertheless Paul tells them that they are temples of the Holy Spirit, even when dealing with them concerning gross immoralities. (See 1 Cor. vi. 15-19.) *The Holy Spirit dwells in every child of God.* In some, however, He dwells way back of consciousness in the hidden sanctuary of their spirit. He is not allowed to take possession as He desires of the whole man, spirit, soul and body. Some therefore are not distinctly conscious of His indwelling, but He is there none the less. What a solemn, and yet what a glorious thought, that in me dwells this august Person, the Holy Spirit. If we are children of God, we are not so much to pray that the Spirit may come and dwell in us, for He does that already, we are rather to recognize His presence, His gracious and glorious indwelling, and give to Him complete control of the house He already inhabits, and strive to so live as not to grieve this holy One, this Divine Guest. We shall see later, however, that it is right to pray for the filling or baptism with the Spirit. What a thought it gives of the hallowedness and sacredness of the body, to think of the Holy Spirit dwelling within us. How considerately we ought to treat these bodies and how sensitively we ought to shun everything that will defile them. How carefully we ought to walk in all things so as not to grieve Him who dwells within us.

This indwelling Spirit is a source of full and everlasting satisfaction and life. Jesus says in John iv. 14, R. V., "Whosoever drinketh of the water that I shall give him shall never thirst; but the water that I shall give him shall become in him a well of water springing up unto (better 'into' as in A. V.) eternal life." Jesus was talking to the woman of Samaria by the well at Sychar. She had said to Him, "Art Thou greater than our father Jacob, who gave us the well and drank thereof himself, and his children and his cattle?" Then Jesus answered and said unto her, "Whosoever drinketh of this water shall thirst again." How true that is of every earthly fountain. No matter how deeply we drink we shall thirst again. No earthly spring of satisfaction ever fully satisfies. We may drink of the fountain of wealth as deeply as we may, it will not satisfy long. We shall thirst again. We may drink of the fountain of fame as deeply as any man ever drank, the satisfaction is but for an hour. We may drink of the fountain of worldly pleasure, of human science and philosophy and of earthly learning, we may even drink of the fountain of human love, none will satisfy long; we shall thirst again. But then Jesus went on to say, "But whosoever drinketh of the water that I shall give him shall never thirst, but the water that I shall give him shall be in him a well of water springing up into everlasting life." The water that Jesus Christ gives is the Holy Spirit. This John tells us in the most explicit language in John vii. 37-39, "In the last day, that great day of the feast, Jesus stood and cried, saying, If any man thirst, let him come unto Me and drink. He that believeth on Me, as the Scripture hath said, out of his belly shall flow rivers of *living water*. (But this *spake He of the Spirit*, which they that believe on Him should receive.)" The Holy Spirit fully and forever satisfies the one who receives Him. He becomes within him a well of water springing up, ever springing up, into everlasting life. It is a great thing to have a well that you can carry with you; to have a well that is within you; to have your source of satisfaction, not in the things outside yourself, but in a well within and that is always within, and that is always springing up in freshness and power; to have our well of satisfaction and joy within us. We are then independent of our environment. It matters little whether we have health or sickness, prosperity or adversity, our source of joy is within and is ever springing up. It matters comparatively little even whether we have our friends with us or are separated from them, separated even by what men call death, this fountain within is always gushing up and our souls are satisfied. Sometimes this fountain within gushes up with greatest power and fullness in the days of deepest bereavement. At such a time all earthly satisfactions fail. What satisfaction is there in money, or worldly pleasure, in the theatre or the opera or the dance, in fame or power or human learning, when some loved one is taken from us? But in the hours when those that we loved dearest upon earth are taken from us, then it is that the spring of joy of the indwelling Spirit of God bursts forth with fullest flow, sorrow and sighing flee away and our own spirits are filled with peace and ecstasy. We have beauty for ashes, the oil of joy for mourning, the garment of praise for the spirit of heaviness (Isa. lxi. 3). If the experience were not too sacred to put in print, I could tell of a moment of sudden and overwhelming bereavement and sorrow, when it seemed as if I would be crushed, when I cried aloud in an agony that seemed unendurable, when suddenly and instantly this fountain of the Holy Spirit within burst forth and I knew such a rest and joy as I had rarely known before, and my whole being was suffused with the oil of gladness.

The one who has the Spirit of God dwelling within as a well springing up into everlasting life is independent of the world's pleasures. He does not need to run after the theatre and the opera and the dance and the cards and the other pleasures without which life does not seem worth living to those who have not received the Holy Spirit. He gives these things up, not so much because he thinks they are wrong, as because he has something so much better. He loses all taste for them.

A lady once came to Mr. Moody and said, "Mr. Moody, I do not like you." He asked, "Why not?" She said, "Because you are too narrow." "Narrow! I did not know that I was narrow." "Yes, you are too narrow. You don't believe in the theatre; you don't believe in cards; you don't believe in dancing." "How do you know I don't believe in the theatre?" he asked. "Oh," she said, "I know you don't." Mr. Moody replied, "I go to the theatre whenever I want to." "What," cried the woman, "you go to the theatre whenever you want to?" "Yes, I go to the theatre whenever I want to." "Oh," she said, "Mr. Moody, you are a much broader man than I thought you were. I am so glad to hear you say it, that you go to the theatre whenever you want to." "Yes, I go to the theatre whenever I want to. I don't want to." Any one who has really received the Holy Spirit, and in whom the Holy Spirit dwells and is unhindered in His working will not want to. Why is it then that so many professed Christians do go after these worldly amusements? For one of two reasons; either because they have never definitely received the Holy Spirit, or else because the fountain is choked. It is quite possible for a fountain to become choked. The best well in one of our inland cities was choked and dry for many months because an old rag carpet had been thrust into the opening from which the water flowed. When the rag was pulled out, the water flowed again pure and cool and invigorating. There are many in the Church to-day who once knew the matchless joy of the Holy Spirit, but some sin or worldly conformity, some act of disobedience, more or less conscious disobedience, to God has come in and the fountain is choked. Let us pull out the old rags to-day that this wondrous fountain may burst forth again, springing up every day and hour into everlasting life.

XI: The Holy Spirit Setting the Believer Free From the Power of Indwelling Sin

In Rom. viii. 2 the Apostle Paul writes, "The law of the Spirit of life in Christ Jesus hath made me free from the law of sin and death." What the law of sin and death is we learn from the preceding chapter, the ninth to the twenty-fourth verses. Paul tells us that there was a time in his life when he was "alive apart from the law" (v. 9). But the time came when he was brought face to face with the law of God; he saw that this law was holy and the commandment holy and just and good. And he made up his mind to keep this holy and just and good law of God. But he soon discovered that beside this law of God outside him, which was holy and just and good, that there was another law inside him directly contrary to this law of God outside him. While the law of God outside him said, "This good thing" and "this good thing" and "this good thing" and "this good thing thou shalt do," the law within him said, "You cannot do this good thing that you would;" and a fierce combat ensued between this holy and just and good law without him which Paul himself approved after the inward man, and this other law in his members which warred against the law of his mind and kept constantly saying, "You cannot do the good that you would." But this law in his members (the law that the good that he would do, he did not, but the evil that he would not he constantly did, v. 19) gained the victory. Paul's attempt to keep the law of God resulted in total failure. He found himself sinking deeper and deeper into the mire of sin, constrained and dragged down by this law of sin in his members, until at last he cried out, "Oh, wretched man that I am, who shall deliver me out of the body of this death?" (v. 24, R. V.). Then Paul made another discovery. He found that in addition to the two laws that he had already found, the law of God without him, holy and just and good, and the law of sin and death within him, the law that the good he would he could not do and the evil he would not, he must keep on doing, there was a third law, "the law of the Spirit of life in Christ Jesus," and this third law read this way, "The righteousness which you cannot achieve in your own strength by the power of your own will approving the law of God, the righteousness which the law of God without you, holy and just and good though it is, cannot accomplish in you, in that it is weak through your flesh, the Spirit of life in Christ Jesus can produce in you so that the righteousness that the law requires may be fulfilled in you, if you will not walk after the flesh but after the Spirit." In other words when we come to the end of ourselves, when we fully realize our own inability to keep the law of God and in utter helplessness look up to the Holy Spirit in Christ Jesus to do for us that which we cannot do for ourselves, and surrender our every thought and every purpose and every desire and every affection to His absolute control and thus walk after the Spirit, the Spirit does take control and set us free from the power of sin that dwells in us and brings our whole lives into conformity to the will of God. *It is the privilege of the child of God in the power of the Holy Spirit to have victory over sin every day and every hour and every moment.*

There are many professed Christians to-day living in the experience that Paul described in Rom. vii. 9-24. Each day is a day of defeat and if at the close of the day, they review their lives they must cry, "Oh, wretched man that I am, who shall deliver me out of the body of this death?" There are some who even go so far as to reason that this is the normal Christian life, but Paul tells us distinctly that this was "when the commandment came" (v. 9), not when the Spirit came; that it is the experience under law and not in the Spirit. The pronoun "I" occurs twenty-seven times in these fifteen verses and the Holy Spirit is not found once, whereas in the eighth chapter of Romans the pronoun "I" is found only twice in the whole chapter and the Holy Spirit appears constantly. Again Paul tells us in the fourteenth verse that this was his experience as "carnal, sold under sin." Certainly, that does not describe the normal Christian experience. On the other hand in Rom. viii. 9 we are told how not to be in the flesh but in the Spirit. In the eighth chapter of Romans we have a picture of the true Christian life, the life that is possible to each one of us and that God expects from each one of us. Here we have a life where not merely the commandment comes but the Spirit comes, and works obedience to the commandment and brings us complete victory over the law of sin and death. Here we have life, not in the flesh, but in the Spirit, where we not only see the beauty of the law (Rom. vii. 22) but where the Spirit imparts power to keep it (Rom. viii. 4). We still have the flesh but we are not in the flesh and we do not live after the flesh. We "through the Spirit do mortify the deeds of the body" (v. 13). The desires of the body are still there, desires which if made the rule of our life, would lead us into sin, but we day by day by the power of the Spirit do put to death the deeds to which the desires of the body would lead us. We walk by the Spirit and therefore do not fulfill the lusts of the flesh (Gal. v. 16, R. V.). We have crucified the flesh with the passions and lusts thereof (Gal. v. 24, R. V.). It would be *going too far to say we had still a carnal nature*, for a carnal nature is a nature governed by the flesh; *but we have the flesh*, but in the Spirit's power, it is our privilege to get daily, hourly, constant victory over the flesh and over sin. But this victory is not in ourselves, nor in any strength of our own. Left to ourselves, deserted of the Spirit of God, we would be as helpless as ever. It is still true that in us, that is in our flesh, dwelleth no good thing (Rom. vii. 18). It is all in the power of the indwelling Spirit, but the Spirit's power may be in such fullness that one is not even conscious of the presence of the flesh. It seems as if it were dead and gone forever, but it is only kept in place of death by the Holy Spirit's power. If for one moment we were to get our eyes off from Jesus Christ, if we were to neglect the daily study of the Word and prayer, down we would go. We must live in the Spirit and walk in the Spirit if we would have continuous victory (Gal. v. 16, 25). The life of the Spirit within us must be maintained by the study of the Word and prayer. One of the saddest things ever witnessed is the way in which some people who have entered by the Spirit's power into a life of victory become self-confident and fancy that the victory is in themselves, and that they can safely neglect the study of the Word and prayer. The depths to which such sometimes fall is appalling. Each of us needs to lay to heart the inspired words of the Apostle, "Wherefore, let him that thinketh he standeth take heed lest he fall" (1 Cor. x. 12). I once knew a man who seemed to make extraordinary strides in the Christian life. He became a teacher of others and was greatly blessed to thousands. It seemed to me that he was becoming self-confident and I trembled for him. I invited him to my room and we had a long heart to heart conversation. I told him frankly that it seemed as if he were going perilously near exceedingly dangerous ground. I said that I found it safer at the close of each day not to be too confident that there had been no failures nor defeats that day but to go alone with God and ask Him to search my heart and show me if there was anything in my outward or inward life that was displeasing to Him, and that very often failures were brought to light that must be confessed as sin. "No," he replied, "I do not need to do that. Even if I should do something wrong, I would see it at once. I keep very short accounts with God, and I would confess it at once." I said it seemed to me as if it would be safer to take time alone with God for God to search us through and through, that while we might not know anything against ourselves, God might know something against us (1 Cor. iv. 4, R. V.), and He would bring it to light and our failure could be confessed and put away. "No," he said, "he did not feel that that was necessary." Satan took advantage of his self-confidence. He fell into most appalling sin, and though he has since confessed and professed repentance, he has been utterly set aside from God's service.

In John viii. 32 we read, "Ye shall know the truth and *the truth shall set you free*." In this verse it is the truth, or the Word of God, that sets us free from the power of sin and gives us victory. And in Ps. cxix. 11 we read, "*Thy Word* have I hid in my heart, that I might not sin against Thee." Here again it is the indwelling Word that keeps us free from sin. In this matter as in everything else what in one place is attributed to the Holy Spirit is elsewhere attributed to the Word. The explanation, of course, is that the Holy Spirit works through the Word, and it is futile to talk of the Holy Spirit dwelling in us if we neglect the Word. If we are not feeding on the Word, we are not walking after the Spirit and we shall not have victory over the flesh and over sin.

XII: The Holy Spirit Forming Christ Within Us

It is a wonderful and deeply significant prayer that Paul offers in Eph. iii. 16-19 for the believers in Ephesus and for all believers who read the Epistle. Paul writes, "For this cause I bow my knees unto the Father, from whom every family in heaven and on earth is named, that He would grant you, according to the riches of His glory, that ye may be strengthened with power through His Spirit in the inward man; that Christ may dwell in your hearts through faith; to the end that ye, being rooted and grounded in love, may be strong to apprehend with all the saints what is the breadth and length, and height and depth, and to know the love of Christ which passeth knowledge, that ye may be filled unto all the fullness of God" (R. V.). We have here an advance in the thought over that which we have just been studying in the preceding chapter. It is the carrying out of the former work to its completion. Here the power of the Spirit manifests itself, not merely in giving us victory over sin but in four things:

I. *In Christ dwelling in our hearts.* The word translated "dwell" in this passage is a very strong word. It means literally, "to dwell down," "to settle," "to dwell deep." It is the work of the Holy Spirit to form the living Christ within us, dwelling deep down in the deepest depths of our being. We have already seen that this was a part of the significance of the name sometimes used of the Holy Spirit, "the Spirit of Christ." In Christ on the cross of Calvary, made an atoning sacrifice for sin, bearing the curse of the broken law in our place, we have *Christ for us*. But by the power of the Holy Spirit bestowed upon us by the risen Christ we have *Christ in us*. Herein lies the secret of a Christlike life. We hear a great deal in these days about doing as Jesus would do. Certainly we ought as Christians to live like Christ. "He that saith he abideth in Him, ought himself so to walk even as He walked" (1 John ii. 6). But any attempt on our part to imitate Christ in our own strength will only result in utter disappointment and despair. There is nothing more futile that we can possibly attempt than to imitate Christ in the power of our own will. If we fancy that we succeed it will be simply because we have a very incomplete knowledge of Christ. The more we study Him, and the more perfectly we understand His conduct, the more clearly will we see how far short we have come from imitating Him. But God does not demand of us the impossible, He does not demand of us that we imitate Christ in our own strength. He offers to us something infinitely better, He offers to form Christ in us by the power of His Holy Spirit. And when Christ is thus formed in us by the Holy Spirit's power, all we have to do is to let this indwelling Christ live out His own life in us, and then we shall be like Christ without struggle and effort of our own. A woman, who had a deep knowledge of the Word and a rare experience of the fullness that there is in Christ, stood one morning before a body of ministers as they plied her with questions. "Do you mean to say, Mrs. H——," one of the ministers asked, "that you are holy?" Quickly but very meekly and gently, the elect lady replied, "Christ in me is holy." No, we are not holy. To the end of the chapter in and of ourselves we are full of weakness and failure, but the Holy Spirit is able to form within us the Holy One of God, the indwelling Christ, and He will live out His life through us in all the humblest relations of life as well as in those relations of life that are considered greater. He will live out His life through the mother in the home, through the day-laborer in the pit, through the business man in his office—everywhere.

II. *In our being rooted and grounded in love* (v. 17). Paul multiplies figures here. The first figure is taken from the tree shooting its roots down deep into the earth and taking fast hold upon it. The second figure is taken from a great building with its foundations laid deep in the earth on the rock. Paul therefore tells us that by the strengthening of the Spirit in the inward man we send the roots of our life down deep into the soil of love and also that the foundations of the superstructure of our character are built upon the rock of love. Love is the sum of holiness, the fulfilling of the law (Rom. xiii. 10); love is what we all most need in our relations to God, to Jesus Christ and to one another; and it is the work of the Holy Spirit to root and ground our lives in love. There is the most intimate relation between Christ being formed within us, or made to dwell in us, and our being rooted and grounded in love, for Jesus Christ Himself is the absolutely perfect embodiment of divine love.

III. *In our being made strong to apprehend with all the saints what is the breadth and length and height and depth, and to know the love of Christ which passeth knowledge.* It is not enough that we love, we must know the love of Christ, but that love passeth knowledge. It is so broad, so long, so high, so deep, that no one can comprehend it. But we can "apprehend" it, we can lay hold upon it; we can make it our own; we can hold it before us as the object of our meditation, our wonder, and our joy. But it is only in the power of the Holy Spirit that we can thus apprehend it. The mind cannot grasp it at all, in its own native strength. A man untaught and unstrengthened by the Spirit of God may talk about the love of Christ, he may write poetry about it, he may go into rhapsodies over it, but it is only words, words, words. There is no real apprehension. But the Spirit of God makes us strong to really apprehend it in all its breadth, in all its length, in all its depth, and in all its height.

IV. *In our being "filled unto all the fullness of God."* There is a very important change between the Authorized and Revised Version. The Authorized Version reads "Filled *with* all the fullness of God." The Revised Version reads more exactly "filled *unto* all the fullness of God." It is no wonder that the translators of the Authorized Version staggered at what Paul said and sought to tone down the full force of his words. To be filled *with* all the fullness of God would not be so wonderful, for it is an easy matter to fill a pint cup with all the fullness of the ocean, a single dip will do it. But it would be an impossibility indeed to fill a pint cup *unto* all the fullness of the ocean, until all the fullness that there is in the ocean is in that pint cup. But it is seemingly a more impossible task that the Holy Spirit undertakes to do for us, to fill us "unto all the fullness" of the infinite God, to fill us until all the intellectual and moral fullness that there is in God is in us. But this is the believer's destiny, we are "heirs of God and joint-heirs with Jesus Christ" (Rom. viii. 17), *i. e.*, we are heirs of God to the extent that Jesus Christ is an heir of God; that is, we are heirs to all God is and all God has. It is the work of the Holy Spirit to apply to us that which is already ours in Christ. It is His work to make ours experimentally all God has and all God is, until the work is consummated in our being "*filled unto all the fullness of God*." This is not the work of a moment, nor a day, nor a week, nor a month, nor a year, but the Holy Spirit day by day puts His hand, as it were, into the fullness of God and conveys to us what He has taken therefrom and puts it into us, and then again He puts His hand into the fullness that there is in God and conveys to us what is taken therefrom, and puts it into us, and this wonderful process goes on day after day and week after week and month after month, and year after year, and never ends until we are "filled *unto* all the fullness of God."

XIII: The Holy Spirit Bringing Forth in the Believer Christlike Graces of Character

There is a singular charm, a charm that one can scarcely explain, in the words of Paul in Gal. v. 22, 23, R. V., "The fruit of the Spirit is love, joy, peace, longsuffering, kindness, goodness, faithfulness, meekness, temperance." What a catalogue we have here of lovely moral characteristics. Paul tells us that they are the fruit of the Spirit, that is, if the Holy Spirit is given control of our lives, this is the fruit that He will bear. All real beauty of character, all real Christlikeness in us, is the Holy Spirit's work; it is His fruit; He produces it; He bears it, not we. It is well to notice that these graces are not said to be the fruits of the Spirit but the fruit, *i. e.*, if the Spirit is given control of our life, He will not bear one of these as fruit in one person and another as fruit in another person, but this will be the one fruit of many flavors that He produces in each one. There is also a unity of origin running throughout all the multiplicity of manifestation. It is a beautiful life that is set forth in these verses. Every word is worthy of earnest study and profound meditation. Think of these words one by one; "love"—"joy"—"peace"—"longsuffering"—"kindness"—"goodness"—"faith" (or "faithfulness," R. V.; faith is the better translation if properly understood. The word is deeper than faithfulness. It is a real faith that results in faithfulness)—"meekness"—"temperance" (or a life under perfect control by the power of the Holy Spirit). We have here a perfect picture of the life of Jesus Christ Himself. Is not this the life that we all long for, the Christlike life? But this life is not natural to us and is not attainable by us by any effort of what we are in ourselves. The life that is natural to us is set forth in the three preceding verses: "Now the works of the flesh are manifest, which are these, fornication, uncleanness, lasciviousness, idolatry, sorcery, enmities, strife, jealousies, wraths, factions, divisions, heresies, envyings, drunkenness, revellings and such like" (Gal. v. 21, R. V.). All these works of the flesh will not manifest themselves in each individual; some will manifest themselves in one, others in others, but they have one common source, the flesh, and if we live in the flesh, this is the kind of a life that we will live. It is the life that is natural to us. But when the indwelling Spirit is given full control in the one He inhabits, when we are brought to realize the utter badness of the flesh and give up in hopeless despair of ever attaining to anything in its power, when, in other words, we come to the end of ourselves, and just give over the whole work of making us what we ought to be to the indwelling Holy Spirit, then and only then, these holy graces of character, which are set forth in Gal. v. 22, 23, are His fruit in our lives. Do you wish these graces in your character and life? Do you really wish them? Then renounce self utterly and all its strivings after holiness, give up any thought that you can ever attain to anything really morally beautiful in your own strength and let the Holy Spirit, who already dwells in you (if you are a child of God) take full control and bear His own glorious fruit in your daily life.

We get very much the same thought from a different point of view in the second chapter and twentieth verse, A. R. V., "I have been crucified with Christ; and it is no longer I that live, but Christ liveth in me: and that life which I now live in the flesh I live in faith, the faith which is in the Son of God, who loved me and gave Himself up for me."

We hear a great deal in these days about "Ethical Culture," which usually means the cultivation of the flesh until it bears the fruit of the Spirit. It cannot be done; no more than thorns can be made to bear figs and the bramble bush grapes (Luke vi. 44; Matt. xii. 33). We hear also a great deal about "character building." That may be all very well if you bear constantly in mind that the Holy Spirit must do the building, and even then it is not so much building as fruit bearing. (See, however, 2 Pet. i. 5-7.) We hear also a great deal about "cultivating graces of character," but we must always bear it clearly in mind that the way to cultivate true graces of character is by submitting ourselves utterly to the Spirit to do His work and bear His fruit. This is "sanctification *of the Spirit*" (1 Pet. i. 2; 2 Thess. ii. 13). There is a sense, however, in which cultivating graces of character is right: viz., we look at Jesus Christ to see what He is and what we therefore ought to be; then we look to the Holy Spirit to make us this that we ought to be and thus, "reflecting as a mirror the glory of the Lord, we are transformed into the same image from glory to glory, even as from the Lord the Spirit" (2 Cor. iii. 18, R. V.). Settle it, however, clearly and forever that the flesh can never bear this fruit, that you can never attain to these things by your own effort that they are "*the fruit of the Spirit.*"

XIV: The Holy Spirit Guiding the Believer Into a Life as a Son

The Apostle Paul writes in Rom. viii. 14, R. V., "For as many as are *led by the Spirit of God*, these are the sons of God." In this passage we see the Holy Spirit taking the conduct of the believer's life. A true Christian life is a personally conducted life, conducted at every turn by a Divine Person. It is the believer's privilege to be absolutely set free from all care and worry and anxiety as to the decisions which we must make at any turn of life. The Holy Spirit undertakes all that responsibility for us. A true Christian life is not one governed by a long set of rules without us, but led by a living and ever-present Person within us. It is in this connection that Paul says, "For ye received not the spirit *of bondage* again *to fear*." A life governed by rules without one is a life of *bondage*. There is always *fear* that we haven't made quite rules enough, and always the dread that in an unguarded moment we may have broken some of the rules which we have made. The life that many professed Christians lead is one of awful bondage; for they have put upon themselves a yoke more grievous to bear than that of the ancient Mosaic law concerning which Peter said to the Jews of his time, that neither they nor their fathers had been able to bear it (Acts xv. 10). Many Christians have a long list of self-made rules, "Thou shalt do this," and "Thou shalt do this," and "Thou shalt do this," and "Thou shalt not do that," and "Thou shalt not do that," and "Thou shalt not do that"; and if by any chance they break one of these self-made rules, or forget to keep one of them, they are at once filled with an awful dread that they have brought upon themselves the displeasure of God (and they even sometimes fancy that they have committed the unpardonable sin). This is not Christianity, this is legalism. "We have not received the spirit of bondage again to fear," we have received the Spirit who gives us the place of sons (Rom. viii. 15). Our lives should not be governed by a set of rules without us but by the loving Spirit of Adoption within us. We should believe the teaching of God's Word that the Spirit of God's Son dwells within us and we should surrender the absolute control of our life to Him and look to Him to guide us at every turn of life. He will do it if we only surrender to Him to do it and trust Him to do it. If in a moment of thoughtlessness, we go our own way instead of His, we will not be filled with an overwhelming sense of condemnation and of fear of an offended God, but we will go to God as our Father, confess our going astray, believe that He forgives us fully because He says so (1 John i. 9) and go on light and happy of heart to obey Him and be led by His Spirit.

Being led by the Spirit of God does not mean for a moment that we will do things that the written Word of God tells us not to do. The Holy Spirit never leads men contrary to the Book of which He Himself is the Author. And if there is some spirit which is leading us to do something that is contrary to the explicit teachings of Jesus, or the Apostles, we may be perfectly sure that this spirit who is leading us is not the Holy Spirit. This point needs to be emphasized in our day, for there are not a few who give themselves over to the leading of some spirit, whom they say is the Holy Spirit, but who is leading them to do things explicitly forbidden in the Word. We must always remember that many false spirits and false prophets are gone out into the world (1 John iv. 1). There are many who are so anxious to be led by some unseen power that they are ready to surrender the conduct of their lives to any spiritual influence or unseen person. In this way, they open their lives to the conduct and malevolent influence of evil spirits to the utter wreck and ruin of their lives.

A man who made great professions of piety once came to me and said that the Holy Spirit was leading him and "a sweet Christian woman," whom he had met, to contemplate marriage. "Why," I said, in astonishment, "you already have one wife." "Yes," he said, "but you know we are not congenial, and we have not lived together for years." "Yes," I replied, "I know you have not lived together for years, and I have looked into the matter, and I believe that the blame for that lies largely at your door. In any event, she is your wife. You have no reason to suppose she has been untrue to you, and Jesus Christ explicitly teaches that if you marry another while she lives you commit adultery" (Luke xvi. 18). "Oh, but," the man said, "the Spirit of God is leading us to love one another and to see that we ought to marry one another." "You lie, and you blaspheme," I replied. "Any spirit that is leading you to disobey the plain teaching of Jesus Christ is not the Spirit of God but some spirit of the devil." This perhaps was an extreme case, but cases of essentially the same character are not rare. Many professed Christians seek to justify themselves in doing things which are explicitly forbidden in the Word by saying that they are led by the Spirit of God. Not long ago, I protested to the leaders in a Christian assembly where at each meeting many professed to speak with tongues in distinct violation of the teaching of the Holy Spirit through the Apostle Paul in 1 Cor. xiv. 27, 28 (that not more than two or at the most, three, shall speak in a tongue in one gathering and that not even one shall speak unless there was an interpreter, and that no two shall speak at the same time). The defense that they made was that the Holy Spirit led them to speak several at a time and many in a single meeting and that they must obey the Holy Spirit, and in such a case as this were not subject to the Word. The Holy Spirit never contradicts Himself. He never leads the individual to do that which in the written Word He has commanded us all not to do. Any leading of the Spirit must be tested by that which we know to be the leading of the Spirit in the Word. But while we need to be on our guard against the leading of false spirits, it is our privilege to be led by the Holy Spirit, and to lead a life free from the bondage of rules and free from the anxiety that we shall not go wrong, a life as children whose Father has sent an unerring Guide to lead them all the way.

Those who are thus led by the Spirit of God are "*sons* of God," that is, they are not merely *children* of God, born it is true of the Father, but immature, but they are the grown children, the mature children of God; they are no longer babes but sons. The Apostle Paul draws a contrast in Gal. iv. 1-7 between the babe under the tutelage of the law and differing nothing from a servant, and the full grown son who is no more a servant but a son walking in joyous liberty. It sometimes seems as if comparatively few Christians to-day had really thrown off the bondage of law, rules outside themselves, and entered into the joyous liberty of sons.

XV: The Holy Spirit Bearing Witness to our Sonship

One of the most precious passages in the Bible regarding the work of the Holy Spirit is found in Rom. viii. 15, 16, R. V., "For ye received not the spirit of bondage again to fear; but ye received the spirit of adoption, whereby we cry Abba, Father. The Spirit Himself beareth witness with our spirit, that we are the children of God." There are two witnesses to our sonship, first, our own spirit, taking God at His Word ("As many as received Him, to them gave He power to become the sons of God," John i. 12), bears witness to our sonship. Our own spirit unhesitatingly affirms that what God says is true that we are sons of God because God says so. But there is another witness to our sonship, namely, the Holy Spirit. He bears witness *together with* our spirit. "Together with" is the force of the Greek used in this passage. It does not say that He bears witness *to* our spirit but "*together* with" it. How He does this is explained in Gal iv. 6, "Because ye are sons, God hath sent forth the Spirit of His Son into your hearts, crying, Abba, Father." When we have received Jesus Christ as our Savior and accepted God's testimony concerning Christ that through Him we have become sons, the Spirit of His Son comes into our hearts filling them with an overwhelming sense of sonship, and crying through our hearts, "Abba, Father." The natural attitude of our hearts towards God is not that of sons. We may call Him Father with our lips, as when for example we repeat in a formal way, the prayer that Jesus taught us, "Our Father, which art in heaven," but there is no real sense that He is our Father. Our calling Him so is mere words. We do not really trust Him. We do not love to come into His presence; we do not love to look up into His face with a sense of wonderful joy and trust because we are talking to our Father. We dread God. We come to Him in prayer because we think we ought to and perhaps we are afraid of what might happen if we did not. But when the Spirit of His Son bears witness together with our spirit to our sonship, then we are filled and thrilled with the sense that we are sons. We trust Him as we never even trusted our earthly Father. There is even less fear of Him than there was of our earthly father. Reverence there is, awe, but oh! such a sense of wonderful childlike trust.

Notice when it is that the Spirit bears witness with our spirit that we are the children of God. We have the order of experience in the order of the verses in Rom. viii. First we see the Holy Spirit setting us free from the law of sin and death, and consequently, the righteousness of the law fulfilled in us who walk not after the law but after the Spirit (vs. 2-4); then we have the believer not minding the things of the flesh but the things of the Spirit (v. 5); then we have the believer day by day through the Spirit putting to death the deeds of the body (v. 13); then we have the believer led by the Spirit of God; then and only then, we have the Spirit bearing witness to our sonship. There are many seeking the witness of the Spirit to their sonship in the wrong place. They practically demand the witness of the Spirit to their sonship before they have even confessed their acceptance of Christ, and certainly before they have surrendered their lives fully to the control of the indwelling Spirit of God. No, let us seek things in their right order. Let us accept Jesus Christ as our Savior, and surrender to Him as our Lord and Master, because God commands us to do so; let us confess Him before the world because God commands that (Matt. x. 32, 33; Rom. x. 9, 10); let us assert that our sins are forgiven, that we have eternal life, that we are sons of God because God says so in His Word and we are unwilling to make God a liar by doubting Him (Acts x. 43; xiii. 38, 39; 1 John v. 10-13; John v. 24; John i. 12); let us surrender our lives to the control of the Spirit of Life, looking to Him to set us free from the law of sin and death; let us set our minds, not upon the things of the flesh but the things of the Spirit; let us through the Spirit day by day put to death the deeds of the body; let us give our lives up to be led by the Spirit of God in all things; and *then* let us simply trust God to send the Spirit of His Son into our hearts filling us with a sense of sonship, crying, "Abba, Father," and He will do it.

God, our Father, longs that we shall know and realize that we are His sons. He longs to hear us call Him Father from hearts that realize what they say, and that trust Him without a fear or anxiety. He is our Father, He alone in all the universe realizes the fullness of meaning that there is in that wonderful word "Father," and it brings joy to Him to have us realize that He is our Father and to call Him so.

Some years ago there was a father in the state of Illinois, who had a child who had been deaf and dumb from her birth. It was a sad day in that home when they came to realize that that little child was deaf and would never hear and, as they thought, would never speak. The father heard of an institution in Jacksonville, Ill., where deaf children were taught to talk. He took this little child to the institution and put her in charge of the superintendent. After the child had been there some time, the superintendent wrote telling the father that he would better come and visit his child. A day was appointed and the child was told that her father was coming. As the hour approached, she sat up in the window, watching the gate for her father to pass through. The moment he entered the gate she saw him, ran down the stairs and ran out on the lawn, met him, looked up into his face and lifted up her hands and said, "Papa." When that father heard the dumb lips of his child speak for the first time and frame that sweet word "Papa," such a throb of joy passed through his heart that he literally fell to the ground and rolled upon the grass in ecstasy. But there is a Father who loves as no earthly father, who longs to have His children realize that they are children, and when we look up into His face and from a heart which the Holy Spirit has filled with a sense of sonship call Him "Abba" (papa), "Father," no language can describe the joy of God.

XVI: The Holy Spirit as a Teacher

Our Lord Jesus in His last conversation with His disciples before His crucifixion said, "But the Comforter which is the Holy Ghost, whom the Father will send in My name, He shall teach you all things, and bring all things to your remembrance, whatsoever I have said unto you" (John xiv. 26).

Here we have a twofold work of the Holy Spirit, teaching and bringing to remembrance the things which Christ had already taught. We will take them in the reverse order.

I. *The Holy Spirit brings to remembrance the words of Christ.*

This promise was made primarily to the Apostles and is the guarantee of the accuracy of their report of what Jesus said; but the Holy Spirit does a similar work with each believer who expects it of Him, and who looks to Him to do it. The Holy Spirit brings to our mind the teachings of Christ and of the Word just when we need them for either the necessities of our life or of our service. Many of us could tell of occasions when we were in great distress of soul or great questioning as to duty or great extremity as to what to say to one whom we were trying to lead to Christ or to help, and at that exact moment the very Scripture we needed—some passage it may be we had not thought of for a long time and quite likely of which we had never thought in this connection—was brought to mind. Who did it? The Holy Spirit did it. He is ready to do it even more frequently, if we only expect it of Him and look to Him to do it. It is our privilege every time we sit down beside an inquirer to point him to the way of life to look up to the Holy Spirit and say, "Just what shall I say to this inquirer? Just what Scripture shall I use?" There is a deep significance in the fact that in the verse immediately following this precious promise Jesus says, "Peace I leave with you, My peace I give unto you." It is by the Spirit bringing His words to remembrance and teaching us the truth of God that we obtain and abide in this peace. If we will simply look to the Holy Spirit to bring to mind Scripture just when we need it, and just the Scripture we need, we shall indeed have Christ's peace every moment of our lives. One who was preparing for Christian work came to me in great distress. He said he must give up his preparation for he could not memorize the Scriptures. "I am thirty-two years old," he said, "and have been in business now for years. I have gotten out of the habit of study and I cannot memorize anything." The man longed to be in his Master's service and the tears stood in his eyes as he said it. "Don't be discouraged," I replied. "Take your Lord's promise that the Holy Spirit will bring His words to remembrance, learn one passage of Scripture, fix it firmly in your mind, then another and then another and look to the Holy Spirit to bring them to your remembrance when you need them." He went on with his preparation. He trusted the Holy Spirit. Afterwards he took up work in a very difficult field, a field where all sorts of error abounded. They would gather around him on the street like bees and he would take his Bible and trust the Holy Spirit to bring to remembrance the passages of Scripture that he needed and He did it. His adversaries were filled with confusion, as he met them at every point with the sure Word of God, and many of the most hardened were won for Christ.

II. *The Holy Spirit will teach us all things.*

There is a still more explicit promise to this effect two chapters further on in John xvi. 12, 13, 14, R. V. Here Jesus says, "I have yet many things to say unto you, but ye cannot bear them now. Howbeit when He, the Spirit of truth, is come, He shall guide you into all the truth: for He shall not speak from Himself; but what things soever He shall hear, these shall He speak: and He shall declare unto you the things that are to come. He shall glorify Me: for He shall take of Mine, and shall declare it unto you." This promise was made in the first instance to the Apostles, but the Apostles themselves applied it to all believers (1 John ii. 20, 27).

It is the privilege of each believer in Jesus Christ, even the humblest, to be "taught of God." Each humblest believer is independent of human teachers—"Ye need not that any teach you" (1 John ii. 27, R. V.). This, of course, does not mean that we may not learn much from others who are taught of the Holy Spirit. If John had thought that he would never have written this epistle to teach others. The man who is the most fully taught of God is the very one who will be most ready to listen to what God has taught others. Much less does it mean that when we are taught of the Spirit, we are independent of the written Word of God; for the Word is the very place to which the Spirit, who is the Author of the Word, leads His pupils and the instrument through which He instructs them (Eph. vi. 17; John vi. 33; Eph. v. 18, 19; cf. Col. iii. 16). But while we may learn much from men, we are not dependent upon them. We have a Divine Teacher, the Holy Spirit.

We shall never truly know the truth until we are thus taught directly by the Holy Spirit. No amount of mere human teaching, no matter who our teachers may be, will ever give us a correct and exact and full apprehension of the truth. Not even a diligent study of the Word either in the English or in the original languages will give us a real understanding of the truth. We must be taught directly by the Holy Spirit and we may be thus taught, each one of us. The one who is thus taught will understand the truth of God better even if he does not know one word of Greek or Hebrew, than the one who knows Greek and Hebrew thoroughly and all the cognate languages as well, but who is not taught of the Spirit.

The Spirit will guide the one whom He thus teaches "into all the truth." The whole sphere of God's truth is for each one of us, but the Holy Spirit will not guide us into all the truth in a single day, nor in a week, nor in a year, but step by step. There are two especial lines of the Spirit's teaching mentioned:

(1) "He shall declare unto you the things that are to come." There are many who say we can know nothing of the future, that all our thoughts on that subject are guesswork. It is true that we cannot know everything about the future. There are some things which God has seen fit to keep to Himself, secret things which belong to Him (Deut. xxix. 29). For example, we cannot "know the times, or the seasons" of our Lord's return (Acts i. 7), but there are many things about the future which the Holy Spirit will reveal to us.

(2) "He shall *glorify Me* (that is, Christ) for He shall take of Mine and shall declare it unto you." This is the Holy Spirit's especial line of teaching with the believer, as with the unbeliever, Jesus Christ. It is His work above all else to reveal Jesus Christ and to glorify Him. His whole teaching centers in Christ. From one point of view or the other, He is always bringing us to Jesus Christ. There are some who fear to emphasize the truth about the Holy Spirit lest Christ Himself be disparaged and put in the background, but there is no one who magnifies Christ as the Holy Spirit does. We shall never understand Christ, nor see His glory until the Holy Spirit interprets Him to us. No amount of listening to sermons and lectures, no matter how able, no amount of mere study of the Word even, would ever give us to see "the things of Christ"; the Holy Spirit must show us and He is willing to do it and He can do it. He is longing to do it. The Holy Spirit's most intense desire is to reveal Jesus Christ to men. On the day of Pentecost when Peter and the rest of the company were "filled with the Holy Spirit," they did not talk much about the Holy Spirit, they talked about Christ. Study Peter's sermon on that day; Jesus Christ was his one theme, and Jesus Christ will be our one theme, if we are taught of the Spirit; Jesus Christ will occupy the whole horizon of our vision. We will have a new Christ, a glorious

Christ. Christ will be so glorious to us that we will long to go and tell every one about this glorious One whom we have found. Jesus Christ is so different when the Spirit glorifies Him by taking of His things and showing them unto us.

III. *The Holy Spirit reveals to us the deep things of God which are hidden from and are foolishness to the natural man.*

We read in 1 Cor. ii. 9-13, "Eye hath not seen, nor ear heard, neither have entered into the heart of man, the things which God hath prepared for them that love Him. But *God hath revealed them unto us by His Spirit*: for *the Spirit searcheth all things, yea, the deep things of God*. For what man knoweth the things of a man, save the spirit of man which is in him? Even so the things of God knoweth no man, but the Spirit of God. Now we have received, not the spirit of the world, but the spirit which is of God; that we might know the things that are freely given to us of God. Which things also we speak, not in the words which man's wisdom teacheth, but which the Holy Ghost teacheth; comparing spiritual things with spiritual." This passage, of course, refers primarily to the Apostles but we cannot limit this work of the Spirit to them. The Spirit reveals to the individual believer the deep things of God, things which human eye hath not seen, nor ear heard, things which have not entered into the heart of man, the things which God hath prepared for them that love Him. It is evident from the context that this does not refer solely to heaven, or the things to come in the life hereafter. The Holy Spirit takes the deep things of God which God hath prepared for us, even in the life that now is, and reveals them to us.

IV. *The Holy Spirit interprets His own revelation. He imparts power to discern, know and appreciate what He has taught.*

In the next verse to those just quoted we read, "But the natural man receiveth not the things of the Spirit of God: for they are foolishness unto him: neither can he know them, because they are spiritually discerned" (1 Cor. iii. 14). Not only is the Holy Spirit the Author of revelation, the written Word of God: He is also the Interpreter of what He has revealed. Any profound book is immeasurably more interesting and helpful when we have the author of the book right at hand to interpret it to us, and it is always our privilege to have the author of the Bible right at hand when we study it. The Holy Spirit is the Author of the Bible and He stands ready to interpret its meaning to every believer every time he opens the Book. To understand the Book, we must look to Him, then the darkest places become clear. We often need to pray with the Psalmist of old, "Open Thou mine eyes, that I may behold wondrous things out of Thy law" (Ps. cxix. 18). It is not enough that we have the revelation of God before us in the written Word to study, we must also have the inward illumination of the Holy Spirit to enable us to apprehend it as we study. It is a common mistake, but a most palpable mistake, to try to comprehend a spiritual revelation with the natural understanding. It is the foolish attempt to do this that has landed so many in the bog of so-called "Higher Criticism." In order to understand art a man must have æsthetic sense as well as the knowledge of colors and of paint, and a man to understand a spiritual revelation must be taught of the Spirit. A mere knowledge of the languages in which the Bible was written is not enough. A man with no æsthetic sense might as well expect to appreciate the Sistine Madonna, because he is not color blind, as a man who is not filled with the Spirit to understand the Bible, simply because he understands the vocabulary and the laws of grammar of the languages in which the Bible was written. We might as well think of setting a man to teach art because he understood paints as to set a man to teach the Bible because he has a thorough understanding of Greek and Hebrew. In our day we need not only to recognize the utter insufficiency and worthlessness before God of our own righteousness, which is the lesson of the opening chapters of the Epistle to the Romans, but also the utter insufficiency and worthlessness in the things of God of our own wisdom, which is the lesson of the First Epistle to the Corinthians, especially the first to the third chapters. (See for example 1 Cor. i. 19-21, 26, 27.)

The Jews of old had a revelation by the Spirit but they failed to depend upon the Spirit Himself to interpret it to them, so they went astray. So Christians to-day have a revelation by the Spirit and many are failing to depend upon the Holy Spirit to interpret it to them and so they go astray. The whole evangelical church recognizes theoretically at least the utter insufficiency of man's own righteousness. What it needs to be taught in the present hour, and what it needs to be made to feel, is the utter insufficiency of man's wisdom. That is perhaps the lesson which this twentieth century of towering intellectual conceit needs most of any to learn. To understand God's Word, we must empty ourselves utterly of our own wisdom and rest in utter dependence upon the Spirit of God to interpret it to us. We do well to lay to heart the words of Jesus Himself in Matt. xi. 25, "I thank thee, O Father, Lord of heaven and earth, because Thou hast hid these things from the wise and prudent, and hast revealed them unto babes." A number of Bible students were once discussing the best methods of Bible study and one man, who was in point of fact a learned and scholarly man, said, "I think the best method of Bible study is the baby method." When we have entirely put away our own righteousness, then and only then, we get the righteousness of God (Phil. iii. 4-7, 9; Rom. x. 3). And when we have entirely put away our own wisdom, then, and only then, we get the wisdom of God. "Let no man deceive himself," says the Apostle Paul. "If any man among you seemeth to be wise in this world, *let him become a fool*, that he may be wise" (1 Cor. iii. 18). And the emptying must precede filling, the self poured out that God may be poured in.

We must daily be taught by the Spirit to understand the Word. We cannot depend to-day on the fact that the Spirit taught us yesterday. Each new time that we come in contact with the Word, it must be in the power of the Spirit for that specific occasion. That the Holy Spirit once illumined our mind to grasp a certain truth is not enough. He must do it each time we confront that passage. Andrew Murray has well said, "Each time you come to the Word in study, in hearing a sermon, or reading a religious book, there ought to be as distinct as your intercourse with the external means, the definite act of self-abnegation, denying your own wisdom and yielding yourself in faith to the Divine teacher" ("The Spirit of Christ," page 221).

V. *The Holy Spirit enables the believer to communicate to others in power the truth he himself has been taught.*

Paul says in 1 Cor. ii. 1-5, "And I, brethren, when I came to you, came not with excellency of speech or of wisdom, declaring unto you the testimony of God. For I determined not to know anything among you, save Jesus Christ, and Him crucified. And I was with you in weakness, and in fear, and in much trembling. And my speech and my preaching was not with enticing words of man's wisdom, but in demonstration of the Spirit and of power: That your faith should not stand in the wisdom of men, but in the power of God." In a similar way in writing to the believers in Thessalonica in 1 Thess. i. 5, "For our Gospel came not unto you in word only, but also in power, and in the Holy Ghost, and in much assurance; as ye know what manner of men we were among you for your sake." We need not only the Holy Spirit to reveal the truth to chosen apostles and prophets in the first place, and the Holy Spirit in the second place to interpret to us as individuals the truth He has thus revealed, but in the third place, we need the Holy Spirit to enable us to effectually communicate to others the truth which He Himself has interpreted to us. We need Him all along the line. One great cause of real failure in the ministry, even when there is seeming success, and not only in the regular ministry but in all forms of service as well, comes from the attempt to teach by "enticing words of man's wisdom" (that is, by the arts of human logic, rhetoric, persuasion and eloquence) what the Holy Spirit has taught us. What is needed is Holy Ghost power, "demonstration of the Spirit and of power." There are three causes of failure in preaching to-day. First, Some other message is taught than the message which the Holy Spirit has revealed in the Word. (Men preach science, art, literature, philosophy, sociology, history, economics, experience, etc., and not the simple Word of God as found in the Holy Spirit's Book,—the Bible.) Second, The Spirit-taught message of the Bible is studied and sought to be apprehended by the natural understanding, that is, without the Spirit's illumination. How common that is, even in institutions where men are being trained for the ministry, even institutions which may be altogether orthodox. Third, The Spirit-given message, the Word, the Bible studied and apprehended under the Holy Ghost's illumination is given out to others with "enticing words of man's wisdom," and not in "demonstration of the Spirit and of power." We need, and we are absolutely dependent upon the Spirit all along the line. He must teach us how to speak as well as what to speak. His must be the power as well as the message.

XVII: Praying, Returning Thanks, Worshipping in the Holy Spirit

Two of the most deeply significant passages in the Bible on the subject of the Holy Spirit and on the subject of prayer are found in Jude 20 and Eph. vi. 18. In Jude 20 we read, "But ye, beloved, building up yourselves on your most holy faith, *praying in the Holy Ghost*," and in Eph. vi. 18, "*Praying* always with all prayer and supplication *in the Spirit*, and watching thereunto with all perseverance and supplication for all saints."

These passages teach us distinctly that *the Holy Spirit guides the believer in prayer*. The disciples did not know how to pray as they ought so they came to Jesus and said, "Lord, teach us to pray" (Luke xi. 1). We to-day do not know how to pray as we ought—we do not know what to pray for, nor how to ask for it—but there is One who is always at hand to help (John xiv. 16, 17) and He knows what we should pray for. He helps our infirmity in this matter of prayer as in other matters (Rom. viii. 26, R. V.). He teaches us to pray. True prayer is prayer in the Spirit (*i. e.*, the prayer that the Holy Spirit inspires and directs). The prayer in which the Holy Spirit leads us is the prayer "according to the will of God" (Rom. viii. 27). When we ask anything according to God's will, we know that He hears us and we know that He has granted the things that we ask (1 John v. 14, 15). We may know it is ours at the moment when we pray just as surely as we know it afterwards when we have it in our actual possession. But how can we know the will of God when we pray? In two ways: First of all, by what is written in His Word; all the promises in the Bible are sure and if God promises anything in the Bible, we may be sure it is His will to give us that thing; but there are many things that we need which are not specifically promised in the Word and still even in that case it is our privilege to know the will of God, for it is the work of the Holy Spirit to teach us God's will and lead us out in prayer along the line of God's will. Some object to the Christian doctrine of prayer; for they say that it teaches that we can go to God in our ignorance and change His will and subject His infinite wisdom to our erring foolishness. But that is not the Christian doctrine of prayer at all; the Christian doctrine of prayer is that it is the believer's privilege to be taught by the Spirit of God Himself to know what the will of God is and not to ask for the things that our foolishness would prompt us to ask for but to ask for things that the never-erring Spirit of God prompts us to ask for. True prayer is prayer "in the Spirit," that is, the prayer which the Spirit inspires and directs. When we come into God's presence, we should recognize our infirmity, our ignorance of what is best for us, our ignorance of what we should pray for, our ignorance of how we should pray for it and in the consciousness of our utter inability to pray aright look up to the Holy Spirit to teach us to pray, and cast ourselves utterly upon Him to direct our prayers and to lead out our desires and guide our utterance of them. There is no place where we need to recognize our ignorance more than we do in prayer. Rushing heedlessly into God's presence and asking the first thing that comes into our minds, or that some other thoughtless one asks us to pray for, is not praying "in the Holy Spirit" and is not true prayer. We must wait for the Holy Spirit and surrender ourselves to the Holy Spirit. The prayer that God, the Holy Spirit, inspires is the prayer that God, the Father, answers.

The longings which the Holy Spirit begets in our hearts are often too deep for utterance, too deep apparently for clear and definite comprehension on the part of the believer himself in whom the Spirit is working—"The Spirit Himself maketh intercession for us *with groanings which cannot be uttered*" (Rom. viii. 26, R. V.). God Himself "must search the heart" to know what is "the mind of the Spirit" in these unuttered and unutterable longings. But God does know what is the mind of the Spirit; He does know what these Spirit-given longings which we cannot put into words mean, even if we do not, and these longings are "according to the will of God," and God grants them. It is in this way that it comes to pass that God is able to do exceedingly abundantly above all that we ask or think, according to the power that worketh in us (Eph. iii. 20). There are other times when the Spirit's leadings are so clear that we pray with the Spirit and with the understanding also (1 Cor. xiv. 15). We distinctly understand what it is that the Holy Spirit leads us to pray for.

II. *The Holy Spirit inspires the believer and guides him in thanksgiving* as well as in prayer. We read in Eph. v. 18-20, R. V., "And be not drunken with wine, wherein is riot, but be filled with the Spirit; speaking one to another in psalms and hymns and spiritual songs, singing and making melody with your heart to the Lord; *giving thanks always* for all things in the name of our Lord Jesus Christ to God, even the Father." Not only does the Holy Spirit teach us to pray, He also teaches us to render thanks. One of the most prominent characteristics of the Spirit-filled life is thanksgiving. On the Day of Pentecost, when the disciples were filled with the Holy Spirit, and spoke as the Spirit gave them utterance, we hear them telling the wonderful works of God (Acts ii. 4, 11), and to-day when any believer is filled with the Holy Spirit, he always becomes filled with thanksgiving and praise. True thanksgiving is "*to* God, even the Father," *through*, or "in the name of" our Lord Jesus Christ, *in* the Holy Spirit.

III. *The Holy Spirit inspires worship* on the part of the believer. We read in Phil. iii. 3, R. V., "For we are the circumcision, who *worship by the Spirit of God*, and glory in Christ Jesus, and have no confidence in the flesh." Prayer is not worship; thanksgiving is not worship. Worship is a definite act of the creature in relation to God. Worship is bowing before God in adoring acknowledgment and contemplation of Himself and the perfection of His being. Some one has said, "In our prayers, we are taken up with our needs; in our thanksgiving we are taken up with our blessings; in our worship, we are taken up with Himself." There is no true and acceptable worship except that which the Holy Spirit prompts and directs. "God is a Spirit and they that worship Him must worship Him *in Spirit* and truth; for such doth the Father seek to be His worshippers" (John iv. 24, 23). The flesh seeks to intrude into every sphere of life. The flesh has its worship as well as its lusts. The worship which the flesh prompts is an abomination unto God. In this we see the folly of any attempt at a congress of religions where the representatives of radically different religions attempt to worship together.

Not all earnest and honest worship is worship in the Spirit. A man may be very honest and very earnest in his worship and still not have submitted himself to the guidance of the Holy Spirit in the matter and so his worship is in the flesh. Oftentimes even when there is great loyalty to the letter of the Word, worship may not be "in the Spirit," *i. e.*, inspired and directed by Him. To worship aright, as Paul puts it, we must have "no confidence in the flesh," that is, we must recognize the utter inability of the flesh (our natural self as contrasted to the Divine Spirit that dwells in and should mold everything in the believer) to worship acceptably. And we must also realize the danger that there is that the flesh intrude itself into our worship. In utter self-distrust and self-abnegation we must cast ourselves upon the Holy Spirit to lead us aright in our worship. Just as we must renounce any merit in ourselves and cast ourselves upon Christ and His work for us upon the cross for justification, just so we must renounce any supposed capacity for good in ourselves and cast ourselves utterly upon the Holy Spirit and His work in us, in holy living, knowing, praying, thanking and *worshipping* and all else that we are to do.

XVIII: The Holy Spirit Sending Men Forth to Definite Lines of Work

We read in Acts xiii. 2-4, "As they ministered to the Lord, and fasted, *the Holy Ghost said, Separate Me* Barnabas and Saul for the work whereunto I have called them. And when they had fasted and prayed, and laid their hands on them, they sent them away. So they, being *sent forth by the Holy Ghost*, departed into Seleucia; and from thence they sailed to Cyprus." It is evident from this passage that *the Holy Spirit calls men into definite lines of work and sends them forth into the work*. He not only calls men in a general way into Christian work, but selects the specific work and points it out. Many a one is asking to-day, and many another ought to ask, "Shall I go to China, to Africa, to India?" There is only one Person who can rightly settle that question for you and that Person is the Holy Spirit. You cannot settle the question for yourself, much less can any other man settle it rightly for you. Not every Christian man is called to go to China; not every Christian man is called to go to Africa; not every Christian man is called to go to the foreign field at all. God alone knows whether He wishes you in any of these places, but He is willing to show you. In a day such as we live in, when there is such a need of the right men and the right women on the foreign field, every young and healthy and intellectually competent Christian man and woman should definitely offer themselves to God for the foreign field and ask Him if He wants them to go. But they ought not to go until He, by His Holy Spirit, makes it plain.

The great need in all lines of Christian work to-day is men and women whom the Holy Ghost calls and sends forth. We have plenty of men and women whom men have called and sent forth. We have plenty of men and women who have called themselves, for there are many to-day who object strenuously to being sent forth by men, by any organization of any kind, but, in fact, are what is immeasurably worse, sent forth by themselves and not by God.

How does the Holy Spirit call? The passage before us does not tell us how the Holy Spirit spoke to the group of prophets and teachers in Antioch, telling them to separate

Barnabas and Saul to the work to which He had called them. It is presumably purposely silent on this point. Possibly it is silent on this point lest we should think that the Holy Spirit must always call in precisely the same way. There is nothing whatever to indicate that He spoke by an audible voice, much less is there anything to indicate that He made His will known in any of the fantastic ways in which some in these days profess to discern His leading—as for example, by twitchings of the body, by shuddering, by opening of the Bible at random and putting his finger on a passage that may be construed into some entirely different meaning than that which the inspired author intended by it. The important point is, He made His will clearly known, and He is willing to make His will clearly known to us to-day. Sometimes He makes it known in one way and sometimes in another, but He will make it known.

But *how shall we receive the Holy Spirit's call*? First of all, by desiring it; second, by earnestly seeking it; third, by waiting upon the Lord for it; fourth, by expecting it. The record reads, "As they *ministered to the Lord, and fasted*." They were waiting upon the Lord for His direction. For the time being they had turned their back utterly upon worldly cares and enjoyments, even upon those things which were perfectly proper in their place. Many a man is saying to-day in justification for his staying home from the foreign field, "I have never had a call." But how do you know that? Have you been listening for a call? God usually speaks in a still small voice and it is only the listening ear that can catch it. Have you ever definitely offered yourself to God to send you where He will? While no man or woman ought to go to China or Africa or other foreign field unless they are clearly and definitely called, they ought each to offer themselves to God for this work and be ready for the call and be listening sharply that they may hear the call if it comes. Let it be borne distinctly in mind that a man needs no more definite call to Africa than to Boston, or New York, or London, or any other desirable field at home.

The Holy Spirit not only calls men and sends them forth into definite lines of work, but He also *guides in the details of daily life and service as to where to go and where not to go, what to do and what not to do*. We read in Acts viii. 27-29, R. V., "And he (Philip) arose and went: and behold, a man of Ethiopia, a eunuch of great authority under Candace, queen of the Ethiopians, who was over all her treasure, who had come to Jerusalem for to worship; and he was returning and sitting in his chariot, and was reading the prophet Isaiah. *And the Spirit said* unto Philip, Go near, and join thyself to this chariot." Here we see the Spirit guiding Philip in the details of service into which He had called him. In a similar way, we read in Acts xvi. 6, 7, R. V., "And they went through the region of Phrygia and Galatia, *having been forbidden of the Holy Ghost to speak the word in Asia*; and when they were come over against Mysia, they assayed to go into Bithynia; and *the Spirit of Jesus suffered them not*." Here we see the Holy Spirit directing Paul where not to go. It is possible for us to have the unerring guidance of the Holy Spirit at every turn of life. Take, for example, our personal work. It is manifestly not God's intention that we speak to every one we meet. To attempt to do so would be to attempt the impossible, and we would waste much time in trying to speak to people where we could do no good that might be used in speaking to people where we could accomplish something. There are some to whom it would be wise for us to speak. There are others to whom it would be unwise for us to speak. Time spent on them would be taken from work that would be more to God's glory. Doubtless as Philip journeyed towards Gaza, he met many before he met the one of whom the Spirit said, "Go near, and join thyself to this chariot." The Spirit is as ready to guide us as He was to guide Philip. Some years ago, a Christian worker in Toronto had the impression that he should go to the hospital and speak to some one there. He thought to himself, "Whom do I know at the hospital at this time?" There came to his mind one whom he knew was at the hospital, and he hurried to the hospital, but as he sat down by his side to talk with him, he realized it was not for this man that he was sent. He got up to lift a window. What did it all mean? There was another man lying across the passage from the man he knew and the thought came to him that this might be the man to whom he should speak. And he turned and spoke to this man and had the privilege of leading him to Christ. There was apparently nothing serious in the man's case. He had suffered some injury to his knee and there was no thought of a serious issue, but that man passed into eternity that night. Many instances of a similar character could be recorded and prove from experience that the Holy Spirit is as ready to guide those who seek His guidance to-day as He was to guide the early disciples. But He is ready to guide us, not only in our more definite forms of Christian work but in all the affairs of life, business, study, everything we have to do. There is no promise in the Bible more plainly explicit than James i. 5-7, R. V., "But if any of you lack wisdom, let him ask of God, who giveth to all liberally and upbraideth not; and it shall be given him. But let him ask in faith, nothing doubting: for he that doubteth is like the surge of the sea driven by the wind and tossed. For let not that man think that he shall receive anything of the Lord." This passage not only promises God's wisdom but tells us specifically just what to do to obtain it. There are really five steps stated or implied in the passage:

1. That we "lack wisdom." We must be conscious of and fully admit our own inability to decide wisely. Here is where oftentimes we fail to receive God's wisdom. We think we are able to decide for ourselves or at least we are not ready to admit our own utter inability to decide. There must be an entire renunciation of the wisdom of the flesh.

2. *We must really desire to know God's way and be willing at any cost to do God's will.* This is implied in the word "*ask.*" The asking must be sincere, and if we are not willing to do God's will, whatever it may be, at any cost, the asking is not sincere. This is a point of fundamental importance. There is nothing that goes so far to make our minds clear in the discernment of the will of God as revealed by His Spirit as an absolutely surrendered will. Here we find the reason why men oftentimes do not know God's will and have the Spirit's guidance. They are not willing to do whatever the Spirit leads at any cost. It is he that "*willeth to* do His will" who shall know, not only of the doctrine, but he shall know his daily duty. Men oftentimes come to me and say, "I cannot find out the will of God," but when I put to them the question, "Are you willing to do the will of God at any cost?" they admit that they are not. The way that is very obscure when we hold back from an absolute surrender to God becomes as clear as day when we make that surrender.

3. *We must definitely "ask" guidance.* It is not enough to desire; it is not enough to be willing to obey; we must *ask*, definitely ask, God to show us the way.

4. *We must confidently expect guidance.* "Let him ask in faith nothing doubting," There are many and many who cannot find the way, though they ask God to show it to them, simply because they have not the absolutely undoubting expectation that God will show them the way. God promises to show it if we expect it confidently. When you come to God in prayer to show you what to do, know for a certainty that He will show you. In what way He will show you, He does not tell, but He promises that He will show you and that is enough.

5. *We must follow step by step as the guidance comes.* As said before, just how it will come, no one can tell, but it will come. Oftentimes only a step will be made clear at a time; that is all we need to know—the next step. Many are in darkness because they do not know and cannot find what God would have them do next week, or next month or next

year. A college man once came to me and told me that he was in great darkness about God's guidance, that he had been seeking, to find the will of God and learn what his life's work should be, but he could not find it. I asked him how far along he was in his college course. He said his sophomore year. I asked, "What is it you desire to know?" "What I shall do when I finish college." "Do you know that you ought to go through college?" "Yes." This man not only knew what he ought to do next year but the year after but still he was in great perplexity because he did not know what he ought to do when these two years were ended. God delights to lead His children a step at a time. He leads us as He led the children of Israel. "And when the cloud was taken up from the tabernacle, then after that the children of Israel journeyed: and in the place where the cloud abode, there the children of Israel pitched their tents. At the commandment of the Lord the children of Israel journeyed, and at the commandment of the Lord they pitched: as long as the cloud abode upon the tabernacle they rested in their tents. And when the cloud tarried long upon the tabernacle many days, then the children of Israel kept the charge of the Lord, and journeyed not. And so it was, when the cloud was a few days upon the tabernacle; according to the commandment of the Lord they journeyed. And so it was, when the cloud abode from even unto the morning, and that the cloud was taken up in the morning then they journeyed: whether it was by day or by night that the cloud was taken up, they journeyed. Or whether it were two days, or a month, or a year, that the cloud tarried upon the tabernacle, remaining thereon, the children of Israel abode in their tents, and journeyed not: but when it was taken up, they journeyed. At the commandment of the Lord they rested in the tents, and at the commandment of the Lord they journeyed: they kept the charge of the Lord, at the commandment of the Lord by the hand of Moses" (Num. ix. 17-23).

Many who have given themselves up to the leading of the Holy Spirit get into a place of great bondage and are tortured because they have leadings which they fear may be from God but of which they are not sure. If they do not obey these leadings, they are fearful they have disobeyed God and sometimes fancy that they have grieved away the Holy Spirit, because they did not follow His leading. This is all unnecessary. Let us settle it in our minds that God's guidance is *clear* guidance. "God is light, and in Him is no darkness at all" (1 John i. 5). And any leading that is not perfectly clear is not from Him. That is, if our wills are absolutely surrendered to Him. Of course, the obscurity may arise from an unsurrendered will. But if our wills are absolutely surrendered to God, we have the right as God's children to be sure that any guidance is from Him before we obey it. We have a right to go to our Father and say, "Heavenly Father, here I am. I desire above all things to do Thy will. Now make it clear to me, Thy child. If this thing that I have a leading to do is Thy will, I will do it, but make it clear as day if it be Thy will." If it is His will, the heavenly Father will make it as clear as day. And you need not, and ought not to do that thing until He does make it clear, and you need not and ought not to condemn yourself because you did not do it. God does not want His children to be in a state of condemnation before Him. He wishes us to be free from all care, worry, anxiety and self-condemnation. Any earthly parent would make the way clear to his child that asked to know it and much more will our heavenly Father make it clear to us, and until He does make it clear, we need have no fears that in not doing it, we are disobeying God. We have no right to dictate to God *how* He shall give His guidance—as, for example, by asking Him to shut up every way, or by asking Him to give a sign, or by guiding us in putting our finger on a text, or in any other way. It is ours to seek and to expect wisdom but it is not ours to dictate how it shall be given. The Holy Spirit divides to "each man severally *as He will*" (1 Cor. xii. 11).

Two things are evident from what has been said about the work of the Holy Spirit. First, how utterly dependent we are upon the work of the Holy Spirit at every turn of Christian life and service. Second, how perfect is the provision for life and service that God has made. How wonderful is the fullness of privilege that is open to the humblest believer through the Holy Spirit's work. It is not so much what we are by nature, either intellectually, morally, physically, or even spiritually, that is important. The important matter is, what the Holy Spirit can do for us and what we will let Him do. Not infrequently, the Holy Spirit takes the one who seems to give the least natural promise and uses him far beyond those who give the greatest natural promise. Christian life is not to be lived in the realm of natural temperament, and Christian work is not to be done in the power of natural endowment, but Christian life is to be lived in the realm of the Spirit, and Christian work is to be done on the power of the Spirit. The Holy Spirit is willing and eagerly desirous of doing for each one of us His whole work, and He will do in each one of us all that we will let Him do.

XIX: The Holy Spirit and the Believer's Body

The Holy Spirit does a work for our bodies as well as for our minds and hearts. We read in Rom. viii. 11, R. V., "But if the Spirit of Him that raised up Jesus from the dead dwelleth in you, He that raised up Christ Jesus from the dead *shall quicken also your mortal bodies through His Spirit* that dwelleth in you."

The Holy Spirit quickens the mortal body of the believer. It is very evident from the context that this refers to the future resurrection of the body (vs. 21-23). The resurrection of the body is the Holy Spirit's work. The glorified body is from Him; it is "a spiritual body." At the present time, we have only the first fruits of the Spirit and are waiting for the full harvest, the redemption of our body (v. 23).

There is, however, a sense in which the Holy Spirit even now quickens our bodies. Jesus tells us in Matt. xii. 28 that He cast out devils by the Spirit of God. And we read in Acts x. 38, "How God anointed Jesus of Nazareth *with the Holy Ghost* and with power, who went about doing good *and healing* all that were oppressed of the devil." In James v. 14, the Apostle writes, "Is any sick among you? Let him call for the elders of the church; and let them pray over him, anointing him with oil in the name of the Lord." The oil in this passage (as elsewhere) is the type of the Holy Spirit, and the truth is set forth that the healing is the Holy Spirit's work. God by His Holy Spirit does impart new health and vigor to these mortal bodies in the present life. To go to the extremes that many do and take the ground that the believer who is walking in fellowship with Christ need never be ill is to go farther than the Bible warrants us in going. It is true that the redemption of our bodies is secured by the atoning work of Christ but until the Lord comes, we only enjoy the first fruits of that redemption; and we are waiting and sometimes groaning for our full place as sons manifested in the redemption of our body (Rom. viii. 23). But while this is true, it is the clear teaching of Scripture and a matter of personal experience on the part of thousands that the life of the Holy Spirit does sweep through these bodies of ours in moments of weakness and of pain and sickness, imparting new health to them, delivering from pain and filling them with abounding life. It is our privilege to know the quickening touch of the Holy Spirit in these bodies as well as in our minds and affections and will. It would be a great day for the Church and for the glory of Jesus Christ, if Christians would renounce forever all the devil's counterfeits of the Holy Spirit's work, Christian Science, Mental Healing, Emmanuelism, Hypnotism and the various other forms of occultism and depend upon God by the power of His Holy Spirit to work that in these bodies of ours which He in His unerring wisdom sees that we most need.

XX: The Baptism With the Holy Spirit

One of the most deeply significant phrases used in connection with the Holy Spirit in the Scriptures is "baptized with the Holy Ghost." John the Baptist was the first to use this phrase. In speaking of himself and the coming One he said, "I indeed baptize you with water unto repentance: but He that cometh after me is mightier than I, whose shoes I am not worthy to bear: *He shall baptize you with the Holy Ghost and with fire*" (Matt. iii. 11). The second "with" in this passage is in italics. It is not found in the Greek. There are not two different baptisms spoken of, the one with the Holy Ghost and one with fire, but one baptism with the Holy Wind and Fire. Jesus afterwards used the same expression. In Acts i. 5, He says, "For John truly baptized with water; but ye shall be *baptized with the Holy Ghost* not many days hence." When this promise of John the Baptist and of our Lord was fulfilled in Acts ii. 3, 4, R. V., we read, "And there appeared unto them tongues parting asunder, like as of fire; and it sat upon each one of them. And they were all filled with the Holy Spirit." Here we have another expression "*filled with the Holy Spirit*" used synonymously with "baptized with the Holy Spirit."

We read again in Acts x. 44-46, "While Peter yet spake these words, *the Holy Ghost fell on* all them which heard the word. And they of the circumcision which believed were astonished, as many as came with Peter, because that on the Gentiles also was *poured out the gift of the Holy Ghost*. For they heard them speak with tongues, and magnify God." Peter himself afterwards describing this experience in Jerusalem tells the story in this way, "And as I began to speak, *the Holy Ghost fell on them*, as on us at the beginning. Then remembered I the word of the Lord, how that He said, John indeed baptized with water; but *ye shall be baptized with the Holy Ghost*. Forasmuch then as *God gave them the like gift as He did unto us* who believed on the Lord Jesus Christ; what was I, that I could withstand God?" (Acts xi. 15-17). Here Peter distinctly calls the experience which came to Cornelius and his household, being *baptized with the Holy Ghost*, so we see that the expression "the Holy Ghost fell" and "the gift of the Holy Ghost" are practically synonymous expressions with "baptized with the Holy Ghost." Still other expressions are used to describe this blessing, such as "receive the Holy Ghost" (Acts ii. 38; xix. 2-6); "the Holy Ghost came on them" (Acts xix. 2-6); "gift of the Holy Ghost" (Heb. ii. 4; 1 Cor. xii. 4, 11, 13); "I send the promise of My Father upon you;" and "endued with power from on high" (Luke xxiv. 49).

What is the baptism with the Holy Spirit?

In the first place *the baptism with the Holy Spirit is a definite experience of which one may and ought to know whether he has received it or not*. This is evident from our Lord's command to His disciples in Luke xxiv. 49 and in Acts i. 4, that they should not depart from Jerusalem to undertake the work which He had commissioned them to do until they had received this promise of the Father. It is also evident from the eighth chapter of Acts, fifteenth and sixteenth verses, where we are distinctly told, "*the Holy Spirit had not as yet fallen upon any of them*." It is evident also from the nineteenth chapter of the Acts of the Apostles, the second verse, R. V., where Paul put to the little group of disciples at Ephesus the definite question, "Did ye receive the Holy Ghost when ye believed?" It is evident that the receiving of the Holy Ghost was an experience so definite that one could answer yes or no to the question whether they had received the Holy Spirit. In this case the disciples definitely answered, "No," that they did not so much as hear whether the Holy Ghost was given. They did not say what our Authorized Version makes them say, that they did not so much as hear whether there was any Holy Ghost. They knew that there was a Holy Ghost; they knew furthermore that there was a definite promise of the baptism with the Holy Ghost, but they had not heard that that promise had been as yet fulfilled. Paul told them that it had and took steps whereby they were definitely baptized with the Holy Spirit before that meeting closed. It is equally evident from Gal. iii. 2 that the baptism with the Holy Spirit is a definite experience of which one may know whether he has received it or not. In this passage Paul says to the believers in Galatia, "This only would I learn of you, Received ye the Spirit by the works of the law, or by the hearing of faith?" Their receiving the Spirit had been so definite as a matter of personal consciousness, that Paul could appeal to it as a ground for his argument. In our day there is much talk about the baptism with the Holy Spirit and prayer for the baptism with the Spirit that is altogether vague and indefinite. Men arise in meeting and pray that they may be baptized with the Holy Spirit, and if you should go afterwards to the one who offered the prayer and put to him the question, "Did you receive what you asked? Were you baptized with the Holy Spirit?" it is quite likely that he would hesitate and falter and say, "I hope so"; but there is none of this indefiniteness in the Bible. The Bible is clear as day on this, as on every other point. It sets forth an experience so definite and so real, that one may know whether or not he has received the baptism with the Holy Spirit, and can answer yes or no to the question, "Have you received the Holy Ghost?"

In the second place it is evident that *the baptism with the Holy Spirit is an operation of the Holy Spirit distinct from and additional to His regenerating work.* This is evident from Acts i. 5, "For John truly baptized with water; but ye *shall be* baptized with the Holy Ghost *not many days hence.*" It is clear then that the disciples had not as yet been baptized with the Holy Ghost, that they were to be thus baptized not many days hence. But the men to whom Jesus spoke these words were already regenerate men. They had been so pronounced by our Lord Himself. He had said to them in John xv. 3, "Now ye are *clean through the word* which I have spoken unto you." But what does clean through the word mean? 1 Peter i. 23 answers the question, "*Being born again*, not of corruptible seed, but of incorruptible, *by the word of God*, which liveth and abideth forever." A little earlier on the same night Jesus had said to them in John xiii. 10, R. V., "He that is bathed needeth not save to wash his feet, but is clean every whit: and *ye are clean but not all.*" The Lord Jesus had pronounced that apostolic company clean—*i. e.*, regenerate men—with the exception of the one who never was a regenerate man, Judas Iscariot who should betray Him (see verse 11). The remaining eleven Jesus Christ had pronounced regenerate men. Yet He tells these same men in Acts i. 5, that the baptism with the Holy Spirit was an experience that they had not as yet realized, that still lay in the future. So it is evident that it is one thing to be born again by the Holy Spirit through the Word and something distinct from this and additional to it to be baptized with the Holy Spirit. The same thing is evident from Acts viii. 12, R. V., compared with the fifteenth and sixteenth verses of the same chapter. In the twelfth verse we read that a large company of disciples had believed the preaching of Philip concerning the kingdom of God *and the name of Jesus Christ*, and "had been baptized into the name of the Lord Jesus" (v. 16, R. V.). Certainly in this company of baptized believers there were at least some regenerate persons. Whatever the true form of water baptism may be, they undoubtedly had been baptized by the true form, for the baptizing had been done by a Spirit-commissioned man, but in the fifteenth and sixteenth verses we read, "When they (that is Peter and John) were come down, they prayed for them, that they might receive the Holy Ghost: for as yet He was fallen upon none of them: only they had been baptized into the name of the Lord Jesus." Baptized believers they were; baptized into the name of the Lord Jesus they had been; regenerate men some of them most assuredly were, and yet not one of them as yet had received, or been baptized with, the Holy Ghost. So again, it is evident that the baptism with the Holy Spirit is an operation of the Holy Spirit distinct from and additional to His regenerating work. A man may be regenerated by the Holy Spirit and still not be baptized with the Holy Spirit. In regeneration, there is the impartation of life by the Spirit's power, and the one who receives it is saved: in the baptism with the Holy Spirit, there is the impartation of power, and the one who receives it is fitted for service. The baptism with the Holy Spirit, however, may take place at the moment of regeneration. It did, for example, in the household of Cornelius. We read in Acts x. 43, that while Peter was preaching, he came to the point where he said concerning Jesus, "To Him bear all the prophets witness, that through His name whosoever believeth in Him shall receive remission of sins," and at that point Cornelius and his household believed and we read immediately, "While Peter yet spake these words, the Holy Ghost fell on all them which heard the word. And they of the circumcision which believed were astonished, as many as came with Peter, because that on the Gentiles also was poured out the gift of the Holy Ghost." The moment they believed the testimony about Jesus, they were baptized with the Holy Ghost, even before they were baptized with water. Regeneration and the baptism with the Holy Spirit took place practically at the same moment, and so they do in many an experience to-day. It would seem as if in a normal condition of the church, this would be the usual experience. But the church is not in a normal condition to-day. A very large part of the church is in the place where the believers in Samaria were before Peter and John came down, and where the disciples in Ephesus were before Paul came and told them of their larger privilege—baptized believers, baptized into the name of the Lord Jesus, baptized unto repentance and remission of sins, but not as yet baptized with the Holy Ghost. Nevertheless *the baptism with the Holy Spirit is the birthright of every believer*. It was purchased for us by the atoning death of Christ, and when He ascended to the right hand of the Father, He received the promise of the Father and shed Him forth upon the church, and if any one to-day has not the baptism with the Holy Spirit as a personal experience, it is because he has not claimed his birthright. Potentially, every member of the body of Christ is baptized with the Holy Spirit (1 Cor. xii. 13), "For in one Spirit, *we were all* baptized into one body, whether we be Jews or Gentiles, whether we be bond or free; and have been all made to drink into one Spirit." But there are many believers with whom that which is potentially theirs has not become a matter of real, actual, personal experience. All men are potentially justified in the atoning death of Jesus Christ on the cross, that is justification is provided for them and belongs to them (Rom. v. 18, R. V.), but what potentially belongs to every man, each man must appropriate to himself by faith in Christ; then justification is actually and experimentally his and just so, while the baptism with the Holy Spirit is potentially the possession of every believer, each individual believer must appropriate it for himself before it is experimentally his. We may go still further than this and say that it is only by the baptism with the Holy Spirit that one becomes in the fullest sense a member of the body of Christ, because it is only by the baptism with the Spirit that he receives power to perform those functions for which God has appointed him as a part of the body.

As we have already seen every true believer has the Holy Spirit (Rom. viii. 9), but not every believer has the baptism with the Holy Spirit (though every believer may have as we have just seen). It is one thing to have the Holy Spirit dwelling within us, perhaps dwelling within us way back in some hidden sanctuary of our being, back of definite consciousness, and something far different, something vastly more, to have the Holy Spirit taking complete possession of the one whom He inhabits. There are those who press the fact that every believer potentially has the baptism with the Spirit, to such an extent that they clearly teach that every believer has the baptism with the Spirit as an actual experience. But unless the baptism with the Spirit to-day is something radically different from what the baptism with the Spirit was in the early church, indeed unless it is something not at all real, then either a very large proportion of those whom we ordinarily consider believers are not believers, or else one may be a believer and a regenerate man without having been baptized with the Holy Spirit. Certainly, this was the case in the early church. It was the case with the Apostles before Pentecost; it was the case with the church in Ephesus; it was the case with the church in Samaria. And there are thousands to-day who can testify to having received Christ and been born again, and then afterwards, sometimes long afterwards, having been baptized with the Holy Ghost as a definite experience. This is a matter of great practical importance, for there are many who are not enjoying the fullness of privilege that they might enjoy because by pushing individual verses in the Scriptures beyond what they will bear and against the plain teaching of the Scriptures as a whole, they are trying to persuade themselves that they have already been baptized with the Holy Spirit when they have not. And if they would only admit to themselves that they had not, they could then take the steps whereby they would be baptized with the Holy Spirit as a matter of definite, personal experience.

The next thing which is clear from the teaching of Scripture is that *the baptism with the Holy Spirit is always connected with, and primarily for the purpose of testimony and service.*

Our Lord in speaking of this baptism which they were so soon to receive in Luke xxiv. 49 said, "And behold I send the promise of My Father upon you: but tarry ye in the city of Jerusalem, until ye be *endued with power from on high.*" And again He said in Acts i. 5, 8, "For John truly baptized with water; but ye shall be baptized with the Holy Ghost not many days hence.... But *ye shall receive power* after that the Holy Ghost is come upon you: and *ye shall be witnesses unto Me*, both in Jerusalem, and in all Judea, and in Samaria, and unto the uttermost part of the earth." In the record of the fulfillment of this promise of our Lord in Acts ii. 4, we read, "And they were all filled with the Holy Ghost and began to speak with other tongues as the Spirit gave them utterance." Then follows the detailed account of what Peter said and of the result. The result was that Peter and the other Apostles spoke with such power that three thousand persons that day were convicted of sin, renounced their sin and confessed their acceptance of Jesus Christ in baptism and continued steadfastly in the Apostles' doctrine and fellowship and in the breaking of bread and in prayers ever afterwards. In the fourth chapter of Acts, the thirty-first to the thirty-third verses, we read that when the Apostles on another occasion were filled with the Holy Spirit, the result was that they "*spake the word of God with boldness*" and that "*with great power gave the Apostles their witness to the resurrection of the Lord Jesus.*" And in the ninth chapter of the Acts of the Apostles, we have a description of Paul's being baptized with the Holy Spirit. We read in the seventeenth to the twentieth verses, "And Ananias went his way, and entered into the house; and putting his hands on him said, Brother Saul, the Lord, even Jesus, that appeared unto thee in the way as thou camest, hath sent me, that thou mightest receive thy sight, and *be filled with the Holy Ghost*. And immediately there fell from his eyes as it had been scales: and he received sight forthwith, and arose, and was baptized. And when he had received meat, he was strengthened.... And *straightway, he preached Christ* in the synagogues, that He is the Son of God," and in the twenty-second verse we read that he "confounded the Jews which dwelt at Damascus, proving that this is the Christ" (R. V.). In 1 Cor. xii. we have the fullest discussion of the baptism with the Holy Spirit found in any passage in the Bible. This is the classical passage on the whole subject. And the results there recorded are gifts for service. The baptism with the Holy Spirit is not primarily intended to make believers happy, but to make them useful. It is not intended merely for the ecstasy of the individual believer, it is intended primarily for his efficiency in service. I do not say that the baptism with the Holy Spirit will not make the believer happy; for as part of the fruit of the Spirit is "joy," if one is baptized with the Holy Spirit, joy must inevitably result. I have never known one to be baptized with the Holy Spirit into whose life there did not come, sooner or later, a new joy, a higher and purer and fuller joy than he had ever known before. But this is not the prime purpose of the baptism nor the most important and prominent result. Great emphasis needs to be laid upon this point, for there are many Christians who in seeking the baptism with the Spirit are seeking personal ecstasy and rapture. They go to conventions and conferences for the deepening of the Christian life and come back and tell what a wonderful blessing they have received, referring to some new ecstasy that has come into their heart, but when you watch them, it is difficult to see that they are any more useful to their pastors or their churches than they were before, and one is compelled to think that whatever they have received, they have not received the real baptism with the Holy Spirit. Ecstasies and raptures are all right in their places. When they come, thank God for them—the writer knows something about them—but in a world such as we live in to-day where sin and self-righteousness and unbelief are so triumphant, where there is such an awful tide of men, women and young people sweeping on towards eternal perdition, I would rather go through my whole life and never have one touch of ecstasy but have power to witness for Christ and win others for Christ and thus to save them, than to have raptures 365 days in the year but no power to stem the awful tide of sin and bring men, women and children to a saving knowledge of my Lord and Savior, Jesus Christ.

The purpose of the baptism with the Holy Spirit is not primarily to make believers individually holy. I do not say that it is not the work of the Holy Spirit to make believers holy, for as we have already seen, He is "the Spirit of Holiness," and the only way we shall ever attain unto holiness is by His power. I do not even say that the baptism with the Holy Spirit will not result in a great spiritual transformation and uplift and cleansing, for the promise is, "He shall baptize you with the Holy Spirit *and fire*" (and the thought of fire as used in this connection is the thought of searching, refining, cleansing, consuming). A wonderful transformation took place in the Apostles at Pentecost, and a wonderful transformation has taken place in thousands who have been baptized with the Holy Spirit since Pentecost, *but the primary purpose of the baptism with the Holy Spirit is efficiency in testimony and service*. It has to do rather with gifts for service than with graces of character. It is the impartation of spiritual power or gifts in service and sometimes one may have rare gifts by the Spirit's power and yet manifest few of the graces of the Spirit. (See 1 Cor. xiii. 1-3; Matt. vii. 22, 23.) In every passage in the Bible in which the baptism with the Holy Spirit is mentioned, it is connected with testimony or service.

We shall perhaps get a clearer idea of just what the baptism with the Holy Spirit is, if we stop to consider what are the results of the baptism with the Holy Spirit.

What Are The Results Of The Baptism With The Holy Spirit?

1. *The specific manifestations of the baptism with the Holy Spirit are not precisely the same in all persons.* This appears very clearly from 1 Cor. xii. 4-13, "Now there are diversities of gifts, but the same Spirit. And there are differences of administrations, but the same Lord. And there are diversities of operations, but it is the same God which worketh all in all. But the manifestation of the Spirit is given to every man to profit withal. For to one is given by the Spirit the word of wisdom; to another the word of knowledge by the same Spirit; to another faith by the same Spirit; to another the gifts of healing by the same Spirit; to another the working of miracles; to another prophecy; to another discerning of spirits; to another divers kind of tongues; to another the interpretation of tongues: but all these worketh that one and the selfsame Spirit, dividing to every man severally as He will. For as the body is one, and hath many members, and all the members of that one body, being many, are one body: so also is Christ. For by one Spirit are we all baptized into one body, whether we be Jews or Gentiles, whether we be bond or free; and have been all made to drink into one Spirit." Here we see one baptism but a great variety of manifestations of the power of that baptism. There are diversities of gifts, but the same Spirit. The gifts vary with the different lines of service to which God calls different persons. The church is a body, and different members of the body have different functions and the Spirit imparts to the one who is baptized with the Spirit those gifts which fit him for the service to which God has called him. It is very important to bear this in mind. Through the failure to see this, many have gone entirely astray on the whole subject. In my early study of the subject, I noticed the fact that in many instances those who were baptized with the Holy Spirit spake with tongues (*e. g.*, Acts ii. 4; x. 46; xix. 6) and I wondered if every one who was baptized with the Holy Spirit would not speak with tongues. I did not know of any one who was speaking with tongues to-day and so I wondered still further whether the baptism with the Holy Spirit were for the present age. But one day I was studying 1 Cor. xii and noticed how Paul said to the believers in that wonderfully gifted church in Corinth, all of whom had been pronounced in the thirteenth verse to be baptized with the Spirit, "And God hath set some in the church, first apostles, secondarily prophets, thirdly teachers, after that miracles, then gifts of healing, helps, governments, diversities of tongues. Are all apostles? Are all prophets? Are all teachers? Are all workers of miracles? Have all the gift of healing? *Do all speak with tongues?* Do all interpret?" So I saw it was clearly taught in the Scriptures that one might be baptized with the Holy Spirit and still not have the gift of tongues. I saw furthermore that the gift of tongues, according to the Scripture, was the last and the least important of all the gifts, and that we were urged to desire earnestly the greater gifts (1 Cor. xiii. 31; 1 Cor. xiv. 5, 12, 14, 18, 19, 27, 28). A little later I was tempted to fall into another error, more specious but in reality just as unscriptural as this, namely, that if one were baptized with the Holy Spirit, he would receive the gift of an evangelist. I had read the story of D. L. Moody, of Charles G. Finney and of others who were baptized with the Holy Spirit, and of the power that came to them as evangelists, and the thought was suggested that if any one is baptized with the Holy Spirit will not he also obtain power as an evangelist? But this was also unscriptural. If God has called a man to be an evangelist and he is baptized with the Holy Spirit, he will receive power as an evangelist, but if God has called him to be something else, he will receive power to become something else. Three great evils come from the error of thinking that every one who is baptized with the Holy Spirit will receive power as an evangelist.

(1) The evil of disappointment. There are many who seek the baptism with the Holy Spirit expecting power as an evangelist, but God has not called them to that work, and though they really meet the conditions of receiving the baptism with the Spirit, and do receive the baptism with the Spirit, power as an evangelist does not come. In many cases this results in bitter disappointment and sometimes even in despair. The one who has expected the power of an evangelist and has not received it sometimes even questions whether he is a child of God. But if he had properly understood the matter, he would have known that the fact that he had not received power as an evangelist is no proof that he has not received the baptism with the Spirit, and much less is it a proof that he is not a child of God.

(2) The second evil is graver still, namely, the evil of presumption. A man whom God has not called to the work of an evangelist or a minister oftentimes rushes into it because he has received, or imagines he has received, the baptism with the Holy Spirit. He thinks all a man needs to become a preacher is the baptism with the Holy Spirit. This is not true. In order to succeed as a minister a man needs a call to that specific work, and furthermore, he needs that knowledge of God's Word that will prepare him for the work. If a man is called to the ministry and studies the Word until he has something to preach, if then he is baptized with the Holy Spirit, he will have success as a preacher, but if he is not called to that work, or if he has not the knowledge of the Word of God that is necessary, he will not succeed in the work, even though he receives the baptism with the Holy Spirit.

(3) The third evil is greater still, namely, the evil of indifference. There are many who know that they are not called to the work of preaching. If then they think that the baptism with the Holy Spirit simply imparts power as an evangelist, or power to preach, the matter of the baptism with the Holy Spirit is one of no personal concern to them. For example, here is a mother with a large family of children. She knows perfectly well, or at least it is hoped that she knows, that she is not called to do the work of an evangelist. She knows that her duty lies with her children and her home. If she reads or hears about the baptism with the Holy Spirit, and gets the impression that the baptism with the Holy Spirit simply imparts power to do the work of an evangelist, or to preach, she will think "The evangelist needs this blessing, my minister needs this blessing, but it is not for me"; but if she understands the matter as it is taught in the Bible, that while the baptism with the Spirit imparts power, the way in which the power will be manifested depends entirely upon the line of work to which God calls us, and that no efficient work can be done without it, and sees still further that there is no function in the church of Jesus Christ to-day more holy and sacred than that of sanctified motherhood, she will say, "The evangelist may need this baptism, my minister may need this baptism; but I must have it to bring up my children in the nurture and admonition of the Lord."

2. *While there are diversities of gifts and manifestations of the baptism with the Holy Spirit, there will be some gift to every one thus baptized.* We read in 1 Cor. xii. 7, R. V., "But to *each one* is given the manifestation of the Spirit to profit withal." Every most insignificant member of the body of Christ has some function to perform in that body. The body grows by that "which every joint supplieth" (Eph. iv. 16), and to each least significant joint, the Holy Spirit imparts power to perform the function that belongs to him.

3. *It is the Holy Spirit who decides how the baptism with the Spirit shall manifest itself in any given case.* As we read in 1 Cor. xii. 11, "But all these worketh the one and the selfsame Spirit dividing to each one severally, *even as He will.*" The Holy Spirit is absolutely sovereign in deciding how, that is, in what special gift, operation, or power, the

baptism with the Holy Spirit shall manifest itself. It is not for us to pick out some field of service and then ask the Holy Spirit to qualify us for that service. It is not for us to select some gift and then ask the Holy Spirit to impart to us this self-chosen gift. It is for us to simply put ourselves entirely at the disposal of the Holy Spirit to send us where He will, to select for us what kind of service He will and to impart to us what gift He will. He is absolute sovereign and our position is that of unconditional surrender to Him. I am glad that this is so. I rejoice that He, in His infinite wisdom and love, is to select the field of service and the gifts, and that this is not to be left to me in my short-sightedness and folly. It is because of the failure to recognize this absolute sovereignty of the Spirit that many fail of the blessing and meet with disappointment. They are trying to select their own gift and so get none. I once knew an earnest child of God in Scotland, who hearing of the baptism with the Holy Spirit and the power that resulted from it, gave up at a great sacrifice his work as a ship plater, for which he was receiving large wages. He heard that there was a great need of ministers in the northwest in America. He came to the northwest. He met the conditions of the baptism with the Holy Spirit and I believe was really baptized with the Holy Spirit, but God had not chosen him for the work of an evangelist, and the power as an evangelist did not come to him. No field seemed to open, and he was in great despondency. He even questioned his acceptance before God. One morning he came into our church in Minneapolis and heard me speak upon the baptism with the Holy Spirit, and as I pointed out that the baptism with the Holy Spirit manifested itself in many different ways, and the fact that one had not power as an evangelist was no proof that he had not received the baptism with the Holy Spirit, light came into his heart. He put himself unreservedly into God's hands for Him to choose the field of labor and the gifts. An opening soon came to him as a Sunday-school missionary, and then, when he had given up choosing for himself and left it with the Holy Spirit to divide to him as He would, a strange thing happened; he did receive power as an evangelist and went through the country districts in one of our northwestern states with mighty power as an evangelist.

4. *While the power may be of one kind in one person and of another kind in another person, there will always be power, the very power of God, when one is baptized with the Holy Spirit.* We read in Acts i. 5, 8, "For John truly baptized with water; but ye shall be baptized with the Holy Ghost not many days hence.... But *ye shall receive power*, after that the Holy Ghost is come upon you: and ye shall be witnesses unto Me both in Jerusalem, and in all Judea, and in Samaria, and unto the uttermost part of the earth." As truly as any one who reads these pages, who has not already received the baptism with the Holy Spirit, seeks it in God's way, he will obtain it, and there will come into his service a power that was never there before, power for the very work to which God has called him. This is not only the teaching of Scripture; it is the teaching of religious experience throughout the centuries. Religious biographies abound in instances of men who have worked along as best they could, until one day they were led to see that there was such an experience as the baptism with the Holy Spirit and to seek it and obtain it and, from that hour, there came into their service a new power that utterly transformed its character. In this matter, one thinks first of such men as Finney, and Moody, and Brainerd, but cases of this character are not confined to the few exceptional men. They are common. The writer has personally met and corresponded with hundreds and thousands of persons around the globe, who could testify definitely to the new power that God has granted them through the baptism with the Holy Spirit. These thousands of men and women were in all branches of Christian service; some of them are ministers of the Gospel, some evangelists, some mission workers, some Y. M. C. A. secretaries, Sunday-school teachers, fathers, mothers,

personal workers. Nothing could possibly exceed the clearness and the confidence and the joyfulness of many of these testimonies.

I shall not soon forget a minister whom I met some years ago at a State Convention of the Young People's Society of Christian Endeavour at New Britain, Conn. I was speaking upon the subject of personal work and as I drew the address to a close, I said that in order to do effective personal work, we must be baptized with the Holy Spirit, and in a very few sentences explained what I meant by that. At the close of the address, this minister came to me on the platform and said, "I have not this blessing you have been speaking about, but I want it. Will you pray for me?" I said, "Why not pray right now?" He said, "I will." We put two chairs side by side and turned our backs upon the crowd as they passed out of the Armory. He prayed and I prayed that he might be baptized with the Holy Spirit. Then we separated. Some weeks after, one who had witnessed the scene came to me at a convention in Washington and told me how this minister had gone back to his church a transformed man, that now his congregations filled the church, that it was largely composed of young men, and that there were conversions at every service. Some years after, this minister was called to another field of service. His most spiritually-minded friends advised him not to go, as all the ruling elements in the church to which he had been called were against aggressive evangelistic work, but for some reason or other, he felt it was the call of God and accepted it. In six months, there were sixty-nine conversions, and thirty-eight of them were business men of the town.

After attending in Montreal some years ago an Inter-provincial Convention of the Young Men's Christian Association of the Provinces of Canada, I received a letter from a young man. He wrote, "I was present at your last meeting in Montreal. I heard you speak upon the Baptism with the Holy Spirit. I went to my rooms and sought that baptism for myself and received it. I am chairman of the Lookout Committee of the Christian Endeavour Society of our church. I called together the other members of the committee. I found that two of them had been at the meeting and had already been baptized with the Holy Spirit. Then we prayed for the other members of the committee and they were baptized with the Holy Spirit. Now we are going out into the church and the young people of the church are being brought to Christ right along."

A lady and gentleman once came to me at a convention and told me how, though they had never seen me before, they had read the report of an address on the Baptism with the Holy Spirit delivered in Boston at a Christian Workers' Convention and that they had sought this baptism and had received it. The man then told me the blessing that had come into his service as superintendent of the Sunday-school. When he had finished, his wife broke in and said, "Yes, and the best part of it is, I have been able to get into the hearts of my own children, which I was never able to do before." Here were three distinctly different lines of service, but there was power in each case. The results of that power may not, however, be manifest at once in conversions. Stephen was filled with the Holy Spirit, but as he witnessed in the power of the Holy Spirit for his risen Lord, he saw no conversions at the time. All he saw was the gnashing of the teeth, the angry looks and the merciless rocks, and so it may be with us. But there was a conversion, even in that case, though it was a long time before it was seen, and that conversion, the conversion of Saul of Tarsus, was worth more than hundreds of ordinary conversions.

5. Another result of the baptism with the Holy Spirit will be *boldness in testimony and service*. We read in Acts iv. 31, "And when they had prayed, the place was shaken where they were assembled together; and they were all filled with the Holy Ghost, and they *spake the word of God with boldness*." The baptism with the Holy Spirit imparts to those who

receive it new liberty and fearlessness in testimony for Christ. It converts cowards into heroes. Peter upon the night of our Lord's crucifixion proved himself a craven coward. He denied with oaths and curses that he knew the Lord. But after Pentecost, this same Peter was brought before the very council that had condemned Jesus to death, and he himself was threatened, but filled with the Holy Ghost, he said, "Ye rulers of the people, and elders of Israel, if we this day be examined of the good deed done to the impotent man, by what means he is made whole; be it known unto you all, and to all the people of Israel, that by the name of Jesus Christ of Nazareth, *whom ye crucified*, whom God raised from the dead, even by Him doth this man stand here before you whole. This is the stone which was set at naught of you builders, which is become the head of the corner. Neither is there salvation in any other: for there is none other name under heaven given among men, whereby we must be saved" (Acts iv. 8-12). A little later when the council commanded him and his companion, John, not to speak or teach in the name of Jesus, they answered, "Whether it be right in the sight of God to hearken unto you more than unto God, judge ye. For we cannot but speak the things which we have seen and heard" (Acts iv. 19, 20). On a still later occasion, when they were threatened and commanded not to speak and when their lives were in jeopardy, Peter told the council to their faces, "We ought to obey God rather than men. The God of our fathers raised up Jesus, *whom ye slew and hanged on a tree*. Him hath God exalted with His right hand to be a Prince and a Savior, for to give repentance to Israel, and forgiveness of sins. And we are His witnesses of these things; and so is also the Holy Ghost, whom God hath given to them that obey Him" (Acts v. 29-32). The natural timidity of many a man to-day vanishes when he is filled with the Holy Spirit, and with great boldness and liberty, with utter fearlessness of consequences, he gives his testimony for Jesus Christ.

6. *The baptism with the Holy Spirit causes the one who receives it to be occupied with God and Christ and spiritual things.* In the record of the day of Pentecost, we read, "They were all filled with the Holy Ghost and began to speak with other tongues as the Spirit gave them utterance. And they were all amazed and marveled, saying one to another, Behold, are not these which speak Galileans? And how hear we every man in our own tongue, wherein we were born? Cretes and Arabians, we do hear them speak in our tongues *the wonderful works of God"* (Acts ii. 4, 7, 8, 11). Then follows Peter's sermon, a sermon that from start to finish is entirely taken up with Jesus Christ and His glory. On a later day we read, "And when they had prayed, the place was shaken where they were assembled together; and they were all filled with the Holy Ghost, and they *spake the word of God* with boldness. And with great power gave the Apostles *witness of the resurrection of the Lord Jesus*: and great grace was upon them all.... Then Peter, *filled with the Holy Ghost*, said unto them, Ye rulers of the people, and elders of Israel, if we this day be examined of the good deed done to the impotent man, by what means he is made whole; be it known unto you all, and to all the people of Israel, that *by the name of Jesus of Nazareth*, whom ye crucified, whom God raised from the dead, even by Him doth this man stand here before you whole" (Acts iv. 31, 33, 8-10). We read of Saul of Tarsus, that when he had been filled with the Holy Spirit, "Straightway in the synagogues *he proclaimed Jesus*" (Acts ix. 17, 20, R. V.). We read of the household of Cornelius, "While Peter yet spake these words, the Holy Ghost fell on them who heard the Word. And they of the circumcision which believed were astonished, as many as came with Peter, because that on the Gentiles also was poured out the gift of the Holy Ghost. For they heard them speak with tongues, and *magnify God*." Here we see the whole household of Cornelius as soon as they were filled with the Holy Spirit magnifying God. In Eph. v. 18, 19, we are

told that the result of being *filled with the Spirit* is that those who are thus filled will speak to one another in psalms and hymns and spiritual songs, singing and making melody in their hearts *to the Lord*. Men who are filled with the Holy Spirit will not be singing sentimental ballads, not comic ditties, nor operatic airs while the power of the Holy Ghost is upon them. If the Holy Ghost should come upon any one while listening to one of the most innocent of the world's songs, he would not enjoy it, he would long to hear something about Christ. Men who are baptized with the Holy Spirit do not talk much about self but much about God, and especially much about Christ. This is necessarily so, as it is the Holy Spirit's office to bear witness to the glorified Christ (John xv. 26; xvi. 14).

To sum up everything that has been said about the results of the baptism with the Holy Spirit; *the baptism with the Holy Spirit is the Spirit of God coming upon the believer, filling his mind with a real apprehension of truths, especially of Christ, taking possession of his faculties, imparting to him gifts not otherwise his but which qualify him for the service to which God has called him.*

The necessity of the baptism with the Spirit.

The New Testament has much to say about the necessity for the baptism with the Holy Spirit. When our Lord was about to leave His disciples to go to be with the Father, He said, "And, behold, I send the promise of My Father upon you: but *tarry ye in the city of Jerusalem, until ye be endued with power from on high*" (Luke xxiv. 49). He had just commissioned them to be His witnesses to all nations, beginning at Jerusalem (vs. 47, 48), but He here tells them that before they undertake this witnessing, they must wait until they receive the promise of the Father, and were thus endued with power from on high for the work of witnessing which they were to undertake. There is no doubt as to what Jesus meant by "the promise of My Father," for which they were to wait before beginning the ministry that He had laid upon them; for in Acts i. 4, 5, we read, "And being assembled together with them (He), commanded them that they should not depart from Jerusalem, but wait for the promise of the Father, which, saith He, ye have heard of Me. For John truly baptized with water; but ye shall be baptized with the Holy Ghost not many days hence." It is evident then that "the promise of the Father" through which the enduement of power was to come was the baptism with the Holy Spirit. He went on to tell His disciples "Ye shall receive power *after that* the Holy Ghost shall come upon you: and ye shall be witnesses unto Me both in Jerusalem, and in all Judea, and in Samaria, and unto the uttermost part of the earth" (Acts i. 8). Now who were the men to whom Jesus said this? The disciples whom He Himself had trained for the work. For more than three years, they had lived in the closest intimacy with Himself; they had been eye-witnesses of His miracles, of His death, of His resurrection, and in a few moments were to be eye-witnesses of His ascension as He was taken up right before their eyes into heaven. And what were they to do? Simply to go and tell the world what their own eyes had seen and what their own ears had heard from the lips of the Son of God. Were they not equipped for the work? With our modern ideas of preparation for Christian work, we should say that they were thoroughly equipped. But Jesus said, "No, you are not equipped. There is another preparation in addition to the preparation already received, so absolutely necessary for effective work that you must not stir one step until you receive it. This other preparation is the promise of the Father, the baptism with the Holy Spirit." If the Apostles with their altogether exceptional fitting for the work which they were to undertake needed this preparation for work, how much more do we? In the light of what Jesus required of His disciples before undertaking the work, does it not seem like the most daring presumption for any of us to undertake to witness and work for Christ until we also have received the promise of the Father, the baptism with the Holy Spirit? There was apparently imperative need that something be done at once. The whole world was perishing and they alone knew the saving truth, nevertheless Jesus strictly charged them "wait." Could there be a stronger testimony to the absolute necessity and importance of the baptism with the Holy Spirit as a preparation for work that should be acceptable to Christ?

But this is not all. In Acts x. 38 we read, "How *God anointed Jesus of Nazareth with the Holy Ghost and power*; who went about doing good, and healing all that were oppressed of the devil; for God was with Him." To what does this refer in the recorded life of Jesus Christ? If we will turn to Luke iii. 21, 22, and Luke iv. 1, 4, 17, 18, we will get our answer. In Luke iii. 21, 22, R. V., we read that after Jesus had been baptized and was praying, "The heaven was opened, and the Holy Spirit descended in a bodily form, as a dove, upon Him, and a voice came out of heaven, Thou art My beloved Son; in Thee I am well pleased." Then the next thing that we read, with nothing intervening but the human genealogy of Jesus, is "And Jesus, *full of the Holy Spirit*, returned from the Jordan, and was led by the Spirit in the wilderness" (Luke iv. 1). Then follows the story of His temptation; then in the fourteenth verse we read, "And Jesus returned *in the power of the Spirit* into Galilee: and a fame went out concerning Him through all the region round about." And in the seventeenth and eighteenth verses, "And there was delivered unto Him the book of the prophet Isaiah. And He opened the book, and found the place where it was written, The Spirit of the Lord is upon Me, because *He hath anointed Me to preach*, etc." Evidently then, it was at the Jordan in connection with His baptism that Jesus was anointed with the Holy Spirit and power, and He did not enter upon His public ministry until He was thus baptized with the Holy Spirit. And who was Jesus? It is the common belief of Christendom that He had been supernaturally conceived through the Holy Spirit's power, that He was the only begotten Son of God, that He was Divine, very God of very God, and yet truly man. If such an One "leaving us an example that we should follow His steps" did not venture upon His ministry, for which the Father had sent Him, until thus definitely baptized with the Holy Spirit, what is it for us to dare to do it? If in the light of these recorded facts we dare to do it, does it not seem like the most unpardonable presumption? Doubtless it has been done in ignorance by many of us, but can we plead ignorance any longer? It is evident that the baptism with the Holy Spirit is an absolutely necessary preparation for effective work for Christ along every line of service. We may have a very clear call to service, as clear it may be as the Apostles had, but the charge is laid upon us as upon them, that before we begin that service we must tarry until we are clothed with power from on high. This enduement of power is through the baptism with the Holy Spirit.

But this is not all even yet. We read in Acts vii. 14-16, "Now when the Apostles which were at Jerusalem heard that Samaria had received the Word of God, they sent unto them Peter and John: who, when they were come down, *prayed for them, that they might receive the Holy Ghost* (for as yet He was fallen upon none of them: only they were baptized in the name of the Lord Jesus)." There was a great company of happy converts in Samaria, but when Peter and John came down to inspect the work, they evidently felt that there was something so essential that these young disciples had not received that before they did anything else, they must see to it that they received it. In a similar way we read in Acts xix. 1, 2, R. V., "And it came to pass, that, while Apollos was at Corinth, Paul having passed through the upper country came to Ephesus, and found certain disciples: and he said unto them, Did ye receive the Holy Ghost when ye believed?" When he found that they had not received the Holy Spirit, the first thing that he saw to was that they should receive the Holy Spirit. He did not go on with the work with the outsiders until that little group of twelve disciples had been equipped for service. So we see that when the Apostles found believers in Christ, the first thing that they always did was to demand whether they had received the Holy Spirit as a definite experience and if not, they saw to it at once that the steps were taken whereby they should receive the Holy Spirit. It is evident then that *the baptism with the Holy Spirit is absolutely necessary in every Christian for the service that Christ demands and expects of him.* There are certainly few greater mistakes that we are making to-day in our various Christian enterprises than that of setting men to teach Sunday-school classes and do personal work and even to preach the Gospel, because they have been converted and received a certain amount of education, including it may be a college and seminary course, but have not as yet been baptized with the Holy Spirit. We think that if a man is hopefully pious and has had a college and seminary education and comes out of it reasonably orthodox, he is now ready that we should lay our hands upon him and ordain him to preach the Gospel. But Jesus Christ says, "No." There is another preparation so all essential that a man must not undertake this work until he has received it. "Tarry ye (literally 'sit ye down') until ye be endued with power from on high." A distinguished theological professor has said that the question ought to be put to every candidate for the ministry, "Have you met God?" Yes, but we ought to go farther than this and be even more definite; to every candidate for the ministry we should put the question, "Have you been baptized with the Holy Spirit?" and if not, we should say to him as Jesus said to the first preachers of the Gospel, "Sit down until you are endued with power from on high."

But not only is this true of ordained ministers, it is true of every Christian, for all Christians are called to ministry of some kind. Any man who is in Christian work, who has not received the baptism with the Holy Spirit, ought to stop his work right where he is and not go on with it until he has been "clothed with power from on high." But what will our work do while we are waiting? The question can be answered by asking another, "What did the world do during these ten days while the early disciples were waiting?" They knew the saving truth, they alone knew it; yet in obedience to the Lord's command they were silent. The world was no loser. Beyond a doubt, when the power came, they accomplished more in one day than they would have accomplished in years if they had gone on in self-confident defiance and disobedience to Christ's command. We too after that we have received the baptism with the Spirit will accomplish more of real work for our Lord in one day than we ever would in years without this power. Even if it were necessary to spend days in waiting, they would be well spent, but we shall see later that there is no need that we spend days in waiting, that the baptism with the Holy Spirit may be received to-day. Some one may say that the Apostles had gone on missionary tours during Christ's lifetime, even before they were baptized with the Holy Spirit. This is true, but that was before the Holy Spirit was given, and before the command was given, "Tarry ye until ye be clothed with power from on high." After that it would have been disobedience and folly and presumption to have gone forth without this enduement, and we are living to-day after the Holy Spirit has been given and after the charge has been given to tarry until clothed.

Who Can Be Baptized With The Holy Spirit?

We come now to the question of first importance, namely, Who can be baptized with the Holy Spirit? At a convention some years ago, a very intelligent Christian woman, a well-known worker in educational as well as Sunday-school work, sent me this question, "You have told us of the necessity of the baptism with the Holy Spirit, but who can have this baptism? The church to which I belong teaches that the baptism with the Holy Spirit was confined to the apostolic age. Will you not tell us who can have the baptism with the Holy Spirit?" Fortunately this question is answered in the most explicit terms in the Bible. We read in Acts ii. 38, 39, R. V., "And Peter said unto them, Repent ye, and be baptized every one of you in the name of Jesus Christ unto the remission of your sins; and ye shall receive the gift of the Holy Ghost. For to you is the promise, and to your children, and to all that are afar off, even as many as the Lord our God shall call unto Him." What is the promise to which Peter refers in the thirty-ninth verse? There are two interpretations of the passage; one is that the promise of this verse is the promise of salvation; the other is that the promise of this verse is the promise of the gift of the Holy Spirit (or the baptism with the Holy Spirit; a comparison of Scripture passages will show that the two expressions are synonymous). Which is the correct interpretation? There are two laws of interpretation universally recognized among Bible scholars. These two laws are the law of usage (or "usus loquendi" as it is called) and the law of context. Many a verse in the Bible standing alone might admit of two or three or even more interpretations, but when these two laws of interpretation are applied, it is settled to a certainty that only one of the various possible interpretations is the true interpretation. The law of usage is this, that when you find a word or phrase in any passage of Scripture and you wish to know what it means, do not go to a dictionary but go to the Bible itself, look up the various passages in which the word is used and especially how the particular writer being studied uses it, and especially how it is used in that particular book in which the passage is found. Thus you can determine what the precise meaning of the word or phrase is in the passage in question. The law of context is this; that when you study a passage, you should not take it out of its connection but should look at what goes before it and what comes after it; for while it might mean various things if it stood alone, it can only mean one thing in the connection in which it is found. Now let us apply these two laws to the passage in question. First of all, let us apply the law of usage. We are trying to discover what the expression "the promise" means in Acts ii. 39. Turning back to Acts i. 4, 5, R. V., we read, "He charged them not to depart from Jerusalem, but to wait for *the promise of the Father*, which, said He, ye heard from Me: for John indeed baptized with water, but ye *shall be baptized with the Holy Ghost not many days hence*." It is evident then, that here the promise of the Father means the baptism with the Holy Spirit. Turn now to the second chapter and the thirty-third verse, R. V., "Being therefore by the right hand of God exalted, and having received *of the Father the promise of the Holy Ghost*, He hath poured forth this, which ye see and hear." In this passage we are told in so many words that the promise is the promise of the Holy Spirit. If this peculiar expression means the baptism with the Holy Spirit in Acts i. 4, 5, and the same thing in Acts ii. 33, by what same law of interpretation can it possibly mean something entirely different six verses farther down in Acts ii. 39? So the law of usage establishes it that the promise of Acts ii. 39 is the promise of the baptism with the Holy Spirit. Now let us apply the law of context, and we shall find that, if possible, this is even more decisive. Turn back to the thirty-eighth verse, "And Peter said unto them, Repent ye, and be baptized every one of you in the name of Jesus Christ unto the remission of your sins; and *ye shall receive the gift of the Holy Ghost; for the promise* is unto you, etc." So it is evident here that the promise is the promise of the gift or baptism with the Holy Spirit. It is settled then by both laws that the promise of Acts ii. 39 is that of the gift of the Holy Spirit, or baptism with the Holy Spirit. Let us then read the verse in that way, substituting this synonymous expression for the expression "the promise," "For the baptism with the Spirit is unto you, and to your children and to all that are afar off, even as many as the Lord our God shall call." "*It is unto you*," says Peter, that is to the crowd assembled before him. There is nothing in that for us. We were not there, and that crowd were all Jews and we are not Jews; but Peter did not stop there, he goes further and says, "And *to your children*," that is to the next generation of Jews, or all future generations of Jews. Still there is nothing in it for us, for we are not Jews; but Peter did not stop even there, he went further and said, "And *to all them that are afar off*." That does take us in. We are the Gentiles who were once "afar off," but now "made nigh by the blood of Christ" (Eph. ii. 13, 17). But lest there be any mistake about it whatever, Peter adds "even as many as the Lord our God shall call unto Him." So on the very day of Pentecost, Peter declares that the baptism with the Holy Spirit is for every child of God in every coming age of the church's history. Some years ago at a ministerial conference in Chicago, a minister of the Gospel from the Southwest came to me after a lecture on the Baptism with the Holy Spirit and said, "The church to which I belong teaches that the baptism with the Holy Spirit was for the apostolic age alone." "I do not care," I replied, "what the church to which you belong teaches, or what the church to which I belong teaches. The only question with me is, What does the Word of God teach?" "That is right," he said. I then handed him my Bible and asked him to read Acts ii. 39, and he read, "For the promise is unto you, and unto your children and to all them that are afar off even as many as the Lord our God shall call unto Him" (R. V.). "Has He called you?" I asked. "Yes, He certainly has." "Is the promise for you then?" "Yes, it is." He took it and the result was a transformed ministry. Some years ago at a student's conference, the gatherings were presided over by a prominent Episcopalian minister, a man greatly honored and loved. I spoke at this conference on the Baptism with the Holy Spirit, and dwelt upon the significance of Acts ii. 39. That night as we sat together after the meetings were over, this servant of God said to me, "Brother Torrey, I was greatly interested in what you had to say to-day on the Baptism with the Holy Spirit. If your interpretation of Acts ii. 39 is correct, you have your case, but I doubt your interpretation of Acts ii. 39. Let us talk it over." We did talk it over. Several years later, in July, 1894, I was at the student's conference at Northfield. As I entered the back door of Stone Hall that day, this Episcopalian minister entered the front door. Seeing me he hurried across the hall and held out his hand and said, "You were right about Acts ii. 39 at Knoxville, and I believe I have a right to tell you something better yet, that I have been baptized with the Holy Spirit." I am glad that I was right about Acts ii. 39, not that it is of any importance that I should be right, but the truth thus established is of immeasurable importance. Is it not glorious to be able to go literally around the world and face audiences of believers all over the United States, in the Sandwich Islands, in Australia and Tasmania and New Zealand, in China and Japan and India, in England and Scotland, Ireland, Germany, France and Switzerland and to be able to tell them, and to know that you have God's sure Word under your feet when you do tell them, "You may all be baptized with the Holy Spirit"? But that unspeakably joyous and glorious thought has its solemn side. If we may be baptized with the Holy Spirit then we *must* be. If we are baptized with the Holy Spirit then souls will be saved through our instrumentality who will not be saved if we are not thus baptized. If then we are not willing to pay the price of this baptism and therefore are not thus baptized we shall be responsible before God for every soul that might have been saved who was not saved because we did not pay the price and therefore did not obtain the blessing. I often tremble for myself and for my brethren in the ministry, and not only for my brethren in the ministry but for my brethren in all forms of Christian work, even the most humble and obscure. Why? Because we are preaching error? No, alas, there are many in these dark days who are doing that, and I do tremble for them; but that is not what I mean now. Do I mean that I tremble because we are not preaching the truth? for it is quite possible not to preach error and yet not preach the truth; many a man has never preached a word of error in his life, but still is not preaching the truth, and I do tremble for them; but that is not what I mean now. I mean that I tremble for those of us who are preaching the truth, the very truth as it is in Jesus, the truth as it is recorded in the written Word of God, the truth in its simplicity, its purity and its fullness, but who are preaching it in "persuasive words of man's wisdom" and not "in demonstration of the Spirit and of power" (1 Cor. ii. 4, R. V.). Preaching it in the energy of the flesh and not in the power of the Holy Spirit. There is nothing more death dealing than the Gospel without the Spirit's power. "The letter killeth, but the Spirit giveth life." It is awfully solemn business preaching the Gospel either from the pulpit or in more quiet ways. It means death or life to those that hear, and whether it means death or life depends very largely on whether we preach it with or without the baptism with the Holy Spirit.

We must be baptized with the Holy Spirit.

Even after one has been baptized with the Holy Spirit, no matter how definite that baptism may be, he needs to be filled again and again with the Spirit. This is the clear teaching of the New Testament. We read in Acts ii. 4, "*They were all filled* with the Holy Ghost and began to speak with other tongues as the Spirit gave them utterance." Now one of those who was present on this occasion and who therefore was filled at this time with the Holy Spirit was Peter. Indeed, he stands forth most prominently in the chapter as a man baptized with the Holy Spirit. But we read in Acts iv. 8, "Then Peter, *filled with the Holy Ghost*, said unto them, etc." Here we read again that Peter was filled with the Holy Ghost. Further down in the chapter we read, in the thirty-first verse, that being assembled together and praying, they were "*all filled with the Holy Ghost*, and they spake the Word of God with boldness." We are expressly told in the context that two of those present were John and Peter. Here then was *a third instance in which Peter was filled with the Holy Spirit.* It is not enough that one be filled with the Holy Spirit once. We, need a new filling for each new emergency of Christian service. The failure to realize this need of constant refillings with the Holy Spirit has led to many a man who at one time was greatly used of God, being utterly laid aside. There are many to-day who once knew what it was to work in the power of the Holy Spirit who have lost their unction and their power. I do not say that the Holy Spirit has left them—I do not believe He has—but the manifestation of His presence and power has gone. One of the saddest sights among us to-day is that of the men and women who once toiled for the Master in the mighty power of the Holy Spirit who are now practically of no use, or even a hindrance to the work, because they are trying to go in the power of the blessing received a year or five years or twenty years ago. For each new service that is to be conducted, for each new soul that is to be dealt with, for each new work for Christ that is to be performed, for each new day and each new emergency of Christian life and service, we should seek and obtain a new filling with the Holy Spirit. We must not "neglect" the gift that is in us (1 Tim. iv. 14), but on the contrary "kindle anew" or "stir into flame" this gift (1 Tim. i. 6, R. V., margin). Repeated fillings with the Holy Spirit are necessary to continuance and increase of power.

The question may arise, "Shall we call these new fillings with the Holy Spirit 'fresh baptisms' with the Holy Spirit?" To this we would answer, the expression "baptism" is never used in the Scriptures of a second experience and there is something of an initiatory character in the very thought of baptism, so if one wishes to be precisely Biblical, it would seem to be better not to use the term "baptism" of a second experience but to limit it to the first experience. On the other hand "*filled* with the Holy Spirit" is used in Acts ii. 4, to describe the experience promised in Acts i. 5, where the words used are "Ye shall be *baptized with the Holy Ghost.*" And it is evident from this and from other passages that the two expressions are to a large extent practically synonymous. However, if we confine the expression "baptism with the Holy Spirit" to our first experience, we shall be more exactly Biblical and it would be well to speak of one baptism but many fillings. But I would a great deal rather that one should speak about new or fresh baptisms with the Holy Spirit, standing for the all-important truth that we need repeated fillings with the Holy Spirit, than that he should so insist on exact phraseology that he would lose sight of the truth that repeated fillings are needed, *i. e.*, I would rather have the right experience by a wrong name, than the wrong experience by the right name. This much is as clear as day, that we need to be filled again and again and again with the Holy Spirit. I am sometimes asked, "Have you received *the second blessing*?" Yes, and the third and the fourth and the fifth and hundreds beside, and I am looking for a new blessing to-day.

We come now to the question of first practical importance, namely, *What must one do in order to obtain the baptism with the Holy Spirit?* This question is answered in the plainest and most positive way in the Bible. A plain path is laid down in the Bible consisting of a few simple steps that any one can take, and it is absolutely certain that any one who takes these steps will enter into the blessing. This is, of course, a very positive statement, and we would not dare be so positive if the Bible were not equally positive. But what right have we to be uncertain when the Word of God is positive? There are seven steps in this path:

1. The first step is that we *accept Jesus Christ as our Savior and Lord.* We read in Acts ii. 38, R. V., "Repent ye, and be baptized every one of you in the name of Jesus Christ for the remission of your sins, and ye shall receive the gift of the Holy Ghost." Is not this statement as positive as that which we made above? Peter says that if we do certain things, the result will be, "Ye *shall receive* the gift of the Holy Ghost." All seven steps are in this passage, but we shall refer later to other passages as throwing light upon this. The first two steps are in the word "repent." "*Repent* ye," said Peter. What does it mean to repent? The Greek word for repentance means "an afterthought" or "change of mind." To repent then means to change your mind. But change your mind about what? About three things; about God, about Jesus Christ, about sin. What the change of mind is about in any given instance must be determined by the context. As determined by the context in the present case, the change of mind is primarily about Jesus Christ. Peter had just said in the thirty-sixth verse, R. V., "Let all the house of Israel know assuredly, that God hath made Him both Lord and Christ, this Jesus whom ye crucified. When they heard this, they were pricked in their heart," as well they might be, "and said unto Peter and the rest of the Apostles, Brethren, what shall we do?" Then it was that Peter said, "Repent ye," "Change your mind about Jesus, change your mind from that attitude of mind that rejected Him and crucified Him to that attitude of mind that accepts Him as Lord and King and Savior." This then is the first step towards receiving the baptism with the Holy Spirit; receive Jesus as Savior and Lord; first of all receive Him as your Savior. Have you done that?

What does it mean to receive Jesus as Savior? It means to accept Him as the One who bore our sins in our place on the cross (Gal. iii. 13; 2 Cor. v. 21) and to trust God to forgive us because Jesus Christ died in our place. It means to rest all our hope of acceptance before God upon the finished work of Christ upon the cross of Calvary. There are many who profess to be Christians who have not done this. When you go to many who call themselves Christians and ask them if they are saved, they reply, "Yes." Then if you put to them the question "Upon what are you resting as the ground of your salvation?" they will reply something like this, "I go to church; I say my prayers, I read my Bible, I have been baptized, I have united with the church, I partake of the Lord's supper, I attend prayer-meeting, and I am trying to live as near right as I know how." If these things are what you are resting upon as the ground of your acceptance before God, then you are not saved, for all these things are your own works (all proper in their places but still your own works) and we are distinctly told in Rom. iii. 20, R. V., that "By the works of the law shall no flesh be justified in His sight." But if you go to others and ask them if they are saved, they will reply "Yes." And then if you ask them upon what they are resting as the ground of their acceptance before God, they will reply something to this effect, "I am not resting upon anything I ever did, or upon anything I am ever going to do; I am resting upon what Jesus Christ did for me when He bore my sins in His own body on the cross. I am resting in His finished work of atonement." If this is what you are really resting upon, then you are saved, you have accepted Jesus Christ as your Savior and you have taken the first step towards the baptism with the Holy Spirit.

The same thought is taught elsewhere in the Bible, for example in Gal. iii. 2. Here Paul asks of the believers in Galatia, "Received ye the Holy Spirit by the works of the law, or *by the hearing of faith*?" Just what did he mean? On one occasion when Paul was passing through Galatia, he was detained there by some physical infirmity. We are not told what it was, but at all events, he was not so ill but that he could preach to the Galatians the Gospel, or glad tidings, that Jesus Christ had redeemed them from the curse of the law by becoming a curse in their place, by dying on the cross of Calvary. These Galatians believed this testimony; this was the hearing of faith, and God set the stamp of His endorsement upon their faith by giving them as a personal experience the Holy Spirit. But after Paul had left Galatia, certain Judaizers came down from Jerusalem, men who were substituting the law of Moses for the Gospel and taught them that it was not enough that they simply believe on Jesus Christ but in addition to this they must keep the law of Moses, especially the law of Moses regarding circumcision, and that without circumcision they could not be saved—*i. e.*, they could not be saved by simple faith in Jesus (cf. Acts xv. 1). These young converts in Galatia became all upset. They did not know whether they were saved or not; they did not know what they ought to do, and all was confusion. It was just as when modern Judaizers come around and get after young converts and tell them that in addition to believing in Jesus Christ, they must keep the Mosaic Seventh Day Sabbath, or they cannot be saved. This is simply the old controversy breaking out at a new point. When Paul heard what had happened in Galatia, he was very indignant and wrote the Epistle to the Galatians simply for the purpose of exposing the utter error of these Judaizers. He showed them how Abraham himself was justified before he was circumcised by simply believing God (Gal. iii. 6), and how he was circumcised after he was justified as a seal of the faith which he already had while he was in uncircumcision. But in addition to this proof of the error of the Judaizers, Paul appeals to their own personal experience. He says to them, "You received the Holy Spirit, did you not?" "Yes." "How did you receive the Holy Spirit, by keeping the law of Moses, or by the hearing of faith, the simple accepting of God's testimony about Jesus Christ that your sins were laid upon Him, and that you are thus justified and saved?" The Galatians had had a very definite experience of receiving the Holy Spirit and Paul appeals to it, and recalls to their mind how it was by the simple hearing of faith that they had received the Holy Spirit. The gift of the Holy Spirit is God's seal upon the simple acceptance of God's testimony about Jesus Christ, that our sins were laid upon Him, and thus trusting God to forgive us and justify us. This then is the first step towards receiving the Holy Spirit. But we must not only receive Jesus as Savior, we must also receive Him as Lord. Of this we shall speak further in connection with another passage in the fourth step.

2. The second step in the path that leads into the blessing of being baptized with the Holy Spirit is *renunciation of sin*. Repentance as we have seen is a change of mind about sin as well as a change of mind about Christ; a change of mind from that attitude of mind that loves sin and indulges sin to that attitude of mind that hates sin and renounces sin. This then is the second step—renunciation of sin. The Holy Spirit is a *Holy* Spirit and we cannot have both Him and sin. We must make our choice between the Holy Spirit and unholy sin. We cannot have both. He that will not give up sin cannot have the Holy Spirit. It is not enough that we renounce one sin or two sins or three sins or many sins, we must *renounce all sin*. If we cling to one single known sin, it will shut us out of the blessing. Here we find the cause of failure in many people who are praying for the baptism with the Holy Spirit, going to conventions and hearing about the baptism with the Holy Spirit, reading books about the baptism with the Holy Spirit, perhaps spending whole nights in prayer for the baptism with the Holy Spirit, and yet obtaining nothing. Why? Because there is some sin to which they are clinging. People often say to me, or write to me, "I have been praying for the baptism with the Holy Spirit for a year (five years, ten years, one man said twenty years). Why do I not receive?" In many such cases, I feel led to reply, "It is sin, and if I could look down into your heart this moment as God looks into your heart, I could put my finger on the specific sin." It may be what you are pleased to call a small sin, but there are no small sins. There are sins that concern small things, but every sin is an act of rebellion against God and therefore no sin is a small sin. A controversy with God about the smallest thing is sufficient to shut one out of the blessing. Mr. Finney tells of a woman who was greatly exercised about the baptism with the Holy Spirit. Every night after the meetings, she would go to her rooms and pray way into the night and her friends were afraid she would go insane, but no blessing came. One night as she prayed, some little matter of head adornment, a matter that would probably not trouble many Christians to-day, but a matter of controversy between her and God, came up (as it had often come up before) as she knelt in prayer. She put her hand to her head and took the pins out of her hair and threw them across the room and said, "There go!" and instantly the Holy Ghost fell upon her. It was not so much the matter of head adornment as the matter of controversy with God that had kept her out of the blessing.

If there is anything that always comes up when you get nearest to God, that is the thing to deal with. Some years ago at a convention in a Southern state, the presiding officer, a minister in the Baptist Church, called my attention to a man and said, "That man is the pope of our denomination in ——; everything he says goes, but he is not at all with us in this matter, but I am glad to see him here." This minister kept attending the meetings. At the close of the last meeting where I had spoken upon the conditions of receiving the baptism with the Holy Spirit, I found this man awaiting me in the vestibule. He said, "I did not stand up on your invitation to-day." I replied, "I saw you did not." "I thought you said," he continued, "that you only wanted those to stand who could say they had absolutely surrendered to God?" "That is what I did say," I replied. "Well, I could not say that." "Then you did perfectly right not to stand. I did not want you to lie to God." "Say," he continued, "you hit me pretty hard to-day. You said if there was anything that always comes up when you get nearest to God, that is the thing to deal with. Now there is something that always comes up when I get nearest to God. I am not going to tell you what it is. I think you know." "Yes," I replied. (I could smell it.) "Well, I simply wanted to say this to you." This was on Friday afternoon. I had occasion to go to another city, and returning through that city the following Tuesday morning, the minister who had presided at the meeting was at the station. "I wish you could have been in our Baptist ministers' meeting yesterday morning," he said; "that man I pointed out to you from the north part of the state was present. He got up in our meeting and said, 'Brethren, we have been all wrong about this matter,' and then he told what he had done. He had settled his controversy with God, had given up the thing which had always come up when he got nearest to God, then he continued and said, 'Brethren, I have received a more definite experience than I had when I was converted.' " Just such an experience is waiting many another, both minister and layman, just as soon as he will judge his sin, just as soon as he will put away the thing that is a matter of controversy between him and God, no matter how small the thing may seem. If any one sincerely desires the baptism with the Holy Spirit, he should go alone with God and ask God to search him and bring to light anything in his heart or life that is displeasing to Him, and when He brings it to light, he should put it away. If after sincerely waiting on God, nothing is brought to light, then we may proceed to take the other steps. But there is no use praying, no use going to conventions, no use in reading books about the baptism with the Holy Spirit, no use in doing anything else, until we judge our sins.

3. The third step is *an open confession of our renunciation of sin and our acceptance of Jesus Christ*. After telling his hearers to repent in Acts ii. 38, Peter continues and tells them to be "baptized every one of you in the name of Jesus Christ unto the remission of your sins." Heart repentance alone was not enough. There must be an open confession of that repentance, and God's appointed way of confession of repentance is baptism. None of those to whom Peter spoke had ever been baptized, and, of course, what Peter meant in that case was water baptism. But suppose one has already been baptized, what then? Even in that case, there must be that for which baptism stands, namely, an open confession of our renunciation of sin and our acceptance of Jesus Christ. The baptism with the Spirit is not for the secret disciple, but for the open confessed disciple. There are many doubtless to-day who are trying to be Christians in their hearts, many who really believe that they have accepted Jesus as their Savior and their Lord and have renounced sin, but they are not willing to make an open confession of their renunciation of sin and their acceptance of Christ. Such an one cannot have the baptism with the Holy Spirit. Some one may ask, "Do not the Friends ('Quakers'), who do not believe in water baptism, give evidence of being baptized with the Holy Spirit?" Doubtless many of them do, but this does not alter the teaching of God's Word. God doubtless condescends in many instances where people are misled as to the teaching of His Word to their ignorance, if they are sincere, but that fact does not alter His Word, and even with a member of the congregation of Friends, who sincerely does not believe in water baptism, there must be before the blessing is received that for which baptism stands, namely, the open confession of our acceptance of Christ and of our renunciation of sin.

4. The fourth step is *absolute surrender to God*. This comes out in what has been already said, namely, that we *must accept Jesus as Lord* as well as Savior. It is stated explicitly in Acts v. 32, "And we are His witnesses of these things; and so is also *the Holy Ghost, whom God hath given to them that obey Him*." That is the fourth step, "obey Him," obedience. But what does obedience mean? Some one will say, doing as we are told. Right, but doing how much that we are told? Not merely one thing or two things or three things or four things, but all things. The heart of obedience is in the will, the essence of obedience is the surrender of the will to God. It is going to God our heavenly Father and

saying, "Heavenly Father, here I am. I am Thy property. Thou hast bought me with a price. I acknowledge Thine ownership, and surrender myself and all that I am absolutely to Thee. Send me where Thou wilt; do with me what Thou wilt; use me as Thou wilt." This is in most instances the decisive step in receiving the baptism with the Holy Spirit. In the Old Testament types it was when the whole burnt offering was laid upon the altar, nothing kept back within or without the sacrificial animal, that the fire came forth from the Holy Place where God dwelt and accepted and consumed the gift upon the altar. And so it is to-day, in the fulfillment of the type, when we lay ourselves, a whole burnt offering, upon the altar, keeping nothing within or without back, that the fire of God, the Holy Spirit, descends from the real Holy Place, heaven (of which the Most Holy Place in the tabernacle was simply a type), and accepts the gift upon the altar. When we can truly say, "My *all* is on the altar," then we shall not have long to wait for the fire. The lack of this absolute surrender is shutting many out of the blessing to-day. People turn the keys of almost every closet in their heart over to God, but there is some small closet of which they wish to keep the key themselves, and the blessing does not come.

At a convention in Washington, D. C., on the last night, I had spoken on How to Receive the Baptism with the Holy Spirit. The Spirit Himself was present in mighty power that night. The chaplain of one of the houses had said to me at the close of the meeting, "It almost seemed as if I could see the Holy Spirit in this place to-night." There were many to be dealt with. About two hours after the meeting closed, about eleven o'clock, a worker came to me and said, "Do you see that young woman over to the right with whom Miss W—— is speaking?" "Yes." "Well, she has been dealing with her for two hours and she is in awful agony. Won't you come and see if you can help?" I went into the seat back of this woman in distress and asked her her trouble. "Oh," she said, "I came from Baltimore to receive the baptism with the Holy Spirit, and I cannot go back to Baltimore until I have received Him." "Is your will laid down?" I asked. "I am afraid not." "Will you lay it down now?" "I cannot." "Are you willing that God should lay it down for you?" "Yes." "Ask Him to do it." She bowed her head in prayer and asked God to empty her of her will, to lay it down for her, to bring it into conformity to His will, in absolute surrender to His own. When the prayer was finished, I said, "Is it laid down?" She said, "It must be. I have asked something according to His will. Yes, it is done." I said, "Ask Him for the baptism with the Holy Spirit." She bowed her head again in brief prayer and asked God to baptize her with the Holy Spirit and in a few moments looked up with peace in her heart and in her face. Why? Because she had surrendered her will. She had met the conditions and God had given the blessing.

5. The fifth step is *an intense desire for the baptism with the Holy Spirit.* Jesus says in John vii. 37-39, "If any man *thirst*, let him come unto Me and drink. He that believeth on Me, as the Scripture hath said, out of his belly shall flow rivers of living water. But this spake He of the Spirit, which they that believe on Him should receive." Here again we have *belief on Jesus* as the condition of receiving the Holy Spirit but we have also this, "If any man thirst." Doubtless when Jesus spake these words He had in mind the Old Testament promise in Isa. xliv. 3, "For I will pour water upon him that is *thirsty*, and floods upon the dry ground: I will pour *My Spirit* upon thy seed, and My blessing upon thine offspring." In both these passages thirst is the condition of receiving the Holy Spirit. What does it mean to thirst? When a man really thirsts, it seems as if every pore in his body had just one cry, "Water! Water! Water!" Apply this to the matter in question; when a man thirsts spiritually, his whole being has but one cry, "The Holy Spirit! The Holy Spirit! The Holy Spirit!" As long as one fancies he can get along somehow without the baptism with

the Holy Spirit, he is not going to receive that baptism. As long as one is casting about for some new kind of church, machinery, or new style of preaching, or anything else, by which he hopes to accomplish what the Holy Spirit only can accomplish, he will not receive the baptism with the Holy Spirit. As long as one tries to find some subtle system of exegesis to read out of the New Testament what God has put into it, namely, the absolute necessity that each believer receive the baptism with the Holy Spirit as a definite experience, he is not going to receive the baptism with the Holy Spirit. As long as a man tries to persuade himself that he has received the baptism with the Holy Spirit when he really has not, he is not going to receive the baptism with the Holy Spirit. But when one gets to the place where he sees the absolute necessity that he be baptized with the Holy Spirit as a definite experience and desires this blessing at any cost, he is far on the way towards receiving it. At a state Young Men's Christian Association Convention, where I had spoken on the Baptism with the Holy Spirit, two ministers went out of the meeting side by side. One said to the other, "That kind of teaching leads either to fanaticism or despair." He did not attempt to show that it was unscriptural. He felt condemned and was not willing to admit his lack and seek to have it supplied, and so he tried to avoid the condemnation that came from the Word by this bright remark, "that kind of teaching leads either to fanaticism or despair." Such a man will not receive the baptism with the Holy Spirit until he is brought to himself and acknowledges honestly his need and intensely desires to have it supplied. How different another minister of the same denomination who came to me one Sunday morning at Northfield. I was to speak that morning on How to Receive the Baptism with the Holy Spirit. He said to me, "I have come to Northfield from —— for just one purpose, to receive the baptism with the Holy Spirit, and I would rather die than go back to my church without receiving it." I said, "My brother, you are going to receive it." The following morning he came very early to my house. He said, "I have to go away on the early train but I came around to tell you before I went that I have received the baptism with the Holy Spirit."

6. The sixth step *is definite prayer for the baptism with the Holy Spirit.* Jesus says in Luke xi. 13, "If ye then, being evil, know how to give good gifts unto your children: how much more shall your heavenly Father give the Holy Spirit *to them that ask Him.*" This is very explicit. Jesus teaches us that the Holy Spirit is given in answer to definite prayer—just ask Him. There are many who tell us that we should not pray for the Holy Spirit, and they reason it out very speciously. They say that the Holy Spirit was given as an abiding gift to the church at Pentecost, and why pray for what is already given? To this the late Rev. Dr. A. J. Gordon well replied that Jesus Christ was given as an abiding gift to the world at Calvary (John iii. 16), but what was given to the world as a whole each individual in the world must appropriate to himself; and just so the Holy Spirit was given to the church as an abiding gift at Pentecost, but what was given to the church as a whole each individual in the church must appropriate to himself, and God's way of appropriation is prayer. But those who say we should not pray for the Holy Spirit go further still than this. They tell us that every believer already has the Holy Spirit (which we have already seen is true in a sense), and why pray for what we already have? To this the very simple answer is, that it is one thing to have the Holy Spirit dwelling way back of consciousness in some hidden sanctuary of the being and something quite different, and vastly more, to have Him take possession of the whole house that He inhabits. But against all these specious arguments we place the simple word of Jesus Christ, "How much more shall your heavenly Father give the Holy Spirit to them that ask Him." It will not do to say, as has been said, that "this promise was for the time of the earth life of our Lord, and to go back

to the promise of Luke xi. 13 is to forget Pentecost, and to ignore the truth that now every believer has the indwelling Spirit;" for we find that after Pentecost as well as before, the Holy Spirit was given to believers in answer to definite prayer. For example, we read in Acts iv. 31, R. V., "*When they had prayed*, the place was shaken wherein they were gathered together, and *they were all filled with the Holy Ghost*, and they spake the Word of God with boldness." Again in Acts viii. 15, 16, we read that when Peter and John were come down and saw the believers in Samaria they "*prayed for them that they might receive the Holy Ghost*, for *as yet He was fallen upon none of them*, only they were baptized in the name of the Lord Jesus." Again in the Epistle of Paul to the Ephesians, Paul tells the believers in Ephesus that he was praying for them that they might be strengthened with power through His Spirit (Eph. iii. 16). So right through the New Testament after Pentecost, as well as before, by specific teaching and illustrative example, we are taught that the Holy Spirit is given in answer to definite prayer. At a Christian worker's convention in Boston, a brother came to me and said, "I notice that you are on the program to speak on the Baptism with the Holy Spirit." "Yes." "I think that is the most important subject on the program. Now be sure and tell them not to pray for the Holy Spirit." I replied, "My brother, I will be sure and not tell them that: for Jesus says, 'How much more shall your heavenly Father give the Holy Spirit to them that ask Him?'" "Yes, but that was before Pentecost." "How about Acts iv. 31, R. V., was that before Pentecost or after?" He said, "It was certainly after." "Well," I said, "take it and read it." "And when they had prayed, the place where they were gathered together was shaken, and they were all filled with the Holy Ghost and spake the Word of God with boldness." "How about Acts viii. 15, 16, was that before Pentecost or after?" "Certainly, it was after." "Take it and read it." "Who when they were come down prayed for them that they might receive the Holy Spirit, for as yet He was fallen on none of them, only they were baptized in the name of Jesus." He had nothing more to say. What was there more to say? But with me, it is not a matter of mere exegesis, that the Holy Spirit is given in answer to definite prayer. It is a matter of personal and indubitable experience. I know just as well that God gives the Holy Spirit in answer to prayer as I know that water quenches thirst and food satisfies hunger. In my first experience of being baptized with the Holy Spirit, it was while I waited upon God in prayer that I was thus baptized. Since then time and again as I have waited on God in prayer, I have been definitely filled with the Holy Spirit. Often as I have knelt in prayer with others, as we prayed the Holy Spirit has fallen upon us just as perceptibly as the rain ever fell upon and fructified the earth. I shall never forget one experience in our church in Chicago. We were holding a noon prayer-meeting of the ministers at the Y. M. C. A. Auditorium, preparatory to an expected visit to Chicago of Mr. Moody. At one of these meetings a minister sprang to his feet and said, "What we need in Chicago is an all-night meeting of the ministers." "Very well," I said. "If you will come up to Chicago Avenue Church Friday night at ten o'clock, we will have a prayer-meeting and if God keeps us all night, we will stay all night." At ten o'clock on Friday night four or five hundred people gathered in the lecture-rooms of the Chicago Avenue Church. They were not all ministers. They were not all men. Satan made a mighty attempt to ruin the meeting. First of all three men got down by the door and knelt down by chairs and pounded and shouted until some of our heads seemed almost splitting, and some felt they must retire from the meeting; and when a brother went to expostulate with them and urge them that things be done decently and in order, they swore at the brother who made the protest. Still later a man sprang up in the middle of the room and announced that he was Elijah. The poor man was insane. But these things were distracting, and there was more or less of confusion until nearly midnight, and some thought they would go home. But it is a poor meeting that the devil can spoil, and some of us were there for a blessing and determined to remain until we received it. About midnight God gave us complete victory over all the discordant elements. Then for two hours there was such praying as I have rarely heard in my life. A little after two o'clock in the morning a sudden hush fell upon the whole gathering; we were all on our knees at the time. No one could speak; no one could pray, no one could sing; all you could hear was the subdued sobbing of joy, unspeakable and full of glory. The very air seemed tremulous with the presence of the Spirit of God. It was now Saturday morning. The following morning, one of my deacons came to me and said, with bated breath, "Brother Torrey, I shall never forget yesterday morning until the latest day of my life." But it was not by any means all emotion. There was solid reality that could be tested by practical tests. A man went out of that meeting in the early morning hours, took a train for Missouri. When he had transacted his business in the town that he visited, he asked the proprietor of the hotel if there was any meeting going on in the town at the time. He said, "Yes, there is a protracted meeting going on at the Cumberland Presbyterian Church." The man was himself a Cumberland Presbyterian. He went to the church and when the meeting was opened he arose in his place and asked the minister if he could speak. Permission was granted, and with the power of the Holy Spirit upon him, he so spoke that fifty-eight or fifty-nine persons professed to accept Christ on the spot. A young man went out of the meeting in the early morning hours and took a train for a city in Wisconsin, and I soon received word from that city that thirty-eight young men and boys had been converted while he spoke. Another young man, one of our students in the Institute, went to another part of Wisconsin, and soon I began to receive letters from ministers in that neighborhood inquiring about him and telling how he had gone into the school-houses and churches and Soldiers' Home and how there were conversions wherever he spoke. In the days that followed men and women from that meeting went out over the earth and I doubt if there was any country that I visited in my tour around the world, Japan, China, Australia, New Zealand, India, etc., in which I did not find some one who had gone out from that meeting with the power of God upon them. For me to doubt that God fills men with the Holy Spirit in answer to prayer would be thoroughly unscientific and irrational. I know He does. And in a matter like this, I would rather have one ounce of believing experience than ten tons of unbelieving exegesis.

7. The seventh and last step is *faith*. We read in Mark xi. 24, "Therefore I say unto you, What things soever ye desire, when ye pray, *believe that ye receive them* and ye shall have them." No matter how definite God's promises are, we only realize these promises experimentally when we believe. For example we read in James i. 5, R. V., "But if any of you lacketh wisdom, let him ask of God, who giveth to all liberally and upbraideth not; and it shall be given him." Now that promise is as positive as a promise can be but we read in the following verses, "But let him *ask in faith nothing doubting*: for he that doubteth is like the surge of the sea driven by the wind and tossed. For let not that man think that he shall receive anything of the Lord; a double-minded man, unstable in all his ways." The baptism with the Spirit, as we have already seen, is for those believers in Christ, who have put away all sin and surrendered absolutely to God, who ask for it, but even though we ask there will be no receiving if we do not believe. There are many who have met the other conditions of receiving the baptism with the Holy Spirit and yet do not receive, simply because they do not believe. They do not expect to receive and they do not receive. But there is a faith that goes beyond expectation, a faith that puts out its hand and takes what it asks on the spot. This comes out in the Revised Version of Mark xi. 24,

"Therefore I say unto you, All things whatsoever ye pray and ask for, *believe that ye have received them* and ye *shall have* them." When we pray for the baptism with the Holy Spirit we should believe that we have received (that is that God has granted our prayer and therefore it is ours) and then we shall have the actual experience of that which we have asked. When the Revised Version came out, I was greatly puzzled about the rendering of Mark xi. 24. I had begun at the beginning of the New Testament and gone right through comparing the Authorized Version with the Revised and comparing both with the best Greek text, but when I reached this passage, I was greatly puzzled. I read the Authorized Version, "What things soever ye desire when ye pray, believe that ye receive them and ye shall have them," and that seemed plain enough. Then I turned to the Revised Version and read, "All things whatsoever ye pray and ask for believe that *ye have received* them and ye *shall have* them." And I said to myself, "What a confusion of the tenses. Believe that ye have already received (past), and ye shall have afterwards (future). What nonsense." Then I turned to my Greek Testament and I found whether sense or nonsense, the Revised Version was the correct rendering of the Greek, but what it meant I did not know for years. But one time I was studying and expounding to my church the First Epistle of John. I came to the fifth chapter, the fourteenth and fifteenth verses (R. V.) and I read, "And this is the boldness which we have towards Him, that, if we ask anything according to His will, He heareth us: and if we know that He heareth us whatsoever we ask, we know that we have the petitions which we have asked of Him." Then I understood Mark xi. 24. Do you see it? If not, let me explain it a little further. When we come to God in prayer, the first question to ask is, Is that which I have asked of God according to His will? If it is promised in His Word, of course, we know it is according to His will. Then we can say with 1 John v. 14, I have asked something according to His will and I know He hears me. Then we can go further and say with the fifteenth verse, Because I know He hears what I ask, I know I have the petition which I asked of Him. I may not have it in actual possession but I know it is mine because I have asked something according to His will and He has heard me and granted that which I have asked, and what I thus believe I have received because the Word of God says so, I shall afterwards have in actual experience. Now apply this to the matter before us. When I ask for the baptism with the Holy Spirit, I have asked something according to His will, for Luke xi. 13 and Acts ii. 39 say so, therefore I know my prayer is heard, and still further I know because the prayer is heard that I have the petition which I have asked of Him, *i. e.*, I know I have the baptism with the Holy Spirit. I may not feel it yet but I have received, and what I thus count mine resting upon the naked word of God, I shall afterwards have in actual experience. Some years ago I went to the student's conference at Lake Geneva, Wisconsin, with Mr. F. B. Meyer, of London. Mr. Meyer spoke that night on the Baptism with the Holy Spirit. At the conclusion of his address, he said, "If any of you wish to speak with Mr. Torrey or myself after the meeting is over, we will stay and speak with you." A young man came to me who had just graduated from one of the Illinois colleges. He said, "I heard of this blessing thirty days ago and have been praying for it ever since but do not receive. What is the trouble?" "Is your will laid down?" I asked. "No," he said, "I am afraid it is not." "Then," I said, "there is no use praying until your will is laid down. Will you lay down your will?" He said, "I cannot." "Are you willing that God should lay it down for you?" "I am." "Let us kneel and ask Him to do it." We knelt side by side and I placed my Bible open at 1 John v. 14, 15 on the chair before him. He asked God to lay down his will for him and empty him of his self-will and to bring his will into conformity with the will of God. When he had finished the prayer, I said, "Is it done?" He said, "It must be. I have asked something according to His will and I know He hears me and I know I have the petition I have asked. Yes, my will is laid down." "What is it you desire?" "The baptism with the Holy Spirit." "Ask for it." Looking up to God he said, "Heavenly Father, baptize me with the Holy Spirit now." "Did you get what you asked?" I asked. "I don't feel it," he replied. "That is not what I asked you," I said. "Read the verse before you," and he read, "This is the boldness which we have towards Him that if we ask anything according to His will He heareth us." "What do you know?" I asked. He said, "I know if I ask anything according to His will He hears me." "What did you ask?" "I asked for the baptism with the Holy Spirit." "Is that according to His will?" "Yes, Acts ii. 39 says so." "What do you know then?" "I know He has heard me." "Read on." "And if we know that if He heareth us whatsoever we ask, we know that we have the petitions which we have asked of Him." "What do you know?" I asked. "I know I have the petition I asked of Him." "What was the petition you asked of Him?" "The baptism with the Holy Spirit." "What do you know?" "I know I have the baptism with the Holy Spirit. I don't feel it, but God says so." We arose from our knees and after a short conversation separated. I left Lake Geneva the next morning, but returned in a few days. I met the young man and asked if he had really received the baptism with the Holy Spirit. He did not need to answer. His face told the story, but he did answer. He went into a theological seminary the following autumn, was given a church his junior year in the seminary, had conversions from the outset, and the next year on the Day of Prayer for Colleges, largely through his influence there came a mighty outpouring of the Spirit upon the seminary of which the president of the seminary wrote to a denominational paper, that it was a veritable Pentecost, and it all came through this young man who received the baptism with the Holy Spirit through simple faith in the Word of God. Any one who will accept Jesus as their Savior and their Lord, put away all sin out of their life, publicly confess their renunciation of sin and acceptance of Jesus Christ, surrender absolutely to God, and ask God for the baptism with the Holy Spirit, and take it by simple faith in the naked Word of God, can receive the baptism with the Holy Spirit right now. There are some who so emphasize the matter of absolute surrender that they ignore, or even deny, the necessity of prayer. It is always unfortunate when one so emphasizes one side of truth that he loses sight of another side which may be equally important. In this way, many lose the blessing which God has provided for them.

The seven steps given above lead with absolute certainty into the blessing. But several questions arise:

1. *Must we not wait until we know we have received the baptism with the Holy Spirit before we take up Christian work?* Yes, but how shall we know? There are two ways of knowing anything in the Christian life. First, by the Word of God; second, by experience or feeling. God's order is to know things first of all by the Word of God. How one may know by the Word of God that they have received the baptism with the Holy Spirit has just been told. We have a right when we have met the conditions and have definitely asked for the baptism with the Holy Spirit to say, "It is mine," and to get up and go on in our work leaving the matter of experience to God's time and place. We get assurance that we have received the baptism with the Holy Spirit in precisely the same way that we get assurance of our salvation. When an inquirer comes to you, whom you have reason to believe really has received Jesus but who lacks assurance, what do you do with him? Do you tell him to kneel down and pray until he gets assurance? Not if you know how to deal with a soul. You know that true assurance comes through the Word of God, that it is through what is "written" that we are to know that we have eternal life (1 John v. 13). So you take the inquirer to the written Word. For example, you take him to John iii. 36. You

tell him to read it. He reads, "He that believeth on the Son hath everlasting life." You ask him, "Who has everlasting life?" He replies from the passage before him, "He that believeth on the Son." "How many who believe on the Son have everlasting life?" "Every one that believes on the Son." "Do you know this to be true?" "Yes." "Why?" "Because God says so." "What does God say?" "God says, 'He that believeth on the Son hath everlasting life.' " "Do you believe on the Son?" "Yes." "What have you then?" He ought to say, "Everlasting life," but quite likely he will not. He may say, "I wish I had everlasting life." You point him again to the verse and by questions bring out what it says, and you hold him to it until he sees that he has everlasting life; sees that he has everlasting life simply because God says so. After he has assurance on the ground of the Word, he will have assurance by personal experience, by the testimony of the Spirit in his heart. Now you should deal with yourself in precisely the same way about the baptism with the Holy Spirit. Hold yourself to the word found in 1 John v. 14, 15, and know that you have the baptism with the Spirit simply because God says so in His Word, whether you feel it or not. Afterwards you will know it by experience. God's order is always: first, His Word; second, belief in His Word; third, experience, or feeling. We desire to change God's order, and have first, His Word, then feeling, then we will believe. But God demands that we believe on His naked Word. "Abraham *believed God* and it was accounted to him for righteousness" (Gal. iii. 6; cf. Gen. xv. 6). Abraham had as yet no feeling in his body of new life and power. He just believed God and feeling came afterwards. God demands of us to-day, as He did Abraham of old, that we simply take Him at His Word and count the thing ours which He has promised, simply because He has promised it. Afterwards we get the feeling and the realization of that which He has promised.

2. The second question that some will ask is, "*Will there be no manifestation of the baptism with the Spirit which we receive?* Will everything be just as it was before, and if it will, where is the reality and use of the baptism?" Yes, there will be manifestation, very definite manifestation, but bear in mind *what the character* of the manifestation will be, *and when* the manifestation is to be expected. When is the manifestation to be expected? After we believe. After we have received on simple faith in the naked Word of God. And what will be the character of the manifestation? Here many go astray. They have read the wonderful experiences of Charles G. Finney, John Wesley, D. L. Moody and others. These men tell us that when they were baptized with the Holy Spirit they had wonderful sensations. Finney, for example, describes it as like great waves of electricity sweeping over him, so that he was compelled to ask God to withhold His hand, lest he die on the spot. Mr. Moody, on rare occasions, described a similar experience. That these men had such experiences, I do not for a moment question. The word of such men as Charles G. Finney, D. L. Moody and others is to be believed, and there is another reason why I cannot question the reality of these experiences, but while these men doubtless had these experiences, there is not a passage in the Bible that describes such an experience. I am inclined to think the Apostles had them, but if they had, they kept them to themselves and it is well that they did, for if they had put them on record, that is what we would be looking for to-day. But what are the manifestations that actually occurred in the case of the Apostles and the early disciples? New power in the Lord's work. We read at Pentecost that they were all filled with the Holy Ghost and *began to speak with other tongues as the Spirit gave them utterance* (Acts ii. 4). Similar accounts are given of what occurred in the household of Cornelius and what occurred in Ephesus. All we read in the case of the Apostle Paul is that Ananias came in and said, "Brother Saul, the Lord, even Jesus, that appeared unto thee in the way as thou camest, hath sent me, that thou mightest receive thy

sight, and be filled with the Holy Ghost." Then Ananias baptized him, and the next thing we read is that Paul went straight down to the synagogue and preached Christ so mightily in the power of the Spirit that he "confounded the Jews which dwelt at Damascus, proving that this is very Christ" (Acts ix. 17-22). So right *through the New Testament, the manifestation that we are taught to expect, and the manifestation that actually occurred was new power in Christian work*, and that is the manifestation that we may expect to-day and we need not look too carefully for that. The thing for us to do is to claim God's promise and let God take care of the mode of manifestation.

3. The third question that will arise with some is, *May we not have to wait for the baptism with the Holy Spirit?* Did not the Apostles have to wait ten days, and may we not have to wait ten days or even more? No, there is no necessity that we wait. We are told distinctly in the Bible why the Apostles had to wait ten days. In Acts ii. 1, we read, "And when the day of Pentecost was fully come" (literally "When the day of Pentecost was being fulfilled," R. V., margin). Way back in the Old Testament types, and back of that in the eternal counsels of God, the day of Pentecost was set for the coming of the Holy Spirit and the gathering of the church, and the Holy Spirit could not be given until the day of Pentecost was fully come, therefore the Apostles had to wait until the day of Pentecost was fulfilled, but there was no waiting after Pentecost. There was no waiting for example in Acts iv. 31; scarcely had they finished the prayer when the place where they were gathered together was shaken and "they were all filled with the Holy Ghost." There was no waiting in the household of Cornelius. They were listening to their first Gospel sermon and Peter said as the climax of his argument "to Him (that is Jesus) bear all the prophets witness that through His name every one that believeth on Him shall receive remission of sins" (R. V.), and no sooner had Peter spoken these words than they believed and "the Holy Ghost fell on them which heard the word." There was no waiting in Samaria after Peter and John came down and told them about the baptism with the Holy Spirit and prayed with them. There was no waiting in Ephesus after Paul came and told them that there was not only the baptism of John unto repentance, but the baptism of Jesus in the Holy Spirit. It is true that they had been waiting some time until then, but it was simply because they did not know that there was such a baptism for them. And many may wait to-day because they do not know that there is the baptism with the Spirit for them, or they may have to wait because they are not resting in the finished work of Christ, or because they have not put away sin, or because they have not surrendered fully to God, or because they will not definitely ask and believe and take; but the reason for the waiting is not in God, it is in ourselves. Any one who will, can lay this book down at this point, take the steps which have been stated and immediately receive the baptism with the Holy Spirit. I would not say a word to dissuade men from spending much time in waiting upon God in prayer for "They that wait upon the Lord shall renew their strength" (Isa. xl. 31). There are few of us indeed in these days who spend as many hours as we should in waiting upon God. The writer can bear joyful testimony to the manifest outpourings of the Spirit that have come time and again as he has waited upon God through the hours of the night with believing brethren, but the point I would emphasize is that the baptism with the Holy Spirit may be had at once. The Bible proves this; experience proves it. There are many waiting for feeling who ought to be claiming by faith. In these days we hear of many who say they are "waiting for their Pentecost"; some have been waiting weeks, some have been waiting months, some have been waiting years. This is not Scriptural and it is dishonoring to God. These brethren have an unscriptural view of what constitutes Pentecost. They have fixed it in their minds that certain manifestations are to occur and as these particular

manifestations, which they themselves have prescribed, do not come, they think they have not received the Holy Spirit. There are many who have been led into the error, already confuted in this book, that the baptism with the Holy Spirit always manifests itself in the gift of tongues. They have not received the gift of tongues and therefore they conclude that they have not received the baptism with the Holy Spirit. But as already seen, one may receive the baptism with the Holy Spirit and not receive the gift of tongues. Others still are waiting for some ecstatic feeling. We do not need to wait at all. We may meet the conditions, we may claim the blessing at once on the ground of God's sure Word. There was a time in the writer's ministry when he was led to say that he would never enter his pulpit again until he had been definitely baptized with the Holy Spirit and knew it, or until God in some way told him to go. I shut myself up in my study and day by day waited upon God for the baptism with the Holy Spirit. It was a time of struggle. The thought would arise, "Suppose you do not receive the baptism with the Holy Spirit before Sunday. How it will look for you to refuse to go into your pulpit," but I held fast to my resolution. I had a more or less definite thought in my mind of what might happen when I was baptized with the Holy Spirit, but it did not come that way at all. One morning as I waited upon God, one of the quietest and calmest moments of my life, it was just as if God said to me, "The blessing is yours. Now go and preach." If I had known my Bible then as I know it now, I might have heard that voice the very first day speaking to me through the Word, but I did not know it and God in His infinite condescension, looking upon my weakness, spoke it directly to my heart. There was no particular ecstasy or emotion, simply the calm assurance that the blessing was mine. I went into my work and God manifested His power in that work. Some time passed, I do not remember just how long, and I was sitting in that same study. I do not remember that I was thinking about this subject at all, but suddenly it was just as if I had been knocked out of my chair on to the floor, and I lay upon my face crying, "Glory to God! Glory to God!" I could not stop. Some power, not my own, had taken possession of my lips and my whole person. The writer is not of an excitable, hysterical or even emotional temperament, but I lost control of myself absolutely. I had never shouted before in my life, but I could not stop. When after a while I got control of myself, I went to my wife and told her what had happened. I tell this experience, not to magnify it, but to say that the time when this wonderful experience (which I cannot really fully describe) came was not the moment when I was baptized with the Holy Spirit. The moment when I was baptized with the Holy Spirit was in that calm hour when God said, "It is yours. Now go and preach."

There is an afternoon that I shall never forget. It was the eighth day of July, 1894. It was at the Northfield Students' Convention. I had spoken that morning in the church on How to Receive the Baptism with the Holy Spirit. As I drew to a close, I took out my watch and noticed that it was exactly twelve o'clock. Mr. Moody had invited us to go up on the mountain that afternoon at three o'clock to wait upon God for the baptism with the Holy Spirit. As I looked at my watch, I said, "Gentlemen, it is exactly twelve o'clock. Mr. Moody has invited us to go up on the mountain at three o'clock to wait upon God for the baptism with the Holy Spirit. It is three hours until three o'clock. Some of you cannot wait three hours, nor do you need to wait. Go to your tent, go to your room in the hotel or in the buildings, go out into the woods, go anywhere, where you can get alone with God, meet the conditions of the baptism with the Holy Spirit and claim it at once." At three o'clock we gathered in front of Mr. Moody's mother's house; four hundred and fifty-six of us in all, all men from the eastern colleges. (I know the number because Mr. Paul Moody counted us as we passed through the gates down into the lots.) We commenced to climb the mountainside. After we had gone some distance, Mr. Moody said, "I do not think we need to go further. Let us stop here." We sat down and Mr. Moody said, "Have any of you anything to say?" One after another, perhaps seventy-five men, arose and said words to this effect, "I could not wait until three o'clock. I have been alone with God and I have received the baptism with the Holy Spirit." Then Mr. Moody said, "I can see no reason why we should not kneel right down here now and ask God that the Holy Spirit may fall on us as definitely as He fell on the Apostles at Pentecost. Let us pray." We knelt down on the ground; some of us lay on our faces on the pine-needles. As we had gone up the mountainside, a cloud had been gathering over the mountain, and as we began to pray the cloud broke and the rain-drops began to come down upon us through the overhanging pine trees, but another cloud, big with mercy, had been gathering over Northfield for ten days and our prayers seemed to pierce that cloud and the Holy Ghost fell upon us. It was a wonderful hour. There are many who will never forget it. But any one who reads this book may have a similar hour alone by himself now. He can take the seven steps one by one and the Holy Spirit will fall upon him.

XXI: The Work of the Holy Spirit in Prophets and Apostles

The work of the Holy Spirit in apostles and prophets is an entirely distinctive work. He imparts to apostles and prophets an especial gift for an especial purpose.

We read in 1 Cor. xii. 4, 8-11, 28, 29, R. V., "Now there are diversities of gifts, but the same Spirit.... For to one is given through the Spirit wisdom; and to another the word of knowledge, according to the same Spirit; to another faith, in the same Spirit; and to another gifts of healings, in the one Spirit; and to another workings of miracles; and to *another prophecy*; and to another discerning of spirits: to another divers kinds of tongues; and to another the interpretation of tongues: but all these worketh the one and the same Spirit, dividing to each severally even as He will.... And God hath set some in the church, *first apostles, secondly prophets*, thirdly teachers, then miracles, then gifts of healing, helps, governments, divers kinds of tongues. *Are all apostles? Are all prophets?* Are all teachers? Are all workers of miracles? Have all gifts of healings? Do all speak with tongues? Do all interpret?" It is evident from these verses that the work of the Holy Spirit in apostles and prophets is of a distinctive character.

The doctrine is becoming very common and very popular in our day that the work of the Holy Spirit in preachers and teachers and in ordinary believers, illuminating them and guiding them into the truth and opening their minds to understand the Word of God is the same in kind and differs only in degree from the work of the Holy Spirit in prophets and apostles. It is evident from the passage just cited that this doctrine is thoroughly unscriptural and untrue. It overlooks the fact so clearly stated and carefully elucidated that while there is "the same Spirit" there are "diversities of gifts" "diversities of administrations" "diversities of workings" (1 Cor. xii. 4-6) and that "not all are prophets" and "not all are apostles" (1 Cor. xii. 29). A very scholarly and brilliant preacher seeking to minimize the difference between the work of the Holy Spirit in apostles and prophets and His work in other men calls attention to the fact that the Bible says that Bezaleel was to be "filled with the Spirit of God" to devise the work of the tabernacle (Ex. xxxi. 1-11). He gives this as a proof that the inspiration of the prophet does not differ from the inspiration of the artist or architect, but in doing this, he loses sight of the fact that the tabernacle was to be built after the "pattern shown to Moses in the Mount" (Ex. xxv. 9, 40) and that therefore it was itself a prophecy and an exposition of the truth of God. It was not mere architecture. It was the Word of God done into wood, gold, silver, brass, cloth, skin, etc. And Bezaleel needed as much special inspiration to reveal the truth in wood, gold, silver, brass, etc., as the apostle or prophet needs it to reveal the Word of God with pen and ink on parchment. There is much reasoning in these days about inspiration that appears at first sight very learned, but that will not bear much rigid scrutiny or candid comparison with the exact statements of the Word of God. There is nothing in the Bible more inspired than the tabernacle, and if the Destructive Critics would study it more, they would give up their ingenious but untenable theories as to the composite structure of the Pentateuch.

2. *Truth hidden from man for ages and which they had not discovered and could not discover by the unaided processes of human reasoning has been revealed to apostles and prophets in the Spirit.*

We read in Eph. iii. 3-5, R. V., "*By revelation* was made known unto me the mystery, as I wrote afore in few words, whereby, when ye read, ye can perceive my understanding in the mystery of Christ; which in other generations was not made known unto the sons of men, *as it hath now been revealed unto His holy Apostles and prophets in the Spirit.*" The Bible contains truth that men had never discovered before the Bible stated it. It contains truth that men never could have discovered if left to themselves. Our heavenly Father, in great grace, has revealed this truth to us His children *through* His servants, *the apostles and the prophets*. The Holy Spirit is the agent of this revelation. There are many who tell us to-day that we should test the statements of Scripture by the conclusions of human reasoning or by the "Christian consciousness." The folly of all this is evident when we bear in mind that the revelation of God transcends human reasoning, and that any consciousness that is not the product of the study and absorption of Bible truth is not really a Christian consciousness. The fact that the Bible does contain truth that man never had discovered we know not merely because it is so stated in the Scriptures, but we know it also as a matter of fact. There is not one of the most distinctive and precious doctrines taught in the Bible that men have ever discovered apart from the Bible. If our consciousness differs from the statements of this Book, which is so plainly God's Book, it is not yet fully Christian and the thing to do is not to try to pull God's revelation down to the level of our consciousness but to tone our consciousness up to the level of God's Word.

3. *The revelation made to the prophets was independent of their own thinking. It was made to them by the Spirit of Christ which was in them. And was a subject of inquiry to their own mind as to its meaning. It was not their own thought, but His.*

We read in 1 Peter i. 10, 11, 12, R. V., "Concerning which salvation the prophets sought and searched diligently, who prophesied of the grace that should come unto you: *searching what time or what manner of time the Spirit of Christ which was in them did point unto*, when it (He) testified beforehand the sufferings of Christ, and the glories that should follow them. *To whom it was revealed*, that not unto themselves, but unto you, did they minister these things, which now have been announced unto you through them that preached the Gospel unto you *by the Holy Ghost* sent forth from heaven; which things angels desire to look into." These words make it plain that a Person in the prophets, and independent of the prophets, and that Person the Holy Spirit, revealed truth which was independent of their own thinking, which they did not altogether understand themselves, and regarding which it was necessary that they make diligent search and study. Another Person than themselves was thinking and speaking and they were seeking to comprehend what He said.

4. *No prophet's utterance was of the prophet's own will, but he spoke from God, and the prophet was carried along in his utterance by the Holy Spirit.*

We read in 2 Peter i. 21, R. V., "For *no prophecy ever came by the will of man*: but men spake *from God, being moved by the Holy Ghost*." Clearly then, the prophet was simply an instrument in the hands of another, as the Spirit of God carried him along, so he spoke.

5. *It was the Holy Spirit who spoke in the prophetic utterances. It was His word that was upon the prophet's tongue.*

We read in Heb. iii. 7, "Wherefore *as the Holy Ghost saith*, To-day if ye will hear His voice." Again we read in Heb. x. 15, 16, "Whereof *the Holy Ghost also is a witness* to us: for *after that He had said* before, This is the covenant that I will make with them after those days, saith the Lord. I will put My laws into their hearts, and in their minds will I write them."

We read again in Acts xxviii. 25, R. V., "And when they agreed not among themselves, they departed, after that Paul had spoken the word, '*Well spake the Holy Ghost* by Isaiah the prophet unto your fathers saying, etc.' " Still again we read in 2 Sam. xxiii. 2, R. V., "The *Spirit of the Lord spake by me*, and *His word* was upon my tongue." Over and over again in these passages we are told that it was the Holy Spirit who was the speaker in the prophetic utterances and that it was His word, not theirs, that was upon the prophet's tongue. The prophet was simply the mouth by which the Holy Spirit spoke. As a man, that is except as the Spirit taught him and used him, the prophet might be as fallible as other men are but when the Spirit was upon him and he was taken up and borne along by the Holy Spirit, he was infallible in his teachings; for his teachings in that case were not his own, but the teachings of the Holy Spirit. When thus borne along by the Holy Spirit it was God who was speaking and not the prophet. For example, there can be little doubt that Paul had many mistaken notions about many things but when he taught as an Apostle in the Spirit's power, he was infallible—or rather the Spirit, who taught through him was infallible and the consequent teaching was infallible—as infallible as God Himself. We do well therefore to carefully distinguish what Paul may have thought as a man and what he actually did teach as an Apostle. In the Bible we have the record of what he taught as an Apostle. There are those who think that in 1 Cor. vii. 6, 25, "But I speak this by permission, not of commandment... yet I give my judgment as one that hath obtained mercy of the Lord," Paul admits that he was not sure in this case that he had the word of the Lord. If this be the true interpretation of the passage (which is more than doubtful) we see how careful Paul was when he was not sure to note the fact and this gives us additional certainty in all other passages. It is sometimes said that Paul taught in his early ministry that the Lord would return during his lifetime, and that in this he was, of course, mistaken. But Paul never taught anywhere that the Lord would return in his lifetime. It is true he says in 1 Thess. iv. 17, "*Then we which are alive and remain*, shall be caught up together with them to meet the Lord in the air, and so shall we ever be with the Lord." As he was still living when he wrote the words, he naturally and properly did not include himself with those who had already fallen asleep in speaking of the Lord's return. But this is not to assert that he would remain alive until the Lord came. Quite probably at this period of his ministry he entertained the hope that he might remain alive and consequently lived in an attitude of expectancy, but the attitude of expectancy is the true attitude in all ages for each believer. It is quite probable that Paul expected that he would be alive to the coming of the Lord, but if he did so expect, he did not so teach. The Holy Spirit kept him from this as from all other errors in his teachings.

6. *The Holy Spirit in the Apostle taught not only the thought (or "concept") but the words in which the thought was to he expressed.* We read in 1 Cor. ii. 13, A. R. V., "Which things also we speak not *in words* which man's wisdom teacheth, but which the Spirit teacheth combining spiritual things with *spiritual words.*" This passage clearly teaches that the words, as well as the thought, were chosen and taught by the Holy Spirit. This is also a necessary inference from the fact that thought is conveyed from mind to mind by words and it is the words which express the thought, and if the words were imperfect, the thought expressed in these words would necessarily be imperfect and to that extent be untrue. Nothing could be plainer than Paul's statement "*in words* which the Spirit teacheth." The Holy Spirit has Himself anticipated all the modern ingenious and wholly unbiblical and false theories regarding His own work in the Apostles. The more carefully and minutely we study *the wording* of the statements of this wonderful Book, the more we will become convinced of the marvelous accuracy of the words used to express the thought. Very often the solution of an apparent difficulty is found in studying the exact words used. The accuracy, precision and inerrancy of the exact words used is amazing. To the superficial student, the doctrine of verbal inspiration may appear questionable or even absurd; any regenerated and Spirit-taught man, who *ponders the words* of the Scripture day after day and year after year, will become convinced that the wisdom of God is in the very words, as well as in the thought which the words endeavor to convey. A change of a word, or letter, or a tense, or case, or number, in many instances would land us into contradiction or untruth, but taking *the words exactly* as written, difficulties disappear and truth shines forth. The Divine origin of nature shines forth more clearly in the use of a microscope as we see the perfection of form and adaptation of means to end of the minutest particles of matter. In a similar manner, the Divine origin of the Bible shines forth more clearly under the microscope as we notice the perfection with which the turn of a word reveals the absolute thought of God.

But some one may ask, "If the Holy Spirit is the author of the words of Scripture, how do we account for variations in style and diction? How do we explain for instance that Paul always used Pauline language and John Johannean language, etc.?" The answer to this is very simple. If we could not account at all for this fact, it would have but little weight against the explicit statement of God's Word with any one who is humble enough and wise enough to recognize that there are a great many things which he cannot account for at all which could be easily accounted for if he knew more. But these variations are easily accounted for. The Holy Spirit is quite wise enough and has quite facility enough in the use of language in revealing truth to and through any given individual, to use words, phrases and forms of expression and idioms in that person's vocabulary and forms of thought, and to make use of that person's peculiar individuality. Indeed, it is a mark of the Divine wisdom of this Book that the same truth is expressed with absolute accuracy in such widely variant forms of expression.

7. *The utterances of the Apostles and the prophets were the Word of God. When we read these words, we are listening not to the voice of man, but to the voice of God.*

We read in Mark vii. 13, "Making *the word of God* of none effect, through your tradition, which ye have delivered; and many such like things do ye." Jesus had been setting the law given through Moses over against the Pharisaic traditions, and in doing this, He expressly says in this passage that the law given through Moses was "*the word of God.*" In 2 Sam. xxiii. 2, we read, "The Spirit of the Lord spake by me, and *His word* was in my tongue." Here again we are told that the utterance of God's prophet was the word of God. In a similar way God says in 1 Thess. ii. 13, "For this cause also thank we God without ceasing, because, when ye *received the word of God which ye heard of us*, ye received it not as the word of men, but as it is *in truth, the word of God*, which effectually worketh also in you that believe." Here Paul declares that the word which he spoke, taught by the Spirit of God, was *the very word of God.*

XXII: The Work of the Holy Spirit In Jesus Christ

Jesus Christ Himself is the one perfect manifestation in history of the complete work of the Holy Spirit in man.

1. *Jesus Christ was begotten of the Holy Spirit.* We read in Luke i. 35, R. V., "And the angel answered and said unto her, The Holy Ghost shall come upon thee; and the power of the Most High shall overshadow thee: wherefore also that which is to be born shall be called holy, the Son of God." As we have already seen, in regeneration the believer is begotten of God, but Jesus Christ was begotten of God in His original generation. He is the only begotten Son of God (John iii. 16). It was entirely by the Spirit's power working in Mary that the Son of God was formed within her. The regenerated man has a carnal nature received from his earthly father and a new nature imparted by God. Jesus Christ had only the one holy nature, that which in man is called the new nature. Nevertheless, He was a real man as He had a human mother.

2. *Jesus Christ led a holy and spotless life and offered Himself without spot to God through the working of the Holy Spirit.* We read in Heb. ix. 14, "How much more shall the blood of Christ, who *through the eternal Spirit offered Himself without spot to God*, purge your conscience from dead works to serve the living God." Jesus Christ met and overcame temptations as other men may meet and overcome them, in the power of the Holy Spirit. He was tempted and suffered through temptation (Heb. iii. 18), He was tempted in all points like as we are (Heb. iv. 15), but never once in any way did He yield to temptation. He was tempted entirely apart from sin (Heb. iv. 15), but He won His victories in a way that is open for all of us to win victory, in the power of the Holy Spirit.

3. *Jesus Christ was anointed and fitted for service by the Holy Spirit.* We read in Acts x. 38, "How God anointed Jesus of Nazareth *with the Holy Ghost and with power*: who went about doing good, and healing all that were oppressed of the devil; for God was with Him." In a prophetic vision of the coming Messiah in the Old Testament we read in Isa. lxi. 1, "*The Spirit of the Lord God is upon me*, because the Lord hath anointed me to preach good tidings unto the meek; He hath sent me to bind up the broken-hearted, to proclaim liberty to the captives, and the opening of the prison to them that are bound." In Luke's record of the earthly life of our Lord in Luke iv. 14, we read "And Jesus returned *in the power of the Spirit* into Galilee, and there went out a fame of Him through all the region round about." In a similar way Jesus said of Himself when speaking in the synagogue in Nazareth, "*The Spirit* of the Lord is upon Me, because He hath anointed Me to preach good tidings unto the poor; He hath sent Me to proclaim release to the captives, and recovering of sight to the blind, to set at liberty them that are bruised, to proclaim the acceptable year of the Lord" (Luke iv. 18, 19, R. V.). All these passages contain the one lesson, that it was by the especial anointing with the Holy Spirit that Jesus Christ was qualified for the service to which God had called Him. As He stood in the Jordan after His baptism, "The Holy Ghost descended in a bodily shape like a dove upon Him," and it was then and there that He was anointed with the Holy Spirit, baptized with the Holy Spirit, and equipped for the service that lay before Him. Jesus Christ received His equipment for service in the same way that we receive ours by a definite baptism with the Holy Spirit.

4. *Jesus Christ was led by the Holy Spirit in His movements here upon earth.* We read in Luke iv. 1, R. V., "And Jesus full of the Holy Ghost returned from Jordan and *was led by the Spirit* in the wilderness." Living as a man here upon earth and setting an example for us, each step of His life was under the Holy Spirit's guidance.

5. *Jesus Christ was taught by the Spirit who rested upon Him. The Spirit of God was the source of His wisdom in the days of His flesh.* In the Old Testament prophecy of the coming Messiah we read in Isa. xi. 2, 3, "*And the Spirit of the Lord shall rest upon Him*, the spirit of wisdom and understanding, the spirit of counsel and might, the spirit of knowledge and of the fear of the Lord. And shall make Him of quick understanding in the fear of the Lord: and He shall not judge after the sight of His eyes, neither reprove after the hearing of His ears." Further on in Isa. xlii. 1, R. V., we read, "Behold My servant, whom I uphold; My chosen in whom My soul delighteth; *I have put My Spirit upon Him*; He shall bring forth judgment to the Gentiles, etc." Matthew tells us in Matt. xii. 17, 18, that this prophecy was fulfilled in Jesus of Nazareth.

6. *The Holy Spirit abode upon Jesus in all His fullness and the words He spoke in consequence were the very words of God.* We read in John iii. 34, R. V., "For He whom God hath sent *speaketh the words of God*: for He giveth not the Spirit by measure."

7. *After His resurrection, Jesus Christ gave commandment unto His Apostles whom He had chosen through the Holy Spirit.* We read in Acts i. 2, "Until the day in which He was taken up, after that He *through the Holy Ghost had given commandment* unto the Apostles whom He had chosen." This relates to the time after His resurrection and so we see Jesus still working in the power of the Holy Spirit even after His resurrection from the dead.

8. *Jesus Christ wrought His miracles here on earth in the power of the Holy Spirit.* In Matt. xii. 28, we read, "I cast out devils by the power of the Spirit of God." It is through the Spirit that miracle working power was given to some in the church after our Lord's departure from this earth (1 Cor. xii. 9, 10), and in the power of the same Spirit, Jesus Christ wrought His miracles.

9. *It was by the power of the Holy Spirit that Jesus Christ was raised from the dead.* We read in Rom. viii. 11, "But if the Spirit of *Him that raised up Jesus from the dead* dwell in you, He that raised up Christ from the dead shall also quicken your mortal bodies by His Spirit that dwelleth in you."

The same Spirit who is to quicken our mortal bodies and is to raise us up in some future day raised up Jesus.

Several things are plainly evident from this study of the work of the Holy Spirit in Jesus Christ:

First of all, we see the completeness of His humanity. He lived and He thought, He worked, He taught, He conquered sin and won victories for God in the power of that very same Spirit whom it is our privilege also to have.

In the second place, we see our own utter dependence upon the Holy Spirit. If it was in the power of the Holy Spirit that Jesus Christ, the only begotten Son of God, lived and worked, achieved and triumphed, how much more dependent are we upon Him at every turn of life and in every phase of service and every experience of conflict with Satan and sin.

The third thing that is evident is the wondrous world of privilege, blessing and victory and conquest that is open to us. The same Spirit by which Jesus was originally begotten, is at our disposal for us to be begotten again of Him. The same Spirit by which Jesus offered Himself without spot to God is at our disposal that we also may offer ourselves without spot to Him. The same Spirit by which Jesus was anointed for service is at our disposal that we may be anointed for service. The same Spirit who led Jesus Christ in His movements here on earth is ready to lead us to-day. The same Spirit who taught Jesus and imparted to Him wisdom and understanding, counsel and might, and knowledge and the fear of the Lord is here to teach us. Jesus Christ is our pattern (1 John ii. 6), "the first born among many brethren" (Rom. viii. 29). Whatever He realized through the Holy Spirit is for us to realize also to-day.

How to Bring Men to Christ

~ ※ ~

By *R. A. Torrey*

~ ※ ~

Preface

This book is written because it seems to be needed. The author has been repeatedly requested by Ministers, Y. M. C. A. Secretaries, Christian Workers, and his own students to put into a permanent and convenient shape the substance of what he has said at Conventions, Summer Schools and in the class–room on personal work. The time has come to yield to these requests. Never before in the history of the Church were there so many who desire to win others to Christ. The good work done by the Young People's Society of Christian Endeavor is in no other direction so evident as in the many thousands of young people in this land who to–day are on fire with a desire to win souls. But while they desire to do this work, many do not know how. This little book aims to tell them. There are several well–known and valuable manuals of texts to be used with inquirers, but this book is intended not only to point out passages to be used but to show how to use them, illustrating this use by cases from actual experience. It is hoped that from a careful study of these pages any earnest Christian can learn how to do efficient work in bringing others to the Savior.

Chapter I. The General Conditions of Success in Bringing Men to Christ

There are certain general conditions, the fulfilment of which is absolutely essential to real success in bringing men to Christ. These conditions, fortunately, are few and simple and such as any one can meet.

1. *The one who would have real success in bringing others to Christ must himself be* A THOROUGHLY CONVERTED PERSON. Jesus said to Peter, "When thou art *converted* strengthen thy brethren." He was in no position to help his brethren until he himself, after his cowardly denial, had turned again to his Lord with his whole heart. If we would bring others to Christ we must turn away from all sin, and worldliness and selfishness with our whole heart, yielding to Jesus the absolute lordship over our thoughts, purposes and actions. If there is any direction in which we are seeking to have our own way and not letting Him have His own way in our lives, our power will be crippled and men lost that we might have saved. The application of this principle to the numerous questions that come up in the life of every young Christian as to whether he should do this or that, each individual can settle for himself if Christ's honor and not his own pleasure is upper–most in his mind and if he looks honestly to God to guide him.

2. *The one who would have real success in bringing others to Christ must have a* LOVE FOR SOULS, *i. e. a longing for the salvation of the lost.* If we have no love for souls, our efforts will be mechanical and powerless. We may know how to approach men and what to say to them, but there will be no power in what we say and it will not touch the heart. But if like Paul we have "great heaviness and unceasing pain in our hearts" for the unsaved, there will be an earnestness in our tone and manner that will impress the most careless. Furthermore if we have a love for souls we will be on the constant watch for opportunities to speak with the unsaved and will find opportunities on the street, in the store, in the home, on the cars and everywhere that would otherwise have entirely escaped our notice.

But how is one to get a love for souls? This question is easily answered. First of all, a love for souls like every other grace of Christian character, is the work of the Holy Spirit. If then we are conscious that we do not have that love for souls that we should have, the first thing to do is to go to God and humbly confess this lack in our lives and ask Him by His Holy Spirit to supply that which we so sorely need, and expect Him to do it (1 John v. 14, 15; Phil. iv. 19). In the second place Jesus Christ had an intense love for souls (Matt. xxiii. 37; Luke xix. 10), and intimate and constant companionship with Him will impart to our lives this grace which was so prominent in His. In the third place feelings are the outcome of thoughts. If we desire any given feeling in our lives we should dwell upon the thoughts which are adapted to produce that feeling. If any saved person will dwell long enough upon the peril and wretchedness of any man out of Christ and the worth of his soul in God's sight as seen in the death of God's Son to save him, a feeling of intense desire for that man's salvation is almost certain to follow. In the fourth place, reflection upon our own ruined and unhappy condition without Christ and the great sacrifice that Christ made to save us, is sure to fill our hearts with a desire to bring others to the Savior we have found.

3. *The one who would have real success in bringing men to Christ must have a* WORKING KNOWLEDGE OF THE BIBLE. The Word of God is the sword of the Spirit (Eph. vi. 17). It is the instrument God uses to convict of sin, to reveal Christ and to regenerate men. If we would work together with God, the Bible is the instrument upon which we must rely and which we must use in bringing men to Christ. We must know how to use the Bible so as (1) to show men their need of a Savior, (2) to show them Jesus as the Savior they need, (3) to show them how to make this Savior their own Savior, (4) to meet the difficulties that stand in the way of their accepting Christ. A large part of the following pages will be devoted to imparting this knowledge.

4. *The one who would have real success in bringing men to Christ must* PRAY MUCH. Solid work in soul winning must be accompanied by prayer at every step. (1). We must pray God to lead us to the right persons to approach. God does not intend that we speak to every one we meet. If we try to do it, we will waste much valuable time in speaking to those whom we cannot help, that we might have used in speaking to those to whom we could have done much good. God alone knows the one to whom He intends us to speak, and we must ask Him to point him out to us, and, expect Him to do it. (Acts viii. 29). (2). We must pray God to show us just what to say to those to whom He leads us. After all our study of the passages to be used in dealing with the various classes of men, we shall need God's guidance in each specific case. Every experienced worker will testify to the many instances in which God has led them to use some text of Scripture that they would not otherwise have used but which proved to be just the one needed. (3). We must pray God to give power to that which He has given us to say. We need not only a message from God but power from God to send the message home. Most workers have to learn this lesson by humiliating experiences. They sit down beside an unsaved man and reason and plead and bring forth texts from the word of God, but the man does not accept Christ. At last it dawns upon them that they are trying to convert the man in their own strength and then they lift an humble and earnest prayer to God for his strength, and God hears and in a short time this "very difficult case" has settled the matter and is rejoicing in Christ. (4). We must pray God to carry on the work after our work has come to an end. After having done that which seems to have been our whole duty in any given instance, whatever may have been the apparent issue of our work, whether successful or unsuccessful, we should definitely commit the case to God in prayer. If there is anything

the average worker in this hurrying age needs to have impressed upon him, it is the necessity of more prayer. By praying more we will not work any less and we will accomplish vastly more.

5. *The one who would have real success in bringing men to Christ must be* "BAPTIZED WITH THE HOLY GHOST." "Ye shall receive power after that the Holy Ghost, is come upon you," said Jesus to his disciples after having given them the great commission to go out and bring men to Himself. The supreme condition of soul winning power is the same to–day: "after that the Holy Ghost is come upon you." A later chapter will be given to a study of what "the Baptism of the Holy Ghost" is and how any Christian can obtain it.

Chapter II. How to Begin

When God has led us to think that He wishes us to make an effort to lead some given individual to Christ, the first question that confronts us is, "How shall I begin?" If the person has gone into an inquiry room, or remained to an after–meeting, or even if they are merely present at prayer–meeting, Sunday–school or other ordinary service of the church, it is comparatively easy. You can then ask him if he is a Christian, or if he would not like to be a Christian, or why he is not a Christian or some other direct and simple question that will lead inevitably to a conversation along this line. But if the person is one in whom you have become interested outside the religious meeting and who is perhaps an entire stranger, it does not at first sight appear so simple, and yet it is not so very difficult. The person can be engaged in conversation on some general topic or on something suggested by passing events, and soon brought around to the great subject. Christ's conversation with the woman of Samaria in the 4th chapter of John is a very instructive illustration of this. Oftentimes even in dealing with entire strangers it is well to broach the subject at once and ask them if they are Christians or if they are saved or some similar question. If this is done courteously and earnestly it will frequently set even careless people to thinking and result in their conversion. It is astonishing how often one who undertakes this work in humble dependence upon God and under His direction, finds the way prepared and how seldom he receives any rebuff. One day the writer met a man on one of the most crowded streets of Chicago. As I passed him the impulse came to speak to him about the Savior. Stopping a moment and asking God to show me if the impulse was from Him, I turned around and followed the man. I overtook him in the middle of the street, laid my hand upon his shoulder and said: "My friend, are you a Christian?" He started and said: "That's a strange question to ask a man." I said, "I know it, and I do not ask that question of every stranger, but God put it into my heart to ask it of you." He then told me that his cousin was a minister and had been urging this very matter upon him, that he himself was a graduate of Amherst college, but had been ruined by drink. After further conversation we separated but later the man accepted Christ as his Savior.

It is often best to win a person's confidence and affection before broaching the subject. It is well to select some one and then lay your plans to win him to Christ. Cultivate his acquaintance, show him many attentions and perform many acts of kindness great and small and at last when the fitting moment arrives take up the great question. An old and thorough going infidel in Chicago was in this way won to Christ by a young woman, who found him sick and alone. She called day after day and showed him many kindnesses and as the consumption fastened itself more firmly upon him she spoke to him of the Savior and had the joy of seeing him accept Christ.

A wisely chosen tract placed in the hand of the one with whom you wish to speak will often lead easily and naturally to the subject. One day I was riding on a train and praying that God would use me to lead some one to His Son. A young lady, daughter of a minister, with whom I had had some conversation on this subject came in with a friend and took the seat immediately in front of me. I took out a little bundle of tracts and selected one that seemed adapted for the purpose and handed it to her and asked her to read it. As she read, I prayed. When she had finished, I leaned over and asked her what she thought about it. She was deeply moved and I asked her if she would not accept Christ right there. Her difficulties were soon met and answered and she accepted Christ. As she left the train she thanked me very heartily for what I had done for her.

You will often meet some one whose face tells the story of unhappiness or discontent: in such a case it is easy to ask the person if he is happy and when he answers "no" you can say, "I can tell you of one who will make you happy if you will only take Him." Skill in beginning a conversation will come with practice. One may be rather awkward about it at first but as we go on we will acquire facility.

When the subject is once opened the first thing to find out is where the person with whom you are dealing stands; then you will know how to wisely treat his case. In the chapters immediately following this all the classes of men one is likely to meet will be given, and the first point to be ascertained is to which class any given individual belongs. But how can we find out to which class any person belongs? First. By asking him questions. Such questions as "Are you a Christian?" "Are you saved?" "Do you know that your sins are forgiven?" "Have you eternal life?" "Are you confessing Christ openly before the world?" "Are you a friend of Jesus?" "Have you been born again?" One may answer these questions untruthfully, either through ignorance or a desire to mislead you. Nevertheless, their answers and the manner of them will show you a great deal about their real state. Second. By watching his face. A man's face will often reveal that which his words try to conceal. Any one who cultivates the study of the faces of those with whom he deals will soon be able to tell in many instances the exact state of those with whom they are dealing irrespective of anything they may say. Third. By the Holy Spirit. The Holy Spirit if we only look to Him to do it will often flash into our minds a view of the man's position, and just the scripture he needs.

When we have learned where the person with whom we are dealing stands, the next thing to do is to lead him as directly as we can to accept Jesus Christ, as his personal Savior and Master. We must always bear in mind that the primary purpose of our work, is not to get persons to join the church or to give up their bad habits or to do anything else than this, to accept Jesus Christ, as their Savior—the one who bore their sins in his own body on the tree and through whom they can have immediate and entire forgiveness,—and as their Master to whom they surrender absolutely the guidance of their thoughts, feelings, purposes and actions. Having led any one to thus accept Christ the next step will be to show him from God's word that he has forgiveness of sins and eternal life. Acts x. 43; xiii. 39; John iii. 36; v. 24, will answer for this purpose. The next step will be to show him how to make a success of the Christian life upon which he has entered. How to do this will be told later. Each person is to be led to accept Christ through a use of the word of God. In the chapters that immediately follow this we will try to show what specific portions of the word to use in given cases and how to use them.

Chapter III. Dealing with the Indifferent or Careless

One of the classes of men most frequently met with, is The Indifferent, or Careless. There are several ways of dealing with them. One is to show them their need of a Savior. A good verse to use for this purpose is Romans iii. 23. Get the person with whom you are dealing to read the verse, "For all have sinned and come short of the glory of God." Then say to him: "Who have sinned?" "All." "Who does that include?" and keep up the questioning until he says, "It includes me." Then ask him what it is that he has done, and keep at it until he comes out plainly and says: "I have sinned and come short of the glory of God." This is likely to make him feel his need of a Savior. Another good verse to use is Isaiah liii. 6. After the verse has been read, ask him who it is that has gone astray and by a series of questions bring him to the point where he will say, "I have gone astray." Then ask him what kind of a sheep one is that has "gone astray" and hold him to it until he says "a lost sheep." "What are you then?" "Lost." Then ask him what the Lord has done with his sin, and hold him to that point until he sees the truth of the verse, that God has laid his sin on Jesus Christ. Now, he is in a position for you to put to him the direct question: "Will you accept this Savior upon whom the Lord has laid your sin?" Still another verse to use is Psalms cxxx. 3. When the verse has been read, ask him, "If the Lord marked iniquities could you stand?" In dealing with this class of men I use Matthew xxii. 37, 38 more frequently than any other passage of Scripture. Before having the person read the verse, it is well to ask him, "Do you know that you have committed the greatest sin that a man can commit?" In all probability he will answer, "No, I have not." Then ask him what he thinks the greatest sin a man can commit. When he has answered, say to him, Now let us see what God considers the greatest sin. Read the verses and ask him, "What is the first and greatest of the commandments?" Then ask him, "What then is the greatest sin?" He will soon answer that the violation of the first and greatest of the commandments must be the greatest sin. Ask him if he has kept that commandment and when he confesses, as sooner or later he must, that he has not, ask him of what he is guilty in the sight of God, and hold him to that point until he admits that he is guilty of committing the greatest sin that a man can commit. An illustration from life may help to make the use of this verse clear. I was dealing with a very bright young man who evidently had no deep sense of sin nor of his need of a Savior. In fact when I asked if he was a Christian he said promptly that he always had been; but there was something in his manner that showed that he had no clear understanding of what it meant to be a Christian. I then asked if he had been born again and he did not even understand what I was talking about. I next asked if he knew he had committed the greatest sin that a man could possibly commit and he at once answered, "No, I never did in my life." I asked what he considered the greatest sin, and he replied "murder." I took my Bible and opened it to Matthew xxii. 37, 38, and asked him to read the verses, which he did. I then asked him, "If this is the first and greatest commandment, what must be the greatest sin?" He answered, "I suppose the breaking of that commandment." I then asked if he had always kept that commandment, if he had always loved God with all his heart, with all his soul, and with all his mind. If he had always put God first in everything. He replied that he had not. I then asked him, "Of what then are you guilty?" The Spirit of God carried the text home and with the greatest earnestness he replied, "I have committed the greatest sin that a man can commit, but I never saw it before in my life." Another verse that can be used with effect is John viii. 34. After the man has read the verse, "Whosoever committeth sin is the servant of sin," ask him "what is one who commits sin?" Then ask him if he commits sin. Then put to him the direct question, "What are you then," and hold him to it until he says "the servant of sin." Then ask him if he does not desire to be delivered from that awful bondage. Hold him to this point until he sees his need of Jesus Christ as a Deliverer from the slavery of sin. The Holy Spirit has used Isaiah lvii. 21 to the salvation of many men who have been indifferent to the claims of the Gospel. After the verse, "There is no peace saith my God to the wicked," has been read slowly, thoughtfully, and earnestly, ask him who it is that says this. Then ask him if it is true; then ask him if it is true in his case. "Have you peace?" One night a careless young man was going out of one of our tents in Chicago and as he passed by me I took him by the hand and said to him, "You need the Savior." He wanted to know why I thought so. I replied, "Because you have no peace." He said, "Yes I have." "No you have not." He then asked me how I knew that. I told him God said so and quoted the above passage. He tried to laugh it off and say the verse was not true in his case. Then he became angry and went out of the tent in a rage, but the next night I saw him kneeling with one of our workers in prayer and when he arose from his knees, the worker came over and said he wished to speak with me. As I approached him he held out his hand and said, "I wanted to beg your pardon for what I said last night; what you said was true, I didn't have peace." I asked him if he had now accepted the Savior. He said he had.

Galatians iii. 10 is a verse which we very frequently use in our work in dealing with the Indifferent. After the one with whom you are dealing has read the verse, "For as many as are of the works of the law are under the curse; for it is written cursed is every one that continueth not in all things which are written in the book of the law to do them" ask him the question, "What is every one that continueth not in all things which are written in the book of the law to do them?" When he answers, "Cursed," ask him if he has continued in all things which are written in the book of the law to do them and when he replies, "No, I have not," put to him the direct question, "What are you then?" and hold him to that point until he says, "I am under the curse." In very many cases the inquirer will be ready at once to be led to the thirteenth verse of the same chapter which shows how he may be saved from that curse under which he rests. Romans vi. 23 can often be used with good effect. "For the wages of sin is death." Ask "what are the wages of sin?" Then, "who earns those wages?" Then, "Are you a sinner?" "What wages then have you earned?" "Do you wish to take your wages?" John iii. 36 is a verse which can be used in a similar way. Ask the question, "Upon whom is it that the wrath of God abides?" Then, "Do you believe on the Son?" "What then abides upon you?" Then put the decisive question, "Are you willing to go away with the wrath of God abiding upon you?" 2 Thes. i. 7–9, and John viii. 24; Rev. xx. 15; xxi. 8; xiv. 10–11, set forth in a most impressive way the awful consequences of sin. If these verses are used they should be read with the deepest earnestness and solemnity and dwelt upon until the person with whom you are dealing realizes their terrible import.

There is another way to arouse a man from his indifference, and that is by showing what Jesus has done for him. I have found Isaiah liii. 5–6 more effectual for this purpose than any other passage in the Bible. An incident from life will illustrate its use. A lady had asked prayers for her daughter, a young woman about twenty years of age. At the close of the services I stepped up to the daughter and asked her if she would not accept Jesus Christ as her Savior at once. She stamped her foot in anger and said, "My mother should have known better than to do that; she knows it will only make me worse." I asked her if she would not sit down for a few minutes and as soon as we were seated I opened my Bible to this passage and began to read, "But he was wounded for our transgressions, he was bruised for our iniquities; the chastisement of our peace was upon him; and with his stripes we are healed. All we like sheep have gone astray; we have turned every one to his own way; and the Lord hath laid on him the iniquity of us all." I made no comment upon the verses whatever, but the Spirit of God carried them home and tears began to roll down the cheeks of the young woman. She did not come out as a Christian that night but did shortly afterward. It is well in using these verses, whenever it is possible, to get the inquirer to change the pronoun from the plural to the singular. "He was wounded for *my* transgressions; he was bruised for *my* iniquities, etc." John iii. 16 can be used in a similar way. I was talking one night to one who was apparently most indifferent and hardened. She told me the story of her sin, with seemingly very little sense of shame, and when I urged her to accept Christ, she simply refused. I put a Bible in her hands and asked her to read this verse. She began to read, "God so loved the world that He gave His only begotten Son," and before she had finished reading the verse she had broken into tears, softened by the thought of God's wondrous love to her. First Peter ii. 24 is a verse of similar character. Ask the inquirer whose sins they were that Jesus bore in his own body on the tree, and hold him to it until he says, "My sins." 1 Peter i. 18–19; Luke xxii. 44; Matt. xxvii. 46, are useful as bringing out in detail what Christ has suffered for us.

There is still another way to arouse indifferent persons, and that is by showing them that the one damning sin is that of which they themselves are guilty—the sin of rejecting Jesus Christ. Heb. x. 28–29 is very effective for this purpose. John xvi. 9; iii. 18, 19, 20, and Acts ii. 36 can also be used.

Oftentimes you will meet one who is not willing to sit down and let you deal with him in this deliberate way. In that case the only thing to do is to look up to God for guidance and power and give him some pointed verse in great earnestness, such for example as Heb. x. 28–29; Romans vi. 23; John iii. 36; Isaiah lvii. 21, and leave it for the Spirit of God to carry the truth home to his heart. A passing shot of this kind has often resulted in the salvation of a soul. The passages given above can be wisely used with one who is not altogether indifferent or careless but who has not a sufficiently deep sense of sin and need to be ready to accept the Gospel.

Chapter IV. Dealing with Those Who Are Anxious to be Saved but Do Not Know How

There is a very large class of persons who are anxious to be saved but simply do not know how. It is not difficult to lead this class of persons to Christ. Perhaps no other passage in the Bible is more used for this purpose than Isaiah liii. 6. It makes the way of salvation very plain. Read the first part of the verse to the inquirer, "All we like sheep have gone astray, we have turned every one to his own way." Then ask, "Is that true of you," and when he has thought it over and said "yes," then say to him, "Now let us see what God has done with your sins," and read the remainder of the verse, "And the Lord hath laid on him the iniquity of us all." "What then is it necessary for you to do to be saved?" Very soon he can be led to see that all that it is necessary for him to do is to accept the sin bearer whom God has provided. Some years ago I noticed in a meeting a white–haired man who did not stand up with the Christians. At the close of the service I walked down to him and said, "Are you not a Christian?" He said he was not. I was sure he was interested, so I put to him the direct question, "Would you become a Christian to–night if I would show you the way?" and he replied that he would. We sat down together and I opened my Bible to Isaiah liii. 6 and read the first part of the verse, "All we like sheep have gone astray, we have turned every one to his own way." I then said to him, "Is that true of you?" and he answered "yes." "Now," I said, "let us read the rest of the verse, 'And the Lord hath laid on him the iniquity of us all.'" "What has the Lord done," I said, "with your sins?" He thought a moment and said "he has laid them on Christ." "What then" I said "is all that you have to do to be saved?" and he replied quite promptly, "Accept him." "Well," I said, "will you accept him to–night?" He said, "I will." "Let us then kneel down and tell God so." We knelt down and I led in prayer and he followed in a very simple way telling God that he was a sinner but that he believed that He had laid his sins upon Jesus Christ, and asking God for Christ's sake to forgive his sins. When he had finished I asked him if he thought God had heard his prayer and that his sins were forgiven, and he said "yes." I then asked him if he would begin to lead a Christian life at once, set up the family altar and openly confess Christ before the world, and he replied that he would. Some months after I met his pastor and made inquiries about him and found that he had gone to his home in a distant village, set up the family altar and united with the church together with his son, the only remaining member of the family out of Christ. Apparently all that this man was waiting for was for some one to make the way of salvation plain to him. I sometimes put it this way in using this verse: "There are two things which a man needs to know and one thing he needs to do in order to be saved. What he needs to *know* is, first, that he is a lost sinner and this verse tells him that; second, that Christ is an all–sufficient Savior and this verse tells him that. What he needs to *do* is simply to accept this all–sufficient Savior whom God has provided." John i. 12 brings out this thought very clearly, "As many as *received him* to them gave he power to become the sons of God, even to them that believe on his name." After the verse has been read you can ask the one with whom you are dealing, "To whom is it that God gives the power to become the sons of God?" "As many as receive him." What must you then do to become a son of God? "Receive him." Well, will you receive him as your Savior and as your master now? Isaiah lv. 7; Acts xvi. 31; John iii. 16 and iii. 36 are all useful in making the way of salvation plain. John iii. 14 compared with Numbers xxi. 8 and the following verses, can often be used with good effect. When they are used you should lead the inquirer to see just what the serpent–bitten Israelite had to do to be saved—that he had simply to look at the brazen serpent lifted up upon the pole—then show him that the sin–bitten man has to do simply the same thing—look at Christ lifted up on the Cross for his sins. Romans i. 16 is another excellent verse to use. It makes the way of salvation very clear. You can ask the inquirer whom it is, according to his verse, that the Gospel saves, and he will see that it is "every one that believeth." Then ask him, "What then is all that is necessary for one to do in order to be saved," and he will see that it is simply to believe. Then ask him "believe what," and the answer is "the Gospel." The next question that naturally arises is, what is the Gospel? This is answered by 1 Cor. xv.; 1–4. These verses show what the Gospel is, "that Christ died for our sins according to the Scriptures; that he was buried and that he rose the third day according to the scriptures" and this is what he must believe in order to be saved. He must believe from his heart that Christ died for his sins and that he rose again. Then ask the inquirer, "do you believe that Christ died for your sins? do you believe that he rose again?" If he says that he does, ask him if he will make this a heart faith and get down and ask God for Christ's sake, to forgive his sins and believe he does it because he says so, and then trust in the living Savior to save him day by day from the power of sin. Romans x. 9–10 also makes the way of salvation clear to many minds where other verses fail. Romans x. 13 makes it, if possible, more simple still. This shows that all that a man has to do to be saved is to "call upon the name of the Lord." You can ask the inquirer "Are you ready now and here to get down and call upon the name of the Lord for salvation and to believe that God saves you because he says he will?" The way of salvation can be made plain by the use of Exodus xii. 7, 13, 23. These verses show that it was the blood that made the Israelites safe and just so it is to–day the blood that makes us safe, and when God sees the blood he passes over us. The only thing for us to do is to get behind the blood. Then show the inquirer that the way to be behind the blood is by simple faith in Jesus Christ. Luke xviii. 10–14 is exceedingly useful in showing what a man may have and yet be lost (the Pharisee) and what a man may lack and yet be saved (the Publican) and that all that a man has to do to be saved is simply to do as the Publican did, that is take the sinner's place and cry to God for mercy and then he will go down to his house justified. This passage can be used in the following manner to make the meaning more clear. Ask the inquirer, "Which one of these two (the Pharisee or the Publican) went down to his house justified?" Then ask him, "What did the Publican do that the Pharisee did not do, that brought him the forgiveness of his sins while the Pharisee went out of the Temple unforgiven?" When he studies the passage he will soon see that what the Publican did was simply to take the sinner's place before God and cry for mercy and that as soon as he did this he was "justified" or forgiven. Then you can ask him, "What is all that it is necessary for you to do to find forgiveness?" Then ask him, "Will you do it now and here?" and when he has done so ask him if he believes God's word and if he is going down to his house justified. What saving faith is, is beautifully illustrated by Luke vii. 48–50. The fiftieth verse tells us that this woman had saving faith. Now ask the inquirer, "What was the faith she had," and show him that her faith was simply such faith that Jesus could and would forgive her sins, that she came to him to do it. This is saving faith. Galatians iii. 10–13 also makes the way of salvation very simple. The tenth verse shows the sinner's position before accepting Christ—"under the curse." The thirteenth verse shows what Christ has done—has been made a curse for us. What the sinner had to do is, evidently, simply to accept Christ.

Chapter V. Dealing with Those Who Are Anxious to be Saved and Know How, but Who Have Difficulties

A very large number of persons whom we try to lead to Christ, we will find are really anxious to be saved and know how, but are confronted with difficulties which they deem insurmountable.

1. One of the difficulties is, "*I am too great a sinner*." 1 Tim. i. 15 meets this fully. One Sunday morning a man who had led a wild and wandering life and who had recently lost $35,000 and been separated from his wife, said to me in response to my question, why he was not Christian, "I am too great a sinner to be saved." I turned at once to 1 Tim. i. 15. "This is a faithful saying and worthy of all acceptation, that Christ Jesus came into the world to save sinners, of whom I am chief." He quickly replied, "well, I am the chief of sinners." "Well," I said, "that verse means you then." He replied, "It is a precious promise." I said, "Will you accept it now?" and he said, "I will." Then I said, "Let us kneel down and tell God so," and we knelt down and he confessed to God his sins, and asked God for Christ's sake to forgive him his sins. I asked him if he had really accepted Christ and he said he had. I asked him if he really believed that he was saved and he said he did. He took an early opportunity of confessing Christ. He left the city in a short time but I was able to follow him. He became a most active Christian, working at his business day times but engaged in some form of Christian work every night in the week. He was reunited to his wife and adopted a little child out of an orphan asylum and had a happy Christian home. Luke xix. 10 is also a very useful passage to use in dealing with this class of men;

especially useful when a man says, "I am lost." You can say, "I have a passage intended expressly for you. If you really mean what you say, you are just the man Jesus is seeking. 'For the Son of man is come to seek and save that which was lost.'" Romans v. 6–8 is a very effective passage. I stopped a man one night as he was hurrying out of a meeting. Laying my hand on his shoulder I said "Did you not hold your hand up to–night for prayers?" He said "yes." I said, "Why then are you hurrying away? Do you know God loves you?" He replied, "You do not know who you are talking to." "I do not care who I am talking to but I know God loves you." He said: "I am the meanest thief in Minneapolis." I said "If you are the meanest thief in Minneapolis, then I know God loves you," and I opened my Bible to Romans v. 8. "But God commendeth his love toward us in that while we were yet sinners Christ died for us." "Now," I said, "If you are the meanest thief in Minneapolis, you are a sinner, and this verse tells that God loves sinners." The man broke down and going into another room with me told me his story. He was just out of confinement for crime; had started out that very night to commit what he said would have been one of the most daring burglaries ever committed in the city of Minneapolis; with his two companions in crime he was passing a corner where he happened to hear an open–air meeting going on and stopped a few minutes to hear and in spite of the protests and oaths of his companions stayed through the meeting and went with us to the Mission. After telling me his story we kneeled in prayer. Through tears he cried to God for mercy, having been led by God's precious promise to believe that God loved a sinner even as vile as he. Matt. ix. 12, 13; Romans x. 13 (Emphasize "whosoever"); John iii. 16 (Emphasize the "whosoever"); Isaiah i. 18; 1 John iv. 14; John ii. 1–2; Isaiah xliv. 22; Isaiah xliii. 25 are also useful passages in dealing with this class of men. Isaiah i. 18 and Ps. li. 14 are especially useful in dealing with men who have committed murder. Never tell any one that his sins are not great. It is well sometimes to say to these men, "Yes, your sins are great, greater than you think, but they have all been settled" and show them Isaiah liii. 6; 1 Peter ii. 24. A woman once came to me in great agitation. After many ineffectual attempts she was at last able to unburden her heart. Fourteen years before she had killed a man and had borne the memory of the act upon her conscience until it had almost driven her crazy. When she told the story to another Christian and myself, we turned to Isaiah liii. 6. After reading the verse very carefully to her, I asked her what the Lord had done with her sin. After a few moments' deep and anxious thought she said, "He has laid it on Christ," I took a book in my hand. "Now," I said "let my right hand represent you, and my left hand Christ, and this book your sin." I laid the book upon my right hand and I said: "Where is your sin now?" She said "On me." "Now," I said, "what has God done with it?" She said "Laid it on Christ," and I laid the book over on the other hand. "Where is your sin now?" I asked. It was long before she could summon courage to answer, and then with a desperate effort she said, "On Christ." I said, "then is it on you any longer?" Slowly the light came into her face and she burst out with a cry, "No, it is on Him, it is on Christ." John i. 29; Acts x. 43; Heb. vii. 25, are also helpful texts in dealing with this class of men.

2. Another difficulty we frequently meet with, is "*I can't hold out*," or "*I am afraid of failure*." 1 Peter i. 5 is useful in showing that we are not to keep ourselves but are "kept by the power of God." John x. 28, 29 shows that the safety of the one who accepts Christ does not depend upon his "holding out" but upon the keeping power of the Father and the Son. 2 Tim. i. 12 shows that it is Christ's business and not ours to keep that which is entrusted to him and that he is able to do it. Isaiah xli. 10, 13 are also helpful. Jude 24 shows that whether we can keep from falling or not, Christ is able to keep us from falling. 2 Chron. xxxii. 7, 8; Romans xiv. 4; 2 Thes. iii. 3, are also good texts to use. 1 Cor. x. 13

is especially useful when one is afraid that some great temptation will overtake him and he will fall.

3. Another difficulty very similar to the preceding one, is "*I am too weak.*" With such a person, use 2 Cor. xii. 9, 10. Ask him "where is it that Christ's strength is made perfect?" When he answers "in weakness," tell him "then the weaker you are in your own strength the better." Philippians iv. 13 shows that however weak we may be, we can do all things through Christ which strengtheneth us. 1 Cor. x. 13 will show that God knows all about our weakness and will not permit us to be tempted above our strength.

4. "*I cannot give up my evil ways or bad habits.*" Gal. vi. 7, 8, will show them that they must give them up or perish. Philippians iv. 13 will show them that they can give them up in Christ's strength. It is an excellent plan to point the one who fears that he cannot give up his bad habits, to Christ, as a risen Savior, 1 Cor. xv. 3, 4. A man once came to me and said: "I come to you to know if there is any way I can get power to overcome my evil habits." He told me his story; he had been converted in childhood but had come to Chicago, fallen in with evil companions and gone down, and now could not break away from his sins. I said to him: "You know only half the gospel, the gospel of a crucified Savior. Through trusting in the crucified Savior you found pardon. But Jesus Christ is also a risen Savior, 1 Cor. xv. 4, 'All power is given unto Him,' Matt. xxviii. 18. He has power to give you victory over your evil habits. Do you believe that?" He said, "yes." "You trusted," I continued, "in the crucified Christ and found pardon, did you not?" "Yes," he replied. "Now," I said, "will you trust the risen Christ to save you from the power of your sins?" "Yes, I will." "Let us kneel down then, and tell him so." We knelt and talked it all over with the Savior. When he arose his very countenance was changed. "I am so glad I came," he said. Some time after I received a letter from him telling me how he found constant victory through trusting in the *risen* Christ.

5. "*I will be persecuted if I become a Christian.*" Never tell any one that he will not be persecuted, but show him from such passages as 2 Tim. ii. 12; 2 Tim. iii. 12; Matt. v. 10, 11, 12; Mark viii. 35; Acts xiv. 22, that persecution is the only path to Glory. Show them from Romans viii. 18 that the sufferings of this present time are not worthy to be compared with the Glory which shall be revealed in us. Show them from Acts v. 41; 1 Peter ii. 20, 21, that it is a privilege to be persecuted for Christ's sake. Heb. xii. 2, 3 is useful in showing them where to look for victory in persecution.

6. "*It will hurt my business,*" or "*I can't be a Christian in my present business.*" Point such an one to Mark viii. 36. This will show him that it is better to lose his business than to lose his soul. After this thought has been sufficiently impressed upon his mind, show him Matt. vi. 32, 33 which contains God's promise that if we put God and His kingdom first, that He will provide for all our real temporal needs. Matt. xvi. 24–27; Luke xii. 16–21; xvi. 24–26 are also very effective passages to use with this class.

7. "*Too much to give up.*" Mark viii. 36 will show them that they had better give up everything than to lose their soul. Philippians iii. 7, 8; Ps. xvi. 11 will show them that what they give up is nothing compared with what they get. Ps. lxxxiv. 11; Romans viii. 32 will show them that God will not ask them to give up any good thing; in other words, that the only things God asks them to give up are the things that are hurting them. A young woman once refused to come to the Savior saying, "There is too much to give up." "Do you think God loves you?" I answered. "Certainly." "How much do you think he loves you?" She thought a moment and answered, "Enough to give his son to die for me." "Do you think, if God loved you enough to give his son to die for you, he will ask you to give up anything it is for your good to keep?" "No." "Do you wish to keep anything that it is not for your

good to keep?" "No." "Then you had better come to Christ at once." And she did. 1 John ii. 17; Luke xii. 16–21 will show them how worthless are the things which they are trying to keep.

8. "*The Christian life is too hard.*" Say to the inquirer, "Let me show you from God's word that you are mistaken about the Christian life being hard." Then turn him to Matt. xi. 30; Prov. iii. 17; Ps. xvi. 11; 1 John v. 3, and show him that a Christian life is not hard but exceedingly pleasant. Then turn him to Prov. xiii. 15, and show him that it is the sinner's life that is hard.

9. "*I am afraid of my ungodly companions*;" or "*I will lose my friends if I take Christ.*" Prov. xxix. 25 will show them the consequence of yielding to the fear of man and the security of the one who trusts in the Lord. Prov. xiii. 20 will show them the result of holding on to their companions, and Ps. i. 1 will show the blessedness of giving up evil companions. 1 John i. 3 shows how much better companionship one gets than he loses by coming to Christ.

10. "*My heart is too hard.*" Ezek. xxxvi. 26, 27, will show them that though their hearts are hard as stone, that will make no difference because God will give them a new heart.

11. "*I have no feeling.*" Ask the inquirer what kind of feeling he thinks he must have before he comes to Christ. If it is the peace of which Christians speak, show him from Gal. v. 22; Eph. i. 13; Acts v. 32; 1 Peter i. 8; Matt. x. 32, that this feeling is the result of accepting Christ and confessing Him, and that he cannot expect it until he accepts and confesses Christ. If the feeling which he thinks he must have is the feeling that he is a sinner, then show him by Is. lv. 7 that it is *not the feeling* that we are sinners that God demands, *but a turning away* from sin. Or, from Acts xvi. 31; John i. 12; that God does not ask us to feel that we are sinners but to confess that we are sinners and trust in Christ as a Savior. Is. lv. 1; Rev. xxii. 17, will show the inquirer that all the feeling he needs is a desire for salvation.

It is often times well, however, with this class of inquirers to show them the passages from Chapter 3 "The Indifferent" until they do feel that they are sinners.

12. "*I am seeking Christ, but cannot find Him.*"

Jer. xxix. 13, shows that when we seek him with the whole heart we shall find him. Speaking with a woman one evening in an after–meeting she said to me, "I have been seeking Christ two years and cannot find Him." I replied, "I can tell you when you will find him." She looked at me in surprise and I turned to Jer. xxix. 13, and read "And ye shall seek me, and find me, when ye shall search for me with all your heart." "There," I said, "that shows you when you will find Christ. You will find him when you search for him with all your heart. Have you done that?" After a little thought she answered "No." "Well, then," I said, "let us kneel right down here now." She did this and in a few moments she was rejoicing in Christ. You can point one who has this difficulty to Luke xv. 1–10; xix. 10. These passages show that Jesus is seeking the sinner and you can say, "if you are really seeking Christ it will not take a seeking Savior and a seeking sinner very long to find each other."

13. "*I cannot believe.*"

In most cases where one says this the real difficulty which lies back of their inability to believe is unwillingness to forsake sin. John v. 44, is a good passage to use with such a one, or Is. lv. 7. In the use of the latter passage, hold the man's attention to the fact that all God asks of him is that he turn away from sin and turn to Him.

14. "*God won't receive me*," or "*I have sinned away the day of grace*," or "*I am afraid I have committed the unpardonable sin.*"

The people who honestly say this, are as a rule about the most difficult class to deal with of any that you will meet. John vi. 37, is the great text to use with them for it shows that Jesus will receive any one who will come to him. Hold him continually to that point, "Him that cometh to me I will in no wise cast out" and if they keep saying "He won't receive me" repeat the text, looking to the Spirit of God to carry the truth home. Many an utterly despondent soul has found light and peace through this verse in God's word. Rev. xxii. 17, is also useful as it shows that any one who will can have the water of life freely. Is. lv. 1, shows that any one who desires salvation can have it. Is. i. 18, shows that no matter how great a man's sins may be still here is pardon. Acts x. 43, and John iii. 16, that "*whosoever*" will believe upon Christ will find pardon and eternal life. Romans x. 13, shows that any one, no matter who or what he is, who will "call upon the name of the Lord shall be saved." It is well sometimes to turn to Heb. vi. 4–6, and Matt. xii. 31–32, and show the inquirer just what the unpardonable sin is and what its results are. Matt. xii. 31, 32, shows that it is blasphemy against the Holy Ghost and put it squarely to him, "have you ever blasphemed against the Holy Ghost?" Heb. vi. 4–6, shows that the difficulty is not in God's unwillingness to forgive, but in the man's unwillingness to repent and that any one who is concerned about his salvation evidently has not committed the unpardonable sin nor sinned away his day of grace. A little instruction along this line is often times all that is needed.

15. "*It is too late.*"

When an inquirer says this, it is often times well to use 2 Cor. vi. 2, and tell him that God says, it is just the time. Luke xxiii. 39–43, is useful as showing that even at the last hour Jesus will hearken to the sinner's cry. 2 Peter iii. 9, will show that His will is that none should perish, but that He is delaying the judgment that He may save as many as will come. Deut. iv. 30, 31, is an especially helpful passage as it says "Even in the latter days" if thou turn to the Lord he will be merciful. Is. i. 18, and Rev. xxii. 17, can alone be used here.

Chapter VI. Dealing with Those Who Entertain False Hopes

1. Among those who entertain false hopes, perhaps the largest class are *those who expect to be saved by their righteous lives*. These persons are easily known by such sayings as these, "I am doing the best I can." "I do more good than evil." "I am not a great sinner." "I have never done anything very bad." Gal. iii. 10, is an excellent passage to use, for it shows that all those who are trusting in their works are under the curse of the law and that there is no hope on the ground of the law for any one who does not "continue in all things which are written in the book of the law to do them." James ii. 10 is also useful. Gal. ii. 16, and Romans iii. 19, 20 are very effective by showing that by the deeds of the law there shall no flesh be justified in God's sight. Matt. v. 20—All these passages show the kind of righteousness God demands and that no man's righteousness comes up to God's standard, and that if a man wishes to be saved he must find some other means of salvation than by his own deeds. It is sometimes well in using these passages to say to the inquirer: "You do not understand the kind of righteousness that God demands or you would not talk as you do. Now let us turn to His word and see what kind of righteousness it is that God demands." There is another way of dealing with this class, by the use of such passages as Luke xvi. 15; Rom. ii. 16; 1 Sam. xvi. 7. These passages show that God looks at the

heart. Hold the inquirer right to that point. Every man when brought face to face with that, must tremble because he knows that whatever his outward life may be, his heart will not stand the scrutiny of God's eye. No matter how self-righteous a man is, we need not be discouraged for somewhere in the depths of every man's heart is the consciousness of sin and all we have to do is to work away until we touch that point. Every man's conscience is on our side. Matt. xxii. 37, 38 can be used when a man says "I am doing the best I can, or doing more good than evil." Say to him, "You are greatly mistaken about that; so far from doing more good than evil, do you know that you have broken the first and greatest of God's laws?" Then show him the passage. Heb. xi. 6, John vi. 29, show that the one thing that God demands is faith and that without that it is impossible to please God, and John xvi. 9, shows that unbelief in Christ is the greatest sin. John iii. 36, shows that the question of eternal life depends solely upon a man's accepting or rejecting Jesus Christ, and Heb. x. 28, 29, that the sin which brings the heaviest punishment is that of treading under foot the Son of God. Before using this latter passage, it would be well to say, "You think you are very good, but do you know that you are committing the most awful sin in God's sight which a man can commit?" If he replies, "No," then say "Well let me show you from God's word that you are;" then turn to this passage and read it with great solemnity and earnestness.

2. Another class of those who entertain false hopes, are *those who think "God is too good to damn anyone*."

When any one says this, you can reply, "We know nothing of God's goodness but what we learn from the Bible, and we must go to that book to find out the character of God's goodness. Let us turn to Romans ii. 2, 4, 5." Having read the verses, you can say something like this, "Now, my friend, you see that the purpose of God's goodness is to lead you to repentance, not to encourage you in sin and when we trample upon his goodness, then we are treasuring up wrath against the day of wrath and revelation of the righteous judgment of God." John viii. 21, 24 and iii. 36, will show the man that however good God may be that he will reject all who reject His Son. Still another way to deal with these men is by showing them from John v. 40; 2 Peter iii. 9–11 or Ezek. xxxiii. 11, that it is not so much God who damns men as men who damn themselves in spite of God's goodness because they will not come to Christ and accept the life freely offered. You can say "God is not willing that any should perish and he offers life freely to you, but there is one difficulty in the way. Let us turn to John v. 40, and see what the difficulty is." Then read the passage: "Ye will not come to me that ye might have life," and say, "My friend here is the difficulty, you won't come; life is freely offered to you but if you will not accept it, you must perish." 2 Peter ii. 4–6, 9; Luke xiii. 3, show how the "good" God deals with persons who persist in sin. Sometimes this last passage can be effectively used in this way: "You say God is too good to damn any one. Now let us see what God Himself says in his word." Then turn to the passage and read, "Except ye repent, ye shall all likewise perish." Repeat the passage over and over again until it has been driven home.

3. A third class of those who entertain false hopes, are *those who say "I am trying to be a Christian."* John i. 12, will show them that it is not "trying" to be a Christian or "trying" to live a better life or "trying" to do anything that God asks of us, but simply to receive Jesus Christ, who did it all, and you can ask the inquirer, "will you now stop your trying and simply receive Jesus as Savior?" Acts xvi. 31, shows that God does not ask us to *try* what we can do but *trust* Jesus and what He has done and will do. Romans iii. 23–25, shows that we are not to be justified by trying to do, "but freely by His grace, through the redemption that is in Christ Jesus" on the simple condition of faith.

4. Still another class of those who entertain false hopes are *those who say, "I feel I am going to Heaven,"* or *"I feel I am saved."* Show them from John iii. 36 that it is not a question of what they feel but what God says, and what God says distinctly in his word is that, "He that believeth not on the Son, shall not see life, but the wrath of God abideth on him." One afternoon I was talking with a lady who a few weeks before had lost her only child. At the time of the child's death she had been deeply interested, but her serious impressions had largely left her. I put to her the question, "Do you not wish to go where your little one has gone?" She replied at once "I expect to." "What makes you think you will?" I said. She replied, "I feel so, I feel that I will go to heaven when I die." I then asked her, if there was anything she could point to in the word of God which gave her a reason for believing that she was going to heaven when she died. "No," she said, "there is not." Then she turned and questioned me, saying, "Do you expect to go to heaven when you die?" "Yes," I replied, "I know I shall." "How do you know it?" she said. "Have you any word from God for it?" "Yes," I answered and turned her to John iii. 36. She was thus led to see the difference between a faith that rested upon her feelings and a faith that rested upon the word of God.

Luke xviii. 9–14, can also be used in the following way; you can say "there was a man in the Bible who felt he was all right, but was all wrong. Let me read you about him." Then read about the Pharisee who was so sure that he was all right, but who was all the time an unforgiven sinner; and make the inquirer see how untrustworthy our feelings are and what the ground of assurance is, viz: God's word. Prov. xiv. 12 can also be used as showing that "there is a way which seemeth right unto a man but the end thereof are the ways of death."

5. The last class of those who entertain false hopes, are *those who say they are saved though they are leading sinful lives*. In the case of many forms of sin, a good passage to use is 1 Cor. vi. 9–10. 1 John ii. 29 will also in many cases sweep away this false hope. 1 John v. 4–5 is useful as showing that one who is really born of God overcomes the world and the fact that they are living in sin and are not overcoming the world is evidence that they have not been born of God.

Chapter VII. Dealing with Those Who Lack Assurance and with Back-sliders

I. Those who Lack Assurance.

Those who lack assurance may be divided into two classes.

1. *Those who lack assurance because of ignorance.* 1 John v. 13, will show all such that we may know that we have eternal life. Often times when you ask people if they know they are saved, or if they know their sins are forgiven, or if they know they have eternal life, they will reply, "Why no one knows that." You can say to them, "Yes the Bible says that all who believe may know it," and then show them 1 John v. 13. John i. 12 shows that Christ gives to as many as receive Him, power to become the Sons of God. A good way to use this verse is to ask the inquirer questions regarding it. "What does every one who receives Him receive power to become?" The inquirer if he is attentively looking at the verse will answer, "A son of God." Then ask the next question, "Have you received Him?" If he replies "Yes," then ask him, "What are you then?" It will probably be necessary to go over it several times but at last the inquirer will see it and say "I am a son of God." John iii. 36 can be used in a similar way. Ask the inquirer "who do these verses say has

everlasting life?" "He that believeth on the Son." "Do you believe on the Son?" "What have you then?" In a little while he will see it and say "Everlasting life." Then have him say over and over again "I have everlasting life," and have him kneel down and thank God for giving him everlasting life. One night I found a young man upon his knees at the close of the service in great distress. I showed him from the Bible how Jesus Christ had borne his sins and asked him if he would accept Christ as his Savior; he said he would; but he seemed to get no light and went out of the meeting in deep distress. The next night he was there again, professing to have accepted Christ but with no assurance that his sins were forgiven. I tried to show him from God's word what God said of those who accepted the Savior, but the light did not come. Finally he rose to leave the meeting. I had just shown him from John iii. 36 that God said that "He that believeth on the Son hath everlasting life." As he turned to leave me, he said, "Will you pray for me?" I said "Yes." He walked a little way down the aisle and I called to him and said, "Do you believe I will pray for you?" He turned with a look of astonishment and replied, "Yes, of course." "Why do you think I will pray for you?" I then asked. "Because you said so," he replied. I said "Isn't God's word as good as mine?" He saw it at once, that while he had been willing to believe my word, he had not been willing to believe God's word, and he received assurance on the spot and knew that he had everlasting life. John v. 24 and 1 John v. 12 can be used in a similar way.

Acts xiii. 39 is very useful in dealing with this class of persons. Ask the inquirer: "What does this verse say that all who believe are?" "Justified." Then ask him, "Do you believe?" "What are you then?" It will probably take two or three times going over it before he sees it and when he answers "I am justified," tell him to thank God for justifying him and confess Christ, and see to it that he does so. Many inquirers of this class stumble over the fact that they have not the witness of the Holy Spirit. Show them from 1 John v. 10 that the witness of the word to their acceptance is sufficient, and that, if they believe not this witness of God in His word, they make Him a liar. Show them further from Eph. i. 13, that it is after we believe the testimony of the word that we are "sealed with the Holy Spirit of promise." The natural order in assurance is this: First, assurance of our justification, *resting on the "Word of God."* Second, public confession of Christ, "with the mouth," Romans x. 10. Third, the witness of the Holy Spirit. The trouble with many is that they wish to invert this order and have the witness of the Holy Spirit before they confess Christ with the mouth. From Matt. x. 32, 33, we learn that when we confess Christ before men, then He confesses us before the Father. We cannot reasonably expect the witness of the Spirit from the Father until we are confessed before the Father. So confession of Christ logically precedes the witness of the Spirit.

It is very important in using these texts to make clear what saving faith is; because many may say that they believe when they do not, in the sense of these texts, and so get a false assurance and entertain false hopes and never find deliverance. There is a great deal of careless dealing with those who lack assurance. Workers are so anxious to have inquirers come out clearly that they urge them on to assurance when they have no right to have assurance of salvation as they have not really accepted Christ.

John i. 12, and 2 Tim. i. 12, make very clear what believing is—receiving Jesus or committing to Jesus. Romans x. 10, will serve a similar purpose by showing that it "is *with the heart* man believeth unto righteousness."

2. *Those who lack assurance because of sin.* The trouble with those who lack assurance is, often, that there is some sin or questionable practice which they ought to confess and give up. John viii. 12; Is. lv. 7; Prov. xxviii. 13; Ps. xxxii. 1–5, are useful

passages in dealing with this class of men, for they show that it is when sin is confessed and forsaken and we follow Christ, that we receive pardon, light and assurance. Often times it is well when one lacks assurance to put the question squarely to him: "Do you know of any sin on to which you are holding or anything in your life which your conscience troubles you about?"

II. Back–sliders. There are two classes of back–sliders and they should be dealt with in different ways.

1. *Careless back–sliders; those who have no great desire to come back to the Savior.* With such persons use Jer. ii. 5, drive the question right home, "What iniquity have you found in the Lord?" Show them the base ingratitude and folly of forsaking such a Savior and Friend. Very likely they have wandered away because of unkind treatment by professed Christians, but hold them right to the point of how *the Lord* treated them and how they are now treating Him. Use also Jer. ii. 13, and show them what they have forsaken and for what. Have them read the verse and ask them, "is not that verse true? When you forsook the Lord did you not forsake the 'fountain of living waters' and turn to 'broken cisterns that can hold no water?'" Illustrate the text by showing how foolish it would be to turn from a fountain of pure living water to broken cisterns or muddy pools. God has greatly honored this verse in bringing back–sliders back to himself. Use Jer. ii. 19. When they have read it ask them whether they have not found it "an evil thing and bitter" having forsaken the Lord their God. Prov. xiv. 14; 1 Kings xi. 9, and Luke xv. 13–17, can often times be used with effect with an impenitent back–slider, showing him the result of his wandering. I have a friend who always uses Amos. iv. 11, 12, and often times with good results.

2. *Back–sliders who are sick of their wanderings and sin and desire to come back to the Lord.* These are perhaps as easy a class to deal with as we ever find. Jer. iii. 12, 13, and 22, will show them how ready the Lord is to receive them back and that all he asks of them is that they acknowledge their sin and return to him. Hos. xiv. 1–4, is full of tender invitation to penitent back–sliders and also shows the way back to God. Is. xliii. 22, 24, 25, and Is. xliv. 20–22; Jer. xxix. 11–13; Deut. iv. 28–31; 2 Chron. vii. 14; 1 John i. 9; ii. 1–2, set forth God's unfailing love for the back–slider and His willingness to receive him back. Mark xvi. 7; 2 Chron. xv. 4; xxxiii. 1–9, 12, 13, give illustrations of great back–sliders who returned to the Lord and how lovingly He received them, 1 John i. 9; Jer. iii. 12–13; 2 Chron. xv. 12, 15; vii. 14, show just what steps the back–slider must take to come back to the Lord and be restored to his favor, viz: humble himself, confess his sins and turn from his sin. Luke xv. 11–24, is perhaps the most useful passage of all in dealing with a back–slider who wishes to return for it has both the steps which the back–slider must take and the kind of reception he will receive.

When a back–slider has returned he should always be given instructions as to how to live so as not to back–slide again. The instruction to be given will be found in Chapter XII. sec. 15.

Chapter VIII. Dealing with Professed Skeptics and Infidels

There are various classes of Sceptics and the same methods of dealing will not answer for all.

1. *Skeptics who are mere triflers.* With such use 1 Cor. i. 18. If a man says the Bible is foolishness to him, you can say "Yes, that is just what the Bible itself says." He will probably be surprised at this reply and then you can show him 1 Cor. i. 18; "the preaching

of the cross is to them that perish foolishness." Then you can say to him, "You see that the Bible says that it is foolishness to some—them that *perish*—and the reason it is foolishness to you is because you are perishing." 1 Cor. ii. 14, can be used in a similar way. A worker was one night dealing with a man who said to him when he was trying to persuade him to come to Christ, "all that you are saying is foolishness to me." The worker quickly replied, "Yes, that is just what the Bible says." The man looked at him in astonishment and said: "What?" "You said all that I have been saying to you was foolishness to you, and that is just what the Bible says." The man was more astonished then than ever and the worker turned him to 1 Cor. ii. 14, "But the natural man receiveth not the things of the Spirit of God; for they are foolishness unto him; neither can he know them because they are spiritually discerned." The man said "I never saw that before; I never thought of it in that light before." 2 Cor. iv. 3, 4, is very useful in showing the trifler that he is lost and that his skepticism arises from the fact that the "god of this world hath blinded his mind." 2 Thes. ii. 10–12, is useful in showing the origin of skepticism, "because they received not the love of the truth" and the consequences of skepticism—delusion and damnation. John viii. 21, 24, is also very searching in dealing with this class of skeptics, showing the terrible consequences of unbelief. John v. 44; iii. 18, 19, 20 expose the origin of skepticism. Ps. xiv. 1, is useful in some cases though one needs to be guarded in its use, using it only when it can be done with earnestness and tenderness. 2 Thes. i. 7, 8 can also be used with good results.

2. *Serious minded skeptics.* There is a large class of men and women in our day who are really desirous of knowing the truth but who are in an utter fog of skepticism. John vii. 17 is a very helpful passage in dealing with such. It shows the way out of skepticism to faith. Get the skeptic to act along the line of that verse. Put to him the question, "Will you surrender your will to God and promise to search honestly and earnestly to find out what God's will is that you may do it, to ask God to show you whether you need a Savior and whether Jesus is a Divine Savior, the Son of God; and will you promise that, if God will show you that Jesus is the Son of God, to accept Him as your Savior and confess Him before the world?" Have him make his promise definite, by putting it down in black and white. If you get him to do this, his skepticism will soon take wings.

One evening at the close of a service I asked a gentleman why he was not a Christian. He replied: "I will tell you. I do not talk much about it; for I am not proud of it as some are, but I am a skeptic. I have lain awake nights thinking about this matter." "Do you believe there is a God?" "Yes, I never gave up my faith that there was a God." "Well, if there is a God you ought to obey him. Will you to–night take your stand upon the will of God to follow it wherever it carries you even if it carries you over the Niagara Falls?" "I try to do as near right as I know how." "That is not what I asked; will you take your stand on the will of God to follow it wherever it carries you?" "I have never put it that way." "Will you put it that way to–night?" "I will." "Do you believe God answers prayer?" "I don't know; I am afraid not." "You don't know that he does not?" "No." "Well, here is a possible clue to the truth, will you follow it, will you ask God to show you whether Jesus is His Son; and what your duty concerning him is?" "I will." Not long after that the man came into a meeting with a new look in his face. He arose and said: "I was all in a mist. I believed nothing." Then he told us what he had done. He had done just as he promised. "And now," he continued, "my doubts are all gone. I don't know where they have gone but they are gone." If the skeptic will not act in this way you can "stop his mouth" by showing him that he is not an honest skeptic and that the trouble with him is not his skepticism but his sin. If the man does not believe there is a God, you can begin one step further back. Ask him if he believes there is an absolute difference between right and wrong (if he does not he is a mere trifler). If he says he does, ask him if he will take his stand upon the right and follow it wherever it carries him. He may try to put you off by saying "What is right?" or that he is doing the right as nearly as he knows how. Get him to promise that he will take his stand upon the right, whatever he may find it to be and follow it whatever the consequence may be. Then show him that if he is honest in this promise, he will try to find out what the right is. Next say to him, "You do not know whether God answers prayer or not. I know He does, and you will admit that here is a possible clue to knowledge. If you are honest in your desire to know the truth, you will follow this possible clue. You can get down and at least pray, 'O my God, if there be a God, teach me thy will and I will do it. Show me whether Jesus is thy son or not. If you show that he is, I will accept Him as my Savior and confess Him before the world.'" Then tell the man to begin reading the Gospel of John, reading slowly and thoughtfully, only a few verses at a time, asking God for light each time before reading and promising God that he will follow the light as fast as He makes it clear. If the man will follow this rational course, it will result in every case in the skeptic coming out into the clear light of faith in the Bible, as the word of God, and Jesus Christ as the Son of God. If the man is not an honest skeptic, this course of treatment will reveal the fact and then you can show him that the difficulty is not with his skepticism but with his rebellious heart.

If the man says that he does not know whether there is an absolute difference between right and wrong, then you can set it down at once that he is bad and turn upon him kindly and earnestly and say to him, "My friend, there is something wrong in your life; no man that is living right doubts that there is a difference between right and wrong. Now you probably know what is wrong and the trouble is not with your skepticism, but with your sin." One afternoon after I had given out an invitation for any skeptic or any one else who wished to talk with me, to remain after the meeting, a young man with whom I had dealt some months before stayed. I asked him what his trouble was. He replied, "The same trouble that I told you in the spring, I cannot believe that there is a God." I asked him if he had done as I had advised him to do in our former conversation; if he had taken his stand upon the right to follow it wherever it carried him. He replied that he did not know that there was any difference between right and wrong. "I do not know that there is such a thing as right." I looked him right in the eyes and said, "Is there some sin your life?"

He said "Yes." I said "what is it?" He replied, "The same that I told you last spring." I said, "You promised to give it up, have you given it up?" He said "No, I have not." "Well," I said, "there is the difficulty, not with your skepticism. Give up that sin and your skepticism will take care of itself." In some confusion he replied, "I guess that is the trouble."

3. *Those who doubt the existence of God.*

The passages under 1 and 2 can also be used with this class and generally it is wise to use them before those given under this head. There are however, three passages that are often times effective with this specific class of skeptics. Ps. xiv. 1; before using this passage you can say to the man, "Let me read you from God's own word what he says about those who deny his existence." Often times it is well to leave the passage to do its own work. Sometimes, however, it is wise to dwell a little upon it. Call the man's attention to the fact that it is "in his heart" that the fool says "there is no God." He does not believe there is a God because he does not wish to. You can add that the folly of saying in one's heart that there is no God is seen in two points; first, there is a God and it is folly to say there is not one, and second, the doctrine that there is not a God always brings misery and wretchedness. Put it right to the man, and ask him if he ever knew a happy atheist. Ps. xix. 1, 2; Romans i. 19–22, are also effective passages.

4. *Those who doubt that the Bible is the word of God.*

Romans iii. 3, 4, is useful in showing that questioning the fact does not alter the fact. Matt. xxiv. 35, is often used by the Spirit to carry to the heart of the skeptic the certainty and immutability of God's word. Mark vii. 13; Matt. v. 18; John x. 35; Luke xxiv. 27, 44, are useful as giving Christ's testimony that the Old Testament is the Word of God. They are especially helpful in dealing with those who say that they accept the authority of Christ but not that of the Old Testament, for in them Christ sets His seal to the Old Testament Scriptures and they show conclusively that if we accept His authority we must accept that of the Old Testament also. Along the same line John xiv. 26, and xvi. 12, 13, are useful as containing Christ's indorsement of the New Testament.

1 Thes. ii. 13, can be used with good effect to meet the statement which is often made, that Paul nowhere claims that his teaching is the word of God. 2 Peter i. 21, John viii. 47; Luke xvi. 30, 31, can also be used in dealing with this class. 2 John v. 10, is very effective in showing the guilt of those who believe not the record that God has given. Before using this last passage you can say, "You doubt, do you, that the Bible is the Word of God? Now let us see what God says about those that believe not His testimony;" then turn them to the passage and have them read it.

5. *Those who doubt a future existence.*

1 Cor. xv. 35–36; John v. 28–29; Dan. xii. 2.

6. *Those who doubt the doctrine of future punishment, or the conscious, endless suffering of the lost.* Rev. xxi. 8, defines what "death" means when used in the scriptures Rev. xvii. 8, compared with Rev. xix. 20, shows what perdition or destruction means in the scriptures. Rev. xix. 20, compared with Rev. xx. 10 shows that "the lake of fire" is not a place where those consigned to it cease to exist, for we find in the latter passage the beast and false prophet are still there at the end of a thousand years and that they, so far from being annihilated or losing conscious existence are tormented night and day forever and ever. Rev. xiii. 7–8 show that those who are subjected to the terrible retribution here described are those whose names are not written in the Book of Life. Matt. x. 28 shows that there is destruction for the soul apart from the destruction of the body. Luke xii. 5, shows that after one is killed and is of course dead, there is a punishment in "hell." Mark iii. 28–29 shows that there is such a thing as eternal sin. Luke xvi. 23–26, shows that the condition of the wicked dead is one of conscious torment. Mark xiv. 21, shows that the retribution visited upon the wicked is of so stern a character that it would be better for him upon whom it is visited if he had never been born.

2 Peter ii. 4; Jude 6, show that hell is not a place where the inhabitants cease to exist, but where they are reserved alive, for the purpose of God. Heb. x. 28–29, show that while the punishment of transgression of the Mosaic law was death, that sorer punishment awaits those who have "trodden under foot the Son of God." Matt. xxv. 41 gives further light upon the subject. It shows that the wicked go to the same place with the Beast and False Prophet and the Devil mentioned in Rev. xix. 20, and xx. 10, and share the same endless, conscious torment.

7. *Those who doubt the divinity of Christ.*

a. In Acts x. 36; 1 Cor. ii. 8, compare Ps. xxiv. 8–10; Heb. i. 8; John xx. 28; Rom. ix. 5; Rev. i. 17, compare Is. xliv. 6, we find several divine titles applied to Christ, the same titles being applied to Christ in the New Testament that are applied to Jehovah in the old.

b. In Heb. i. 10, 3, we find divine offices attributed to Christ.

c. In John v. 22–23, compare Rev. v. 13; Heb. i. 6; Phil. ii. 10, we find it taught that Jesus Christ should be worshiped as God.

d. In John v. 22–23 we find Jesus claiming the same honor as his Father, and either He was Divine or the most blasphemous impostor that ever lived. Drive it home that the one who denies Christ's Divinity puts Him in the place of a blasphemous imposter. Mark xiv. 61, 62, can be used in a similar way.

e. 1 John ii. 22, 23, compared with 1 John v. 1, 5, shows that the one who denies the Divinity of Christ, no matter who he may be, is a liar and an antichrist. 1 John v. 10–12, shows that he who does not believe that Jesus is divine makes God a liar, "Because he believeth not the record that God gave of His Son." Heb. x. 28–29, shows the folly, guilt and punishment of rejecting Christ as the Son of God. John viii. 24, shows beyond a question that no one who does not believe in the Divinity of Jesus Christ will be saved. John xx. 31, shows that we have life through believing that Jesus is the Christ, the son of God.

(Note. It is best as a rule before taking up specific difficulties to deal with the inquirer with the passage under the head here in this chapter of "Skeptics who are mere triflers," or those under "Serious minded skeptics.")

Often times there is no need to take up specific questions as for example about future punishment until the inquirer has first settled the matter whether he will accept Christ as his Savior.

Chapter IX. Dealing with the Complaining

1. Those who complain of God.

Many that you wish to lead to Christ will say something to the effect that God is unjust and cruel, Job. xl. 2, and Romans ix. 20, are very pointed passages to use with inquirers of this class and need no comment. It might be well to preface the reading of the passages with some remark like this; "Do you know of how enormous a sin you are guilty in accusing God of being unjust and cruel? Let me read what God says about it in His Word." Then read the passages. Romans xi. 33 will serve to show the complaining that the reason God's ways seem unjust and cruel is because they are so deep and unsearchable; and that the trouble is not with God's ways but the limitation of their understanding. Heb. xii. 5, 7, 10, 11 are especially useful in cases where the inquirer complains because of his own misfortunes or sorrows. Is. lv. 8–9 will often times prove helpful. Not infrequently you will meet with one who will say that "God is unjust to create men and then damn them." Turn such an one to Ezek. xxxiii. 11. This passage meets this complaint by showing that God has no pleasure in the death of the wicked, but desires their welfare and that the wicked bring damnation upon themselves by their stubborn refusal to repent. 1 Tim. ii. 3–4, shows that God, so far from creating man to damn him, desires that all men be saved. 2 Peter iii. 9, teaches that God is not willing that any should perish and is delaying His purposes in order that all may come to repentance. John v. 40, and Matt. xxiii. 37, show that the whole cause of man's damnation is his own willful and persistent refusal to come to Christ. John iii. 36, and iii. 16, are also helpful in many cases.

2. Those who complain of the bible. Men will often times say, "The Bible is contradictory and absurd;" or "the Bible seems foolish to me." Two classes of passages can be used in dealing with such inquirers.

a. 1 Cor. i. 18; ii. 14; 2 Cor. iv. 3–4; Dan. xii. 10; Rom. xi. 33, 34 and in extreme cases 2 Thes. ii. 10, 11, 12.

b. John vii. 17; Ps. xxv. 14; Matt. xi. 25, (see remarks in Chapter VIII under Serious minded skeptics and Skeptics who are mere triflers.) Sometimes the best thing to do with a man who says the Bible is full of contradictions, is to hand him your Bible and ask him to show you one. In most cases he will not attempt to do it; as people who complain about the Bible, as a rule know nothing about its contents. One day a man was brought to me to deal with and when I asked him why he was not a Christian he replied, "The Bible is full of contradictions." I at once asked him to show me one. "Oh!" he said, "it's full of them." I said, "If it is full of them you ought to be able to show me one." He said, "Well, there is one in Psalms." I said, "Show it to me." He commenced looking in the back of the New Testament for the book of Psalms. I said, "You are not looking in the right part of the Bible for Psalms. Let me find it for you." I found him the book of Psalms and handed it to him. After fumbling around he said, "I could find it, if I had my own Bible here." "Well," I said, "Will you bring your Bible to–night?" He promised he would and agreed to meet me at a certain place in the church. The appointed hour came, but he did not. Some months afterwards in another series of meetings in the same church one of the workers stopped me and said, "Here's a man I wish you would deal with; he is a skeptic." I looked at him and recognized him as the same man. "Oh!" I said, "you are the man that lied to me here;" and with much confusion he admitted that he was, but he was still playing his old game of saying that the Bible was full of contradictions. In nine cases out of ten, men who say this, know nothing about the Bible, and when you ask them to show you a contradiction in the Bible they are filled with confusion.

3. Those who complain of God's way of Salvation.

A great many men will say, "I do not see why God could not save men in some other way than by the death of His son." Is. lv. 8, 9, Romans xi. 33 are useful in dealing with such. I have used Romans ix. 20 with effect with men of this sort. A young student said to me one night, when I asked why he was not a Christian, that he did not see why it was necessary for Christ to die for him; why God did not save him in some other way. I opened my Bible and read to him Romans ix. 20, and put the question right to him, "Who art thou that repliest against God?" and then said to him, "Do you realize what you are doing, that you are condemning God?" The young man very much confused said "I did not mean to do that." "Well," I said; "that is what you are doing." "If that is so," he replied, "I will take it back." A good way to do with such men is to show them by the use of passages given under Chapter III, "Dealing with the Indifferent" that they are lost sinners. When any one is led to see this, God's way of salvation will approve itself as just the thing.

4. Those who complain of Christians. Very frequently when we try to persuade men to accept Christ as their Savior, they reply; "*There are too many hypocrites in church.*" Romans xiv. 4 and 12, especially the latter verse, are exceedingly effective in dealing with such.

Romans ii. 1, and Matt. vii. 1–5, are also excellent. John xxi. 21, 22 is useful in showing the objector that he is solely responsible for his own relation to Christ and that what others do is none of his affairs. Sometimes the inquirer will *complain of the way Christian people have treated him.* In such a case turn the attention of the inquirer from the way in which Christian people have treated him to the way in which God has treated him. For this purpose use Jer. ii. 5; Is. liii. 5; Romans v. 6–8. Then ask him if the fact that Christians have treated him badly is any excuse for his treatment of a Heavenly Father who has treated him so well. One night turning to an aged man I asked him if he was a Christian. He replied that he was not, that he was a back–slider. I asked him why he back–slid. He replied that Christian people had treated him badly. I opened my Bible and read

Jer. ii. 5, to him, "Thus saith the Lord, what iniquity have your fathers found in *me*, that they are gone far from *me*, and have walked after vanity and are become vain?" I said, "Did you find any iniquity in God? Did God not use you well?" With a good deal of feeling the man admitted that God had not treated him badly and I held him right to this point of God's treatment of him, and not man's treatment, and his treatment of God. Matt. xviii. 23–35; Eph. iv. 30–32; Matt. vi. 14–15, are also useful as showing the absolute necessity of our forgiving men.

Chapter X. Dealing with Those Who Wish to Put Off a Decision Until Some Other Time

1. There are several classes of those who wish to put off a decision. One of the largest is composed of *those who say "I want to wait," or "Not to–night," or "I will think about it," or "I will come to–morrow night,"* or some such thing. Use Is. lv. 6. The inquirer having read the passage, ask him when it is that he is to seek the Lord, and when he answers "While he may be found," ask him when that is and then drive it home. Ask him if he is sure that he can find Him to–morrow if he does not seek Him to–day. Or you can use Prov. xxix. 1. It is well after he has read this verse to ask the one with whom you are dealing what becomes of the one who "being often reproved hardeneth his neck" and when he answers "He shall be destroyed," ask him how he shall be destroyed, and when he answers "Suddenly," ask him if he is willing to run the risk. Or you can use Matt. xxv. 10–12. Ask him who it was that went into the marriage? and when he answers "They that were ready" ask him if he is ready. Then ask him what happened after those who were ready went in. Then ask him where "those who were not ready" were. Then put it to him, "Are you willing to be on the out–side?" Or you can use Luke xii. 19, 20. Ask the inquirer for how long a time this man thought he had made provision. Then ask him: "If God should call you to–night would you be ready?" Matt. xxiv. 44, is especially effective in dealing with those who say "I am not ready." 1 Kings xviii. 21, can be used with good effect. An excellent way to use this verse is by asking the person whether he would be willing to wait a year and not have an opportunity under any circumstances, no matter what came up, of accepting Christ. When he answers, "No, I might die within a year," ask him if he would be willing to wait a month. Then bring it down to a week and finally to a day, and ask him if he would like God and the Holy Spirit and all Christians to leave him alone for a day and he not have an opportunity, under any circumstances of accepting Christ? Almost any thoughtful person will say, "No." Then tell him that if that is the case he had better accept Christ at once. Dr. Chalmers was the first one to use this method and it has been followed by many others with great success. Prov. xxvii. 1; James iv. 13, 14; Job. xxxvi. 18; Luke xiii. 24–28; xii. 19, 20; John viii. 21; xii. 35; vii. 33–34, can also be used with this class.

2. Those who say "*I must get fixed in business first, then I will become a Christian*," or "*I must do something else first.*" Matt. vi. 33, is the great passage to use in such cases; for it shows that we must seek the kingdom of God first.

3. Those who say "*I am waiting God's time.*" If one says this, ask him if he will accept Christ in God's time if you will show him when God's time is. Then turn to 2 Cor. vi. 2, or Heb. iii. 15.

4. Those who say "*I am too young*," or "*I want to wait until I am older.*" Ecc. xii. 1, is an all–sufficient answer to such. Matt. xix. 14, and xviii. 3, are also good passages to

use as they show that youth is the best time to come to Christ and that all must become children, even if they are old, before they can enter into the kingdom of Heaven. It is often times wise in dealing with persons who wish to put off a decision until some time in the future to use the passages given in Chapter III for "The Indifferent," until such a deep impression is made of their need of Christ that they will not be willing to postpone accepting Christ.

In dealing with those under "1" above, it is best to use only one passage and drive that home by constant repetition. One night I was dealing with a man who was quite interested but who kept saying "I cannot decide to–night." I quoted Prov. xxix. 1. To every answer he made I would come back to this passage. I must have repeated it a great many times in the course of the talk until the man was made to feel not only his need of Christ but the danger of delaying and the necessity of a prompt decision. He tried to get away from the passage but I held him to this one point. The passage lingered with him and it was emphasized by the providence of God; for that very night he was assaulted and quite seriously injured, and he came the next night with his head bandaged and accepted Christ. The pounding which he received from his assailant would probably have done him little good if the text of scripture had not been pounded into his mind.

Chapter XI. Dealing with the Willful and the Deluded

1. The Willful

There are several varieties of the Willful. There are those for example who say "*I do not wish you to talk to me.*" In such a case it is usually best to give some pointed passage of scripture and let it talk for itself and then leave the person alone to reflect upon it. Romans vi. 23; Heb. x. 28, 29; Heb. xii. 25; Mark xvi. 16; Prov. xxix. 1, and Prov. i. 24–33, are passages which are good for this purpose.

Then there are those who say "*I cannot forgive.*" Matt. vi. 15 and xviii. 23–35, are good to use as showing that they must forgive or be lost. Phil. iv. 13, and Ezek. xxxvi. 26, will show them how they can forgive. There are a great many people who are kept from Christ by an *unforgiving* spirit. Some times this difficulty can be removed by getting the person to kneel in prayer and ask God to take away their unforgiving spirit. I once reasoned a long time with an inquirer who was under deep conviction, but was held back from accepting Christ by a hatred in her heart toward some one who had wronged her. She kept insisting that she could not forgive. Finally I said, "let us get down and tell God about this matter." To this she consented and scarcely had we knelt when she burst into a flood of tears, and the difficulty was removed and she accepted Christ immediately.

There are those again who say "*I love the world too much.*" Mark viii. 36, is the great text to use with this class. Luke xiv. 33, will show the absolute necessity that the world be given up. Luke xii. 16–20; 1 John ii. 15, 16, 17, will show the folly of holding on to the world and Ps. lxxxiv. 11, Romans viii. 32, will show that the Lord will hold back no good thing from them.

There are those who say "*I cannot acknowledge a wrong that I have done.*" Prov. xxviii. 13, will show the wretchedness and woe that is sure to follow unless the wrong is acknowledged. Others will say "*I do not want to make a public confession.*" Romans x. 10; Matt. x. 32, 33, will show that God will accept nothing else. Mark viii. 38; John xii. 42, 43, and Prov. xxix. 25, will show the peril of not making it. There are those who say "*I want to have my own way.*" Is. lv. 8–9, will show how much better God's way is, and Prov. xiv. 12, shows the consequences of having our own way. Finally there are those who say "*I neither accept Christ nor reject Him.*" Matt. xii. 30, will show that they must do one or the other. This verse has been used to the conviction of a great many.

2. The Deluded

a. Under this head come the *Roman Catholics*. A good way to deal with a Roman Catholic is to show him the necessity of the new birth and what the new birth is. John iii. 3, 5, 7, shows the necessity of the new birth. What the new birth is, is shown in Ezek. xxxvi. 25–27; 2 Cor. v. 17; 2 Peter i. 4. Many Roman Catholics understand the new birth to mean baptism, but it can be easily shown them that the language used does not fit baptism. Further than this, in 1 Cor. iv. 15, Paul says to the Corinthian Christians he had begotten them again through the gospel. If the new birth meant baptism he must have baptized them, but in 1 Cor. i. 14, he declares he had not baptized them. Acts viii. 13, 21, 23, shows that a man may be baptized, and yet his heart not be "right in the sight of God" so he has "neither part nor lot in this matter." It is well to take a step further and show the inquirer what the evidences of the new birth are. 1 John ii. 29; iii. 9, 14–17; v. 1, 4, give the Biblical evidences of the new birth. The next question that will arise is "How to be born again." This question is answered in John i. 12; 1 Peter i. 23; Jas. i. 18.

Acts iii. 19, is a good text to use with Roman Catholics as it shows the necessity of repentance and conversion. What repentance is, will be shown by Is. lv. 7; Jonah iii. 10. Still another way of dealing with Roman Catholics is by showing them that it is the believer's privilege to know that he has eternal life. Roman Catholics almost always lack assurance. They do not know that they are forgiven, but hope to be forgiven some day. If you can show them that we may *know* that we are forgiven and that we have eternal life, it will awaken in a great many of them a desire for this assurance. 1 John v. 13, shows that it is the believer's privilege to know. Acts xiii. 38, 39; x. 43, John iii. 36, are very useful in leading them into this assurance. Still another way of dealing with them (but it is not best to use it until you have already made some progress with them) is to show them the advantage of Bible study. Good texts for this purpose are John v. 39; 1 Peter ii. 1, 2; 2 Tim. iii. 13–17; Jas i. 21, 22; Ps. i. 1, 2; Josh. i. 8; Mark vii. 7, 8, 13; Matt. xxii. 29. These texts, excepting the one in 1 Peter ii. 1, 2, are all practically the same in the "Douay" or Roman Catholic Bible as they are in the Protestant Bible and it is well oftentimes in dealing with a Catholic to use the Catholic Bible.

Still another way of dealing with a Roman Catholic is to use the same method that you would in dealing with an impenitent sinner—that is to awaken a sense that he is a sinner and needs Christ. For this purpose use Matt. xxii. 37, 38; Gal. iii. 10, 13; Is. liii. 6.

Many people think that there is no use of talking with Roman Catholics, that they cannot be brought to Christ. This is a great mistake. Many of them are longing for something they do not find in the Roman Catholic church, and, if you can show them from the word of God how to find it, they come along very easily and they make very earnest Christians. Do not attack the Roman Catholic church. Give them the truth, and the errors in time will take care of themselves. Often times our attacks only expose our ignorance.

There is one point at which we always have the advantage in dealing with a Roman Catholic; that is that there is peace and power in Christianity as we know it that there is not in Christianity as they know it, and they appreciate the difference.

b. Jews. The best way to deal with a Jew is to show him that his own Bible points to Christ. The most helpful passages to use are Is. liii.; Dan. ix. 26; Zech. xii. 10. There are also useful passages in the New Testament; the whole book of Hebrews, especially the ninth and tenth chapters and the seventh chapter, 25th to 28th verses, and the whole Gospel of Matthew. A great many Jews to–day are inquiring into the claims of Jesus of Nazareth, and are open to approach upon this subject. The great difficulty in the way of the Jew coming out as a Christian is the terrific persecution which he must endure if he does. This difficulty can be met by the passages already given in Chapter V, Section 5 under the head of "Those Who are Afraid of Persecution."

(Note. There are a number of good tracts for Jews which can be had from the Mildmay Mission to the Jews, 79 Mildmay Road, London.)

c. *Spiritualists.* Lev. xix. 31; xx. 6; Deut. xviii. 10–12; 2 Kings xxi. 1, 2, 6; 1 Chron. x. 13; Is. viii. 19, 20; 1 John iv. 1–3; 2 Thes. ii. 9–12, are passages to be used with this class.

In dealing with all classes of deluded people it is well to begin by using John vii. 17, and bring them to a place where they heartily desire to know the truth. There is no hope of bringing a man out of his delusion, unless he desires to know the truth.

Chapter XII. Some Hints and Suggestions

There are a few general suggestions to be made that will prove helpful to the worker.

1. *As a rule choose persons to deal with of your own sex and about your own age.* There are exceptions to this rule. One should be always looking to the Holy Spirit for his guidance as to whom to approach, and He may lead us to one of the opposite sex, but unless there is clear guidance in the matter, it is quite commonly agreed among those who have had large experience in Christian work that men do, on the whole, most satisfactory work with men, and women with women. Especially is this true of the young. Many unfortunate complications oftentimes arise when young men try to lead young women to Christ or vice versa. Of course, an elderly motherly woman may do excellent work with a young man or boy, and an elderly, fatherly man may do good work with a young woman or girl. It is not wise ordinarily for a young and inexperienced person to approach one very much older and maturer and wiser than themselves on this subject.

2. *Whenever it is possible, get the person with whom you are dealing alone.* No one likes to open his heart freely to another on this most personal and sacred of all subjects when there are others present. Many will from pride defend themselves in a false position when several are present, who would fully admit their error or sin or need, if they were alone with you. As a rule it is far better for a single worker to deal with a single unconverted person, than for several workers to deal with a single inquirer or for a single worker to deal with several inquirers at once. If you have several to deal with take them one by one. Workers often find that when they have made no headway while talking to several at once, by taking individuals off by themselves they soon succeed in leading them one by one to Christ.

3. *Let your reliance be wholly in the Spirit of God and the Word of God.*

4. *Do not content yourself with merely reading passages from the Bible—much less in merely quoting them, but have the one with whom you are dealing read them himself that the truth may find entrance into the heart through the eye as well as the ear.*

5. *It is ofttimes well to use but a single passage of scripture, drive that home and clinch it* so that the one with whom you have been dealing cannot forget it, but will hear it ringing in his memory long after you have ceased talking. Dr. Ichabod Spencer once in dealing with a young man who had many difficulties kept continually quoting the passage "now is the accepted time, behold now is the day of salvation." The young man tried to get Dr. Spencer on to something else, but over and over again he rang out the words. The next day the young man returned rejoicing in Christ and thanking the doctor that he had

"hammered" him with that text. The words kept ringing in his ears during the night and he could not rest until he had settled the matter by accepting Christ. It is a good thing when a person can point to some definite verse in the word of God and say "I know on the authority of that verse that my sins are forgiven and I am a child of God." There are times, however when a powerful effect is produced by a piling up of passages along some line until the mind is convinced and the heart conquered.

6. *Always hold the person with whom you are dealing to the main point of accepting Christ.* If he wishes to discuss the claims of various denominations, or the question of baptism, or theories of future punishment or any other question other than the central one of his need of a Savior and Christ the Savior he needs; tell him that those questions are proper to take up in their right place and time, but the time to settle them is after he has settled the first and fundamental question of accepting or rejecting Christ. Many a case has been lost by an inexperienced worker allowing himself to be involved in a discussion of some side issue which it is utter folly to discuss with an unregenerated person.

7. *Be courteous.* Many well–meaning but indiscreet Christians by their rudeness and impertinence repel those whom they would win to Christ. It is quite possible to be at once perfectly frank and perfectly courteous. You can point out to men their awful sin and need without insulting them. Your words may be very searching, while your manner is very gentle and winning. Indeed, the more gentle and winning our manner is, the deeper our words will go, for they will not stir up the opposition of those with whom we deal. Some zealous workers approach those with whom they wish to deal in such a manner that the latter at once assume the defensive and clothe themselves with an armor that it is impossible to penetrate.

8. *Be dead in earnest.* Only the earnest man can make the unsaved man feel the truth of God's word. It is well to let the passages that we would use with others first sink into our own souls. I know of a very successful worker who for a long time used the one passage, "prepare to meet thy God," with every one with whom she dealt, but that passage had taken such complete possession of her heart and mind that she used it with tremendous effect. A few passages that have mastered us are better than many passages that we have mastered from some text book.

The reader of this book is advised to ponder, upon his knees, such of the passages suggested in it as he decides to use until he himself feels their power. We read of Paul that he "ceased not to warn every one night and day, with tears." (Acts xx. 31.) Genuine earnestness will go farther than any skill learned in a training class or from the study of such a book as this.

9. *Never lose your temper when trying to lead a soul to Christ.* Some persons are purposely exasperating, but even such may be won, by patience, forbearance and gentleness.

They certainly cannot be won if you lose your temper. Nothing delights them more, or gives them more comfort in their sins. The more extremely irritating they are in their words and actions the more impressed they will be if you return insults with kindness. Often times the one who has been most insufferable will come back in penitence. One of the most insulting men I ever met afterwards became one of the most patient, persistent and effective of workers.

10. *Never have a heated argument with one whom you would lead to Christ.* This always comes from the flesh and not from the spirit. (Gal. v. 20, 22, 23.) It arises from pride and unwillingness to let the other person get the best of you in argument. Refuse to argue. If the one with whom you are talking has mistaken notions that must be removed

before he can be led to Christ quietly and pleasantly show him their error. If the error is not essential refuse to discuss it and hold the person to the main question.

11. *Never interrupt any one else who is dealing with a soul.* You may think he is not doing it in the wisest way, but if you can do it any better, bide your time and you will have the opportunity. Many an unskilled worker has had some one at the very point of decision when some meddler has broken in and upset the whole work. On the other hand, do not let others, if you can help it, interrupt you. Just a little word plainly but courteously spoken will usually prevent it.

12. *Don't be in a hurry.* One of the great faults of Christian work to–day is haste. We are too anxious for immediate results and so do superficial work. It is very noticeable how many of those with whom Christ dealt came out slowly. Nicodemus, Joseph, Peter and even Paul—though the final step in his case seems very sudden—are cases in point. It was three days even after the personal appearance of Jesus to Paul on the way to Damascus before the latter came out into the light and openly confessed Christ. (Acts xxii. 16.) One man with whom slow but thorough work has been done, and who at last has been brought out clearly for Christ, is better than a dozen with whom hasty work has been done, who think they have accepted Christ when in reality they have not. It is often a wise policy to plant a truth in a man's heart and leave it to work. The seed on rocky ground springs up quickly but withers as quickly.

13. *Whenever it is possible and wise, get the person with whom you are dealing on his knees before God.* It is wonderful how many difficulties disappear in prayer, and how readily stubborn people yield when they are brought into the very presence of God himself. I remember talking with a young woman, in an inquiry room, for perhaps two hours and making no apparent headway; but, when at last we knelt in prayer, in less than five minutes she was rejoicing in her Savior.

14. *Whenever you seem to fail in any given case go home and pray over it and study it to see why you failed.* If you have been at a loss as to what scripture to use, study that portion of this book that describes the different classes we meet and how to deal with them and see where this case belongs and how you ought to have treated it. Then go back if you can and try again. In any case you will be better prepared next time. The greatest success in this work comes through many apparent defeats. It will be well to frequently study these hints and suggestions to see if your failures come through neglect of them.

15. *Before parting from the one who has accepted Christ, be sure to give him definite instructions as to how to succeed in the Christian life.* The following are points that should be always insisted upon. (a.) Confess Christ with the mouth before men every opportunity you get. Rom. x. 9, 10; Matt. x. 32, 33. (b.) Be baptized and partake regularly of the Lord's supper. Acts ii. 38, 42; Luke xxii. 19; 1 Cor. xi. 24–26. (c.) Study the Word of God daily. 1 Pet. ii. 2; Acts xx. 32; 2 Tim. iii. 13–17; Acts xvii. 11. (d.) Pray daily, often and in every time of temptation. Luke xi. 9–13; xxii. 40; 1 Thes. v. 17. (e.) Put away out of your life every sin, even the smallest, and everything you have doubts about, and obey every word of Christ 1 John i. 6, 7; Rom. xiv. 23; John xiv. 23. (f.) Seek the society of Christians. Eph. iv. 12–16; Acts ii. 42, 47; Heb. x. 24, 25. (g.) Go to work for Christ. Matt. xxv. 14–29. (h.) When you fall into sin don't be discouraged, but confess it at once, believe it is forgiven because God says so and get up and go on. 1 John i. 9; Phil. iii. 13–14. It would be well to give these instructions in some permanent form to the one whom you have led to Christ. You can write them out or get a little tract called the "Christian Life Card" published by John C. Collins, Bureau of Supplies, New Haven, Conn. This contains them and some other matter.

16. *When you have led any one to Christ, follow him up and help him in the development of his Christian life.* Many are led to Christ and then neglected and get on very poorly. This is a great mistake. The work of following up those who are converted is as important as the work of leading them to Christ, and as a rule no one can do it so well as the person whom God used in their conversion.

Chapter XIII. The Baptism of the Holy Spirit

There is one condition of success in bringing men to Christ that is of such cardinal importance, and so little understood, that it demands a separate chapter. I refer to the Baptism of the Holy Spirit. In Acts i. 5; Luke xxiv. 49 (comp. Acts i. 8), and Acts ii. 4, we have three expressions; "baptized with the Holy Spirit," "endured with power from on high" and "filled with the Holy Spirit." By a careful comparison of these and related passages we will find that these various expressions refer to one and the same experience. This experience we shall see as we proceed in the study of this subject is an absolutely necessary condition of acceptable and effective service for Christ.

1. What is the Baptism of the Holy Spirit?

1. *It is a definite and distinct operation of the Holy Spirit of which one may know whether it has been wrought in him or not.* This is evident from the fact that Jesus bade His disciples tarry in Jerusalem until they had received this enduement, (Luke xxiv. 49, comp. Acts i. 8), and if it was not a definite and distinct operation of which they might know whether they had received it or not, of course, they would not know when this command of Christ had been complied with and when they were ready to begin their witnessing.

2. *It is an operation of The Holy Spirit separate from His regenerating work.* This appears from Acts i. 5, where the disciples are told "ye shall be baptized with the Holy Spirit not many days hence." But from John xv. 3; xiii. 10 we learn that the disciples were already regenerated. It appears also from Acts viii. 15, 16 where we are told of certain who had already believed and were baptized with water, but upon whom the Holy Spirit had not yet fallen. The same thing is shown by Acts xix. 1–6, where we are told of certain who were disciples, but who had not received the Holy Spirit since they believed. *One may then be regenerated by the Holy Spirit without being baptized with the Holy Spirit. Such an one is saved but he is not yet fitted for service.* Every believer has the Holy Spirit, Rom. viii. 9, but not every believer has the Baptism of the Holy Spirit, (Acts viii. 12–16; xix. 1–2). We shall see very soon that every believer may have the baptism of the Holy Spirit.

3. *The Baptism of the Holy Spirit is always connected with testimony or service*, (see 1 Cor. xii. 4–13; Acts i. 5–8; Luke xxiv. 49; Acts ii. 4; iv. 8, 31; vii. 55; ix. 17, 20; x. 45–46; xix. 6.) The Baptism of the Holy Spirit has no direct reference to cleansing from sin. This is an important point to bear in mind for many reasons. There is a line of teaching on this subject that leads men to expect that if they receive the Baptism of the Holy Spirit, the old carnal nature will be eradicated. There is not a line of scripture to support this position. As said above, and as any one can learn for himself if he will examine all the passages in which the baptism of the Holy Spirit is mentioned, it is always connected with testimony and service. It is indeed accompanied with a great moral and spiritual uplifting and pre–supposes, as we shall see, an entire surrender of the will to Christ, but its primary and immediate purpose is fitting for service. We will get a more definite idea of what the Baptism of the Holy Spirit is, if we consider its manifestations and results as stated in the

Bible. (a.) Let us look first at the passage that goes most into detail on this subject, 1 Cor. xii. 4–13. We see at once that *the manifestations or results of the Baptism of the Holy Spirit are not precisely the same in all persons*. For example, the Baptism of the Holy Spirit will not make every one who receives it a successful evangelist or teacher. Some quite different gift may be imparted. This fact is often overlooked and much disappointment and doubt are the result. The manifestations or results vary with the lines of service to which God has called different individuals. One receives the gift of an evangelist, another of a teacher, another of government, another of a helper, another of a mother, (1 Cor. xii. 28–31; Eph. iv. 8, 11.) (b.) 1 Cor. xii. 7, 11. *There will be some gift in every case.* Not the same gift but some gift, of an evangelist, or a pastor, or of a teacher or some other. (c.) 1 Cor. xii. 11. *The Holy Spirit is Himself the one who decides what the gift or gifts shall be which he will impart to each individual.* It is not for us to select some place of service and then ask the Holy Spirit to qualify us for that service, nor for us to select some gift, and then ask the Spirit to impart to us that gift. It is for us to put ourselves entirely at the disposal of the Holy Spirit to send us where "He will," into what line of service "He will" (Acts xiii. 2,) and to impart what gift "He will." He is absolutely sovereign and our rightful position is that of absolute and unconditional surrender to Him. This is where many fail of a blessing and meet with disappointment. I know a most sincere and self–sacrificing man who gave up a lucrative business and took up the work of an evangelist. He had heard of the Baptism of the Holy Spirit; and had been led to suppose that, if he received it, it would qualify him for the work of an evangelist. The man came more than four thousand miles to this country, but the work did not open to him. He was in much perplexity and doubt until he was led to see that it was not for him to select the work of an evangelist, as good as that work was, and then expect the Holy Spirit to qualify him for this self–chosen work. He gave himself up to be sent into whatever work the Spirit might will. Into the work in which he was sent the power of the Spirit came upon him and he received this very gift of an evangelist which he had coveted. (d.) Acts i. 5, 8. *The Baptism of the Holy Spirit always imparts power for service, the services to which God calls us.* In a certain city was an uneducated boy who was led to Christ. In his very lowly occupation he began witnessing for Jesus. He went on from step to step in Christ's work. My attention was called to him by a gentleman who was interested in him, and who said he would like to have me meet him. The gentleman brought him to Chicago, and I invited him one night to speak in one of our tents. It was in an exceedingly hard neighborhood. Into the same tent an organized mob once came to break up the meeting. It was a difficult audience to hold. The young man began in what appeared to me to be a very commonplace way, and I was afraid I had made a mistake in asking him to speak, but I prayed and watched the audience. There was nothing remarkable in his address as he went on—excepting the bad grammar. But I noticed that all the people were listening. They continued to listen to the end. When I asked if there was any one who wished to accept Christ, people rose in different parts of the tent to signify that they did. Thinking it all over, I told the facts to a man who had known the speaker before. "It is just so wherever he goes" was the reply. What was the explanation? This uneducated boy had received the Baptism of the Holy Ghost and had received power. One night at the close of an address on the Baptism of the Holy Spirit, a minister came to me on the platform and said: "I need this power, won't you pray for me?" "Let us kneel right down here now," I replied, and we did. A few weeks after I met a gentleman who had been standing by. "Do you remember," he said "the minister with whom you prayed at New Britain. He went back to his church; his church is packed Sunday evenings, a large part of the audience are young men and he is having conversions right along." He had received the Baptism of the Holy Spirit and "power." (e.) Acts iv. 29–31. *The Baptism of the Holy Spirit always imparts boldness in testimony and service.* Peter is a notable example of this. Contrast Peter in Acts iv. 8–12 with Peter in Mark xiv. 66–72. Perhaps some one who reads this book has a great desire to speak to others and win them to Christ, but an insuperable timidity stands in the way. If you will only get the Baptism of the Holy Spirit, all that will be overcome.

We are now in a position to define the baptism of the Holy Spirit. *The Baptism of the Holy Spirit, is the Spirit of God falling upon the believer, taking possession of his faculties, imparting to him gifts not naturally his own, but which qualify him for the service to which God has called him.*

2. The necessity of the baptism of the Holy Spirit as a preparation for Christian work.

(1.) *In Luke xxiv. 49. Jesus bade the apostles to tarry in Jerusalem until they were "endued with power from on high."* These men had been appointed to be witnesses of the life, death and resurrection of Christ. (Luke xxiv. 45–48. Acts; i. 22; x. 39–41.) They had received what would seem to be a splendid and sufficient training for this work. For more than three years they had been to school to the best of teachers, Jesus Himself. They had been eye witnesses of his miracles, death, burial, resurrection and ascension. But there was still one thing needed. And this need was of such vital importance that Jesus would not permit them to enter upon their appointed work until that need had been met. That need was the Baptism of the Holy Spirit. If the apostles with their unparalleled fitting for service, were not permitted to enter that service until all their other training had been supplemented by the Baptism of the Holy Spirit, what daring presumption it is for any of us with our inferior training to dare to do it. But this is not all, *even Jesus Himself did not enter upon his ministry until specially anointed with the Holy Spirit and with power.* (Acts x. 38, comp. Luke iii. 22 and iv. 1, 14). *This baptism is an absolutely essential preparation for Christian work.* It is either ignorance of the plain requirements of God's word or the most daring presumption on our part when we try to do work for Christ until we know we have been Baptized with the Holy Spirit.

(2.) *It is the privilege of every believer to be baptized with the Holy Spirit.* This appears from Acts ii. 39, "To you is the promise and to your children and to all that are afar off, even as many as the Lord our God shall call unto him." The context, the use of the word "promise" in this and the preceding chapter (ch. i. 4; ii. 16, 33.) and the use of the expression "gift of the Holy Spirit" throughout the book, all prove conclusively that "the promise" of this verse means the promise of the Baptism of the Holy Spirit; and the verse tells us that this promise is for all in all ages of the church's history whom God shall call unto him, *i. e.* for every believer. If we have not this baptism it is our own fault. It is for us and we are responsible before God for all the work we might have done, and all the souls we might have won if we were so baptized, and we are guilty to the extent that the work is not done and the souls not won.

3. How can we obtain the Baptism of the Holy Spirit?

We now come to the practical question: how can we obtain this Baptism of the Holy Spirit which is such an absolute necessity in our work for Christ? Fortunately the answer to this question is very plainly stated in the Bible.

(1) "Repent ye and be baptized every one of you in the name of Jesus Christ unto the remission of your sins; and ye shall receive the gift of the Holy Spirit" (Acts ii. 38) *The first step toward obtaining this Baptism is repentance.* Repentance means "a change of mind," a change of mind about sin, about God, and in this case especially (as the context shows) a change of mind about Christ. A real change of mind such as leads to action—to

our turning away from all sin, our turning to God, our turning away from rejecting Jesus Christ to accepting Him. *The second step is the confession of our renunciation of sin and acceptance of Jesus Christ in God's appointed way by baptism in the name of Jesus Christ.* The Baptism with the Holy Spirit in at least one instance (Acts x. 44–48) preceded the baptism with water but this was manifestly an exceptional case and God says "repent ye and be baptized every one of you in the name of Jesus Christ unto the remission of your sins; and ye shall receive the gift of the Holy Spirit," (Acts ii. 38).

(2) "The Holy Spirit whom God hath given to them that obey him." (Acts v. 32). *The condition of the gift of the Holy Ghost here stated is that we "obey Him."* Obedience means more than the mere performance of some of the things that God bids us do. It means the entire surrender of our wills, ourselves and all we have, to Him. It means that we come to Him and say from the heart, "here I am, I am thine, thou hast bought me with a price, I acknowledge thine ownership. Take me, do with me what thou wilt, send me where thou wilt, use me as Thou wilt." This entire yielding of ourselves to God is the condition of our receiving the Baptism of the Holy Spirit, and it is at this point that many fail of this blessing. At the close of a convention a gentleman hurried to the platform and said there was a lady in great distress who wished to speak with me. It was an hour before I could get to her, but I found her still in great mental suffering in the intensity of her desire for the Baptism of the Holy Spirit. Others had talked to her but it had seemed to do no good. I sat down behind her and said, "Is your will wholly surrendered?" She did not know. "You wish to be a Christian worker do you not?" "Yes." "Are you willing to go back to Baltimore and be a servant girl if it is God's will?" "No!" "You will never receive this blessing until your own will is wholly laid down." "I can't lay it down." "Would you like to have God lay it down for you?" "Yes." "Well, let us ask Him to do it." We did, he heard the prayer, the will was laid down, the Baptism of the Holy Spirit was received and she went from the church rejoicing.

Obedience means also the doing in all matters great and small, the will of God as revealed in His Word or by His Spirit. Any refusal to do what God bids us do, any conscious doing of what he bids us not do, even in very little matters, is sufficient to shut us out of this blessing. If there is anything no matter how little, that comes up before us to trouble us as we pray over this matter, we should set it right with God at once. Mr. Finney tells of one who, in great agony prayed for days for the Baptism of the Holy Spirit but received no answer. At last as she was praying one night she put her hand to her head and took off some little adornment that always came up before her when she prayed and cast it from her. Immediately she received the long desired blessing. It seemed a very little thing but it was a matter of controversy with God and hindered the blessing.

(3.) "How much more shall your Heavenly Father give the Holy Spirit to them that ask Him." (Luke xi. 13.)

(a.) There must be definite prayer for this Baptism. It is often said that the Holy Spirit is already here and that every believer has the Spirit and so we ought not to pray for the Holy Spirit. This argument overlooks the distinction between having the Holy Spirit and having this specific operation of the Holy Spirit. (see Section 1.2 above.) It also contradicts the plain teaching of God's word that He gives "the Holy Spirit to them that ask Him." It is furthermore shown to be fallacious by the fact that the Baptism of the Holy Spirit in the book of Acts was constantly given in connection with and in answer to prayer. (Acts i. 14; ii. 1–4; iv. 31; viii. 15,17.)

(b.) Prayer implies desire. There is no real prayer for the Baptism of the Spirit unless there is *a deep desire for it.* As long as a man thinks he can get along somehow without this blessing, he is not likely to get it; but when a man reaches the place where he feels he must have this no matter what it costs, he is far on the way toward receiving it. Many a minister of the gospel and other worker has been brought to a place where he has felt he could not go on with his ministry without this gift and then the gift has soon followed and the character of his work has been entirely transformed.

(c.) *The prayer to be effectual must be in faith (Mark xi. 24).* James says in regard to the prayer for wisdom, "Let him ask in faith, nothing wavering. For he that wavereth is like a wave of sea driven with the wind and tossed. For let not that man think that he shall receive anything of the Lord." (Jas. i. 6, 7.) The same principle, of course, holds in regard to the prayer for the Holy Spirit. It is at this very point that many miss the blessing. How to approach God in faith is clearly taught by 1 John v. 14, 15. "This is the confidence that we have in Him, that, if we ask anything according to his will He heareth us, and if we know that he hear us whatsoever we ask, we know that we have the petitions that we desired of him." When we ask Him for the Baptism of the Holy Spirit we know that we have asked something according to His will for it is definitely promised in His word. Therefore we know that "He heareth us; and if we know that He hear us we know that we have the petition" which we have asked of him. As soon then as I am sure I have met the conditions stated above of the gift of the Holy Spirit, and asked it of God I have a right to count this blessing mine—the prayer is heard and I have the petition I asked of him—and get up and enter into my work assured that in my work will be seen the Spirit's power. "But," some one will say, "shall we expect no manifestations?" Yes, but where? In service. When I know on the authority of God's word that my prayer is heard, I have the right to enter upon any service to which He calls me and confidently expect the manifestation of the Spirit's power in that service. It is a mistake to wait or look for, as so many do, the manifestation in electric shocks or peculiar emotional experiences. They may and often do accompany the Baptism of the Holy Spirit. But the Bible clearly teaches us (i Cor. xii. 4–11) that the place to look for manifestations, is in service and the most important, reliable and scriptural manifestations are found in our work. "Must we not wait," it may be asked, "until we know that we have received the baptism of the Holy Spirit?" Most assuredly, but how are we to know? The same way in which we know we are saved, *by the testimony of God's word*. When I know I have met the conditions and have asked this gift which is "according to his will" I know by God's word (1 John v. 14, 15.) that my prayer is heard, and that I have the petition I desired of him. I have a right to arise with no other evidence than the all–sufficient evidence of God's word, and enter into the service to which God calls me. "Did not the early disciples wait ten days?" it may again be asked. Yes, and the reason why is clearly given in Acts ii. 1.—"When the day of Pentecost was fully come." In the O. T. types the day of Pentecost had been appointed as the day in God's economy for the first giving of the Holy Spirit and the offering of the first–fruits (the church) and so the Holy Spirit could not be given until that day. (Lev. xxiii. 9–17.) But after the Spirit was once given we find no protracted period of waiting on the part of those who sought this blessing. (Acts iv. 31; viii. 15, 17; ix. 17, 20; xix. 6.) Men are obliged to wait to–day, but it is only because they have not met the conditions, or do not believe and claim the blessing simply on the Word of God. The moment we meet the conditions and claim the blessing it is ours. (Mark xi. 24 R.V.) Any child of God may lay down this book, meet the conditions, ask the blessing, claim it and have it. In a Students' Summer School at Lake Geneva after a talk by F. B. Meyer on the Baptism of the Holy Spirit, a student remained to talk with me. He said he had heard of this before and had been seeking it for months but could not get it. I found his will was not surrendered, but that was soon settled. Then I said, "Let us kneel down and ask God for the Baptism of the Holy Spirit." He did so. Was that petition "according to his will?" I asked. "Yes." "Was the prayer heard?" After some hesitation, "It must have been." "Have you what you asked of Him?" "I don't feel it." I read 1 John v. 15 from the Bible that lay open before us: "If we know that he hears us, whatsoever we ask, we know that *we have* the petition we desired of him." "Was the prayer heard?" "Yes." "Have you what you asked?" "I must have; for God says so." We arose and soon separated. Going back to the school in a few days I met the young man again. His face was now all aglow and he knew he had received what at first he took upon the bare word of God.

4. The Repetition of the Baptism of the Holy Spirit.

One thing more needs to be said before we leave this subject. *The Baptism of the Holy Spirit is an experience that needs frequent repeating.* This appears from a comparison of Acts ii. 4—where Peter with others was filled with the Holy Spirit—with Acts iv. 8.—where Peter was filled again,—and with Acts iv. 31 where Peter with others was filled yet again. A new filling is needed and should be sought for each new emergency of Christian service. There are many who once knew experimentally what the Baptism of the Holy Spirit meant who are trying to work to-day in the power of that old experience and are working without God. They need and must have a new Baptism before God can use them.

How to Succeed in The Christian Life

~ ※ ~

By *R. A. Torrey*

~ ※ ~

Dedicated to the many thousands in many lands who have professed Christ in our meetings.

Introduction

I have for years felt the need of a book to put in the hands of those beginning the Christian life that would tell them just how to make a complete success of this new life upon which they were entering. I could find no such book, so I have been driven to write one. This book aims to tell the young convert just what he most needs to know. I hope that pastors and evangelists and other Christian workers may find it a good book to put in the hands of young converts. I hope that it may also prove a helpful book to many who have long been Christians but have not made that headway in the Christian life that they long for.

Chapter I. Beginning Right

There is nothing more important in the Christian life than beginning right. If we begin right we can go on right. If we begin wrong the whole life that follows is likely to be wrong. If any one who reads these pages has begun wrong, it is a very simple matter to begin over again and begin right. What the right beginning in the Christian life is we are told in John 1: 12, "But as many as received Him, to them gave He power to become the sons of God, even to them that believe on His name." The right way to begin the Christian life is by receiving Jesus Christ. To any one who receives Him, He at once gives power to become a child of God. If the reader of this book should be the wickedest man on earth and should at this moment receive Jesus Christ, that very instant he would become a child of God. God says so in the most unqualified way in the verse quoted above. No one can become a child of God in any other way. No man, no matter how carefully he has been reared, no matter how well he has been sheltered from the vices and evils of this world, is a child of God until he receives Jesus Christ. We are "sons of God through faith in Christ Jesus" (Gal. 3: 26), and in no other way.

What does it mean to receive Jesus Christ? It means to take Christ to be to yourself all that God offers Him to be to everybody. Jesus Christ is God's gift. "For God so loved the world that He gave His only begotten Son that whosoever believeth in Him should not perish but have everlasting life" (John 3: 16). Some accept this wondrous gift of God. Every one who does accept this gift becomes a child of God. Many others refuse this wondrous gift of God, and every one who refuses this gift of God perishes. He is condemned already. "He that believeth on the Son is not condemned, but he that believeth not is condemned already because he hath not believed in the name of the only begotten Son of God" (John 3: 18).

What does God offer His Son to be to us?

1. First of all, *God offers Jesus to us to be our sin-bearer.* We have all sinned. There is not a man or woman or a boy or a girl who has not sinned (Romans 3: 22, 23). If any of us say that we have not sinned we are deceiving ourselves and giving the lie to God (1 John 1: 8, 10). Now we must each of us bear our own sin or some one else must bear it in our place. If we were to bear our own sins, it would mean we must be banished forever from the presence of God, for God is holy. "God is light and in Him is no darkness at all" (1 John 1:5). But God Himself has provided another to bear our sins in our place so that we should not need to bear them ourselves. This sin-bearer is God's own Son, Jesus Christ,

"For He hath made Him to be sin for us who knew no sin that we might be made the righteousness of God in Him" (2 Cor. 5:21). When Jesus Christ died upon the cross of Calvary He redeemed us from the curse of the law by being made a curse in our stead (Gal. 3:13). To receive Christ then is to believe this testimony of God about His Son, to believe that Jesus Christ did bear our sins in His own body on the cross (1 Pet. 2:24), and to trust God to forgive all our sins because Jesus Christ has borne them in our place. "All we like sheep have gone astray; we have turned every one to his own way; and the Lord hath laid on Him the iniquity of us all" (Is. 53:6). Our own good works, past, present or future have nothing to do with the forgiveness of our sins. Our sins are forgiven, not because of any good works that we do, they are forgiven because of the atoning work of Christ upon the cross of Calvary in our place. If we rest in this atoning work we shall do good works, but our good works will be the outcome of our being saved and the outcome of our believing on Christ as our sin-bearer. Our good works will not be the ground of our salvation, but the result of our salvation, and the proof of it. We must be very careful not to mix in our good works at all as the ground of salvation. We are not forgiven because of Christ's death *and our good works*, we are forgiven solely and entirely because of Christ's death. To see this clearly is the right beginning of the true Christian life.

2. *God offers Jesus to us as our deliverer from the power of sin.* Jesus not only died, He rose again. To-day He is a living Savior. He has all power in heaven and on earth (Matt. 28: 18). He has power to keep the weakest sinner from falling (Jude 24). He is able to save not only from the uttermost but "to the uttermost" all that come unto the Father through Him. (Wherefore He is able to save to the uttermost them that draw near unto God through Him, seeing that He ever liveth to make intercession for them.—Heb. 7: 25) "If the Son therefore shall make you free, ye shall be free indeed" (John 8: 36). To receive Jesus is to believe this that God tells us in His Word about Him, to believe that He did rise from the dead, to believe that He does now live, to believe that He has power to keep us from falling, to believe that He has power to keep us from the power of sin day by day, and just trust Him to do it.

This is the secret of daily victory over sin. If we try to fight sin in our own strength, we are bound to fail. If we just look up to the risen Christ to keep us every day and every hour, He will keep us. Through the crucified Christ we get deliverance from the guilt of sin, our sins are all blotted out, we are free from all condemnation; but it is through the risen Christ that we get daily victory over the power of sin. Some receive Christ as a sin-bearer and thus find pardon, but do not get beyond that, and so their life is one of daily failure. Others receive Him as their risen Savior also, and thus enter into an experience of victory over sin. To begin right we must take Him not only as our sin-bearer, and thus find pardon; but we must also take Him as our risen Savior, our Deliverer from the power of sin, our Keeper, and thus find daily victory over sin.

3. But *God offers Jesus to us, not only as our sin-bearer and our Deliverer from the power of sin, but He also offers Him to us as our Lord and King.* We read in Acts 2: 36, "Let all the house of Israel know assuredly, that God hath made that same Jesus, whom ye have crucified, both Lord and Christ." Lord means Divine Master, and Christ means anointed King. To receive Jesus is to take Him as our Divine Master, as the One to whom we yield the absolute confidence of our intellects, the One whose word we believe absolutely, the One whom we will believe though many of the wisest of men may question or deny the truth of His teachings; and as our King to whom we gladly yield the absolute control of our lives, so that the question from this time on is never going to be, what would I like to do or what do others tell me to do, or what do others do, but the whole question

is what would my King Jesus have me do? A right beginning involves an unconditional surrender to the Lordship and Kingship of Jesus.

The failure to realize that Jesus is Lord and King, as well as Savior, has led to many a false start in the Christian life. We begin with Him as our Savior, as our sin-bearer and our Deliverer from the power of sin, but we must not end with Him merely as Savior, we must know Him as Lord and King. There is nothing more important in a right beginning of the Christian life than an unconditional surrender, both of the thoughts and the conduct to Jesus. Say from your heart and say it again and again, "*All* for Jesus." Many fail because they shrink back from this entire surrender. They wish to serve Jesus with half their heart, and part of themselves and part of their possessions. To hold back anything from Jesus means a wretched life of stumbling and failure.

The life of entire surrender is a joyous life all along the way. If you have never done it before, go alone with God to-day, get down on your knees and say, "All for Jesus," and mean it. Say it very earnestly; say it from the bottom of your heart. Stay there until you realize what it means and what you are doing. It is a wondrous step forward when one really takes it. If you have taken it already, take it again, take it often. It always has fresh meaning and brings fresh blessedness. In this absolute surrender is found the key to the truth. Doubts rapidly disappear for one who surrenders all (John 7: 17). In this absolute surrender is found the secret of power in prayer (1 John 3: 22). In this absolute surrender is found the supreme condition of receiving the Holy Ghost (Acts 5: 32).

Taking Christ as your Lord and King involves obedience to His will as far as you know it in each smallest detail of life. There are those who tell us that they have taken Christ as their Lord and King who at the same time are disobeying Him daily in business, in domestic life, in social life and in personal conduct Such persons are deceiving themselves. You have not taken Jesus as your Lord and King if you are not striving to obey Him in everything each day. He Himself says, "Why call ye Me 'Lord, Lord!' and do not the things that I say?" (Luke 6: 46).

To sum it all up, the right way to begin the Christian life is to accept Jesus Christ as your sin-bearer and to trust God to forgive your sins because Jesus Christ died in your place; to accept Him as your risen Savior who ever lives to make intercession for you, and who has all power to keep you, and to trust Him to keep you from day to day; and to accept Him as your Lord and King to whom you surrender the absolute control of your thoughts and of your life. This is the right beginning, the only right beginning of the Christian life. If you have made this beginning, all that follows will be comparatively easy. If you have not made this beginning, make it now.

Chapter II. The Open Confession of Christ

Having begun the Christian life right by taking the proper attitude towards Christ in a private transaction between Himself and yourself, the next step is an open confession of the relationship that now exists between yourself and Jesus Christ. Jesus says in Matt. 10: 32, "Whosoever therefore shall confess Me before men, him will I confess also before My Father which is in heaven." He demands a public confession. He demands it for your own sake. This is the path of blessing. Many attempt to be disciples of Jesus and not let the world know it. No one has ever succeeded in that attempt. To be a secret disciple means to be no disciple at all. If one really has received Christ he cannot keep it to himself. "For out of the abundance of the heart the mouth speaketh" (Matt. 12: 34). So important is the public confession of Christ that Paul puts it first in his statement of the conditions of salvation. He says, "If thou shalt *confess with thy mouth* the Lord Jesus and shalt believe in thine heart that God hath raised Him from the dead, thou shalt be saved. For with the heart man believeth unto righteousness; and with the mouth confession is made unto salvation" (Rom. 10: 9, 10). The life of confession is the life of full salvation. Indeed, the life of confession is the life of the only real salvation. When we confess Christ before men down here, He confesses us before the Father in heaven and the Father gives us the Holy Spirit as the seal of our salvation.

It is not enough that we confess Christ just once, as, for example, when we are confirmed, or when we unite with the church, or when we come forward in a revival meeting. We should confess Christ constantly. We should not be ashamed of our Lord and King. We should let people know that we are on His side. In the home, in the church, at our work, and at our play, we should let others know where we stand. Of course, we should not parade our Christianity or our piety, but we should leave no one in doubt whether we belong to Christ. We should let it be seen that we glory in Him as our Lord and King.

The failure to confess Christ is one of the most frequent causes of backsliding. Christians get into new relationships where they are not known as Christians and where they are tempted to conceal the fact; they yield to the temptation and they soon find themselves drifting. The more you make of Jesus Christ, the more He will make of you. It will save you from many a temptation if the fact is clearly known that you are one who acknowledges Christ as Lord in all things.

Chapter III. Assurance of Salvation

If one is to have the fullest measure of joy and power in Christian service, he must know that his sins are forgiven, that he is a child of God, and that he has eternal life. It is the believer's privilege to *know* that he has eternal life. John says in 1 John 5: 13, "These things have I written unto you, *that ye may know* that ye have eternal life, even unto you that believe on the name of the Son of God." John wrote this first epistle for the express purpose that any one who believes on the name of the Son of God *might know* that he has eternal life.

There are those who tell us that no one can know that he has eternal life until he is dead and has been before the judgment seat of God, but God Himself tells us that we may know. To deny the possibility of the believer's knowing that he has eternal life is to say that the First Epistle of John was written in vain, and it is to insult the Holy Spirit who is its real author. Again Paul tells us in Acts 13: 39, "By Him (that is by Christ) every one that believeth *is justified* from all things." So every one that believeth in Jesus may know that he is justified from all things. He may know it because the Word of God says so. Again John tells us in John 1: 12, "But *as many as received Him* (that is Jesus Christ) to them gave He the right to become children of God, even to them that believe on His name." Here is a definite and unmistakable declaration that every one who receives Jesus becomes a child of God. Therefore every believer in Jesus may know that he is a child of God. He may know it on the surest of all grounds, *i. e.*, because the Word of God asserts that he is a child of God.

But how may any individual know that he has eternal life? He may know it on the very best ground of knowledge, that is through the testimony of God Himself as given in the Bible. The testimony of Scripture is the testimony of God. What the Scriptures say is absolutely sure. What the Scriptures say God says. Now in John 3: 36 the Scriptures say, "He that believeth on the Son *hath* everlasting life." Any one of us may know whether we believe on the Son or not. Whether we have that real faith in Christ that leads us to receive Him. If we have this faith in Christ we have God's own written testimony that we have eternal life, that our sins are forgiven, that we are the children of God. We may feel forgiven, or we may not feel forgiven, but that does not matter. It is not a question of what we feel but of what God says. God's Word is always to be believed. Our own feelings are oftentimes to be doubted. There are many who are led to doubt their sins are forgiven, to doubt that they have everlasting life, to doubt that they are saved, because they do not feel forgiven, or do not feel that they have everlasting life, or do not feel that they are saved. Because you do not feel it is no reason why you should doubt it.

Suppose that you were sentenced to imprisonment and that your friends secured a pardon for you. The legal document announcing your pardon is brought to you. You read it and know you are pardoned because the legal document says so, but the news is so good and so sudden that you are dazed by it. You do not realize that you are pardoned. Some one comes to you and says, "Are you pardoned?" What would you reply? You would say, "Yes, I am pardoned." Then he asks, "Do you feel pardoned?" You reply, "No, I do not feel pardoned. It is so sudden, it is so wonderful, I cannot realize it." Then he says to you, "But how can you know that you are pardoned if you do not feel it?" You would hold out the document and you would say, "This says so." The time would come, after you had read the document over and over again and believed it, when you would not only know you were pardoned because the document said so but you would feel it. Now the Bible is God's authoritative document declaring that every one that believeth in Jesus is justified; declaring that every one that believeth on the Son hath everlasting life; declaring that every one who receives Jesus is a child of God. If any one asks you if your sins are all forgiven, reply, "Yes, I know they are because God says so." If they ask you if you know that you are a child of God, reply, "Yes, I know I am a child of God because God says so." If they ask you if you have everlasting life, reply, "Yes, I know I have everlasting life because God says so. God says, 'He that believeth on the Son hath everlasting life.' I know I believe on the Son, and therefore I know I have eternal life—because God says so." You may not feel it yet but if you will keep meditating upon God's statement and believing what God says, the time will come when you will feel it.

For one who believes on the Son of God to doubt that he has eternal life is for him to make God a liar. "He that believeth on the Son of God hath the witness in him. He that believeth not God, hath made Him a liar because he hath not believed in the witness that God hath borne concerning His Son and the witness is this, that God gave unto us eternal life, and this life is in His Son. He that hath the Son hath the life: he that hath not the Son of God hath not the life" (1 John 5: 10-12). Any one who does not believe God's testimony that He has given unto us eternal life and that this life is in His Son and that he that hath the Son hath the life, makes God a liar.

It is sometimes said "it is presumption for any one to say that he knows he is saved, or to say that he knows that he has eternal life." But is it presumption to believe God? Is it not rather presumption not to believe God, to make God a liar? When you who believe on the Son of God and yet doubt that you have eternal life, you make God a liar. When Jesus said to the woman who was a sinner, "Thy sins are forgiven" (Luke 7: 48), was it presumption for her to go out and say, "I know my sins are all forgiven"? Would it not have been presumption for her to have doubted for a moment that her sins were all forgiven? Jesus had said that they were forgiven. For her to doubt it would have been for her to give the lie to Jesus. Is it then any more presumption for the believer to-day to say, "My sins are all forgiven, I have eternal life," when God says in His written testimony to every one that believeth, "You are justified from all things" (Acts 13: 39), "You have eternal life" (John 3: 36; 1 John 5: 13)?

Be very sure first of all that you really do believe on the name of the Son of God; that you really have received Jesus. If you are sure of this then never doubt for a moment that your sins are all forgiven, never doubt for a moment that you are a child of God, never doubt for a moment that you have everlasting life. If Satan comes and whispers, "Your sins are not forgiven," point Satan to the Word of God and say, "God says my sins are forgiven and I know they are." If Satan whispers, "Well perhaps you don't believe on Him," then say, "Well if I never did before I will now." And then go out rejoicing, knowing that your sins are forgiven, knowing that you are a child of God, knowing that you have everlasting life.

There are doubtless many who say they know they have eternal life who really do not believe on the name of the Son of God, who have not really received Jesus. This is not true assurance. It has no sure foundation in the Word of God who cannot lie. If we wish to get assurance of salvation we must first get saved. The reason why many have not the assurance that they are saved is because they are not saved. They ought not to have assurance. What they need first is salvation. But if you have received Jesus in the way described in the first chapter, YOU ARE SAVED, you are a child of God, your sins are forgiven. Believe it, know it. Rejoice in it.

Having settled it, let it remain settled. Never doubt it. You may make mistakes, you may stumble, you may fall, but even if you do, if you have really received Jesus, know that your sins are forgiven and rise from your fall and go forward in the glad assurance that there is nothing between you and God.

Chapter IV. Receiving the Holy Spirit

When the Apostle Paul came to Ephesus, he found a little group of twelve disciples of Christ. There was something about these twelve disciples that struck Paul unfavorably. We are not told what it was. It may be that he did not find in them that overflowing joyfulness that one learns to expect in all Christians who have really entered into the fullness of blessing that there is for them in Christ. It may be that Paul was troubled at the fact that there were only twelve of them, thinking that if these twelve were what they ought to be, there would certainly have been more than twelve of them by this time. Whatever it may have been that impressed Paul unfavorably, he went right to the root of the difficulty at once by putting to them the question, "Did ye receive the Holy Ghost when ye believed?" (Acts 19: 2). It came out at once that they had not received the Holy Ghost, that in fact they did not know that the Holy Ghost had been given. Then Paul told them that the Holy Ghost had been given, and also showed them just what they must do to receive the Holy Ghost then and there, and before that gathering was over the Holy Ghost came upon them. From that day on there was a different state of affairs in Ephesus. A great revival sprang up at once so that the whole city was shaken, "So mightily grew the Word of God and prevailed" (Acts 19: 20). Paul's question to these young disciples in Ephesus should be put to young disciples everywhere, "Have ye received the Holy Ghost?" In *receiving the Holy Spirit* is the great secret of joyfulness in our own hearts, of victory over sin, of power in prayer, and of effective service.

Every one who has truly received Jesus must have the Holy Spirit dwelling in him in some sense; but in many believers, though the Holy Spirit dwells in them, He dwells way back in some hidden sanctuary of their being, back of consciousness. It is something quite different, something far better than this, to receive the Holy Spirit in the sense that Paul meant in his question. To receive the Holy Spirit in such a sense that one knows experimentally that he has received the Holy Spirit, to receive the Holy Spirit in such a sense that we are conscious of the joy with which He fills our hearts different from any joy that we have ever known in the world; to receive the Holy Spirit in such a sense that He rules our life and produces within us in ever increasing measure the fruit of the Spirit, love, joy, peace, long-suffering, gentleness, goodness, faith, meekness, temperance; to receive the Holy Spirit in such a sense that we are conscious of His drawing our hearts out in prayer in a way that is not of ourselves; to receive the Holy Spirit in such a sense that we are conscious of His help when we witness for Christ, when we speak to others individually and try to lead them to accept Christ, or when we teach a Sunday-school class, or speak in public, or do any other work for the Master. Have you received the Holy Spirit? If you have not, let me tell you how you may.

1. First of all in order to receive the Holy Spirit, one must be resting in the death of Christ on the cross for us as the sole and all-sufficient ground upon which God pardons all our sins and forgives us.

2. In order to receive the Holy Spirit we must put away every known sin. We should go to our heavenly Father and ask Him to search us through and through and bring to light anything in our life, our outward life or our inward life, that is wrong in His sight, and if He does bring anything to light that is displeasing to Him, we should put it away, no matter how dear it is to us. There must be a complete renunciation of all sin in order to receive the Holy Spirit.

3. In the third place, in order to receive the Holy Spirit, there must be an open confession of Christ before the world. The Holy Spirit is not given to those who are trying to be disciples in secret, but to those who obey Christ and publicly confess Him before the world.

4. In the fourth place, in order to receive the Holy Spirit, there must be an absolute surrender of our lives to God. You must go to Him and say, "Heavenly Father, here I am. Thou hast bought me with a price. I am Thy property. I renounce all claim to do my own will, all claim to govern my own life, all claim to have my own way. I give myself up unreservedly to Thee—all I am and all I have. Send me where Thou wilt, use me as Thou wilt, do with me what Thou wilt—I am Thine." If we hold anything back from God, no matter how small it may seem, that spoils it all. But if we surrender all to God, then God will give all that He has to us. There are some who shrink from this absolute surrender to God, but absolute surrender to God is simply absolute surrender to infinite love. Surrender to the Father, to the Father whose love is not only wiser than any earthly father's, but more tender than any earthly mother's.

5. In order to receive the Holy Spirit there should be definite asking for the Holy Spirit. Our Lord Jesus says in Luke 11: 13, "If ye then, being evil, know how to give good gifts unto your children: how much more shall your heavenly Father give the Holy Spirit to them that ask Him?" Just ask God to give you the Holy Spirit and expect Him to do it, because He says He will.

6. Last of all, in order to receive the Holy Spirit, there must be faith, simply taking God at His Word. No matter how positive any promise of God's Word may be, we enjoy it personally only when we believe. Our Lord Jesus says, "All things whatsoever ye pray and ask for, believe that ye have received them, and ye shall have them" (Mark 11: 24). When you pray for the Holy Spirit you have prayed for something according to God's will and therefore you may know that your prayer is heard and that you have what you asked

of Him (1 John 5: 14, 15). You may feel no different, but do not look at your feelings but at God's promise. Believe the prayer is heard, believe that God has given you the Holy Spirit and you will afterwards have in actual experience what you have received in simple faith on the bare promise of God's Word.

It is well to go often alone and kneel down and look up to the Holy Spirit and put into His hands anew the entire control of your life. Ask Him to take the control of your thoughts, the control of your imagination, the control of your affections, the control of your desires, the control of your ambitions, the control of your choices, the control of your purposes, the control of your words, the control of your actions, the control of everything, and just expect Him to do it. The whole secret of victory in the Christian life is letting the Holy Spirit who dwells within you, have undisputed right of way in the entire conduct of your life.

Chapter V. Looking Unto Jesus

If we are to run with patience the race that is set before us, we must always keep looking unto Jesus (Heb. 12: 1-3). One of the simplest and yet one of the mightiest secrets of abiding joy and victory is to *never lose sight of Jesus*.

1. First of all *we must keep looking at Jesus as the ground of our acceptance before God*. Over and over again Satan will make an attempt to discourage us by bringing up our sins and failures and thus try to convince us that we are not children of God, or not saved. If he succeeds in getting us to keep looking at and brooding over our sins, he will soon get us discouraged, and discouragement means failure. But if we will keep looking at what God looks at, the death of Jesus Christ in our place that completely atones for every sin that we ever committed, we will never be discouraged because of the greatness of our sins. We shall see that while our sins are great, very great, that they have all been atoned for. Every time Satan brings up one of our sins, we shall see that Jesus Christ has redeemed us from its curse by being made a curse in our place (Gal. 3: 13). We shall see that while in ourselves we are full of unrighteousness, nevertheless in Christ we are made the righteousness of God, because Christ was made to be sin in our place (2 Cor. 5: 21). We will see that every sin that Satan taunts us about has been borne and settled forever (1 Pet. 2: 24; Is. 53: 6). We shall always be able to sing,

"Jesus paid my debt,
All the debt I owe;
Sin had left a crimson stain,
He washed it white as snow."

If you are this moment troubled about any sin that you have ever committed, either in the past or in the present, just look at Jesus on the cross; believe what God tells you about Him, that this sin which troubles you was laid upon Him (Is. 53: 6). Thank God that the sin is all settled; be full of gratitude to Jesus who bore it in your place and trouble about it no more. It is an act of base ingratitude to God to brood over sins that He in His infinite love has cancelled. Keep looking at Christ on the cross and walk always in the sunlight of God's favor. This favor of God has been purchased for you at great cost. Gratitude demands that you should always believe in it and walk in the light of it.

2. In the second place, *we must keep looking at Jesus as our risen Savior, who has all power in heaven and on earth and is able to keep us every day and every hour*. Are you tempted to do some wrong at this moment? If you are, remember that Jesus rose from the dead, remember that at this moment He is living at the right hand of God in the glory;

remember that He has all power in heaven and on earth, and that, therefore, He can give you victory right now. Believe what God tells you in His Word that Jesus has power to save you this moment "to the uttermost" (Heb. 7: 25). Believe that He has power to give you victory over this sin that now besets you. Ask Him to give you victory, expect Him to do it. In this way by looking unto the risen Christ for victory you may have victory over sin every day, every hour, every moment. "Remember Jesus Christ risen from the dead" (2 Tim. 2: 8).

God has called every one of us to a victorious life, and the secret of this victorious life is always looking to the risen Christ for victory. Through looking to Christ crucified we obtain pardon and enjoy peace. Through looking to the risen Christ we obtain present victory over the power of sin. If you have lost sight of the risen Christ and have yielded to temptation, confess your sin and know that it is forgiven because God says so (1 John 1: 9) and look to Jesus, the risen One, again to give you victory now and keep looking to Him.

3. In the third place, *we must keep looking to Jesus as the One whom we should follow in our daily conduct.* Our Lord Jesus says to us, His disciples to-day, as He said to His early disciples, "Follow Me." The whole secret of true Christian conduct can be summed up in these two words "Follow Me." "He that saith he abideth in Him ought himself so to walk *even as He walked*" (1 John 2: 6). One of the commonest causes of failure in Christian life is found in the attempt to follow some good man, whom we greatly admire. No man and no woman, no matter how good, can be safely followed. If we follow any man or woman, we are bound to go astray. There never has been but one absolutely perfect Man upon this earth—the Man Christ Jesus. If we try to follow any other man we are more sure to imitate his faults than his excellencies. Look at Jesus and Jesus only as your Guide.

If at any time you are in any perplexity as to what to do, simply ask the question, What would Jesus do? Ask God by His Holy Spirit to show you what Jesus would do. Study your Bible to find out what Jesus did do and follow Jesus. Even though no one else seems to be following Jesus, be sure that you follow Him. Do not spend your time or thought in criticizing others because they do not follow Jesus. See that you follow Him yourself. When you are wasting your time criticizing others for not following Jesus, Jesus is always saying to you, "What is that to thee; follow THOU Me" (John 21: 22). The question for you is not what following Jesus may involve for other people. The question is what does following Jesus mean for you?

This is the really simple life, the life of simply following Jesus. Many perplexing questions will come to you, but the most perplexing question will soon become as clear as day if you determine with all your heart to follow Jesus in everything. Satan will always be ready to whisper to you, "Such and such a good man does it," but all you need to do is to answer, "It matters not to me what this or that man may do or not do. The only question to me is, What would Jesus do?" There is wonderful freedom in this life of simply following Jesus. This path is straight and plain. But the path of the one who tries to shape his conduct by observing the conduct of others is full of twists and turns and pitfalls. Keep looking at Jesus. Follow on trustingly where He leads. This is the path of the just which shineth more and more unto the perfect day (Prov. 4: 18). He is the Light of the World, any one who follows Him shall not walk in darkness, but shall have the light of life all along the way (John 8: 12).

Chapter VI. Church Membership

No young Christian and no old Christian can have real success in the Christian life without the fellowship of other believers. The church is a divine institution, built by Jesus Christ Himself. It is the one institution that abides. Other institutions come and go; they do their work for their day and disappear, but the church will continue to the end. "The gates of hell shall not prevail against it" (Matt. 16: 18). The church is made up of men and women, imperfect men and women, and consequently is an imperfect institution, but none the less it is of divine origin and God loves it, and every believer should realize that he belongs to it and should openly take his place in it and bear his responsibilities regarding it.

The true church consists of all true believers, all who are united to Jesus Christ by a living faith in Himself. In its outward organization at the present time, it is divided into numberless sects and local congregations, but in spite of these divisions the true church is one. It has one Lord, Jesus Christ. It has one faith, faith in Him as Savior, Divine Lord and only King; one baptism, the baptism in the one Spirit into the one body (Eph. 4: 4, 5; 1 Cor. 12: 13). But each individual Christian needs the fellowship of individual fellow believers. The outward expression of this fellowship is in membership in some organized body of believers. If we hold aloof from all organized churches, hoping thus to have a broader fellowship with all believers belonging to all the churches, we deceive ourselves. We will miss the helpfulness that comes from intimate union with some local congregation. I have known many well-meaning persons who have held aloof from membership in any specific organization, and I have never known a person who has done this, whose own spiritual life has not suffered by it. On the day of Pentecost the three thousand who were converted were at once baptized and were added to the church (Acts 2: 41, 47), and "They continued steadfastly in the apostle's doctrine and fellowship, and in breaking of bread and in prayers." Their example is the one to follow. If you have really received Jesus Christ, hunt up as soon as possible some company of others who have received Jesus Christ and unite yourself with them.

In many communities there may be no choice of churches, for there is only one. In other communities one will be faced with the question, "With what body of believers shall I unite?" Do not waste your time looking for a perfect church. There is no perfect church. If you wait until you find a perfect church before you unite with any, you will unite with none, and thus you will belong to a church in which you are the only member and that is the most imperfect church of all. I would rather belong to the most imperfect Christian church I ever knew than not to belong to any church at all. The local churches in Paul's day were very imperfect institutions. Let one read the epistles to the Corinthians and see how imperfect was the church in Corinth, see how much there was that was evil in it, and yet Paul never thought of advising any believer in Corinth to get out of this imperfect church. He did tell them to come out of heathenism, to come out from fellowship with infidels (2 Cor. 6: 14-18), but not a word on coming out of the imperfect church in Corinth. He did tell the church in Corinth to separate from their membership certain persons whose lives were wrong (1 Cor. 5: 11, 12), but he did not tell the individual members of the church in Corinth to get out of the church because these persons had not yet been separated from their fellowship.

As you cannot find a perfect church, find the best church you can. Unite with a church where they believe in the Bible and where they preach the Bible. Avoid the churches where words are spoken open or veiled that have a tendency to undermine your faith in the Bible as a reliable revelation from God Himself, the all-sufficient rule of faith and practice. Unite with a church where there is a spirit of prayer, where the prayer-meetings are well kept up. Unite with a church that has a real active interest in the salvation of the lost, where young Christians are looked after and helped, where minister and people have a love for the poor and outcast, a church that regards its mission in this world to be the same as the mission of Christ, "to seek and to save the lost." As to denominational differences, other things being equal, unite with that denomination whose ideas of doctrine and of government and of the ordinances are most closely akin to your own. But it is better to unite with a live church of some other denomination than to unite with a dead church of your own. We live in a day when denominational differences are becoming ever less and less, and oftentimes they are of no practical consequence whatever; and one will often feel more at home in a church of some other denomination than in any accessible church of his own denomination. The things that divide the denominations are insignificant compared with the great fundamental truths and purposes and faith that unite them.

If you cannot find the church that agrees with the pattern set forth above, find the church that comes nearest to it. Go into that church and by prayer and by work try to bring that church as nearly as you can to the pattern of what you think a church of Christ ought to be. But do not waste your strength in criticism against either church or minister. Seek for what is good in the church and in the minister and do your best to strengthen it. Hold aloof firmly, though unobtrusively, from what is wrong and seek to correct it. Do not be discouraged if you cannot correct it in a day or a week or a month or a year. Patient love and prayer and effort will tell in time. Drawing off by yourself and snarling and grumbling will do no good. They will simply make you and the truths for which you stand repulsive.

Chapter VII. Bible Study

There is nothing more important for the development of the spiritual life of the Christian than regular, systematic Bible study. It is as true in the spiritual life as it is in the physical life that health depends upon what we eat and how much we eat. The soul's proper food is found in one book, the Bible. Of course, a true minister of the gospel will feed us on the Word of God, but that is not enough. He feeds us but one or two days in the week and we need to be fed every day. Furthermore, it will not do to depend upon being fed by others. We must learn to feed ourselves. If we study the Bible for ourselves as we ought to study it, we shall be in a large measure independent of human teachers. Even if we are so unfortunate as to have for our minister a man who is himself ignorant of the truth of God we shall still be safe from harm.

We live in a day in which false doctrine abounds on every hand and the only Christian who is safe from being led into error is the one who studies his Bible for himself daily. The Apostle Paul warned the elders of the church in Ephesus that the time was soon coming when grievous wolves should enter in among them not sparing the flock and when of their own selves men should arise speaking perverse things to draw away the disciples after them, but he told them how to be safe even in such perilous times as these. He said, "I commend you to God and to the Word of His grace, which is able to build you up and to give you an inheritance among them which are sanctified." Through meditation on the Word of God's grace they would be safe even in the midst of abounding error on the part of the leaders in the church (Acts 20: 29-32). Writing later to the Bishop of the church in Ephesus Paul said, "But evil men and impostors shall wax worse and worse, deceiving and being deceived" (2 Tim. 3: 13) but he goes on to tell Bishop Timothy how he and his fellow believers could be safe even in such times of increasing peril as were coming. That way was through the study of the Holy Scriptures, which are able to make wise unto salvation (2 Tim. 3: 14, 15). "All Scripture," he adds, "is given by inspiration of God and is profitable for doctrine, for reproof, for correction, for instruction in righteousness that the man of God may be perfect, thoroughly furnished unto all good works." That is to say, through the study of the Bible one will be sound in doctrine, will be led to see his sins and put them away, will find discipline in the righteous life and attain unto complete equipment for all good works. Our spiritual health, our growth, our strength, our victory over sin, our soundness in doctrine, our joy and peace in Christ, our cleansing from inward and outward sin, our fitness for service, all depend upon the study of the Word of God. The one who neglects his Bible is bound to make a failure of the Christian life. The one who studies his Bible in the right spirit and by a true method is bound to make a success of the Christian life.

This brings us face to face with the question, "What is the right way to study the Bible?"

1. First of all, we should *study it daily* (Acts 17: 11). This is of prime importance. No matter how good the methods of Bible study that one follows may be, no matter how much time one may put into Bible study now and then, the best results can only be secured when one makes it a matter of principle never to let a single day go by without earnest Bible study. This is the only safe course. Any day that is allowed to pass without faithful Bible study is a day thrown open to the advent into our hearts and lives of error or of sin. The writer has been a Christian for more than a quarter of a century and yet to-day he would not dare to allow even a single day to pass over his head without listening to the voice of God as it speaks to him through the pages of His Book. It is at this point that many fall away. They grow careless and let a day pass, or even several days pass, without going alone with God and letting Him speak to them through His Word. Mr. Moody once wisely said, "In prayer we talk to God. In Bible study, God talks to us, and we had better let God do most of the talking."

A regular time should be set apart each day for the study of the Bible. I do not think it is well as a rule to say that we shall study so many chapters in a day, for that leads to undue haste and skimming and thoughtlessness, but it is well to set apart a certain length of time each day for Bible study. Some can give more time to Bible study than others, but no one ought to give less than fifteen minutes a day. I set the time so low in order that no one may be discouraged at the outset. If a young Christian should set out to give an hour or two hours a day to Bible study, there is a strong probability that he would not keep to the resolution and he might become discouraged. Yet I know of many very busy people who have given the first hour of every day for years to Bible study and some who have given even two hours a day. The late Earl Cairns, Lord Chancellor of England, was one of the busiest men of his day, but Lady Cairns told me a few months ago that no matter how late he reached home at night he always arose at the same early hour for prayer and Bible study. She said, "We would sometimes get home from Parliament at two o'clock in the morning, but Lord Cairns would always arise at the same early hour to pray and study the Bible." Lord Cairns is reported as saying, "If I have had any success in life, I attribute it to the habit of giving the first two hours of each day to Bible study and prayer."

It is important that one choose the right time for this study. Wherever it is possible, the best time for this study is immediately after arising in the morning. The worst time of all is the last thing at night. Of course, it is well to give a little while just before we retire to Bible reading, in order that God's voice may be the last to which we listen, but the bulk of our Bible study should be done at an hour when our minds are clearest and strongest. Whatever time is set apart for Bible study should be kept sacredly for that purpose.

2. We should *study the Bible systematically*. Much time is frittered away in random study of the Bible. The same amount of time put into systematic study would yield far larger results. Have a definite place where you are studying and have a definite plan of study. A good way for a young Christian to begin the study of the Bible is to read the Gospel of John. When you have read it through once, begin and read it again until you have gone over the Gospel five times. Then read the Gospel of Luke five times in the same way; then read the Acts of the Apostles five times, then 1 Thessalonians five times, then 1 John five times, then Romans five times, then Ephesians five times.

By this time you will be ready to take up a more thorough method of Bible study. A good method is to begin at Genesis and read the Bible through chapter by chapter. Read each chapter through several times and then answer the following questions on the chapter:

(1) What is the principal subject of the chapter? (State the principal contents of the chapter in a single phrase or sentence.)

(2) What is the truth most clearly taught and most emphasized in the chapter?

(3) What is the best lesson?

(4) What is the best verse?

(5) Who are the principal people mentioned?

(6) What does the chapter teach about Jesus Christ? Go through the entire Bible in this way.

Another and more thorough method of Bible chapter study, which cannot be applied to every chapter in the Bible, but which will yield excellent results when applied to some of the more important chapters of the Bible, is as follows:

(1) Read the chapter for to-day's study five times, reading it aloud at least once. Each new reading will bring out some new point.

(2) Divide the chapter into its natural divisions and find headings for each division that describes in the most striking way the contents of that division. For example, suppose the chapter studied is 1 John 5. You might divide it in this way: First division, verses 1-3, The Believer's Noble Parentage. Second division, verses 4, 5, The Believer's Glorious Victory. Third division, verses 6-10, The Believer's Sure Ground of Faith. Fourth division, verses 11, 12, The Believer's Priceless Possession. Fifth division, verse 13, The Believer's Blessed Assurance. Sixth division, verses 14, 15, The Believer's Unquestioning Confidence. Seventh division, verses 16, 17, The Believer's Great Power and Responsibility. Eighth division, verses 18, 19, The Believer's Perfect Security. Ninth division, verse 20, The Believer's Precious Knowledge. Tenth division, verse 21, The Believer's Constant Duty.

(3) Note the important differences between the Authorized Version and the Revised.

(4) Write down the leading facts of the chapter in their proper order.

(5) Make a note of the persons mentioned in the chapter and of any light thrown upon their character.

(6) Note the principal lessons of the chapter. It would be well to classify these. For instance lessons about God; lessons about Christ, lessons about the Holy Spirit, etc.

(7) Find the central truth of the chapter.

(8) The key verse of the chapter, if there is one.

(9) The best verse in the chapter. Mark it and memorize it.

(10) Write down what new truth you have learned from the chapter.

(11) Write down what truth already known has come to you with new power.

(12) What definite thing have you resolved to do as a result of studying this chapter. It would be well to study in this way, all the chapters in Matthew, Mark, Luke, John and Acts; the first eight chapters of Romans; 1 Cor. 12, 13 and 15; first six chapters of 2 Corinthians; all the chapters in Galatians, Ephesians, Philippians, First Thessalonians and First Epistle of John. It would be well at times to vary this by taking up other methods of study for a time.

Another profitable method of Bible study is the topical method. This was Mr. Moody's favorite method of study. Take up the great topics of which the Bible teaches such as, the Holy Spirit, Prayer, the Blood of Christ, Sin, Judgment, Grace, Justification, the New Birth, Sanctification, Faith, Repentance, the Character of Christ, the Resurrection of Christ, the Ascension of Christ, the Second Coming of Christ, Assurance, Love of God, Love (to God, to Christ, to Christians, to all men), Heaven, Hell. Get a Bible text-book and go through the Bible on each one of these topics. (Other methods of Bible study, and more thorough methods for the advanced student, will be found in the author's book "How to Study the Bible for Greatest Profit.")

3. We should *study the Bible comprehensively*—the whole Bible. Many who read their Bibles make the great mistake of confining all their reading to certain portions of the Bible that they enjoy, and in this way they get no knowledge of the Bible as a whole. They miss altogether many of the most important phases of Bible truth. Begin and go through the Bible again and again—a certain portion each day from the Old Testament and a portion from the New Testament. Read carefully at least one Psalm every day.

It is well oftentimes to read a whole book of the Bible through at a single sitting. Of course, with a few books of the Bible this would take one or two hours, but with most of the books of the Bible it can be done in a few minutes. With the shorter books of the Bible they should be read through again and again at a single sitting.

4. *Study the Bible attentively.* Do not hurry. One of the worst faults in Bible study is haste and heedlessness. The Bible only does good by the truth that it contains. It has no magic power. It is better to read one verse attentively than to read a dozen chapters thoughtlessly. Sometimes you will read a verse that takes hold of you. Don't hurry on. Linger and ponder that verse. As you read, mark in your Bible what impresses you most. One does not need an elaborate system of Bible marking, simply mark what impresses you. Meditate upon what you mark. God pronounces that man blessed who "meditates" in God's law day and night (Ps. 1: 2). It is wonderful how a verse of Scripture will open if one reads it over and over again and again, paying attention to each word as he reads it, trying to get its exact meaning and its full meaning. Memorize the passages that impress you most (Ps. 119: 11). When you memorize a passage of Scripture, memorize its location as well as its words. Fix in your mind chapter and verse where the words are found. A busy but spiritually-minded man who was hurrying to catch a train once said to me, "Tell me in a word how to study my Bible." I replied, "Thoughtfully."

5. *Study your Bible comparatively.* That is compare Scripture with Scripture. The best commentary on the Bible is the Bible itself. Wherever you find a difficult passage in the Bible, there is always some passage elsewhere that explains its meaning. The best book to use in this comparison of Scripture with Scripture is "The Treasury of Scripture Knowledge." On every verse in the Bible this book gives a large number of references. It is well to take up some book of the Bible and go through that book verse by verse, looking up carefully and studying every reference given in "The Treasury of Scripture Knowledge." This is a very fruitful method of Bible study. It is also well in studying the

Bible by chapters to look up the references on the more important verses in the chapter. One will get more light on passages of Scripture by looking up the references given in "The Treasury of Scripture Knowledge," than in any other way I know.

6. *Study your Bible believingly.* The Apostle Paul in writing to the Christians in Thessalonica says, "For this cause also thank we God without ceasing, because, when ye received the Word of God which ye heard of us, ye received it not as the Word of men, but as it is in truth, the Word of God, which effectually worketh also in you that believe" (1 Thess. 2: 13). Happy is the one who receives the Word of God as these believers in Thessalonica received it, who receives it as what it really is, the Word of God. In such a one it "works effectually." The Bible is the Word of God and we get the most out of any book by studying it as what it really is. It is often said that we should study the Bible just as we study any other book. That principle contains a truth, but it also contains a great error. The Bible, it is true, is a book as other books are books, the same laws of grammatical and literary construction hold here as in other books, but the Bible is a unique book. It is what no other book is, the Word of God. This can be easily proven to any candid man.[1] The Bible ought then to be studied as no other book is. It should be studied as the Word of God. This involves five things:

(1) A greater eagerness and more careful and candid study to find out just what it teaches than is bestowed upon all other books. It is important to know the mind of man. It is absolutely essential to know the mind of God. The place to discover the mind of God is the Bible. This is the book in which God reveals His mind.

(2) A prompt and unquestioning acceptance of, and submission to its teachings when definitely ascertained. These teachings may appear to us unreasonable or impossible, nevertheless we should accept them. If this book is the Word of God, how foolish it is to submit its teachings to the criticism of our finite reasoning. A little boy who discredits his wise father's statements simply because to his infant mind they appear unreasonable, is not a philosopher, but a fool. But the greatest of human thinkers is only an infant compared with the infinite God. And to discredit God's statements found in His Word because they appear unreasonable to our infantile minds is not to act the part of the philosopher, but the part of a fool. When we are once satisfied that the Bible is the Word of God, its clear teachings must be for us the end of all controversy and discussion.

(3) Absolute reliance upon all its promises in all their length and breadth and depth and height. The one who studies the Bible as the Word of God will say of any promise, no matter how vast and beyond belief it appears, "God who cannot lie has promised this, so I will claim it for myself." Mark the promise you thus claim. Look each day for some new promise from your infinite Father. He has put "His riches in glory" at your disposal (Phil. 4: 19). I know of no better way to grow rich spiritually than to search daily for promises, and when you find them appropriate them to yourself.

(4) Obedience. Be a doer of the Word and not a hearer only deceiving your own soul (James 1: 22). Nothing goes farther to help one understand the Bible than the purpose to obey it. Jesus said, "If any man willeth to do His will, he shall know of the teaching" (John 7: 17). The surrendered will means the clear eye. If our eye is single (that is, our will is absolutely surrendered to God) our whole body shall be full of light. But if our eye be evil (that is, if we are trying to serve two masters and are not absolutely surrendered to one Master, God) our whole body shall be full of darkness (Matt. 6: 22-24). Many a passage

[1] The author has given some of the proofs that the Bible is the Word of God in his book, "Talks to Men."

that looks obscure to you now would become as clear as day if you were willing to obey in all things what the Bible teaches. Each commandment discovered in the Bible that is really intended as a commandment to us should be obeyed instantly. It is remarkable how soon one loses his relish for the Bible and how soon the mind becomes obscured to its teachings when we disobey the Bible at any point. Many a time I have known persons who have loved their Bibles and have been useful in God's service and clear in their views of the truth who have come to something in the Bible that they were unwilling to obey, some sacrifice was demanded that they were unwilling to make, and their love for the Bible has rapidly waned, their faith in the Bible began to weaken, and soon they were drifting farther and farther away from clear views of the truth. Nothing clears the mind like obedience; nothing darkens the mind like disobedience. To obey a truth you see prepares you to see other truths. To disobey a truth you see darkens your mind to all truths.

Cultivate prompt, exact, unquestioning, joyous obedience to every command that it is evident from its context applies to you. Be on the lookout for new orders from your King. Blessing lies in the direction of obedience to them. God's commands are but sign-boards that mark the road to present success and blessedness and to eternal glory.

(5) Studying the Bible as the Word of God involves studying it as His own voice speaking directly to you. When you open the Bible to study realize that you have come into the very presence of God and that now He is going to speak to you. Realize that it is God who is talking to you as much as if you saw Him standing there. Say to yourself, "God is now going to speak to me." Nothing goes farther to give a freshness and gladness to Bible study than the realization that as you read God is actually talking to you. In this way Bible study becomes personal companionship with God Himself. That was a wonderful privilege that Mary had one day, of sitting at the feet of Jesus and listening to His voice, but if we will study the Bible as the Word of God and as if we were in God's very presence, then we shall enjoy the privilege of sitting at the feet of God and having Him talk to us every day. How often what would otherwise be a mere mechanical performance of a duty would become a wonderfully joyous privilege if one would say as he opens the Bible, "Now God, my Father, is going to speak to me." Oftentimes it helps us to a realization of the presence of God to read the Bible on our knees. The Bible became in some measure a new book to me when I took to reading it on my knees.

7. *Study the Bible prayerfully.* God, who is the author of the Bible, is willing to act as interpreter of it. He does so when you ask Him to. The one who prays with earnestness and faith the Psalmist's prayer, "Open Thou mine eyes that I may behold wondrous things out of Thy law" (Ps. 119: 18) will get his eyes opened to see new beauties and wonders in the Word of God that he never dreamed of before. Be very definite about this. Each time you open the Bible to study it, even though it is but for a few minutes, ask God to give you an open and discerning eye, and expect Him to do it. Every time you come to a difficulty in the Bible, lay it before God and ask an explanation and expect it. How often we think as we puzzle over hard passages, "Oh, if I only had some great Bible teacher here to explain this to me!" God is always present. He understands the Bible better than any human teacher. Take your difficulty to Him and ask Him to explain it. Jesus said, "When He the Spirit of Truth is come, He shall guide you into all the truth" (John 16: 13). It is the privilege of the humblest believer in Christ to have the Holy Spirit for his guide in his study of the Word. I have known many very humble people, people with almost no education, who got more out of their Bible study than most of the great theological teachers that I have known; simply because they had learned that it was their privilege to have the Holy Spirit for their teacher as they studied the Bible. Commentaries on the Bible

are oftentimes of great value, but one will learn more of real value from the Bible by having the Holy Spirit for his teacher when he studies his Bible than he will from all the commentaries that were ever published.

8. *Improve spare moments for Bible study.* In almost every man's life many minutes each day are lost, while waiting for meals, riding on trains, going from place to place in street-cars and so forth. Carry a pocket Bible or Testament with you and save these golden moments by putting them to the very best use, listening to the voice of God.

9. *Store away the Scripture in your mind and heart.* It will keep you from sin (Ps. 119: 11); from false doctrine (Acts 20: 29, 30, 32; 2 Tim. 3: 13-15). It will fill your heart with joy (Jer. 15: 16); and peace (Ps. 85: 8). It will give you victory over the evil one (1 John 2: 14); it will give you power in prayer (John 15: 7); it will make you wiser than the aged and your enemies (Ps. 119: 98, 100, 130); it will make you "complete, furnished completely unto every good work" (2 Tim. 3: 16, 17). Try it. Do not memorize at random but memorize Scripture in a connected way; memorize texts bearing on various subjects in proper order; memorize by chapter and verse that you may know where to put your finger on the text if any one disputes it. You should have a good Bible for your study. One of the best is "The Oxford Two Version Bible, Workers' Edition."

Chapter VIII. Difficulties in the Bible

Sooner or later every young Christian comes across passages in the Bible which are hard to understand and difficult to believe. To many a young Christian, these difficulties become a serious hindrance in the development of their Christian life. For days and weeks and months oftentimes faith suffers partial or total eclipse. At just this point wise counsel is needed. We have no desire to conceal the fact that these difficulties exist. We rather desire to frankly face and consider them. What shall we do concerning these difficulties that every thoughtful student of the Bible will sooner or later encounter.

1. *The first thing we have to say about these difficulties is that from the very nature of the case difficulties are to be expected.* Some people are surprised and staggered because there are difficulties in the Bible. I would be more surprised and more staggered if there were not. What is the Bible? It is a revelation of the mind and will and character and being of the infinitely great, perfectly wise, and absolutely holy God. But to whom is this revelation made? To men and women like you and me, to finite beings. To men who are imperfect in intellectual development and consequently in knowledge, and in character and consequently in spiritual discernment.

There must, from the very necessities of the case, be difficulties in such a revelation made to such persons. When the finite tries to understand the infinite there is bound to be difficulty. When the ignorant contemplate the utterances of one perfect in knowledge there must be many things hard to be understood and some things which to their immature and inaccurate minds appear absurd. When sinful beings listen to the demands of an absolutely holy being they are bound to be staggered at some of His demands, and when they consider His dealings they are bound to be staggered at some of His dealings. These dealings will necessarily appear too severe, stern, harsh, terrific. It is plain that there must be difficulties for us in such a revelation as the Bible is proven to be. If some one should hand me a book that was as simple as the multiplication table and say, "This is the Word of God, in which He has revealed His whole will and wisdom," I would shake my head and say, "I cannot believe it. That is too easy to be a perfect revelation of infinite wisdom."

There must be in any complete revelation of God's mind and will and character and being, things hard for a beginner to understand, and the wisest and best of us are but beginners.

2. *The second thing to be said about these difficulties is that a difficulty in a doctrine, or a grave objection to a doctrine, does not in any wise prove the doctrine to be untrue.* Many thoughtless people fancy that it does. If they come across some difficulty in the way of believing in the divine origin and absolute inerrancy and infallibility of the Bible, they at once conclude that the doctrine is exploded. That is very illogical. Stop a moment and think and learn to be reasonable and fair. There is scarcely a doctrine in science commonly believed to-day that has not had some great difficulty in the way of its acceptance. When the Copernican theory, now so universally accepted, was first proclaimed, it encountered a very grave difficulty. If this theory were true the planet Venus should have phases as the moon has. But no phases could be discovered by the best glass then in existence. But the positive argument for the theory was so strong that it was accepted in spite of this apparently unanswerable objection. When a more powerful glass was made, it was discovered that Venus had phases after all. The whole difficulty arose, as all those in the Bible arise, from man's ignorance of some of the facts in the case. According to the common sense logic recognized in every department of science, if the positive proof of a theory is conclusive, it is believed by rational men, in spite of any number of difficulties in minor details. Now the positive proof that the Bible is the Word of God, that it is an absolutely trustworthy revelation from God Himself of Himself, His purposes and His will, of man's duty and destiny, of spiritual and eternal realities, is absolutely conclusive. Therefore every rational man and woman must believe it in spite of any number of difficulties in minor details. He is a shallow thinker who gives up a well-attested truth because of some facts which he cannot reconcile with that truth. And he is a very shallow Bible scholar who gives up the divine origin and inerrancy of the Bible because there are some supposed facts that he cannot reconcile with that doctrine.

3. *The third thing to be said about the difficulties in the Bible is that there are many more and much greater difficulties in the way of a doctrine that holds the Bible to be of human origin, and hence fallible, than are in the way of the doctrine that holds the Bible to be of divine origin and hence altogether trustworthy.* A man may bring you some difficulty and say, "How do you explain that if the Bible is the Word of God?" and perhaps you may not be able to answer him satisfactorily. Then he thinks he has you, but not at all. Turn on him and ask him how do you account for the fulfilled prophecies of the Bible if it is of human origin? How do you account for the marvelous unity of the Book? How do you account for its inexhaustible depth? How do you account for its unique power in lifting men up to God? How do you account for the history of the Book, its victory over all men's attacks, etc., etc., etc. For every insignificant objection he can bring to your view, you can bring many deeply significant objections to his view, and no candid man will have any difficulty in deciding between the two views. The difficulties that confront one who denies that the Bible is of divine origin and authority are far more numerous and weighty than those that confront the ones who believes it is of divine origin and authority.

4. *The fourth thing to be said about the difficulties in the Bible is the fact that you cannot solve a difficulty does not prove that it cannot be solved, and the fact that you cannot answer an objection does not prove at all that it cannot be answered.* It is passing strange how often we overlook this very evident fact. There are many who, when they meet a difficulty in the Bible and give it a little thought and can see no possible solution, at once jump at the conclusion that a solution is impossible by any one, and so throw up their faith in the reliability of the Bible and in its divine origin. A little more of that

modesty that is becoming in beings so limited in knowledge as we all are would have led them to say, "Though I see no possible solution to this difficulty, some one a little wiser than I might easily find one." Oh! if we would only bear in mind that we do not know everything, and that there are a great many things that we cannot solve now that we could easily solve if we only knew a little more. Above all, we ought never to forget that there may be a very easy solution to infinite wisdom of that which to our finite wisdom—or ignorance—appears absolutely insoluble. What would we think of a beginner in algebra who, having tried in vain for half an hour to solve a difficult problem, declared that there was no possible solution to the problem because he could find none? A man of much experience and ability once left his work and came a long distance to see me in great perturbation of spirit because he had discovered what seemed to him a flat contradiction in the Bible. It had defied all his attempts at reconciliation, but in a few moments he was shown a very simple and satisfactory solution of the difficulty.

5. *The fifth thing to be said about the difficulties in the Bible is that the seeming defects in the book are exceedingly insignificant when put in comparison with its many and marvelous excellencies.* It certainly reveals great perversity of both mind and heart that men spend so much time expatiating on the insignificant points that they consider defects in the Bible, and pass by absolutely unnoticed the incomparable beauties and wonders that adorn and glorify almost every page. What would we think of any man, who in studying some great masterpiece of art, concentrated his entire attention upon what looked to him like a fly-speck in the corner. A large proportion of what is vaunted as "critical study of the Bible" is a laborious and scholarly investigation of supposed fly-specks and an entire neglect of the countless glories of the book.

6. *The sixth thing to be said about the difficulties in the Bible is that the difficulties in the Bible have far more weight with superficial readers of it than with profound students.* Take a man who is totally ignorant of the real contents and meaning of the Bible and devotes his whole strength to discovering apparent inconsistencies in it, to such superficial students of the Bible these difficulties seem of immense importance; but to the one who has learned to meditate on the Word of God day and night they have scarce any weight at all. That mighty man of God, George Müller, who had carefully studied the Bible from beginning to end more than a hundred times, was not disturbed by any difficulties he encountered. But to the one who is reading it through carefully for the first or second time there are many things that perplex and stagger.

7. *The seventh thing to be said about the difficulties in the Bible is that they rapidly disappear upon careful and prayerful study.* How many things there are in the Bible that once puzzled us and staggered us that have been perfectly cleared up, and no longer present any difficulty at all! Is it not reasonable to suppose that the difficulties that still remain will also disappear upon further study?

How shall we deal with the difficulties which we do find in the Bible?

1. First of all, *honestly.* Whenever you find a difficulty in the Bible, frankly acknowledge it. If you cannot give a good honest explanation, do not attempt as yet to give any at all.

2. *Humbly.* Recognize the limitations of your own mind and knowledge, and do not imagine there is no solution just because you have found none. There is in all probability a very simple solution. You will find it some day, though at present you can find no solution at all.

3. *Determinedly.* Make up your mind that you will find the solution if you can by any amount of study and hard thinking. The difficulties in the Bible are your heavenly Father's challenge to you to set your brains to work.

4. *Fearlessly.* Do not be frightened when you find a difficulty, no matter how unanswerable it appears upon first glance. Thousands have found such before you. They were seen hundreds of years ago and still the Old Book stands. You are not likely to discover any difficulty that was not discovered and probably settled long before you were born, though you do not know just where to lay your hand upon the solution. The Bible which has stood eighteen centuries of rigid examination and incessant and awful assault, is not going under before any discoveries that you make or any attacks of modern infidels. All modern infidel attacks upon the Bible are simply a revamping of old objections that have been disposed of a hundred times in the past. These old objections will prove no more effective in their new clothes than they did in the cast-off garments of the past.

5. *Patiently.* Do not be discouraged because you do not solve every problem in a day. If some difficulty defies your best effort, lay it aside for awhile. Very likely when you come back to it, it will have disappeared and you will wonder how you were ever perplexed by it. The writer often has to smile to-day when he thinks how sorely he was perplexed in the past over questions which are now as clear as day.

6. *Scripturally.* If you find a difficulty in one part of the Bible, look for other Scripture to throw light upon it and dissolve it. Nothing explains Scripture like Scripture. Never let apparently obscure passages of Scripture darken the light that comes from clear passages, rather let the light that comes from the clear passage illuminate the darkness that seems to surround the obscure passage.

7. *Prayerfully.* It is wonderful how difficulties dissolve when one looks at them on his knees. One great reason why some modern scholars have learned to be destructive critics is because they have forgotten how to pray.

Chapter IX. Prayer

The one who would succeed in the Christian life must lead a life of prayer. Very much of the failure in Christian living to-day, and in Christian work, results from neglect of prayer. Very few Christians spend as much time in prayer as they ought. The Apostle James told believers in his day that the secret of the poverty and powerlessness of their lives and service was neglect of prayer. "Ye have not," says God through the Apostle James, "because ye ask not." So it is to-day. Why is it, many a Christian is asking, that I make such poor headway in my Christian life? Why do I have so little victory over sin? Why do I accomplish so little by my effort? and God answers, "You have not because you ask not."

It is easy enough to lead a life of prayer if one only sets about it. Set apart some time each day for prayer. The rule of David and of Daniel is a good one; three times a day. "Evening and morning and at noon," says David, "will I pray and cry aloud and He shall hear my voice" (Ps. 55: 17). Of Daniel we read, "Now when Daniel knew that the writing was signed, he went into his house; and his windows being open in his chamber towards Jerusalem, he kneeled upon his knees three times a day, and prayed, and gave thanks before his God as he did aforetime" (Dan. 6: 10). Of course, one can pray while walking the street, or riding in the car, or sitting at his desk, and one should learn to lift his heart to God right in the busiest moments of his life, but we need set times of prayer, times when we go alone with God, shut to the door and talk to our Father in the secret place (Matt. 6: 6). God is in the secret place and will meet with us there and listen to our petitions.

Prayer is a wonderful privilege. It is an audience with the King. It is talking to our Father. How strange it is that people should ask the question, "How much time ought I to spend in prayer?" When a subject is summoned to an audience with his king, he never asks, "How much time must I spend with the king?" His question is rather, "How much time will the king give me?" And with any true child of God who realizes what prayer really is, that it is an audience with the King of Kings, the question will never be, "How much time must I spend in prayer," but "How much time may I spend in prayer with a due regard to other duties and privileges?"

Begin the day with thanksgiving and prayer. Thanksgiving for the definite mercies of the past, prayer for the definite needs of the present day. Think of the temptations that you are likely to meet during the day; ask God to show you the temptations that you are likely to meet and get from God strength for victory over these temptations before the temptations come. The reason why many fail in the battle is because they wait until the hour of battle. The reason why others succeed is because they have gained their victory on their knees long before the battle came. Jesus conquered in the awful battles of Pilate's judgment hall and of the cross because He had the night before in prayer anticipated the battle and gained the victory before the struggle really came. He had told His disciples to do the same. He had bidden them "Pray that ye enter not into temptation" (Luke 22: 40), but they had slept when they ought to have prayed, and when the hour of temptation came they fell. Anticipate your battles, fight them on your knees before temptation comes and you will always have victory. At the very outset of the day, get counsel and strength from God Himself for the duties of the day.

Never let the rush of business crowd out prayer. The more work that any day has to do, the more time must be spent in prayer in preparation for that work. You will not lose time by it, you will save time by it. Prayer is the greatest time saver known to man. The more the work crowds you the more time take for prayer.

Stop in the midst of the bustle and hurry and temptation of the day for thanksgiving and prayer. A few minutes spent alone with God at midday will go far to keep you calm in the midst of the worries and anxieties of modern life.

Close the day with thanksgiving and prayer. Review all the blessings of the day and thank God in detail for them. Nothing goes farther to increase faith in God and in His Word than a calm review at the close of each day of what God has done for you that day. Nothing goes further towards bringing new and larger blessings from God than intelligent thanksgiving for blessings already granted.

The last thing you do each day ask God to show you if there has been anything in the day that has been displeasing in His sight. Then wait quietly before God and give God an opportunity to speak to you. Listen. Do not be in a hurry. If God shows you anything in the day that has been displeasing in His sight, confess it fully and frankly as to a holy and loving Father. Believe that God forgives it all, for He says He does (1 John 1: 9). Thus at the close of each day all your accounts with God will be straightened out. You can lie down and sleep in the glad consciousness that there is not a cloud between you and God. You can arise the next day to begin life anew with a clean balance sheet. Do this and you can never backslide for more than twenty-four hours. Indeed, you will not backslide at all. It is very hard to straighten out accounts in business that have been allowed to get crooked through a prolonged period. No bank ever closes its business day until its balance is found to be absolutely correct. And no Christian should close a single day until his accounts with God for that day have been perfectly adjusted alone with Him.

There should be special prayer in special temptation—that is when we see the temptation approaching. If you possibly can, get at once alone somewhere with God and fight your battle out. Keep looking to God. "Pray without ceasing" (1 Thess. 5: 17). It is not needful to be on your knees all the time but the heart should be on its knees all the time. We should be often on our knees or on our faces literally. This is a joyous life, free from worry and care. "In nothing be anxious; but in everything by prayer and supplication with thanksgiving, let your request be made known unto God, and the peace of God which passeth all understanding shall guard your hearts and thoughts in Christ Jesus" (Phil. 4: 6, 7).

There are three things for which one who would succeed in the Christian life must especially pray. 1. For wisdom. "If any of you lack wisdom (and we all do) let him ask of God" (James 1: 5). 2. For strength. "For they that wait upon the Lord shall renew their strength" (Is. 40: 31). 3. For the Holy Spirit. "Your heavenly Father shall give the Holy Spirit to them that ask Him" (Luke 11: 13). Even if you have received the Holy Spirit, you should constantly pray for a new filling with the Holy Spirit and definitely expect to receive it. We need a new filling with the Spirit for every new emergency of Christian life and Christian service. The Apostle Peter was baptized and filled with the Holy Spirit on the Day of Pentecost (Acts 2: 1-4) but he was filled anew in Acts 4: 8 and Acts 4: 31. There are many Christians in the world who once had a very definite baptism with the Holy Spirit and had great joy and were wonderfully used, but who have tried to go ever since in the power of that baptism received years ago, and to-day their lives are comparatively joyless and powerless. We need constantly to get new supplies of oil for our lamps. We get these new supplies of oil by asking for them.

It is not enough that we have our times of secret prayer to God alone with Him, we also need fellowship with others in prayer. If they have a prayer-meeting in your church attend it regularly. Attend it for your own sake; attend it for the sake of the church. If it is a prayer-meeting only in name and not in fact, use your influence quietly and constantly (not obtrusively) to make it a real prayer-meeting. Keep the prayer-meeting night sacredly for that purpose. Refuse all social engagements for that night. A major-general in the United States army once took command of the forces in a new district. A reception was arranged for him for a certain night in the week. When he was informed of this public reception he replied that that was prayer-meeting night and everything else had to give way for prayer-meeting, that he could not attend the reception on that night. That general had proved himself a man that can be depended upon. The Church of Christ in America owes more to him than to almost any other officer in the American army. Ministers learn to depend upon their prayer-meeting members. The prayer-meeting is the most important meeting in the church. If your church has no prayer-meeting, use your influence to have one. It does not take many members to make a good prayer-meeting. You can start with two but work for many.

It is well to have a little company of Christian friends with whom you are in real sympathy and with whom you meet regularly every week simply for prayer. There has been nothing of more importance in the development of my own spiritual life of recent years than a little prayer-meeting of less than a dozen friends who have met every Saturday night for years. We met and together we waited upon God. If my life has been of any use to the Master, I attribute it largely to that prayer-meeting. Happy is the young Christian that has a little band of friends like that that meet together regularly for prayer.[2]

Chapter X. Working for Christ

One of the important conditions of growth and strength in the Christian life is work. No man can keep up his physical strength without exercise and no man can keep up his spiritual strength without spiritual exercise, *i. e.*, without working for his Master. The working Christian is the happy Christian. The working Christian is the strong Christian. Some Christians never backslide because they are too busy about their Master's business to backslide. Many professed Christians do backslide because they are too idle to do anything but backslide. Jesus said to the first disciples, "Follow Me and I will make you fishers of men" (Matt. 4: 19). Any one who is not a fisher of men is not following Christ. Bearing fruit in bringing others to the Savior is the purpose for which Jesus has chosen us and is one of the most important conditions of power in prayer. Jesus says in John 15: 16, "Ye have not chosen Me, but I have chosen you and ordained you *that ye should go and bring forth fruit*, and that your fruit should remain, *that whatsoever ye shall ask of the Father in My name He may give it you*." These words of Jesus are very plain. They tell us that the one who is bearing fruit is the one who can pray in the name of Christ and get what he asks in that name. In the same chapter Jesus tells us that bearing fruit in His strength is the condition of fullness of joy. He says, "These things have I spoken unto you (that is, the things about abiding in Him and bearing fruit in His strength) that My joy might remain in you and that your joy might be full" (John 15: 11). Experience abundantly proves the truth of these words of our Master. Those who are full of activity in winning others to Christ are those who are full of joy in Christ Himself.

If you wish to be a happy Christian; if you wish to be a strong Christian, if you wish to be a Christian who is mighty in prayer, begin at once to work for the Master and never let a day pass without doing some definite work for Him. But how can a young Christian work for Him? How can a young Christian bear fruit? The answer is very simple and very easy to follow. You can bear fruit for your Master by going to others and telling them what your Savior has done for you, and by urging them to accept this same Savior and showing them how to do it. There is no other work in the world that is so easy to do, so joyous, and so abundant in its fruitfulness, as personal hand to hand work. The youngest Christian can do personal work. Of course, he cannot do it so well as he will do it later, after he has had more practice. But the way to learn how to do it is by doing it. I have known thousands of Christians all around the world who have begun to work for Christ, and to bring others to Christ, the very day that they were converted. How often young men and young women, yes, and old men and old women too, have come to me and said, "I accepted Jesus Christ last night as my Savior, my Lord and my King, and to-night I have led a friend to Christ." Then the next day they would come and tell me of some one else they had led to Christ. When we were in Sheffield, a young man working in a warehouse accepted Christ. Before the month's mission in Sheffield was over he had led thirty others to Christ, many of them in the same warehouse where he himself worked. This is but one instance among many. There are many books that tell how to do personal work.[3]

---

2 If any reader desires more full and definite instruction on the subject of prayer he is referred to the author's book, "How to Pray."

3 The author has written a little book on this line named "How to Bring Men to Christ" that has proved

But one does not need to wait until they have read some book on the subject before they begin. One of the commonest and greatest mistakes that is made is that of frittering one's life away in getting ready to get ready to get ready. Some never do get ready. The way to get ready is to begin at once. Make up your mind that you will speak about accepting Christ to at least one person every day. Early in his Christian life Mr. Moody made this resolution that he would never let a day pass over his head without speaking to at least one person about Christ. One night he was returning late from his work. As he got near home it occurred to him that he had not spoken to any one that day. He said to himself, "It is too late now. I will not get an opportunity. Here will be one day gone without my speaking to any one about Christ." But a little ways ahead of him he saw a man standing under a lamp-post. He said, "Here is my last opportunity." The man was a stranger to him, though he knew who Mr. Moody was. Mr. Moody hurried up to him and asked him, "Are you a Christian?" The man replied, "That is none of your business. If you were not a sort of a preacher I would knock you into the gutter." But Mr. Moody spoke a few faithful words to him and passed on. The next day this man called on one of Mr. Moody's business friends in Chicago in great indignation. He said, "That man Moody of yours over on the Northside is doing more harm than he is good. He has zeal without knowledge. He came up to me last night, a perfect stranger, and asked me if I was a Christian. He insulted me. I told him if he had not been a sort of preacher I would have knocked him into the gutter." Mr. Moody's friend called him in and said to him, "Moody, you are doing more harm than good. You have zeal without knowledge. You insulted a friend of mine on the street last night." Mr. Moody went out somewhat crestfallen, feeling that perhaps he was doing more harm than good, that perhaps he did have zeal without knowledge. But some weeks after, late at night, there was a great pounding on his door. Mr. Moody got out of bed and rushed to the door supposing that the house was on fire. That same man stood at the door. He said, "Mr. Moody, I have not had a night's rest since you spoke to me that night under the lamp-post and I have come around for you to tell me what to do to be saved." Mr. Moody had the joy that night of leading that man to Christ. It is better to have zeal without knowledge than to have knowledge without zeal, but it is better yet to have zeal with knowledge, and any one may have this. The way to get knowledge is by experience, and the way to get experience is by doing the work. The man who is so afraid of making blunders that he never does anything, never learns anything. The man who goes ahead and does his best and is willing to risk the blunders, is the man who learns to avoid the blunders in the future. Some of the most gifted men I have ever known have never really accomplished anything, they were so fearful of making blunders. Some of the most useful men I have ever known were men who at the outset were the least promising, but who had a real love for souls and went on, at first in a blundering way, but they blundered on until they learned by experience to do things well. Do not be discouraged by your blunders. Pitch in and keep pegging away. Every honest mistake is but a stepping-stone to future success. Try every day to lead some one else to Christ. Of course, you will not succeed every day, but the work will do you good any way, and years after you will often find that where you thought you have made the greatest blunders, you have accomplished the best results. The man who gets angriest at you, will often turn out in the end the man who is most grateful to you. Be patient and hope on. Never be discouraged.

Make a prayer list. Go alone with God. Write down at the top of a sheet of paper, "God helping me, I promise to pray daily and to work persistently for the conversion of

---

helpful to many.

the following persons." Then kneel down and ask God to show you who to put on that list. Do not make the list so long that your prayer and work become mechanical and superficial. After you have made the list keep your covenant, really pray for them every day. Watch for opportunities to speak to them—improve these opportunities. You may have to watch long for your opportunities with some of them, and you may have to speak often, but never give up. I prayed about fifteen years for one man, one of the most discouraging men I ever met, but I saw that man converted at last, and I saw him a preacher of the gospel, and many others were converted through his preaching, and now he is in the Glory.

Learn to use tracts. Get a few good tracts that are fitted to meet the needs of different kinds of people. Then hand these tracts out to the people whose needs they are adapted to meet. Follow your tracts up with prayer and with personal effort.

Go to your pastor and ask him if there is some work he would like to have you do for him in the church. Be a person that your pastor can depend upon. We live in a day in which there are many kinds of work going on outside the church, and many of these kinds of work are good and you should take part in them as you are able, but never forget that your first duty is to the church of which you are a member. Be a person that your pastor can count on. It may be that your pastor may not want to use you, but at least give him the chance of refusing you. If he does refuse you, don't be discouraged, but find work somewhere else. There is plenty to do and few to do it. It is as true to-day as it was in the days of our Savior, "The harvest truly is plenteous but the laborers are few" (Matt. 9: 37), "Pray therefore the Lord of the harvest that He will send forth laborers into His harvest," and pray that He will send you (Matt. 9: 38). The right kind of men are needed in the ministry. The right kind of men and women are needed for foreign mission work, but you may not be the right kind of a man or woman for foreign missionary work, but none the less there is work for you to do just as important in its place as the work of the minister or the missionary is. See that you fill your place and fill it well.[4]

Chapter XI. Foreign Missions

In order to have the largest success in the Christian life one must be interested in foreign missions. The last command of our Lord before leaving this earth was, "Go ye therefore, and make disciples of all the nations, baptizing them into the name of the Father, and of the Son and of the Holy Ghost: teaching them to observe all things whatsoever I have commanded you: and lo, I am with you alway even unto the end of the world" (Matt. 28: 19, 20). Here is a command and a promise. It is one of the sweetest promises in the Bible. But the enjoyment of the promise is conditioned upon obedience to the command. Our Lord commands every one of His disciples to go and "make disciples" of all the nations. This command was not given to the apostles alone, but to every member of Christ's church in all ages. If we go, then Christ will be with us even unto the end of the age; but, if we do not go, we have no right to count upon His companionship. Are you going? How can we go? There are three ways in which we can go, and in at least two of these ways we must go if we are to enjoy the wonderful privilege of the personal companionship of Jesus Christ every day unto the end of the age.

1. First, *many of us can go in our own persons*. Many of us ought to go. God does not call every one of us to go as foreign missionaries, but He does call many of us to go who

[4] The author's book, "How to Work for Christ," is a large work describing at length many ways of working for our Master.

are not responding to the call. Every Christian should offer himself for the foreign field and leave the responsibility of choosing him or refusing him to the all-wise One, God Himself. No Christian has a right to stay at home until he has gone and offered himself definitely to God for the foreign field. If you have not done it before, do it to-day. Go alone with God and say, "Heavenly Father, here I am, Thy property, purchased by the precious blood of Christ. I belong to Thee. If Thou dost wish me in the foreign field, make it clear to me and I will go." Then keep watching for the leading of God. God's leading is clear leading. He is light and in Him is no darkness at all (1 John 1: 5). If you are really willing to be led, He will make it clear as day. Until He does make it clear as day, you need have no morbid anxiety that perhaps you are staying at home when you ought to go to the foreign field. If He wants you, He will make it clear as day in His own way and time. If He does make it clear, then prepare to go step by step as He leads you. And when His hour comes, go, no matter what it costs. If He does not make it clear that you ought to go in your own person, stay at home and do your duty at home and go in the other ways that will now be told.

2. *We all can go, and all ought to go to the foreign field by our gifts.* There are many who would like to go to the foreign field in their own person, but whom God providentially prevents, but who are still going in the missionaries they support or help to support. It is possible for you to preach the Gospel in the remotest corners of the earth by supporting or helping to support a foreign missionary or a native worker in that place. Many who read this book are able financially to support a foreign missionary out of their own pocket. If you are able to do it, do it. If you are not able to support a foreign missionary, you may be able to support a native helper—do it. You may be able to support one missionary in Japan and another in China, and another in India and another in Africa and another somewhere else—do it. Oh! the joy of preaching the Gospel in lands that we shall never see with our own eyes. How few in the church of Christ to-day realize their privilege of preaching the Gospel and saving men and women and children in distant lands by sending substitute missionaries to them, that is, by sending some one that goes for you where you cannot go yourself. They could not go but for your gifts by which they are supported and you could not go but for them, by their going in your place. You may be able to give but very little to foreign missions, but every little counts. Many insignificant streams together make a mighty river. If you cannot be a river, at least be a stream.

Learn to give largely. The large giver is the happy Christian. "The liberal soul shall be made fat" (Prov. 11: 25). "He which soweth sparingly shall reap also sparingly, and he which soweth bountifully shall reap also bountifully," and "God is able to make all grace abound towards you, that ye, always having all sufficiency in all things may abound to every good work" (2 Cor. 9: 8, 9). Success and growth in the Christian life depend upon few things more than upon liberal giving. The stingy Christian cannot be a growing Christian. It is wonderful how a Christian man begins to grow when he begins to give. Power in prayer depends on liberality in giving. One of the most wonderful statements about prayer and its answers is 1 John 3: 22. John says there that, whatsoever he asked of God he received; and he tells us why, because he on his part, kept God's commandments and did those things which were pleasing in His sight, and the immediate context shows that the special commandments he was keeping were the commandments about giving. He tells us in the twenty-first verse that when our heart condemns us not in the matter of giving then have we confidence in our prayers to God. God's answers to our prayers come in through the same door that our gifts go out to others, and some of us open the door such a little ways by our small giving that God is not able to pass in to us any large answers to our prayers. One of the most remarkable promises in the Bible is that found in Phil. 4: 19, "My God shall supply, (fulfill, that is fill full) all your need according to His riches in glory by Christ Jesus," but this promise was made to believers who had distinguished themselves above their fellows by the largeness and the frequency of their giving (Cf. vs. 14-18). Of course, we should not confine our giving to foreign missions. We should give to the work of the home church: we should give to rescue work in our large cities. We should do good to all men as we have opportunity, especially to those who are of the household of faith (Gal. 6: 10). But foreign missions should have a large part in our gifts.

Give systematically. Set aside for Christ a fixed proportion of all the money or goods you get. Be exact and honest about it. Don't use that part of your income for yourself under any circumstances. The Christian is not under law, and there is no law binding on the Christian that he should give a tenth of his income, but as a matter of free choice and glad gratitude a tenth is a good proportion to begin with. Don't let it be less than a tenth. God required that of the Jews and the Christian ought not to be more selfish than a Jew. After you have given your tenth, you will soon learn the joy of giving free will offerings in addition to the tenth.

3. But there is another way in which we can go to the foreign field, that is by our prayers. We can all go in this way. Any hour of the day or night you can reach any corner of the earth by your prayers. I go to Japan, to China and to Australia and to Tasmania and to New Zealand and to India and to Africa and to other parts of the earth every day, by my prayers. And prayer really brings things to pass where you go. Do not make prayer an excuse for not going in your own person if God wishes you, and do not make prayer an excuse for small giving. There is no power in that kind of prayer. If you are ready to go yourself if God wishes you, and if you are actually going by your gifts as God gives you ability, then you can go effectually by your prayers also. The greatest need of the work of Jesus Christ to-day is prayer. The greatest need of foreign missions to-day is prayer. Foreign missions are a success, but they are no such success as they ought to be and might be. They are no such success as they would be if Christians at home, as well as abroad, were living up to the full measure of their opportunity in prayer.

Be definite in your prayers for foreign missions. Pray first of all that God will send forth laborers into His harvest, the right sort of laborers. There are many men and women in the foreign field that ought never to have gone there. There was not enough prayer about it. More foreign missionaries are greatly needed, but only more of the right kind of missionaries. Pray to God daily and believingly to send forth laborers into the harvest.

Pray for the laborers who are already on the field. No class of men and women need our prayers more than foreign missionaries. No class of men and women are objects of more bitter hatred from Satan than they. Satan delights to attack the reputation and the character of the brave men and women who have gone to the front in the battle for Christ and the Truth. No persons are subjected to so numerous and to such subtle and awful temptations as foreign missionaries. We owe it to them to support them by our prayers. Do not merely pray for foreign missionaries in general. Have a few special missionaries of whose work you make a study that you may pray intelligently for them.

Pray for the native converts. We Christians at home think we have difficulties and trials and temptations and persecutions, but the burdens that we have to bear are nothing to what the converts in heathen lands have to bear. The obstacles oftentimes are enormous and discouragements crushing. Christ alone can make them stand, but He works in answer to the prayers of His people. Pray often, pray earnestly, pray intensely and pray believingly for native converts. How wonderfully God has answered prayer for native converts we are beginning to learn from missionary literature. It is well to be definite here again and to have some definite field about whose needs you keep yourself informed and pray for the converts of that field. Do not have so many that you become confused and mechanical. Pray for conversions in the foreign field. Pray for revivals in definite fields. The last few years have been years of special prayer for special revival in foreign fields and from every corner of the earth tidings have come of how amazingly God is answering these prayers. But the great things that God is beginning to do are small indeed in comparison with what He will do if there is more prayer.

Chapter XII. Companions

Our companions have a great deal to do with determining our character. The companionships that we form create an intellectual, moral and spiritual atmosphere that we are constantly breathing, and our spiritual health is helped or hindered by it. Every young Christian should have a few wisely chosen friends, intimate friends, with whom he can talk freely. Search out for yourself a few persons of about your own age with whom you can associate intimately. Be sure that they are spiritual persons in the best sense. Persons who love to study the Bible, persons who love to converse on spiritual themes, persons who know how to pray and do pray, persons who are really working to bring others to Christ.

Do not be at all uneasy about the fact that some Christian people are more agreeable to you than others. God has made us in that way. Some are attracted to some persons and some to others, and it proves nothing against the others and nothing against yourself that you are not attracted to them as you are to some people. Cultivate the friendship of those whose friendship you find helpful to your own spiritual life.

On the other hand avoid the companionships that you find spiritually and morally hurtful. Of course, we are not to withdraw ourselves utterly from unconverted people, or even of very bad people. We are to cultivate oftentimes the acquaintance of unspiritual people, and even of very bad people, in order that we may win them for Christ; but we must always be on our guard in such companionships to bear always in mind to seek to lift them up or else they will be sure to drag us down. If you find in spite of all your best effort that any companionship is doing harm to your own spiritual life, then give it up. Some people are surrounded with such an atmosphere of unbelief or cynicism or censoriousness or impurity or greed or some other evil thing that it is impossible to associate with them to any large extent without being contaminated. In such a case, the path of wisdom is plain; stop associating with them to any large extent. Stop associating with them at all except in so far as there is some prospect of helping them.

But there are other companionships that mold our lives besides the companionships of living persons. The books that we read are our companions. They exert a tremendous influence for good or for evil. There is nothing that will help us more than a good book, and there is nothing that will hurt us more than a bad book. Among the most helpful books are the biographies of good men. Read again and again the lives of such good and truly great men as Wesley and Finney and Moody. We live in a day in which good biographies abound. Read them. Well written histories are good companions. No study is more practical and instructive than the study of history, and it is not only instructive but spiritually helpful if we only watch to see the hand of God in history, to see the inevitable triumph of right and the inevitable punishment of wrong in individuals and in nations.

Some few books of fiction are helpful, but here one needs to be very much on his guard. A large portion of modern fiction is positively pernicious morally. Books of fiction that are not positively bad, at least give false views of life and unfit one for life as it really is. Much reading of fiction is mentally injurious. The inveterate novel reader ruins his powers of close and clear thinking. Fiction is so fascinating that it always tends to drive out other reading that is more helpful mentally and morally. We should be on our guard in even reading good literature, that the good does not crowd out the best; that is that the best of man's literature does not crowd out the very best of all—God's Book. God's Book, the Bible, must always have the first place.

Then there is another kind of companionship that has a tremendous influence over our lives, that is the companionship of pictures. The pictures that we see every day of our lives, and the pictures that we see only occasionally, have a tremendous power in the shaping of our lives. A mother had two dearly loved sons. It was her dream and ambition that these sons should enter the ministry, but both of them went to sea. She could not understand it until a friend one day called her attention to the picture of a magnificent ship in full sail careening through the ocean that hung above the mantel in the dining-room. Every day of their lives her boys had gazed upon that picture, had been thrilled by it, and an unconquerable love for the sea and longing for it had thus been created and this had determined their lives. How many a picture that is a masterpiece of art, but in which there is an evil suggestion, has sent some young men on the road to ruin. Many of our art collections are so polluted with improper pictures that it is not safe for a young man or a young woman to visit them. The evil thought that they suggest may be but for a moment, and yet Satan will know how to bring that picture back again and again and work injury by it. Don't look for a moment at any picture, no matter how praised by art critics, that taints your imagination with evil suggestion. Avoid as you would poison every painting, or engraving, every etching, every photograph that leaves a spot of impurity on your mind, but feast your soul upon the pictures that make you holier, kinder, more sympathetic and more tender.

Chapter XIII. Amusements

Young people need recreation. Our Savior does not frown upon wholesome recreation. He was interested in the games of the children when He was here upon earth. He watched the children at their play (Matt. 12: 16-19), and He watches the children at their play to-day, and delights in their play when it is wholesome and elevating. In the stress and strain of modern life older people too need recreation if they are to do their very best work. But there are recreations that are wholesome, and there are amusements that are pernicious. It is impossible to take up amusements one by one, and it is unnecessary. A few principles can be laid down.

1. *Do not indulge in any form of amusement about whose propriety you have any doubts.* Whenever you are in doubt, always give God the benefit of the doubt. There are plenty of recreations about which there can be no question. "He that doubteth is condemned: for whatsoever is not of faith is sin" (Rom. 14: 32). Many a young Christian will say, "I am not sure that this amusement is wrong." Are you sure it is right? If not, leave it alone.

2. *Do not indulge in any amusement that you cannot engage in to the glory of God.* "Whether therefore ye eat or drink, or whatsoever ye do, do all to the glory of God" (1

Cor. 10: 31). Whenever you are in doubt as to whether you should engage in any amusement ask yourself, Can I do this at this time to the glory of God?

3. *Do not engage in any amusement that will hurt your influence with anybody.* There are amusements, which perhaps are all right in themselves, but which we cannot engage in without losing our influence with some one. Now every true Christian wishes his life to tell with everybody to the utmost. There is so much to be done and so few to do it that every Christian desires every last ounce of power for good that he can have with everybody, and, if any amusement will injure your influence for good with any one, the price is too great. Do not engage in it. A Christian young lady had a great desire to lead others to Christ. She made up her mind that she would speak to a young friend of hers about coming to Christ, and while resting between the figures of a dance she said to the young man who was her companion in the dance, "George, are you a Christian?" "No," he said, "I am not, are you?" "Yes," she replied, "I am." "Then," he said, "what are you doing here?" Whether justly or unjustly the world discounts the professions of those Christians who indulge in certain forms of the world's own amusements. We cannot afford to have our professions thus discounted.

4. *Do not engage in any amusement that you cannot make a matter of prayer*, that you cannot ask God's blessing upon. Pray before your play just as much as you would pray before your work.

5. *Do not go to any place of amusement where you cannot take Christ with you, and where you do not think Christ would feel at home.* Christ went to places of mirth when He was here upon earth. He went to the marriage feast in Cana (John 2), and contributed to the joy of the occasion, but there are many modern places of amusement where Christ would not be at home. Would the atmosphere of the modern stage be congenial to that holy One whom we call "Lord"? If it would not, don't you go.

6. *Don't engage in any amusement that you would not like to be found enjoying if the Lord should come.* He may come at any moment. Blessed is that one whom when He cometh, He shall find watching and ready, and glad to open to Him immediately (Luke 12: 36, 40). I have a friend who was one day walking down the street thinking upon the return of his Lord. As he thought he was smoking a cigar. The thought came to him, "Would you like to meet Christ now with that cigar in your mouth?" He answered honestly, "No, I would not." He threw that cigar away and never lighted another.

7. *Do not engage in any amusement, no matter how harmless it would be for yourself, that might harm some one else.* Take for example card playing. It is probable that thousands have played cards moderately all their lives and never suffered any direct moral injury from it, but every one who has studied the matter knows that cards are the gamblers' chosen tools. He also knows that most, if not all, gamblers took their first lessons in card playing at the quiet family card table. He knows that if a young man goes out into the world knowing how to play cards and indulging at all in this amusement that before long he is going to be put into a place where he is going to be asked to play cards for money, and if he does not consent he will get into serious trouble. Card playing is a dangerous amusement for the average young man. It is pretty sure to lead to gambling on a larger or a smaller scale, and one of the most crying social evils of our time is the evil of gambling. Some young man may be encouraged to play cards by your playing who will afterwards become a gambler and part of the responsibility will lie at your door. If I could repeat all the stories that have come to me from broken-hearted men whose lives have been shipwrecked at the gaming table; if I could tell of all the broken-hearted mothers who have come to me, some of them in high position, whose sons have committed suicide at Monte

Carlo and other places, ruined by the cards, I think that all thoughtful and true Christians would give them up forever.

For most of us the recreations that are most helpful are those that demand a considerable outlay of physical energy. Recreations that take us into the open air, recreations that leave us refreshed in body and invigorated in mind. Physical exercises of the strenuous kind, but not over-exercise, is one of the great safeguards of the moral conduct of boys and young men. There is very little recreation in watching others play the most vigorous game of football but there is real health for the body and for the soul in a due amount of physical exercise for yourself.

Chapter XIV. Persecution

One of the discouragements that meets every true Christian before he has gone very far in the Christian life is persecution. God tells us in His Word that "All that will live godly in Christ Jesus shall suffer persecution" (2 Tim. 3: 12). Sooner or later every one who surrenders absolutely to God and seeks to follow Jesus Christ in everything will find that this verse is true. We live in a God-hating world and in a compromising age. The world's hatred of God in our day is veiled. It does not express itself in our land in the same way that it expressed itself in Palestine in the days of Jesus Christ, but the world hates God to-day as much as it ever did, and it hates the one who is loyal to Christ. It may not imprison him or kill him but in some way it will persecute him. Persecution is inevitable for a loyal follower of Jesus Christ. Many a young Christian when he meets with persecution is surprised and discouraged and not a few fall away. Many a one seems to run well for a few days but like those of whom Jesus spoke, "They have no root in themselves, but endure for a while; then when tribulation or persecution ariseth because of the Word straightway they stumble" (Mark 4: 17). I have seen many an apparently promising Christian life brought to an end in this way. But if persecution is rightly received, it is no longer a hindrance to the Christian life but a help to it.

Do not be discouraged when you are persecuted. No matter how fierce and hard the persecution may be, be thankful for it. Jesus says, "Blessed are they which are persecuted for righteousness' sake: for theirs is the kingdom of heaven. Blessed are ye, when men shall revile you, and persecute you, and shall say all manner of evil against you falsely, for My sake. Rejoice, and be exceeding glad: for great is your reward in heaven: for so persecuted they the prophets which were before you" (Matt. 5: 10-12). It is a great privilege to be persecuted for Christ and for the truth. Peter found this out and wrote to the Christians of his day: "Beloved, think it not strange concerning the fiery trial which is to try you, as though some strange thing happened unto you. But rejoice, inasmuch, as ye are partakers of Christ's suffering; that, when His glory shall be revealed, ye may be glad also with exceeding joy. If ye be reproached for the name of Christ, happy are ye; for the spirit of glory and of God resteth upon you: on their part He is evil spoken of, but on your part He is glorified" (1 Peter 4: 12-14). Be very sure that the persecution is really for Christ's sake and not because of some eccentricity of your own, or because of your stubbornness. There are many who bring upon themselves the displeasure of others because they are stubborn and cranky and then flatter themselves that they are being persecuted for Christ's sake and for righteousness' sake. Be considerate of the opinions of others and be considerate of the conduct of others. Be sure that you do not push your opinions upon others in an unwarrantable way, or make your conscience a rule of life for other people. But never yield a jot of principle. Stand for what you believe to be the truth. Do it in love, but do it at any cost. And if when you are standing for conviction and principle you are disliked for it and slandered for it and treated with all manner of unkindness because of it, do not be sad but rejoice. Do not speak evil of those who speak evil of you, "because Christ also suffered for us, leaving us an example, that ye should follow His steps: who, when He was reviled, reviled not again, when He suffered, He threatened not; but committed Himself to Him that judgeth righteously" (1 Peter 2: 21, 23).

At this point many a Christian makes a mistake. He stands loyally for the truth, but he receives the persecution that comes for the truth with harshness, he grows bitter, he gets to condemning every one but himself. There is no blessing in bearing persecution in that way. Persecution should be borne meekly, lovingly, serenely. Don't talk about your own persecutions. Rejoice in them. Thank God for them, and go on obeying God. And don't forget to love and pray for them who persecute you (Matt. 5: 44).

If at any time the persecution seems harder than you can bear, remember how abundant the reward is, "If we suffer, we shall also reign with Him. If we deny Him, He also will deny us" (2 Tim. 2: 12). Every one must enter into the kingdom of God through much tribulation (Acts 14: 22), but do not go back on that account. Remember always however fiercely the fire of persecution may burn, "That the sufferings of this present time are not worthy to be compared with the glory which shall be revealed in us" (Rom. 8: 18). Remember too that your light affliction is but for the moment, and that it worketh out for you "a far more exceeding and eternal weight of glory" (2 Cor. 4: 17). Keep looking, not at the things which are seen, but at the things which are not seen, for the things which are seen are but for a time, but the things which are not seen are for eternity (2 Cor. 4: 18). When the apostles were persecuted, even unto imprisonment and stripes, they departed from the presence of the council that had ordered their terrible punishment, rejoicing that they were counted worthy to suffer shame for the name of Jesus, and they continued daily in the temple and every house teaching and preaching Jesus Christ (Acts 5: 40-42).

The time may come when you think that you are being persecuted more than others, but you do not know what others may have to endure. Even if it were true,—that you were being persecuted more than any one else, you ought not to complain but to humbly thank God that He has bestowed upon you such an honor. Keep your eyes fixed upon "Jesus, the Author and Finisher of our faith; who for the joy that was set before Him endured the cross, despising the shame, and is set down at the right hand of the throne of God. For consider Him that endured such contradiction of sinners against Himself, lest ye be wearied and faint in your mind" (Heb. 12: 2, 3). I was once talking with an old colored man who in the slave days had found his Savior. The cruel master had him flogged again and again for his loyalty to Christ but he said to me, "I simply thought of my Savior dying on the cross in my place, and I rejoiced to suffer persecution for Him."

Chapter XV. Guidance

I have met a great many who are trying to lead a Christian life who are much troubled over the question of guidance. They wish to do the will of God in all things, but what puzzles them is to tell what the will of God may be in every case. When any one starts out with the determination to obey God in everything and to be led by the Holy Spirit, Satan seeks to trouble him by perplexing him as to what the will of God is. Satan comes and suggests that something is the will of God that is probably not the will of God at all, and then when he does not do it, Satan says, "There you disobeyed God." In this way, many a conscientious young Christian gets into a very morbid and unhappy state of mind, fearing that he has disobeyed God and has lost His favor. This is one of the most frequent devices of the devil to keep Christians from being cheerful.

How may we know the will of God?

First of all let me say that a true Christian life is not a life governed by a whole lot of rules about what one shall eat, and what one shall drink, and what one shall do, and what one shall not do. A life governed by a lot of rules is a life of bondage. One is sure sooner or later to break some of these man-made rules and to get into condemnation. Paul tells us in Rom. 8: 15, "Ye have not received the spirit of bondage again to fear; but ye have received the spirit of adoption (placing us a son), whereby we cry, Abba, Father." The true Christian life is the life of a trusting, glad, fear-free child; not led by rules, but led by the personal guidance of the Holy Spirit who dwells within us. "As many as are led by the Spirit of God these are sons of God" (Rom. 8: 14). If you have received the Holy Spirit, He dwells within you and is ready to lead you at every turn of life. A life governed by a multitude of rules is a life of bondage and anxiety. A life surrendered to the control of the Holy Spirit is a life of joy and peace and freedom. There is no anxiety in such a life, there is no fear in the presence of God. We trust God and rejoice in His presence just as a true child trusts his earthly father and rejoices in his presence. If we make a mistake at any point, even if we disobey God, we go and tell Him all about it as trustfully as a child and know that He forgives us and that we are restored at once to His full favor (1 John 1: 9).

But how can we tell the Holy Spirit's guidance that we may obey Him and thus have God's favor at every turn of life? This question is answered in James 1: 5-7, "But if any of you lacketh wisdom, let him ask of God, who giveth to all liberally and upbraideth not; and it shall be given him, but let him ask in faith, nothing doubting: for he that doubteth is like the surge of the sea driven by the wind and tossed. For let not that man think that he shall receive anything of the Lord." This is very simple. It includes five points.

(1) That you recognize your own ignorance and your own inability to guide your own life—that you lack wisdom.

(2) The surrender of your will to God, and a real desire to be led by Him.

(3) Definite prayer to Him for guidance.

(4) Confident expectation that God will guide you. You "ask in faith, nothing doubting."

(5) That you follow step by step as He guides. God may only show you a step at a time. That is enough. All you need to know is the next step. It is here that many make a mistake. They wish God to show them the whole way before they take the first step. A university student once came to me over the question of guidance. He said, "I cannot find out the will of God. I have been praying but God does not show me His will." This was in the month of July. I said, "About what is it that you are seeking to know the will of God?" "About what I should do next summer." I said, "Do you know what you ought to do to-morrow?" "Yes." "Do you not know what you ought to do next autumn?" "Yes, finish my course. But what I want to know is what I ought to do when my university course is over." He was soon led to see that all he needed to know for the present was what God had already shown him. That when he did that, God would show him the next step. Do not worry about what you ought to do next week. Do what God shows you you ought to do to-day. Next week will take care of itself. Indeed, to-morrow will take care of itself. Obey the Spirit of God for to-day. "Be not therefore anxious for the morrow; for the morrow will be anxious for the things of itself. Sufficient unto the day is the evil thereof" (Matt. 6: 34). It is enough to live a day at a time, if we do our very best for that day.

God's guidance is clear guidance, "God is light and in Him is no darkness at all" (1 John 1: 5). Do not be anxious over obscure leadings. Do not let your soul be ruffled by the thought, "Perhaps this obscure leading is what God wants me to do." Obscure leadings are not divine leadings. God's path is as clear as day. Satan's path is full of obscurity and uncertainty and anxiety and questioning. If there comes some leading of which you are not quite sure whether it is the will of God or not, simply go to your Heavenly Father and say, "Heavenly Father, I desire to know Thy will. I will do Thy will if Thou wilt make it clear. But Thou art light and in Thee is no darkness at all. If this is Thy will make it clear as day and I will do it." Then wait quietly upon God and do not act until God makes it clear, but the moment it is made clear, act at once.

The whole secret of guidance is an absolutely surrendered will, a will that is given up to God and ready to obey Him at any cost. Many of our uncertainties about God's guidance are simply because we are not really willing to do what God is really guiding us to do. We are tempted to say, "I cannot find out what God's will is," when the real trouble is we have found out His will and it is something we do not wish to do and we are trying to make ourselves think that God wants us to do something else.

All supposed leadings of God should be tested by the Word of God. The Bible is God's revealed will. Any leading that contradicts the plain teaching of the Bible is certainly not the leading of the Holy Spirit. The Holy Spirit does not contradict Himself. A man once came to me and said that God was leading him to marry a certain woman. He said that she was a very devoted Christian woman and they had been greatly drawn towards one another and they felt that God was leading them to be married. But I said to the man, "You already have a wife." "Yes," he said, "but we have never lived happily and we have not lived together for years." "But," I replied, "that does not alter the case. God in His Word has told us distinctly the duty of the husband to the wife and how wrong it is in His sight for a husband to divorce his wife and marry another." "Yes," said the man, "but the Holy Spirit is leading us to one another." I indignantly replied that "Whatever spirit is leading you to marry one another, it is certainly not the Holy Spirit but the spirit of the evil one. The Holy Spirit never leads any one to disobey the Word of God."

In seeking to know the guidance of the Spirit always search the Scriptures, study them prayerfully. Do not make a book of magic out of the Bible. Do not ask God to show you His will and then open your Bible at random and put your finger upon some text and take it out of its connection without any relation to its real meaning and decide the will of God in that way. This is an irreverent and improper use of Scripture. You may open your Bible at just the right place to find right guidance, but if you do, it will not be by some fanciful interpretation of the passage you find. It will be by taking the passage in its context and interpreting it to mean just what it says as seen in its context. All sorts of mischief has arisen from using the Bible in this perverse way. I knew an earnest Christian woman once who was somewhat concerned about the predictions made by a false prophetess that Chicago was to be destroyed on a certain day. She opened her Bible at random. It opened to the twelfth chapter of Ezekiel, "Son of man, eat thy bread with quaking, and drink thy water with trembling and with carefulness.… And the cities that are inhabited shall be laid waste, and the land shall be desolate" (Ezek. 12: 18, 20). Now this seemed to exactly fit the case and the woman was considerably impressed, but if the verses had been studied in their connection, it would have been evident at once that God was not speaking about Chicago and that they were not applicable to Chicago. It was not an intelligent study of the Word of God and therefore led to a false conclusion.

To sum up, lead a life not led by rules but by the personal guidance of the Holy Spirit. Surrender your will absolutely to God. Whenever you are in doubt as to His guidance, go to Him and ask Him to show you His will, expect Him to do it, follow step by step as He leads. Test all the leadings by the plain and simple teachings of the Bible. Live free from anxiety and worry lest in some unguarded moment you have not done the right thing.

After you have done what you think God led you to do, do not be always going back and wondering whether you did the right thing. You will get into a morbid state if you do. If you really wished to do God's will and sought His guidance, and did what you thought He guided you to do, you may rest assured you did the right thing, no matter what the outcome has been. Satan is bound that we shall not be happy, cheerful Christians if he can prevent it, but God wishes us to be happy, cheerful, bright Christians every day and every hour. He does not wish us to brood but to rejoice (Phil. 4: 4). A most excellent Christian man came to me one Monday morning in great gloom over the failures of the work of the preceding day. He said to me, "I made wretched work of teaching my Sunday-school class yesterday." I said, "Did you honestly seek wisdom from God before you went to your class?" He said, "I did." I said, "Did you expect to receive it?" He said, "I did." "Then," I said, "in the face of God's promise what right have you to doubt that God did give you wisdom?" (James 1: 5-7). His gloom disappeared and he looked up with a smile and said, "I had no right to doubt." Let us learn to trust God. Let us remember that if our wills are surrendered to Him He is ever more willing to guide us than we are to be guided. Let us trust that He does guide us at every step and even though what we do does not turn out as we expected, let us never brood over it but trust God. Let us walk in the light of simple trust in God. In this way we shall be glad and peaceful and strong and useful at every turn of life.

The Baptism with the Holy Spirit

~ ※ ~

By *R. A. Torrey*

~ ※ ~

"Wait for the promise of the Father."—Acts i: 4.

"Ye shall be baptized with the Holy Spirit not many days hence."—Acts 1:5.

"Ye shall receive power after that the Holy Ghost is come upon you."—Acts 1:6.

"For to you is the promise, and to your children, and to all that are afar off, even as many as the Lord thy God shall call unto him."—Acts 11:36

Introduction.

It was a great turning point in my ministry when, after much thought and study and meditation, I became satisfied that the Baptism with the Holy Spirit was an experience for to-day and for me, and set myself about obtaining it. Such blessing came to me personally, that I began giving Bible readings on the subject, and with increasing frequency as the years have passed. God in his wondrous grace has so greatly blessed these readings, and so many have asked for them in printed form, convenient for circulation among their friends, that I have decided to write them out in full for publication. It is an occasion of great joy that so many and such excellent books on the person and work of the Holy Spirit have appeared of late. I wish to call especial attention to two of these: "Through the Eternal Spirit," by James Elder Cumming and "The Spirit of Christ," by Andrew Murray.

In the following pages I speak uniformly of the Holy Spirit, but in the quotations from the Bible retain the less desirable phraseology there used—"The Holy Ghost"—except in those instances where the translators themselves varied their usage. Probably most of the readers of this book already know that "the Holy Spirit" and "the Holy Ghost" are simply two different translations of precisely the same Greek words. It seems very unfortunate, and almost unaccountable, that the English revisors did not follow the suggestion of the American Committee and for "Holy Ghost" adopt uniformly the rendering "Holy Spirit."

Chapter I. The Baptism with the Holy Spirit: What it is and What it Does.

While a great deal is said in these days concerning the Baptism with the Holy Spirit, it is to be feared that there are many who talk about it and pray for it, who have no clear and definite idea of what it is. But the Bible, if carefully studied, will give us a view of this wondrous blessing that is perfectly clear and remarkably definite.

1. We find first of all *that there are a number of designations in the Bible for this one experience.* In Acts i:5, Jesus said, *"Ye shall be baptized with the Holy Ghost not many days hence."* In Acts ii:4, when this promise was fulfilled, we read *"they were all filled with the Holy Ghost."* In Acts i:4, the same experience is spoken of as *"the promise of the Father,"* and in Luke xxiv:49 as *"the promise of my Father"* and *"endued with power from on high."* By a comparison of Acts x:44, 45, 47 with Acts xi:15, 16, we find that the expressions *"the Holy Spirit fell on them"* and *"the gift of the Holy Ghost"* and *"received the Holy Ghost"* are all equivalent to *"baptized with the Holy Ghost."*

2. We find in the next place that *the Baptism with the Holy Spirit is a definite experience of which one may know whether he has received it or not.* This is evident from our Savior's com- mand to the Apostles: "Tarry ye in the city, until ye be endued with power from on high." (Luke xxiv:49.) If this enduement with power or Baptism with the Holy Ghost were not an experience so definite that one could know whether he had received it or not, how could they tell when those commanded days of tarrying were at an end? The same thing is clear from Paul's very definite question to the disciples at Ephesus. "Did ye receive the Holy Ghost when ye believed?" (Acts xix:2, R. V.) Paul evidently expected a definite "yes" or a definite "no" for an answer. Unless the experience were definite and of such a character that one could know whether he had received it or not, how could these disciples answer Paul's question? In point of fact they knew they had not

"received" or been "baptized with" the Holy Ghost, and a short time afterward they knew they had "received" or been "baptized with" the Holy Ghost. (Acts xix:6.) Ask many a man to-day who prays that he may be baptized with the Holy Ghost: "Well, my brother, did you get what you asked, were you baptized with the Holy Ghost," and he would be dumb-founded. He did not expect anything so definite that he could answer positively to a question like that, "yes" or "no." But we find in the Bible nothing of that vagueness and indefiniteness which we find in much of our modern prayer and speech regarding this subject. The Bible is a very definite book. It is very definite about salvation: so definite that a man who knows his Bible can say positively "yes" or "no" to the question "are you saved." It is equally definite about "the Baptism with the Holy Ghost:" so that a man who knows his Bible can say positively, "yes," or "no," to the question, "have you been baptized with the Holy Ghost." There may be those who are saved who do not know it, because they do not understand their Bibles, but it is their privilege to know it. So there may be those who have been Baptized with the Holy Ghost, who do not know the Bible name for what has come to them, but it is their privilege to know.

3. *The Baptism with the Holy Spirit is a work of the Holy Spirit separate and distinct from His regenerating work.* To be regenerated by the Holy Spirit is one thing, to be baptized with the Holy Spirit is something different, something further. This is evident from Acts i:5. There Jesus said: "Ye shall be baptized with the Holy Ghost *not many days hence.*" They were not then as yet "baptized with the Holy Ghost." But they were *already* regenerated. Jesus Himself had already pronounced them so. In John xv:3, he had said to the same men, "Now are ye clean through the Word." (Comp. Jas. i:18; 1 Pet. i:23) and in John xiii:10: "Ye are clean, but not all," excepting by the "but not all" the one unregenerate man in the Apostolic company, Judas Iscariot, from the statement "Ye are clean." (See John xiii:11.) The Apostles, excepting Judas Iscariot, were then already regenerate men, but they were not yet "baptized with the Holy Ghost." From this it is evident that regeneration is one thing, and that the baptism with the Holy Spirit is something different, something further. One can be regenerated and still not yet be baptized with the Holy Ghost. The same thing is evident from Acts viii:12-16. Here we find a company of believers who had been baptized. Surely in this company of baptized believers there were some regenerate men. But the record informs us that when Peter and John came down they "prayed for them that they might receive the Holy Ghost: (for *as yet he was fallen upon none of them*)." It is clear then that one may be a believer, may be a regenerate man, and yet not have the Baptism with the Holy Spirit. In other words, the Baptism with the Holy Spirit is something distinct from and beyond His regenerating work. Not every regenerate man has the Baptism with the Holy Spirit, though as we shall see later, every regenerate man may have this Baptism. If a man has experienced the regenerating work of the Holy Spirit he is a saved man, but he is not fitted for service until in addition to this he has received the Baptism with the Holy Spirit.

4. *The Baptism with the Holy Spirit is always connected with testimony and service.* Look carefully at every passage in which the Baptism with the Holy Spirit is mentioned and you will see it is connected with and is for the purpose of testimony and service. (For example, Acts i:5, 8; ii:4; iv:31, 33.) This will come out very clearly when we come to consider what the Baptism with the Holy Spirit does. The Baptism with the Holy Spirit is not for the purpose of cleansing from sin, but for the purpose of empowering for service. There is a line of teaching, put forward by a very earnest but mistaken body of people, that has brought the whole doctrine of the Baptism with the Holy Spirit into disrepute. It runs this way: First proposition: there is a further experience (or second blessing) after

regeneration, namely, the Baptism with the Holy Spirit. This proposition is true and can be easily proven from the Bible. Second proposition: this Baptism with the Holy Spirit can be instantaneously received. This proposition is also true and can be easily proven from the Bible. Third proposition: this Baptism with the Holy Spirit is the eradication of the sinful nature. This proposition is untrue. Not a line of Scripture can be adduced to show that the Baptism with the Holy Spirit is the eradication of the sinful nature. The conclusion drawn from these three propositions, two true and one false, is necessarily false. The Baptism with the Holy Spirit is not for the purpose of cleansing from sin, but for the purpose of empowering for service. It is indeed the work of the Holy Spirit to cleanse from sin. Further than this there is a work of the Holy Spirit where the believer is strengthened with might in the inner man: that Christ may dwell in his heart by faith... that he might be filled unto all the fullness of God. (Eph. iii:16-19) There is a work of the Holy Spirit of such a character that the believer is "made free from the law of sin and death," (Rom. Viii:2) and through the Spirit does "mortify (put to death) the deeds of the body." (Rom. viii:13.) It is our privilege to so walk daily and hourly in the power of the Spirit, that the carnal nature is kept in the place of death. But this is not the Baptism with the Spirit, neither is it the *eradication* of the sinful nature. It is not something done once for all, it is something that must be momentarily maintained. "*Walk* in the Spirit, and ye shall not fulfil the lust of the flesh." (Gal. v:16.) While insisting that the Baptism with the Spirit is primarily, for the purpose of empowering for service, it should be added that the Baptism is accompanied by a great moral uplift. (See Acts ii:44-46; iv:31-35.) This is necessarily so, from the steps one must take to obtain this blessing.

5. We will get a still clearer and fuller view of what the Baptism with the Holy Spirit is, if we will notice what this Baptism does. This is stated concisely in Acts i:8. "Ye shall receive *power* after that the Holy Ghost is come upon you; and ye shall be witnesses," etc. The Baptism with the Holy Spirit imparts "*power,*" power for service. This power will not manifest itself in precisely the same way in each individual. This is brought out very clearly in 1 Cor. xii:4-13. "Now there are diversities of gifts but the same spirit. For to one is given, through the Spirit, the word of wisdom; and to another the word of knowledge, according to the same spirit, to another faith, in the same spirit; and to another gifts of healings, in the one spirit; to another diverse kinds of tongues; but all these worketh the one and the same spirit, dividing to each one severally even as He will." In my early study of the Baptism with the Holy Spirit I noticed that in many instances those who were so baptized "spoke with tongues," and the question came often into my mind, if one is baptized with the Holy Spirit will he not speak with tongues. But I saw no one so speaking and I often wondered, is there any one to-day who actually is baptized with the Holy Spirit. This twelfth chapter of 1st Corinthians cleared me up on that, especially when I found Paul asking of those who had been baptized with the Holy Spirit, "Do all speak with tongues?" (1 Cor. xii:30.) But I fell into another error, namely, that any one who received the Baptism with the Holy Spirit would receive power as an evangelist, or as a preacher of the Word. This is equally contrary to the teaching of the chapter, that "there are *diversities of gifts*, but the one Spirit." There are three evils arising from the mistake just mentioned. First, disappointment. Many will seek the Baptism with the Holy Spirit, expecting power as an evangelist, but God has not called them to that work and the power that comes from the Baptism with the Holy Spirit manifests itself in another way in them; many cases of bitter disappointment and almost despair have arisen from this cause. The second evil is graver than the first, presumption. A man whom God has not called to the work of an evangelist or minister rushes into it because he has received, or thinks he has

received, the Baptism with the Holy Spirit. Many a man has said, "All a man needs to succeed as a preacher is the Baptism with the Holy Spirit." This is not true: he needs a call to that specific work, and he needs the study of the Word of God that will prepare him for the work. The third evil is still greater, indifference. There are many who know they are not called to the work of preaching. For example, a mother with a large family of children knows this. If then, they think that the Baptism with the Holy Spirit simply imparts power to preach, it is a matter of no personal concern to them; but when we come to see the truth that, while the Baptism with the Spirit imparts power, the way in which that power will be manifested, depends upon the work to which God has called us, and that no efficient work can be done without it, then the mother will see that she equally with the preacher needs this Baptism—needs it for that most important and hallowed of all work, to bring up her children "in the nurture and admonition of the Lord." I have recently met a very happy mother. A few months ago she heard of the Baptism with the Holy Spirit, sought it and received it. "Oh," she joyfully exclaimed as she told me the story, "Since I received it, I have been able to get into the hearts of my children which I was never able to do before."

It is the Holy Spirit Himself who decides how the power will manifest itself in any given case; "the spirit dividing to each one severally as *He* will." (1 Cor. xii:11 R. V.) We have a right "to desire earnestly the greater gifts." (1 Cor. xii:31.), but the Holy Spirit is sovereign, and He, not we, must determine in the final issue. It is not for us then to select some gift and look to the Holy Spirit to impart the self-chosen gift; it is not for us to select some field of service and then look to the Holy Spirit to impart to us power in that field which we, and not He, have chosen. It is rather for us to recognize the divinity and sovereignty of the Spirit, and put ourselves unreservedly at His disposal; for Him to select the gift that "He will" and impart to us that gift, for Him to select for us the field that "He will" and impart to us the power that will qualify us for the field He has chosen. I once knew a child of God, who, hearing of the Baptism with the Holy Spirit and the power that resulted from it, gave up at a great sacrifice, the secular work in which he was engaged, and entered upon the work of an evangelist. But the expected power in that line did not follow. The man fell into great doubt and darkness until he was led to see that the Holy Spirit divideth "to each one severally, even as He will." Then, giving up selecting his own field and gifts, he put himself at the Holy Spirit's disposal for Him to choose. In the final outcome the Holy Spirit did impart to this man power as an evangelist and a preacher of the Word. We must then surrender ourselves absolutely to the Holy Spirit to work as He will.

But, while the power that the Baptism with the Holy Spirit brings, manifests itself in different ways in different individuals, there will always be power. Just as surely as a man is baptized with the Holy Spirit there will be new power, a power not his own, "the power of the Highest!" Religious biography abounds in instances of men who have worked along as best they could until one day they were led to see there was such an experience as the Baptism with the Holy Spirit and to seek it and obtain it; from that hour there came into their service a new power that utterly transformed its character. Finney, Brainerd and Moody are cases in point. But cases of this character are not confined to a few exceptional men, they are becoming common. The writer has personally met and corresponded with hundreds during the past twelve months, who could testify to the new power that God had granted them through the Baptism with the Holy Spirit. These hundreds of men and women were in all branches of Christian service. Many of them were ministers of the gospel, others mission workers, others Y.M.C.A. secretaries, others Sunday-school teachers, others personal workers, others fathers and mothers. Nothing could exceed the clearness, confidence and joyfulness of many of these testimonies. What we have in promise in the words of Christ many have, and all may have, in glad experience: "Ye shall receive power, after that the Holy Ghost is come upon you."

To sum up the contents of this chapter: The Baptism with the Holy Spirit is the Spirit of God coming upon the believer, taking possession of his faculties, imparting to him gifts not naturally his own, but which qualify him for the service to which God has called him.

Chapter II. The Necessity and Possibility of the Baptism with the Holy Spirit.

Shortly before Christ was received up into heaven, having committed the preaching of the gospel to his disciples, He laid upon them this very solemn charge concerning the beginning of the great work He had committed to their hands: "Behold, I send forth the promise of my father upon you; but tarry ye in the city, until ye be clothed with power from on high." (Luke xxiv:49.) There is no doubt as to what Jesus meant by the "promise of my Father" for which they were to wait before beginning the ministry which He had entrusted to them; for in Acts i:4, 5, we read that Jesus "charged them not to depart from Jerusalem, but to wait for *the promise of the Father*," which, said he, "Ye heard from me: for John indeed baptized with water: but ye shall be *baptized with the Holy Ghost* not many days hence." "The promise of the Father," through which the enduement of power was to come, was the Baptism with the Holy Spirit. (Comp. Acts i:8.) Christ then strictly charged his disciples not to presume to undertake the work to which He had called them until they had received as the necessary and all-essential preparation for that work, the Baptism with the Holy Spirit. The men to whom Jesus said this, seemed to have already received very thorough preparation for the work in hand. They had been to school to Christ Himself for more than three years. They had heard from His own lips the great truths that they were to proclaim to the world. They had been eye witnesses of His miracles, of His death and of His resurrection and were about to be eye-witnesses of His ascension. The work before them was simply to go forth to proclaim what their own eyes had seen and what their own ears had heard from the lips of Christ Himself. Were they not fully prepared for this work? It would seem so to us. But Christ said, "No. You are so utterly unprepared you must not stir a step yet. There is a further preparation, so all-essential to effective service, you must abide at Jerusalem until you receive it. This further preparation is the Baptism with the Holy Spirit. When you receive that—and *not until then*—you will be prepared to begin the work to which I have called you." If Christ did not permit these men who had received so rare and unparalleled a schooling for the work to which He had so definitely and clearly called them to undertake this work without receiving in addition to that the Baptism with the Holy Spirit, what is it for us to undertake the work to which He has called us until we have received, in addition to any amount of schooling we may have had for the work, the Baptism with the Holy Spirit? Is it not most daring presumption?

But this is not all. In Acts x:38, we read "how God anointed Jesus of Nazareth with the Holy Ghost and with power: who went about doing good, and healing all that were oppressed of the devil." When we look into the gospels for an explanation of these words, we find it in Luke iii:21, 22; iv:1, 14, 15, 18, 21. We find that at the Baptism of Jesus at Jordan, *as He prayed*, the Holy Spirit came upon Him. Then, "*full* of the Holy Ghost," He has the temptation experience. Then, "*in the power of the Spirit,*" He begins his ministry, and proclaims Himself "*anointed* to preach" because "*the Spirit of the Lord is upon* Him." In other words, Jesus the Christ, never entered upon the ministry for which He came into this world until He was baptized with the Holy Spirit. If Jesus Christ, who had been supernaturally conceived through the Holy Spirit's power, who was the only begotten Son of God, who was divine, very God of very God, and yet truly man, if such an one, "leaving us an example that we should follow in His steps," did not venture upon the ministry for which the Father had sent Him until thus baptized with the Holy Ghost, what is it for us to dare to do it? If, in the light of these recorded facts, we dare to do it, it seems like an offence going beyond presumption. Doubtless it has been done in ignorance by many, but can we plead ignorance any longer? *The Baptism with the Holy Spirit is an absolutely necessary preparation for effective service for Christ along every line of service.* We may have a very clear call to service, as clear it may be as the Apostles had, but the charge is laid upon us, as upon them, that before we begin that service we must "tarry until ye be clothed with power from on high." This enduement with power is through the Baptism with the Holy Spirit. There are certainly few greater mistakes that we are making to-day, than that of setting men to teach Sunday-school classes, and do personal work, and even to preach the gospel, simply because they have been converted and received a certain amount of education—perhaps including a college and seminary course—but have not as yet been baptized with the Holy Spirit. Any man who is in Christian work, who has not received the Baptism with the Holy Spirit, ought to stop his work right where he is, and not go on with it until he has been "clothed with power from on high." But what will our work do while we are waiting? What did the world do those ten days while the early disciples were waiting? They alone knew the saving truth, yet, in obedience to the Lord's command, they were silent. The world was no loser. When the power came they accomplished more in one day than they would have accomplished in years, if they had gone on in presumptuous disobedience to Christ's charge; so will we after we have received the Baptism with the Holy Spirit accomplish more in one day than we ever would in years without His power. Days spent in waiting, if it were necessary, would be well spent, but we shall see further on that there is no need that we spend days in waiting. It may be said that the Apostles had gone out on missionary tours during Christ's lifetime before they were baptized with the Holy Spirit. This is true, but that was before the Holy Ghost was given, and before the charge, "tarry until ye be clothed with power from on high" was given. After that it would have been disobedience and presumption to have gone forth without this enduement, and we are living to-day after the Holy Ghost has been given and after the charge to "tarry until clothed" has been given.

We come now to the question of the Possibility of the Baptism with the Holy Spirit. Is the Baptism with the Holy Spirit for us? This is a question that has a most plain and explicit answer in the Word of God. In Acts ii:39, we read: "For to you is the promise, and to your children, and to all that are afar off, *even as many as the Lord our God shall call unto him.*" What is "the promise" of this passage? Turning back to the fourth and fifth verses of the preceding chapter we read: "Wait for *the promise* of the Father, which saith he, ye have heard of me. For John truly baptized with water; but *ye shall be baptized with the Holy Ghost* not many days hence." Again in the thirty-third verse of the second chapter we read: "Having received of the Father *the promise of the Holy Ghost.*" It would seem to be perfectly clear that "the promise" of the thirty-ninth verse must be the same as "the promise" of the thirty-third verse, and "the promise" of the fourth and fifth verses of the preceding chapter; *i.e.* the promise of the Baptism with the Holy Spirit. This conclusion is rendered absolutely certain by the context: "Repent and be baptized every one of you in the name of Jesus Christ unto the remission of your sins, and *ye shall receive the gift of the Holy Ghost.* For to you is the promise," etc. The promise then of this verse is the promise of the gift or Baptism with the Holy Ghost. (Comp. Acts x:45 with Acts xi:15, 16.) Who is this gift for? "To you," says Peter to the Jews whom he was immediately addressing. Then looking over their heads to the next generation, "And to your children." Then looking down all the coming ages of the Church's history to Gentile as well as Jew, "And to all that are afar off, even as many as the Lord our God shall call unto him." The Baptism with the Holy Spirit is for every child of God in every age of the Church's history. If it is not ours in experimental possession, it is because we have not taken (the exact force of the word "receive" in verse 38 is *take*) what God has provided for us in our exalted Savior. (Acts ii:33; John vii:38, 39.) A minister of the Gospel once came to me after a lecture on the Baptism with the Holy Spirit and said: "The church to which I belong, teaches that the Baptism with the Holy Spirit was for the Apostolic age alone." "It matters not," was replied, "what the church to which you belong or the church to which I belong teaches. What says the Word of God?" Acts ii:39 was read: "To you is the promise, and to your children, and to all that are afar off, even as many as the Lord our God shall call unto him." "Has he called you?" I asked. "Yes, he certainly has." "Is the promise for you?" "Yes, it is." And it was. And it is for every child of God who reads these pages. What a thrilling thought it is that the Baptism with the Holy Spirit, the enduement with *power from on high* is for us, is FOR ME individually. But that unspeakably joyous thought has its solemn side. If I *may* be baptized with the Holy Spirit, I *must* be. If I am baptism with the Holy Spirit, then will souls be saved through my instrumentality who are not so saved if I am not so baptized. If then I am not willing to pay the price of this Baptism, and therefore am not so baptized, I am responsible before God for all the souls that might have been saved but were not saved through me because I was not baptized with the Holy Spirit. I oftentimes tremble for my brethren in Christian work and myself. Not because we are teaching deadly error to men; some are guilty of even that, but I do not refer to that now. Not that we are not teaching the full truth as it is in Jesus. It must be confessed that there are many who do not teach positive error who do not preach a full gospel, but I do not refer to that. I tremble for those who are preaching the truth, the truth as it is in Jesus, the Gospel in its simplicity, in its purity, in its fullness, but preaching it "in persuasive words of wisdom" and not "in demonstration of the spirit and of power" (1 Cor. ii:4.), preaching it in the energy of the flesh and not in the power of the Holy Spirit. There is nothing more deadly than the gospel without the Spirit's power. "The letter killeth, but the Spirit giveth life." It is awfully solemn business preaching the gospel either from the pulpit or in more quiet ways. It means death or life to those who hear, and whether it means death or life, depends very largely on whether we preach it without or with the Baptism with the Holy Spirit. We must be baptism with the Holy Spirit.

~ ※ ~

Note: It is sometimes argued that "the Baptism with the Holy Spirit" was for the purpose of imparting miracle-working power and for the Apostolic age alone. In favor of this position it is asserted that the Baptism with the Holy Spirit was followed quite uniformly by miracles. The untenableness of this position is seen:

1. By the fact, that Christ Himself asserted that the purpose of the Baptism with the Holy Spirit was to impart power for witnessing—not especially power to work miracles. (Acts i:5, 8; Luke xxiv:48, 49.)

2. By the fact that Paul distinctly taught that there were diversities of gifts, and that "workings of miracles" was only one of the manifold manifestations of the Baptism with the Holy Spirit. (1 Cor. xii:4, 8-10.)

3. By the fact, that Peter distinctly asserts that "the gift of the Holy Ghost," "the promise," is for all believers in all generations (Acts ii:38, 39), and it is evident from a comparison of Acts ii:39 with Luke xxiv:49; Acts i:4, 5; ii:33, and of Acts ii:38 with Acts x:45 and Acts xi:15, 16, that each of these two expressions, "the promise," and "the gift of the Holy Ghost," refers to the Baptism with the Holy Spirit. If we take miracles in a broad sense of all results wrought by supernatural power, then it is true that each one baptized with the Holy Spirit does receive miracle-working power; for each one so baptized does receive a power not naturally his own supernatural power, God's own power. The result of the Baptism with the Holy Spirit that was most noticeable and essential was convincing, convicting and converting power. (Acts ii:4, 37, 41. Acts iv:8-13. Acts iv:31, 33. Acts ix:17, 20-22.) There seem to have been no displays of miracle-working power immediately following Paul's Baptism with the Holy Spirit, even though he became so singularly gifted in this direction at a later day—it was power to witness for Jesus as the Son of God that he received in immediate connection with the Baptism with the Holy Spirit.

Chapter III. How the Baptism with the Holy Spirit Can Be Obtained.

We have now come to a place where there is a deep sense that we must be baptized with the Holy Spirit. The practical question confronts us; how can we obtain this baptism with the Holy Spirit which we so sorely need. This question also the Word of God answers very plainly and very explicitly. There is pointed out in the Bible a path, consisting of seven simple steps, which any one who will can take, and whoever takes these seven steps will, with absolute certainty, enter into this blessing. This statement may seem very positive, but the Word of God is equally positive regarding the outcome of taking these steps which it points out. All seven steps are stated or implied in Acts. ii:38: "Repent ye, and be baptized every one of you in the name of Jesus Christ unto the remission of your sins, *and ye shall receive* the gift of the Holy Ghost." The first three steps are brought out with especial definiteness and distinctness in this verse. The others which are clearly implied in the verse are brought out more explicitly by other passages to which we shall refer later.

1. The first two steps are found in the word "repent." What does "repent" mean? *Change your mind;* change your mind about what? About God, about Christ, about sin. As to what the change of mind is about in any given case must be determined by the context. Here the first and most prominent thought is a change of mind about Christ. Peter has just brought against his hearers the awful charge that they had crucified Him whom God had made both Lord and Christ. "Pricked in their heart" by this charge, carried home by the power of the Holy Spirit, his hearers had cried out, "Men and brethren, what shall we do?" "Repent," Peter answered. Change your mind about Christ. Change from a Christ-hating and Christ-crucifying attitude of mind to a Christ-accepting attitude of mind. Accept Jesus as Christ and Lord. *This then is the first step toward the Baptism with the Holy Spirit: Accept Jesus as Christ and Lord.*

2. The second step is also found in the word "repent." While the change of mind about Jesus is the first and prominent thought, there must also be a change of mind about sin. A change of mind from a sin-loving or sin-indulging attitude of mind to a sin-hating and sin-renouncing attitude of mind. This is the second step; *renounce sin,* all sin, every sin. Here we come upon one of the commonest obstacles to receiving the Holy Spirit—*Sin.* Something is held on to that in our inmost hearts we more or less definitely feel to be not pleasing to God. If we are to receive the Holy Spirit, there must be very honest and very thorough heart searching. We cannot do satisfactory searching ourselves, God must do it. If we wish to receive the Holy Spirit we should go alone with God and ask Him to search us thoroughly and bring to light anything that displeases Him. (Ps. cxxxix:23, 24.) Then we should wait for him to do it. When the displeasing thing is revealed it should be put away at once. If, after patient and honest waiting, nothing is brought to light, we may conclude there is nothing of this kind in the way, and proceed to the further steps. But we should not conclude this too hurriedly. The sin that hinders the blessing may be something that appears very small and insignificant in itself. Mr. Finney tells of a young woman who was in deep concern regarding the Baptism with the Holy Spirit. Night after night she agonized in prayer, but the desired blessing did not come. One night as she was in prayer there came up before her some matter of head adornment that had often troubled her before; putting her hand to her head, she took the pins out and threw them away and immediately the blessing came. This was a small matter in itself, a matter that would not have appeared to many as sin, but yet a matter of controversy between this woman and God, and when this was settled the blessing came. "Whatsoever is not of faith is sin" (Rom. xiv:23), and it matters not how little the thing may be, if there are questions regarding it, it must be put away if we are to have the Baptism with the Holy Spirit. *The second step then toward the Baptism with the Holy Spirit is to put away every sin.*

3. The third step is found in this same verse: "*Be baptized in the name of Jesus Christ unto the remission of your sins.*" It was immediately after His baptism that the Holy Spirit descended upon Jesus. (Luke iii:21, 22.) In His baptism, Jesus, though Himself sinless, humbled Himself to take the sinner's place, and then God highly exalted Him by the giving of the Holy Spirit and by the audible testimony, "Thou art my beloved son; in thee I am well pleased." So we must humble ourselves to make open confession of our sin and renunciation of it and acceptance of Jesus Christ, in God's appointed way, by Baptism. The Baptism with the Holy Spirit is not for the one who secretly takes his place as a sinner and believer in Christ, but for the one who does so openly. Of course, the Baptism with the Holy Spirit may precede water baptism as in the case of the household of Cornelius. (Acts x:47.) But this was evidently an exceptional case and water baptism immediately followed. I have little doubt that there have been those, among Christians who did not believe in or practice water baptism—as for example "the Friends" or "Quakers"—who have had and given evidence of the Baptism with the Holy Spirit, but the passage before us certainly presents the normal order.

4. The fourth step is clearly implied in the verse we have been studying, (Acts ii:38), but it is brought out more explicitly in Acts v:32: "The Holy Ghost, whom God hath given to them that *obey Him.*" *The fourth step is obedience.* What does obedience mean? It does not mean merely doing some of the things, or many of the things, or most of the things, that God bids us do. It means *total surrender to the will of God.* Obedience is an attitude of the will lying back of specific acts of obedience. It means that I come to God and say: "Heavenly Father, here I am and all I have. Thou hast bought me with a price and I acknowledge thine absolute ownership. Take me and all I have, and do with me

whatsoever thou wilt. Send me where thou wilt, use me as thou wilt. I surrender myself and all I possess absolutely, unconditionally, for ever, to thy control and use." It was when the burnt offering, *whole,* no part held back, was laid upon the altar that "there came forth fire from before the Lord" and accepted the gift (Lev. ix:24), and it is when we bring ourselves a *whole* burnt offering to the Lord, and lay ourselves thus upon the altar, that the fire comes and God thus accepts the gift. Here we touch upon the hindrance to the Baptism with the Holy Spirit in many lives: there is not total surrender, the will is not laid down, the heart does not cry, "Lord, where thou wilt, what thou wilt, as thou wilt." One man desires the Baptism with the Holy Spirit that he may preach or work with power in Boston, when God wishes him in Bombay. Another, that he may preach to popular audiences, when God wishes him to plod among the poor. A young woman at a convention expressed a strong desire that some one would speak on the Baptism with the Holy Spirit. The address went home with power to her heart. She had been for some time in deep travail of soul when I asked her what it was that she desired. "Oh," she cried, I "cannot go back to Baltimore until I am baptized with the Holy Spirit." "Is your will laid down?" "I don't know." "You wish to go back to Baltimore to be a Christian worker?" "Yes." "Are you willing to go back to Baltimore and be a servant girl if that is where God wishes you?" "No, I am not." "Well, you will never get the Baptism with the Holy Spirit until you are. Will you lay your will down?" "I can't." "Are you willing God should lay it down for you?" "Yes." "Well, then, ask Him to do it." The head was bowed in brief but earnest prayer. "Did God hear that prayer?" "He must have, it was according to His will; He did." "Now ask Him for the Baptism with the Holy Spirit." Again the head was bowed and the brief, earnest prayer ascended to God. There was a brief silence and the agony was over, the blessing had come—when the will was surrendered. There are many who hold back from this total surrender because they fear God's will. They are afraid God's will may be something dreadful. Remember who God is. He is our Father. Never an earthly father had so loving and tender a will regarding his children as He has toward us. "No good thing will He withhold from them that walk uprightly." (Ps. lxxxiv:11.) "He that spared not His own Son, but delivered him up for us all, how shall he not with him also freely give us all things?" There is nothing to be feared in God's will. God's will will always prove in the final outcome the best and sweetest thing in all God's universe.

5. The fifth step is found in Luke xi:13. "If ye, being evil know how to give good gifts unto your children, how much more shall your heavenly Father give the Holy Spirit to them that ask him?" The asking of this verse is the asking that springs from real and intense desire. This is brought out by the context: "Ask, and it shall be given you; seek and ye shall find; knock, and it shall be opened unto you." Note also the parable of the importunate friend that immediately precedes. Evidently the asking that Christ has in mind is not the asking of a passing and half-hearted whim, but the asking of intense desire. There is a very suggestive passage in Isaiah, the forty-fourth chapter and third verse: "I will pour water upon him that is *thirsty*… I will pour my Spirit upon thy seed." What does it mean to be thirsty? When one is thirsty there is but one cry: "Water! water! water!" Every pore in the body seems to have a voice and cry out "water." So when our hearts have one cry, "the Holy Spirit, the Holy Spirit, the Holy Spirit," then it is that God pours floods upon the dry ground, pours His Spirit upon us. *This then is the fifth step—intense desire for the Baptism with the Holy Spirit.* To what a pitch of longing the early disciples had been brought by the tenth day of their eager waiting, and their thirsty souls were filled that day when "Pentecost was fully come." As long as one thinks he can get along somehow without the Baptism with the Holy Spirit, as long as he casts about for

something in the way of education or cunningly concocted methods of work, he is not going to received it. There are many ministers who are missing the fullness of power God has for them, simply because they are not willing to admit the lack there has been all these years in their ministry. It is indeed a humiliating thing to confess, but that humiliating confession would be the precursor of a marvelous blessing. But there are not a few, who, in their unwillingness to make this wholesome confession, are casting about for some ingenious device of exegesis to get around the plain and simple meaning of God's Word, and thus they are cheating themselves of the fullness of the Spirit's power that God is so eager to bestow upon them; and, furthermore, they are imperiling the eternal interests of the souls that are dependent upon their ministrations, that might be won for Christ, if they had the power of the Holy Spirit which they might have. But there are others whom God in His grace has brought to see that there was a something their ministry lacked, and this something nothing less than that all-essential Baptism with the Holy Spirit, without which one is utterly unqualified for acceptable and effective service, and they have humbly and frankly confessed their lack, sometimes they have been led to the God-taught resolution that they would not go on in their work until this lack was supplied, they have waited in eager longing upon God the Father for the fulfilment of His promise, and the result has been a transformed ministry for which many have risen to bless God.

It is not enough that the desire for the Baptism with the Holy Spirit be intense; it must also have the right motive. There is a desire for the Baptism with the Holy Spirit that is purely selfish. There is many a one who has an intense desire for the Baptism with the Holy Spirit simply that he may be a great preacher, or great personal worker, or renowned in some way as a Christian. It is simply his own gain or glory that he is seeking. After all it is not the Holy Spirit that he seeks, but his own honor and the Baptism with the Holy Spirit simply as a means to that end. One of the subtlest and most dangerous snares into which Satan leads us, is that, where we are seeking the Holy Spirit, this most solemn of all gifts, for our own ends. The desire for the Holy Spirit must not be in order to make that sublime and divine Person the servant of our low ends, but for the glory of God. It must arise from a recognition that God and Christ are being dishonored by my powerless ministry and by the sin of the people about me, against which I now have no power, and that He will be honored, if I have the Baptism with the Spirit of God. One of the most solemn passages in the New Testament bears upon this point. (Acts viii:18-24.) "When Simon saw that through the laying on of the Apostles' hands the Holy Ghost was given, he offered them money, saying, Give me also this power, that on whomsoever I lay my hands, he may receive the Holy Ghost." Here was a strong desire on Simon's part, but it was entirely unhallowed and selfish, and Peter's terrific answer is worthy of note and meditation. Is there not many a one to-day who, with equally unhallowed and selfish purpose desires the Baptism with the Holy Spirit? Each one who is desiring and seeking the Baptism with the Holy Spirit, would do well to ask himself *why* he desires it. If you find that it is merely for your own gratification or glory, then ask God to forgive you the thought of your heart, and to enable you to see how you need it for His glory and to desire it to that end.

6. The sixth step is in this same verse. (Luke xi:13.) "If ye then, being evil, know how to give good gifts unto your children, how much more shall your heavenly Father give the Holy Spirit to them that *ask* Him." *The sixth step is to ask.* Definite asking for a definite blessing. When Christ has been accepted as Savior and Master, and confessed as such, when sin has been put away, when there has been the definite, total surrender of the will, when there is real and holy desire, then comes the simple act of asking God for this definite

blessing. It is given in answer to earnest, definite, specific, believing prayer. It has been earnestly contended by some that we should not pray for the Holy Spirit. They reason this out in this way: "The Holy Spirit was given to the Church at Pentecost, as an abiding gift." This is true, but what was given to the Church each believer must appropriate for himself. It has been well said on this point, that God has already given Christ to the world, (John iii; 16), but that each individual must appropriate Him by a personal act to get the personal advantage of the gift, and so must each individual personally appropriate God's gift of the Holy Spirit to get the personal advantage of it. But it is argued, still further that each believer has the Holy Spirit. This is also true in a sense. "If any man have not the Spirit of Christ, he is none of His." (Rom. viii:9.) But as we have already seen, it is quite possible to have something, yes much, of the Spirit's presence and work in the heart and yet come short of that special fullness and work known in the Bible as the Baptism or Filling with the Holy Spirit. In answer to all specious reasonings on this subject we put the simple statement of Christ: "How much more shall your heavenly Father give the Holy Spirit to them that *ask* Him." At a convention at which the author was announced to speak on this subject, a brother said to him: "I see you are to speak on the Baptism with the Holy Spirit." "Yes." "It is the most important subject on the program; now be sure and tell them not to pray for the Holy Spirit." "I shall certainly not tell them that; for Jesus said, 'How much more shall your heavenly Father give the Holy Spirit to them that *ask* Him.'" "Oh, but that was before Pentecost." "How about Acts iv:31? was that before Pentecost or after?" "After it, of course." "Well, read it." It was read: "When they had *prayed*, the place was shaken where they were assembled together, and they were all filled with the Holy Ghost." "How about the eighth chapter of Acts? Was that before Pentecost or after?" "After, of course." "Well, read the fourteenth to the sixteenth verses." The verses were read: "Peter and John, when they were come down, *prayed* for them, *that they might receive the Holy Ghost;* for *as yet He was fallen upon none of them*, and they received the Holy Ghost." Against all inferences is this clear teaching of the Word by precept and example, that the Holy Spirit is given in answer to prayer. It was so at Pentecost; it has been so since. Those whom I have met who give most evidence of the Spirit's presence and power in their life and work believe in praying for the Holy Spirit. It has been the author's unspeakable privilege to pray with many ministers and Christian workers for this great blessing, and afterward to learn from them or from others of the new power that has come into their service, none other than the power of the Holy Spirit.

7. The seventh and last step is found in Mark xi:24. "What things soever ye desire, when ye pray, *believe* that ye receive them, and ye shall have them." God's most positive and unqualified promises must be appropriated by faith. In James i:5, we read: "If any of you lack wisdom, let him ask of God that giveth to all members liberally, and upbraideth not; and it shall be given him." Now, that is certainly positive and unqualified enough, but listen to what the writer says next: "But let him ask *in faith, nothing wavering*, for he that wavereth is like a wave of the sea driven with the wind and tossed. For let not that man think that he shall receive anything of the Lord." There must then be faith in order to make our own the most positive and unqualified promises of God, such as that in Luke xi:13, and Acts ii:38, 39. Here then we discover the cause of failure in many cases to enter into the blessing of the Baptism with the Holy Spirit. The failure is because the last step is not taken—the simple step of faith. They do not believe, they do not confidently expect, and we have another instance of how men "Entered not in because of unbelief." (Heb. iv:6.) There are many, very many, who are kept out of this land of milk and honey just by this unbelief. It should be added that there is a faith that goes beyond expectation, a faith that

just puts out its hand and takes what it asks. This is brought out very clearly by the Revised Version (R. V.) of Mark xi:24. "All things whatsoever ye pray and ask for, believe that ye have received them and ye shall have them." I remember how greatly I was perplexed by this rendering of the R. V. when I first noticed it. On examining the Greek of the passage I saw that the R. V. was correct, but what did it mean? It seemed like a singular confusion of the tenses. "Believe that ye *have* (already) *received* them, and ye *shall have* them." This seeming enigma was solved long after, while studying the First Epistle of John. I read in the fifth chapter, fourteenth and fifteenth verses: "This is the boldness which we have toward Him, that, if we ask anything according to his will, he heareth us: and if we know that he heareth us whatsoever we ask, we know that that *we have* the petitions which we have asked of him." (R. V.) When I ask anything of God the first thing to find out is, is this petition according to his will? When that is settled, when I find it is according to His will when, for example, the thing asked is definitely promised in His word—then I know the prayer is heard, and I know further, "I have the petition which I have asked of him." I know it because He plainly says so, and what I have thus appropriated on simple, childlike faith in His naked Word "I shall have" in actual experience. When one who has a clear title to a piece of property deeds it to me it is mine as soon as the deed is properly executed and recorded, though it may be some time before I enter into the experimental enjoyment of it. I have it in the one sense as soon as the deed is recorded. I shall have it in the other sense later. In like manner, as soon as we, having met the conditions of prevailing prayer, put up to God a petition for "anything according to his will," it is our privilege to know that the prayer is heard, and that the thing which we have asked of Him is ours. Now apply this to the Baptism with the Holy Spirit. I have met the conditions of obtaining this blessing already mentioned. I simply, definitely, ask God, the Father, for the Baptism with the Holy Spirit. Then I stop and say was that prayer "according to his will?" Yes, Luke xi:13 says so. "If ye then being evil, know how to give good gifts unto your children, how much more shall your heavenly Father give the Holy Spirit to them that ask him?" Acts ii:38, 39 says: "Repent ye, and be baptized every one of you in the name of Jesus Christ unto the remission of your sins; and ye shall receive the gift of the Holy Ghost. For to you is the promise, and to your children, and to all that are afar off, even as many as the Lord our God shall call unto him." (R. V.) It is clear that the prayer for the Baptism with the Holy Spirit is "according to His will," for it is definitely and plainly promised. I know then that the prayer is heard and that *I have the petition which I have asked of Him.* (1 John v:14, 15.) That is, I have the Baptism with the Holy Spirit. I have then the right to arise from my knees and say, on the all-sufficient authority of God's Word, "I have the Baptism with the Holy Spirit," and *afterwards* I shall have in experimental enjoyment what I have appropriated by simple faith; for God has said and He cannot lie, "All things whatsoever ye pray and ask for, believe that ye have received them, *and ye shall have them.*" Any reader of this book may at this point lay it down, and, if Christ has been accepted as Savior and Lord, and openly confessed as such in God's way, and if sin has been searched out and put away, and if there has been total surrender of the will and of self to God, and if there is a true desire for God's glory to be Baptized with the Holy Spirit—if these conditions have been met, you may get down just now before God, and ask him to baptize you with the Holy Spirit, and you can then say, when the prayer has gone up, "That prayer was heard, I have what I have asked, I *have the baptism with the Holy Spirit,*" and you have a right to get up and go out to your work, assured that in that work you will have the Holy Spirit's power. But some one will ask, "Must I not know that I have the Baptism with the Holy Spirit before I begin the work?" Certainly, but how shall we know? I know of no better way of knowing anything than by God's Word. I would believe God's word before my feelings any day. How do we deal with an inquirer who has accepted Christ, but who lacks assurance that he has eternal life? We do not ask him to look at his feelings, but we take him to some such passage as John iii:36. We tell him to read it and he reads: "He that believeth on the Son hath everlasting life." "Who says that?" we ask. "God says it." "Is it true?" "Oh, certainly it is true; God says it." "Who does God say has everlasting life?" "He that believeth on the Son." "Do you believe on the Son?" "Yes." "What have you then?" "Oh, I don't know, I don't feel yet that I have eternal life." "But what does God say?" "He that believeth on the Son hath everlasting life." "Are you going to believe God or your feelings?" We hold the inquirer right there until on the simple, naked word of God, feeling or no feeling, he says, "I know I have eternal life because God says so," and afterward the feeling comes. Deal with yourself in this matter of the Baptism with the Holy Spirit just as you deal with an inquirer in the matter of assurance. *Be sure you have met the conditions*, and then simply *ask, claim, act*. But some one will say, "Will it be just as it was before, won't there be any manifestation?" Most assuredly there will be some manifestation. "To each one is given the manifestation of the Spirit to profit withal." (1 Cor. xii:7.) But what will the character of the manifestation be and where shall we see it? It is at this point that many make a mistake. They have, perhaps, read the life of Mr. Finney or of Jonathan Edwards, and recall how great waves of electric emotion swept over these men until they were obliged to ask God to withdraw His hand lest they die from the ecstasy. Or they have gone to some meeting, and heard testimonies to similar experiences, and they expect something like this. Now I do not deny the reality of such experiences. I cannot. The testimony of such men as Finney and Edwards is to be believed. There is a stronger reason why I cannot deny them. But while admitting the reality of these experiences, I would ask, where is there a single line of the New Testament that describes any such experience in connection with the Baptism with the Holy Spirit? Every manifestation of the Baptism with the Holy Spirit in the New Testament was in new power in service. Look, for example, at 1 Cor. xii, where this subject it is treated in the most thorough way, and note the character of the manifestations mentioned. It is quite probable that the Apostles had similar experiences to those of Finney and Edwards and others, but, if they had, the Holy Spirit kept them from recording them. It is well He did, for if they had told of such things we would have looked for these things rather than the more important manifestation of power in service.

But another question will be asked: "Did not the Apostles wait ten days and may we not have to wait?" The Apostles were kept waiting ten days, but the reason is given in Acts ii:1. "When the Day of Pentecost was now come" (literally was being fulfilled, R. V.). In the eternal purposes and plans of God and in the Old Testament types the Day of Pentecost was set as the time for the giving of the Holy Spirit, and the Spirit could not be given until the Day of Pentecost was fulfilled to come, but we read of no waiting after Pentecost, in Acts. iv:31, there was no waiting. "*When they had prayed* the place was shaken where they were assembled together, and they were all filled with the Holy Ghost." In Acts viii, there was no waiting. When Peter and John came down to Samaria and found that none of the young converts had been baptized with the Holy Spirit they "prayed for them, that they might receive the Holy Ghost," and they did then and there. (Acts viii:15, 17.) Paul of Tarsus was not obliged to wait in the ninth chapter of the Acts. Ananias came in and told him of this wondrous gift, and baptized him, and laid his hands upon him, and "*straightway* in the synagogue he proclaimed Jesus, that he is the Son of God." (Acts ix:17, 20.) There was no waiting in Acts x. Before Peter had fairly got through his sermon the Baptism with the Holy Spirit came. (Acts x:44-46; Comp. chap. xi:15, 16.) In the nineteenth chapter of the Acts there was no waiting. As soon as Paul had declared to the Ephesian disciples the gift of the Holy Spirit, and the conditions were met, the blessing followed. (Acts xix:1-6.) Men only have to wait when they do not meet the conditions, when Christ is not fully accepted, or sin is not put away, or there is not total surrender, or true desire, or definite prayer, or simple faith, just taking upon the naked Word. The absence of some of these things keeps many waiting for more than ten days sometimes. But there is no need that any reader of this book wait ten hours. You can have the Baptism with the Holy Spirit just now, if you will. A young man once came to me in great earnestness about this matter. "I heard of the Baptism with the Holy Spirit," he said, "some time ago and have been seeking it, but have not received it." "Is your will laid down?" "I am afraid that is the trouble." "Will you lay it down?" "I am afraid I cannot." "Are you willing God should lay it down for you?" "Yes." "Ask Him to." We knelt in prayer, and he asked God to lay down his will for him. "Did God hear that prayer?" "He must have, it was according to His will." "Is your will laid down?" "It must be." "Then ask God for the Baptism with the Holy Spirit." He did this. "Was that prayer according to His will?" "Yes." "Was it heard?" "It must have been." "Have you the Baptism with the Holy Spirit?" "I don't feel it." "That is not what I asked you; read those verses again." The Bible lay open at 1 John v:14, 15 before him and he read: "This is the confidence we have in him, that, if we ask anything according to his will, He heareth us." "Wait a moment; was that prayer according to His will?" "It certainly was." "Was it heard?" "It was." "Read on." "And if we know that he hear us whatsoever we ask, we know that we have the petitions that we desired of Him." "Know what?" "That we have the petitions we desired of Him." "What was the petition?" "The Baptism with the Holy Spirit." "Have you it?" "I don't feel it, but God says so, and I must have." A few days later I met him again and asked if he really had received what he took on simple faith. With a happy look in his face he answered, "Yes." I lost sight of him for perhaps two years, and then found him preparing for the ministry, and already preaching and God was honoring his preaching with souls saved, and a little later used him with others as a means of great blessing to the theological seminary where he was studying. He had also decided to serve Christ in the foreign field. What he claimed on simple faith and received, any reader of this book can claim and receive in the same way.

Chapter IV. "Fresh Baptisms with the Holy Spirit" Or the Refilling with the Holy Spirit.

In the second chapter of the Acts of the Apostles, fourth verse, we read: "They were all filled with the Holy Ghost, and began to speak," etc. This was the fulfillment of Acts i:5. "Ye shall be baptized with the Holy Ghost not many days hence." One of those mentioned by name as being "filled with the Holy Ghost," (Acts ii:4), or "baptized with the Holy Ghost" (Acts i:5), at this time was Peter. Turning over to the fourth chapter, the eighth verse, we read: "Then Peter, filled with the Holy Ghost, said unto them," etc. Here Peter experienced a new filling with the Holy Spirit. Again, in the thirty-first verse of this same chapter, we read: "When they had prayed the place was shaken where they were assembled together; and they were all filled with the Holy Ghost." Peter is named as one of this company (verses 19 and 23), so we see that Peter here experienced a third filling with the Holy Spirit. It is evident that it is not sufficient that one be once "baptized with the Holy Spirit." As new emergencies of service arise, there must be new fillings with the Spirit. The failure to realize this has led to most sad and serious results in many a man's service. He has been baptized at some period in his life with the Holy Spirit, and strives to get through his whole future life in the power of this past experience. It is largely for this reason that we see so many men who once unquestionably worked in the Holy Spirit's power, who give little evidence of the possession of that power to-day. For each new service that is to be conducted, for each new soul that is to be dealt with, for each new service for Christ that is to be performed, for each new day and each new emergency of Christian life and service, we should definitely seek a new filling with the Holy Spirit. I do not deny that there is an "anointing that abideth," (1 John ii:27), nor the permanency of the gifts that the Holy Spirit bestows; I simply assert with clear and abundant Scripture proof, to say nothing of proof from experience and observation; that this gift must not be "neglected" (1 Tim. iv:14), but rather "kindled anew" or "stirred into a flame" (2 Tim. i:6); and that repeated fillings with the Holy Spirit are necessary to continuance and increase of power. Now arises the question, ought these new *fillings* with the Holy Spirit to be called "fresh *baptisms* with the Holy Spirit?" While, on the one hand, it must be admitted that in Acts ii:4, the expression "*filled* with the Holy Ghost" is used to describe the experience promised in Acts i:5, in the words, "Ye shall be *baptized* with the Holy Ghost," and that therefore the two expressions are to this extent synonymous; on the other hand, it should be noticed, that the expression, "Baptized with the Holy Spirit" is nowhere used in the Bible of any experience but the first, and that, furthermore, the word "baptized" of itself suggests an initial or initiatory experience. While, therefore, we stand for the truth that those who speak of "fresh baptisms with the Holy Spirit" are aiming at, it would seem wisest to follow the uniform Bible usage and speak of the experiences that succeed the first, as being "*filled* with the Holy Spirit," and not as being "baptized with the Holy Spirit."

Chapter V. How Spiritual Power is Lost.

Any discussion of the Baptism with the Holy Spirit and the power which results from it, would be incomplete if attention were not called to the fact that spiritual power may be lost.

One of the strangest and saddest stories of the Old Testament history is that of Samson. It is also one of the most instructive. He was by far the most remarkable man of his day. The grandest opportunities were open to him, but after striking temporary victories, his life ended in tragic failure, all through his own inexcusable folly. Time and again it is said of him that "the Spirit of the Lord came mightily upon him," and in the power of that Spirit he wrought to the astonishment of his people and the discomfiture of the enemies of the Lord; but in Judges xvi:19, 20, we see him deserted of the Lord, though unconscious of it, his strength gone from him and he about to be taken into wretched captivity, the sport of the godless, and to die with the enemies of the Lord a violent and dishonored death.

Unfortunately Samson is not the only man in Christian history, who, having once known the power of the Holy Spirit, has afterward been shorn of this power and laid aside. There have been many Samsons, and I presume there will be many more—men whom God has once used and has afterward been forced to lay aside. One of the saddest sights on earth is such a man. Let us consider when it is the Lord departs from a man or withdraws His power from him, or in other words, "How power is lost."

1. *First of all God withdraws His power from men when they go back upon their separation to Him.* This was the precise case with Samson himself. (Judges xvi:19. Comp. Num. vi:2, 5.) His uncut hair was the outward sign of his Nazarite vow by which "he separated himself unto the Lord." The shearing of his hair was the surrender of his separation. His separation given up he was shorn of his power. It is at this same point that many a man to-day is shorn of his power. There was a day when he separated himself unto God. He turned his back utterly upon the world and its ambitions, its spirit, its purposes; he set himself apart to God as holy unto Him, to be His, for God to take him and use him and do with him what He would. God has honored his separation, He has anointed him with the Holy Ghost and power. He has been used of God. But Delilah has come to him. The world has captured his heart again. He has listened to the world's siren voice and allowed her to shear him of the sign of separation. He is no longer a man separated, or wholly consecrated, to the Lord, and the Lord leaves him. Are there not such persons among those who read this? Men and women the Lord once used, but He does not use you now. You may still be outwardly in Christian work, but there is not the old time liberty and power in it, and this is the reason—you have been untrue to your separation, to your consecration to God; you are listening to Delilah, to the voice of the harlot, to the world and its allurements. Would you get the old power back again? There is but one thing to do. Let your hair grow again as Samson did. Renew your consecration to God.

2. *Power is lost through the incoming of sin.* It was so with Saul, the son of Kish. The Spirit of God came upon Saul and he wrought a great victory for God. (1 Samuel xi:6.) He brought the people of God forward to a place of triumph over their enemies, who had held them under for years. But Saul disobeyed God in two distinct instances (1 Samuel xiii:13, 14; xv:3, 9-11, 23), and the Lord withdrew His favor and His power, and Saul's life ended in utter defeat and ruin. This is the history of many men whom God has once used. Sin has crept in. They have done that which God has told them not to do, or they have refused to do that which God bade them do, and the power of God has been withdrawn. The one who has known God's power in service and would continue to know it, must walk very softly before Him. He must be listening constantly to hear what God bids him do or not do. He must respond promptly to the slightest whisper of God. It would seem as if any one who had once known God's power would rather die than lose it. But it is lost through the incoming of sin. Are there those among the readers of this book who are passing through this dreadful experience of the loss of God's power? Ask yourself if this be the reason; has sin crept in somewhere? Are you doing something, some little thing, perhaps, that God tells you not to do? Are you leaving undone something God bids you do? Set this matter right with God and the old power will come back. David was guilty of an awful sin, but when that sin was confessed and put away, he came to know again the power of the Spirit. (Ps. xxxii:1-5; li:11-13.)

If we would continuously know the power of God we should go often alone with Him, at the close of each day at least, and ask Him to show us if any sin, anything displeasing in His sight, has crept in that day, and if He shows us that there has, we should confess it and put it away then and there.

3. *Power is lost again through self-indulgence.* The one who would have God's power must lead a life of self-denial. There are many things which are not sinful in the ordinary understanding of the word sin, but which hinder spirituality and rob men of power. I do not believe that any man can lead a luxurious life, over-indulge his natural appetites, indulge extensively in dainties, and enjoy the fullness of God's power. The gratification of the flesh and the fullness of the Spirit do not go hand in hand. "The flesh lusteth against

the Spirit, and the Spirit against the flesh: and these two are contrary the one to the other." (Gal v:17.) Paul wrote, "I keep under my body, and bring it into subjection." (1 Cor. ix:27, see R. V. Greek. Note also Eph. v:18.)

We live in a day when the temptation to the indulgence of the flesh is very great. Luxuries are common. Piety and prosperity not seldom go hand in hand, and in many a case the prosperity that piety and power have brought has been the ruin of the man to whom it has come. Not a few ministers of power have become popular and in demand. With the increasing popularity has come an increase of pay and of the comforts of life. Luxurious living has come in, and the power of the Spirit has gone out. It would not be difficult to cite specific instances of this sad truth. If we would know the continuance of the Spirit's power, we need to be on guard to lead lives of simplicity, free from indulgence and surfeiting, ever ready to "endure hardness, as a good soldier of Jesus Christ." (2 Tim. ii:3.) I frankly confess I am afraid of luxury;—not as afraid of it as I am of sin, but it comes next as an object of dread. It is a very subtle but a very potent enemy of power. There are devils to-day that "go not out but by prayer and fasting."

4. *Power is lost through greed for money.* It was through this that a member of the original apostolic company, the twelve whom Jesus Himself chose to be with Him, fell. The love of money, the love of accumulation, got into the heart of Judas Iscariot, and proved his ruin. "The love of money is a root of all kinds of evil," (1 Tim. vi:10.) but one of the greatest evils of which it is the root is that of the loss of spiritual power. How many a man there is to-day who once knew what spiritual power was, but money began to come. He soon felt its strange fascination. The love for accumulation, covetousness, the love for more, little by little took possession of him. He has accumulated his money honestly; but it has absorbed him, and the Spirit of God is shut out, and his power has departed. Men who would have power, need to have the words of Christ, "Take heed and beware of covetousness," writ large and graved deep upon their hearts. One does not need to be rich to be covetous. A very poor man may be very much absorbed in the desire for wealth—just as much so as any greedy millionaire.

5. *Power is lost through pride.* This is the subtlest and most dangerous of all the enemies of power. I am not sure but that more men lose their power at this point, than at any of those mentioned thus far. There is many a man who has not consciously gone back upon his consecration, he has not let sin, in the sense of conscious doing of that which God forbade or conscious refusal to do that which God commanded, creep into his life, he has not given way to self-indulgence, he has utterly, persistently and consistently refused the allurements of money accumulation, but still he has failed, *pride has come in.* He has become puffed up because of the very fact that God has given him power and used him, puffed up, it may be, over the consistency and simplicity and devotion of his life, and God has been forced to set him aside. God cannot use a proud man (1 Pet. v:5.) "God resisteth the proud and giveth grace to the humble." The man who is puffed up with pride, self-esteem, cannot be filled up with the Holy Spirit. Paul saw this danger for himself. God saw it for him, and "lest he be exalted above measure, through the abundance of the revelations, there was given to (him) a thorn in the flesh, the messenger of Satan to buffet (him), lest (he) should be exalted above measure." (2 Cor. xii:7.) How many men has failed here! They have sought God's power, sought it in God's way, it has come. Men have testified of the blessing received through their Word, and pride has entered and been indulged, and all is lost. Moses was the meekest of men, and yet he failed at this very point. "Must we fetch you water out of this rock?" he cried, and then and there God laid him aside (Num. xx:10-12). If God is using us at all, let us get down very low before Him.

The more he uses us the lower let us get. May God keep his own words ringing in our ears: "Be clothed with humility, for God resisteth the proud, and giveth grace to the humble." (1 Pet. v:5.)

6. *Power is lost through neglect of prayer.* It is in prayer especially that we are charged with the energy of God. It is the man who is much in prayer into whom God's power flows mightily. John Livingston spent a night with some Christians in conference and prayer. The next day, June 21st, 1630, he so preached at the Kirk of Shotts, that the Spirit fell upon his hearers in such a way that five hundred could either date their conversion or some remarkable confirmation from that day forward. This is but one instance among thousands to show how power is given in prayer. Virtue or power is constantly going from us, as from Christ (Mark v:30), in service and blessing; and if power would be maintained, it must be constantly renewed in prayer. When electricity is given off from a charged body it must be recharged. So must we be recharged with the Divine energy, and this is effected by coming into contact with God in prayer. Many a man whom God has used has become lax in his habits of prayer, and the Lord departs from him and his power is gone. Are there not some of us who have not to-day the power we once had, and simply because we do not spend the time on our faces before God that we once did?

7. *Power is lost through neglect of the Word.* God's power comes through prayer, it comes also through the Word (Ps. i:2, 3; Josh. i:8). Many have known the power that comes through the regular, thoughtful, prayerful, protracted meditation upon the Word, but business and perhaps Christian duties have multiplied, other studies have come in, the Word has been in a measure crowded out, and power has gone. We must meditate daily, prayerfully, profoundly upon the Word if we are to maintain power. Many a man has run dry through its neglect.

I think the seven points mentioned give the principal ways in which spiritual power is lost. I think of no others. If there is one dread that comes to me more frequently than any other, it is that of losing the power of God. Oh, the agony of having known God's power, of having been used of Him, and then of having that power withdrawn, to be laid aside as far as any real usefulness is concerned. Men may still praise you, but God can't use you. To see a perishing world around you and to know there is no power in your words to save. Would not to die be better than that? I have little fear of losing eternal life. Every believer in Christ has that already. I am in the hand of Jesus Christ and in the hand of God the Father and no one can pluck me out of their hand, (John x:28-30), *but* I see so many men from whom God has departed, men once eminently used of God, I walk with fear and trembling, and cry unto Him daily to keep me from the things that would make the withdrawal of his power necessary. But what those things are I think he has made plain to me, and I have tried in the words here written to make them plain to both you and myself. To sum them up they are these: the surrender of our separation, sin, self-indulgence, greed for money, pride, the neglect of prayer, and the neglect of the Word. Shall we not, by God's grace, from this time be on our guard against these things, and thus make sure of the continuance of God's power in our life and service until that glad day comes when we can say with Paul: "I have fought a good fight, I have finished my course, I have kept the faith; henceforth there is laid up for me a crown of righteousness, which the Lord, the righteous judge, shall give me at that day," (2 Tim. iv:7, 8,) or better yet with Jesus, "I have glorified thee on the earth, having accomplished the work which thou hast given me to do." (John xvii:4.)

CPSIA information can be obtained
at www.ICGtesting.com
Printed in the USA
LVHW101119230123
737753LV00006B/403

9 781640 322745